2002 DEDICATION

I would like to dedicate this book to a number of people.

First must come my wife, Vicky, and my children, Matthew and Emily, who had to make sacrifices of their time while this book was written. I would also like to thank David, Rachel, Sam and Megan Bunce who, too, found that the production process impacted on their lives. Matthew Thompson, the commissioning editor, deserves a dedication for the problems I caused him by being a slower-than-expected author, and Ramona Lamport deserves a medal for her perseverance with the editing process.

Finally, however, I would like to dedicate this book to the victims of the World Trade Center disaster of 11 September 2001. The destruction of both so many lives and one of the most striking examples of the output of the development process was shocking. I hope, perhaps, that some of the readers of this book will use some of the ideas, concepts and techniques contained within it in the rebirth of a new WTC that will be even more beautiful than the original and will enrich the lives of future generations, as well as forming a fitting memorial to those lives so senselessly ended.

Tim Havard
Oxford
March 2002

2008 DEDICATION

To Vicky. Thanks for putting up with me!

SPONSOR'S FOREWORD

ARGUS Software is the world's leading provider of property appraisal software. Formed from the merger of the UK's Circle Software Ltd and the US companies Realm Business Solutions and Treesoft, ARGUS Software provides a range of products for appraisal and valuation, investment analysis and budgeting, many of which represent the industry standard in the countries where they are used.

This is the case with ARGUS Developer (formally known as CircleDeveloper), which is the world's primary development appraisal modelling tool, with users in the UK, Europe, the USA and Canada as well as the Middle East and Australasia. This wide user base allied to the wealth of experience the program development team has gained since the product was launched in 1990 has meant that the software has continuously evolved to meet the changing needs of the market.

ARGUS Software is keen to promote education and understanding of the property markets in general and the development sector in particular and is therefore particularly pleased to be associated with *Contemporary Property Development*.

ARGUS Software Ltd
2/6 Granard Business Centre
Bunns Lane
Mill Hill
London
NW7 2DQ
www.argussoftware.com

PREFACE TO THE SECOND EDITION

It seems a long time ago that I wrote the original dedication to *Contemporary Property Development*! Much has happened in these six years, yet much has stayed the same.

The World Trade Center site remains, in the main, to be redeveloped while the world is still feeling the impact of the events of 11 September. The site itself is perhaps the greatest indication of how long-term, complex and emotive the development process is, with conflict between the competing aims and requirements of the landowners, the city authorities, the people of New York and the victims of the attack leading to a series of competitions, designs, redesigns and much debate generated in all media about what should be built. It is an extreme example of what property development can be like. It is such an important factor in life. Property is more than habitation, more than a place to work and play, it is our very environment, one of the things that define us as humans. Debates such as these will always rage around development. This was true in 2002, is true in 2008 and will almost certainly be true in the future.

One thing that has changed in the past six years has been at the other end of the financial scale. The trend to invest in residential investment property by small investors has grown enormously. Hand in hand with this, and aided by myriad lifestyle programmes on TV, has come a boom in small-scale development. Suddenly everybody seems to either be a developer or has aspirations to be one. I have tried to reflect this in the new edition of the book, with more emphasis on residential-type developments. This also reflects the wider market with a wider involvement of larger developers in residential development, usually on 'brownfield' sites in inner urban areas. Again, I have tried to slightly alter the book's focus to reflect this, as well as to cover the impact that the internet has had on the property markets. Finally, I have tried to keep pace with legislative changes and changes in the wider economic environment.

I hope the reader will find the book useful. I would like to apologise in advance for any errors or omissions. The responsibility for those is all mine!

Tim Havard

Culcheth, Warrington
January 2008

Contents

INTRODUCTION

WHAT THIS BOOK AIMS TO DO

Property development can be defined as the process that sees the transformation of real property from one state to another.

The property development process is viewed in different ways by the various groups of people involved. Developers, planners and environmentalists have different, possibly opposing objectives, and will therefore have different views of the merits or faults of any proposed development. Property development is therefore a potentially divisive subject, and one fraught with political implications. However, while the social and political aspects are important, the focus of this book is on the tactical issues of property development. This book is intended to be a practical guide to property development, rather than an academic discourse on the subject.

Property development, like many aspects of society, has changed markedly in recent years. Many of the traditional roles in development have changed, with the divisions between the participants becoming blurred. The end market for the product is volatile, with user requirements ever-changing. Development has always been a contentious process but it is now increasingly intertwined with political, social and environmental policy issues. At the same time, development has also become more accessible, with more participants from a wide variety of backgrounds either undertaking developments themselves or taking key parts in the development process.

The book was designed with these observations in mind and it therefore has two main objectives. First, for those wishing to undertake development, the book aims to give the reader a sound practical guide to the process and environment of property development. Depending on the requirements of the reader, the book will provide a basic level of knowledge, but will also provide the opportunity to acquire more advanced skills. The book covers all stages of the development process. Each stage is explored at a theoretical or explanatory level, but case studies that provide the link between the theory and practice of development are also included. Property development can be a relatively simple process, particularly with small-scale 'entry level' schemes like house refurbishments. It can also be extremely complex at the larger end of the scale. The book is aimed at all levels, although the complex cases will, inevitably, form the bulk of the consideration.

Second, the book is aimed at people who are involved in the development process or decision-making, either as members of the development team or people who are outside development itself but need to understand the process. Contemporary members of the development team need to develop wider skills and knowledge to successfully complete their tasks. In many cases, projects would benefit from the wider participation of all the members of the construction team in the development process. Individual components of the team, be they architects, planners, engineers, contractors, etc., have, however, sometimes found their role limited due to their lack of knowledge of aspects of the development process as a whole. Similarly, decision-makers in the corporate and public sector need to understand development in order to make informed and sound decisions. Many of the controversial decisions in public life in the UK in recent years, such as the Millennium Dome, Wembley Stadium and the London Olympics site, are essentially property development decisions. A better understanding of the mechanics, process and economics should lead to better decisions. This book aims to filling this gap in the knowledge base.

THE STRUCTURE OF THE BOOK

The book is made up of seven chapters that cover aspects of the theory of development, and a case study chapter that shows how the theory relates to practice. The theory chapters are, however, strongly rooted in practice.

The seven theory chapters are:

> *Chapter 1: The background to property development in the UK.* In this chapter the players in the development markets are reviewed, as are the various forms that development can take. In particular, however, the property markets are reviewed, as an understanding of how these markets work is vital to understanding how development can take place.
> *Chapter 2: Development inception.* In this chapter a number of issues connected with what enables development to take place are examined. This includes how development starts and what factors have to be in place to make it viable; how market research is carried out in order to establish whether there is a demand for the type of development proposed and to determine the final form of development; and how development interacts with the land use planning system with a concentration on the process of obtaining planning consent.
> *Chapter 3: The finance and economics of development.* Property and finance are inextricably linked. Property tends to be expensive and development is particularly capital-intensive. Raising funds for development is a vital issue. Many viable schemes have failed to proceed from the planning stage for want of financial backing. This chapter explores the vital area of development finance, covering simple development loans to corporate financing of major developments. The impact of tax on development is covered in this area.
> *Chapter 4: Financial appraisal of development projects.* Development appraisal is a vital specialist area. It gives information about how much the developer can afford to bid for a site. It tells them how much profit they can make if everything goes as expected. It can be used to explore the downside risk of development. In particular, however, it forms a vital component in the process of obtaining development finance.

> *Chapter 5: Executing the development.* The majority of development ideas do not proceed beyond the planning phase. Putting all the components in place for development to get underway forms the bulk of the work in many developments. However, the execution of the development itself is a vital component to the success of the scheme. This chapter looks at the construction of the development team, the roles and characters of the key players and the way they should work together. It also reviews how building work should be procured and how the contracts should be administered in order to successfully complete the development.
> *Chapter 6: Post completion.* This chapter examines how the completed development is handled after the construction works have finished. It covers the choices available to the developer, including selling the completed scheme and setting up the completed development as an investment vehicle. It covers aspects such as selecting an agent and also lease structures.
> *Chapter 7: Risk appraisal and risk mitigation: a common-sense approach.* Finally, in the theory part of the book, a chapter specifically devoted to risk and its management is included. Risk and development are common partners, therefore it is important to be aware of what can go wrong and the consequences. In particular, it is important to appreciate what can be done to reduce the chance of the bad events occurring or to mitigate their effects if they cannot be avoided.

The book concludes with an examination of a series of case studies drawn from real development examples. A range of projects has been selected to illustrate how the theory relates to reality and how real developers have brought schemes to fruition.

THE SCOPE OF THE BOOK

Although simple compared with other engineering-type projects (such as developing a new car or aircraft), property development is highly complex in that it requires many strands of skills, knowledge and resources to be brought together. Even a simple project requires some involvement and knowledge of basic economics, the planning system, finance, construction technology, design skills and management. Larger projects mean greater complexity.

This is reflected in a book on the subject. Each of the chapters of the book could have formed the topic for a substantial book on their own, and indeed often do. A book that attempts to cover the whole process is bound to be a compromise. None of the chapters are as comprehensive as they could be, even though some of them are very large! The book is intended to provide the reader with something more than an introduction but it cannot impart expert knowledge in any area because of its natural limitations. In actual fact this reflects what many successful developers are like. They are often a 'Jack-of-all-trades'. They need to know something about most aspects of what they do but they do not need to be experts in any.

A classic developer is a catalyst, a ringmaster or an entrepreneur, depending on the metaphor that the reader prefers. To use another one, a developer can be imagined to be someone doing a jigsaw: he or she will be able to visualise the end picture, he or she will know how the pieces need to be assembled, but they do not need to know how the picture was put onto the board or how the pieces were cut out.

This book tries to impart the ability to assemble the pieces of the jigsaw and to have some understanding of what each piece represents. It may fail – that is a risk that all project developers face. That is part of the fun of trying.

THE BACKGROUND TO PROPERTY DEVELOPMENT IN THE UK
CHAPTER 1

The diverse nature of development in the UK

Property development is taken in general to be the process that involves the transformation of property from one state to another.

The property development process can be looked at in several different ways. Adams, for example, reviews a number of models that try to take a dispassionate view of the process, breaking it down into a number of streams and stages.[1] These academic models have their uses but it must be recognised that any party involved with the process, either directly or indirectly, will have a different point of view. For example, the development of a decentralised office park can be fitted into any of the models reviewed by Adams, but the interpretation of the process in practice is multi-fold.

To a developer, process equates to the ways that an identified opportunity is realised and the profit extracted. The developer may attempt to short cut the process where possible to achieve this end. To a local planning department the process may represent steps towards the realisation of a master plan or vision for an area that will achieve the goals of the community as they see it. To an environmentalist, the scheme may represent a process of destruction, another contribution to the degradation of the natural environment and, therefore, one to be opposed at every step.

Property development is a terribly emotive, divisive issue and it is easy to become bogged down in the political and social issues related to aspects of the process. This aspect is largely beyond the scope of this book, which is intended as a practical guide to development. Whether an individual development is politically correct or socially acceptable is for others to comment on. This book largely concentrates on the tactical rather than the strategic level. The strategic does, however, influence the tactical at many levels and to understand the process properly it is important to have a good grasp of the widely differing characteristics of development. This introductory section gives something of an overview of the strategic element, looking at the background and characteristics of development in three broad sections.

Section 1 examines how property development can take many different forms. The overall process reviewed in the models above is fundamentally the same for all but can differ quite markedly in detail from one situation to another. This section

1

reviews the different forms that property development can take, examines how different motives affect the final form of development and looks at some of the different ways that the parties to development come together to actually undertake development.

Section 2 examines exactly who is involved in development. The book gives pencil sketches of these parties, looking at their roles, motives and behaviour. These factors are often complex and interrelated. They also vary in different circumstances.

Section 3 examines the background to development, perhaps the most important part of the process – the property markets themselves. Property is an amazingly diverse asset of great complexity which can involve several sectors and entail a web of legal interests; indeed, a single individual property may serve several markets and contain several tiers of legal interests within it. Anyone involved in property development must have an understanding of these markets for they have a significant impact on the process of property development.

Section 1: different forms of property development

Some of the diversity covered by the catch-all phrase 'property development' can be appreciated when the different types of development are reviewed. These can be classified by the type of change in the property considered, as detailed below:

> *new build*: development on a previously undeveloped site
> *new build – brownfield*: development on a previously used site
> *redevelopment – demolition*: clearance and new build of a functional and similar building
> *redevelopment – partial demolition*: partial new build
> *refurbishment*: retention of existing structure which is renewed or rebuilt
> *conversion/change of use*: existing structure substantially retained but for different use (e.g. from office to residential use).

It is immediately obvious that these divisions are not absolutes. It is easy to get combinations of these classifications in the same development, but they are useful sub-divisions.

In addition to this classification, it is important to consider the motives of the body initiating the development which, again, can influence the process quite markedly. The common theme is that all development releases some kind of 'latent' profit. This profit may be in the 'normal' mode of money return, but it might also be in the form of 'social profit' in terms of additional value to the community.

Some of the motives for development can be broken down into the following categories:

Private sector development – for profit

Initiator	Purpose	Motives
Private sector property developer	Develop property for sale or letting to third parties	Development profit
Investor	Develop property for letting to third parties and for selling on to other investors in the long term	Return on capital invested
Corporate sector	Develop property for own occupation and use	1. Enhance profit-making potential of business operations 2. Acquire valuable tangible asset

Public sector development – for profit

Initiator	Purpose	Motives
Government or other public sector or quasi-public sector body	Develop property for sale or letting to third parties or for own use	1. Meet occupational/operational requirements 2. Enhance local or national economic development

Public sector development – not for profit

Initiator	Purpose	Motives
Government or other public sector or quasi-public sector body	Develop property for sale or letting to third parties or for own use	1. To meet needs of society not met by private sector development 2. To provide infrastructure or environmental enhancement to encourage economic development

In addition to these broad motives for development there are also hybrids. Examples are Private Finance Initiative (PFI)/Public Private Partnership (PPP) projects where the Government or some other public body is the initiator while the private sector is the executor.

A number of different mechanisms of development also exist. Many books on this subject do not recognise that development takes place in a variety of different environments or through different routes. Some might term these 'environment-different' routes of procurement, and indeed we will be returning to look at these when we examine development execution. However, at a strategic level, to comprehend the development process more completely, some appreciation of the differences must be obtained. Each environment or route produces a developed property of some kind as its outcome and each involves different players, or the same players with different responsibilities and different roles.

This is probably easier to illustrate than explain in a handful of paragraphs. Seven of the most common development routes are illustrated below.

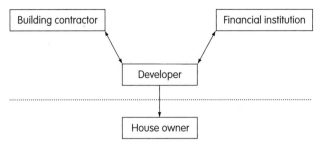

FIGURE 1.1 Private sector house builder

PRIVATE SECTOR HOUSE BUILDER

In this environment developers act as initiator, catalyst and project manager. They may have the same identity as the building contractor but are usually separate in the UK house building market. Developers find the land, obtain planning consent and building control approval and arrange all other necessary components for the development to go ahead. They then enter into a contract with a building contractor to construct the dwellings, usually at a fixed cost per unit (the contract is represented by the double arrow in Figure 1.1). Developers also arrange finance to pay the majority of development costs. Commonly this will be debt finance raised from commercial lenders but the larger builders may obtain finance through other sources (e.g. the stock market, bond issues or retained profits). This type of development does not have a specific known end user at the time of the development; hence, the product will tend to be unadventurous and fairly uniform in order to appeal to a wide variety of end users, although it will be targeted at certain income/socioeconomic groups from the outset. Developers usually sell the freehold interest in the property to the end user and thus retain no long-term interest in the development, other than any guarantee that runs with the property. The dotted line represents the division between those who have an interest in the conduct of the development and those who retain an interest in it afterwards. The development finance is normally repaid with the procedes of the sale.

RESIDENTIAL DEVELOPMENT FOR LETTING

This type of development route (Figure 1.2) is a relatively recent innovation in the UK. Residential investment and development is common in other countries where owner occupation does not dominate the market. An example of this are cities in the USA where high costs of ownership allied to the need for flexibility in the labour market lead to high levels of leasing in the apartment market. Such tenure arrangements need to be supported by legislation, particularly in regard to the characteristics of the landlord and tenant legislation and the tax system.

The trend in UK legislation throughout most of the 20th century was to protect the tenant's rights over those of the landlord. Rents were controlled and tenants received statutory rights and rights of succession in title of relatives. Much of the legislation was well intended and did protect vulnerable groups from the unscrupulous landlord.

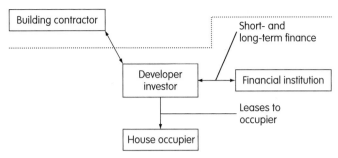

FIGURE 1.2 Residential development for letting

The net result, however, was to prevent residential owners from receiving sufficient income from lettings to maintain the stock and to receive an acceptable return. This encouraged the trend towards owner occupation as investors were driven out of the 'middle ground' of the letting market; this type of tenure in the UK being confined to the top and bottom ends of the market. It was not until the 1980s, with the introduction of assured short-hold tenancies at market rents, that private landlords were attracted back into this market, and even then it has taken many years for a substantial new build market to develop.

The development of this market may have been limited by the lack of encouragement from the UK Treasury. In many countries, such as the USA and Australia, the landlord can claim tax breaks such as depreciation allowances to offset tax that is liable elsewhere. Residential investment thus becomes a tax shelter for people who would otherwise not invest in property – for example, the wealthy professional. There are limited tax concessions in the UK, but they are largely confined to capital allowances on plant and machinery and on industrial buildings (at the time of writing).

Returning to this route of development, there has been an increasing number of this type of scheme over recent years. Many of the schemes have involved the conversion and refurbishment of redundant office or industrial/warehouse buildings in the centres of major cities. These schemes are frequently disposed of on long leaseholds to the individual apartment occupiers[2] but they are also increasingly being developed by investors, or else the freehold interest sold on to investors, with the flats being leased at market rents on shorter leases to occupiers. This type of development has also taken place in the housing association market for many years (see Section 3 on *Property markets* below), particularly as this sector has taken over from the council house sector in terms of new build provision.

CORPORATE CLIENT REQUIRING BUILDING FOR OWN OCCUPATION

In the commercial market[3] there are several routes to development. The one represented diagrammatically in Figure 1.3 is the simplest. This is where a corporate occupier (although others, such as government departments or functions, use this route) requires a new building. In these cases it is the corporate occupier who is the development initiator, driver and coordinator. Clients, in the traditional form of

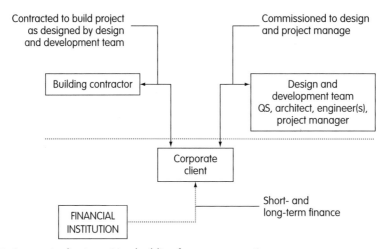

FIGURE 1.3 Corporate client requiring building for own occupation

this route, employ their own design and development team to detail the scheme based on their own brief. This team prepares the designs and tender documents which the construction sector uses to prepare bids in competition to secure the work. The design and development team then manages the development process to its conclusion. Traditionally, the project management role has been fulfilled by the architect, although more commonly in larger schemes professional project managers have taken over this role. The funding arrangements for this type of project are diverse. Often, funds will be derived from internal sources, i.e. the corporate concern uses part of its own resources to develop the building. In other cases, individual project funding is obtained from normal lending sources, either through mortgage or normal corporate loan arrangements.

The type of building produced by this route is quite diverse. The corporate sector direct development route can produce very functional buildings designed merely to meet the requirements of the occupier and little else. It can also produce bold and innovative products as the company seeks to project an image or to make a statement. The advantage of this route is that the building only has to meet the needs of a single occupier – the commissioner – and need not appeal to a wide market (as in buildings that are produced for sale or lease without a specific end occupier in mind, i.e. speculatively). It is perhaps not a coincidence that some of the most bold, advanced and often controversial buildings produced in the UK over the past 25 years have been procured by this route. These include the Lloyd's of London building, the Cable and Wireless training building,[4] and Portcullis House, the new offices for Westminster MPs. It is interesting that these buildings are often some of the most expensive in terms of cost per square metre compared with their market-led contemporaries.

VARIATION: DESIGN AND BUILD TYPE CONTRACTS

This route to development is a variation on the procurement route outlined immediately above, being the contemporary route to direct building procurement.

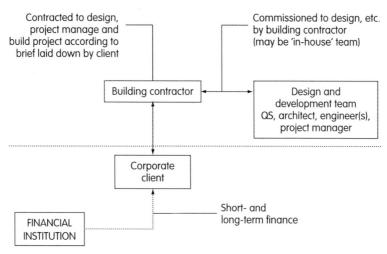

FIGURE 1.4 Design and build type contracts

The concept behind design and build type projects (Figure 1.4) is that the client seeking the building has a 'one stop shop' arrangement with the contractor, who is commissioned to both construct the building and provide the detailed design realisation of the client's broad concept for the building. It is argued by the proponents of this method that this provides a cheaper and faster route to the finished building. The client must prepare a brief and then usually offer a handful of contractors the opportunity to bid competitively for the contract, bringing forward their concepts to meet the brief.

This route to development occurs most frequently in this type of situation, where the building is for a defined end user and where there is no entrepreneurial developer involved.

VARIATION: PFI- AND PPP-TYPE PROJECTS

A further variation on the corporate, known end user development routes is the PFI/PPP-type arrangement. Public sector bodies (government departments, hospitals, prisons, schools, etc.) formerly used the traditional routes outlined in the two immediately preceeding sections, but for a number of reasons the PFI/PPP route has been the preferred option in recent years. The principal reason is that this route takes spending off the Government's public sector capital spending budget. The public body procuring the building pays a 'rent' type annual fee to the provider for the provision of the building and its services rather than having to find the funds for the whole building out of the public purse. Another reason for the adoption of this route is that the specialist skills of facilities management are removed from the responsibility of the public sector, again reducing government costs. Also, this method gives the occupier the ability to more accurately budget future costs. In general, the public sector body may also receive best value following this route, although this is less clearly established.

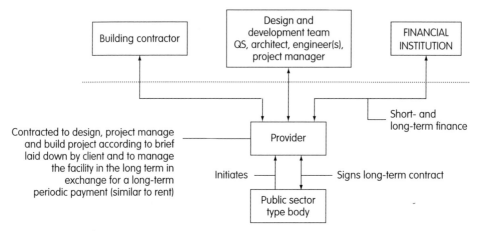

FIGURE 1.5 PFI- and PPP-type projects

The principle underlying PFI/PPP should be apparent from Figure 1.5. Rather than construct and run a building to carry out the public sector function, the body seeks a provider who will provide the building and a specified list of services for a set period of time, after which the building will revert back to the provider/owner. This period of time is often quite long, 25 years being the norm, and it is also common for the provider to set the fee received for the entire period of the occupation of the public body. PFI/PPP contracts tend to be individual to each project and wide variations in form exist. The documentation is invariably complex and the process often takes a considerable period of time to negotiate.

SPECULATIVE DEVELOPMENT: DEVELOPER INVESTOR

The final two main development routes that will be outlined cover the situations where the traditional 'property developer' operates. In many, but not all cases, the end user of the development is not known at the inception of the process. In the vast majority of cases in both routes the occupier of the building leases the property with the long-term freehold interest being vested in another party. Both of these routes are very common. There is a tendency for most corporate occupiers not to own their premises as this is viewed as tying up financial resources outside the core activities of the business; there is also a ready investment market where owners seek to receive an income from their property holdings. Although many of the routes outlined above in the commercial sector receive a large amount of publicity, the latter two routes dominate the market.

There are two main variations on the route, largely defined by the characteristics of the developer. In the first, the developer seeks to retain the long-term beneficial ownership of the building, i.e. they are building to invest and are termed *developer investors* (Figure 1.6). This group of developers includes some of the largest UK property companies. The developer acts as the catalyst and focus of the development, commissioning the design, construction and finance of the development, and finding the end user. The actual financial arrangements depend

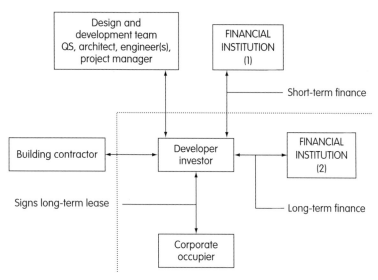

FIGURE 1.6 Speculative development: developer investor

on the characteristics of the developer, the larger companies funding developments using a variety of corporate finance sources such as long-term stock market debenture stock, while smaller developers rely on commercial, often project-specific loans to undertake the schemes. Sometimes this results in the developer needing to secure two sources of finance – short-term finance to construct the building and long-term, mortgage-type finance, which repays the original loan and which is serviced from the rents received.

SPECULATIVE DEVELOPMENT: DEVELOPER TRADER

The second 'traditional' development route is illustrated in Figure 1.7. This route is perhaps the most complex that has been outlined to date but is also the most common in the context of the UK market. Here, the developer acts as the ultimate entrepreneur developer – in the project for the short-term return only. The roles taken by the *developer trader* are similar to the developer investor, except that the former is also seeking a long-term owner for the freehold of the scheme, i.e. they aim to sell the finished development as a completed investment.

Both of these routes have common features. It is relatively uncommon for either developer traders or developer investors to procure buildings by the design and build route. This is because the developer feels the need to closely control the output of the design process, given that the product is often targeted at specific market sectors or sub-sectors. A second common feature of these routes is that the product is designed to appeal to as wide a variety of occupiers as possible, thus reducing the risk to the developer of ending up with an empty building. A by-product of this is that the buildings produced tend to be bland and mediocre.

The seven development routes outlined above are the principal but certainly not the only ones. There tends to be considerable variation among them, with hybrid

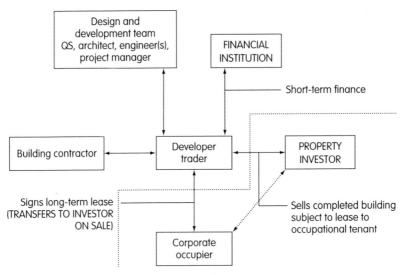

FIGURE 1.7 Speculative development: developer trader

routes existing. Some developers act as developer traders and as developer investors depending on the individual scheme and the prevailing market conditions. Whatever the case, appreciating what routes to development exist assists greatly in understanding how the development process works.

Section 2: players in the development market

One of the features of the past century in the UK was the widening of involvement in the property market in general, and property development in particular. By the beginning of the 21st century a wider variety of people and bodies had been, or currently were, players in the development market. A list of players in the market would be almost infinite; if, however, we concentrate on those bodies that have a consistently significant influence on the market and the process, then a more manageable list may result:

> landowners
> financial institutions
> local authorities
> central government
> property consultants and agents
> pressure groups
> developers.

It is useful to attempt to identify who the chief players are, what their role is within the development process and what the future trends may be. It should be noted that this book is intended as a practically based book, rather than one that concentrates on the philosophies and motives of the players. Hence, there will not be an intensive concentration on this section.

LANDOWNERS

Who are they?

There are a number of different categories of landowner, although ultimately it is the Crown from which the roots of land ownership arise. This section attempts to summarise the key players. The landowner is stated first, followed by examples, nature of holdings and comments.

The Crown estates

Examples

> Royal palaces
> Royal estates.

Nature of holdings

Traditional estates in many parts of England, Wales and Scotland.

Comments

Landowners tend not to release land for major scale development. The role of these estates is largely for the preservation of the status quo. Exceptions do exist, such as Poundbury, Prince Charles's experiment in sustainable development.

Traditional landed estates

Examples

> Grosvenor estates
> Howard de Walden estates.

Nature of holdings

Traditional estates had significant rural and urban land holdings. With the development of urban centres many of these land holdings are now located in high-value locations close to city centres. This is particularly true in the centre of London where significant parts of the West End are owned by the landed estates.

Comments

Some of the landed estates have little or no involvement in development or the land and property markets. Others, including the two listed above, are significant players and have used their landowning as a springboard for the establishment of major property companies. In the case of Grosvenor, this has extended far beyond the original estate boundaries.

Central government

Examples

> Direct government-owned land, e.g. Ministry of Defence estate
> Land owned by agencies of central government.

Nature of land holdings

These landowners own large areas of country, particularly as part of the defence estate, including army bases, ports, air bases and associated residential areas housing the staff. They also own major areas of rural land such as Salisbury Plain, for testing, training and exercises, and live firing. The secret arms of government (MI5 and MI6, defence research, etc.) also fall within this category. Agencies of central government include air traffic control, the civil service commission, offices of government agencies like job centres and part of the health estate.

Comments

Governments in recent years have become less directly involved in property development. This trend has increased with the development of the Private Finance Initiative and Public Private Partnerships. The extent of their land holdings, however, still makes them highly influential in the development market. This has been notable in recent years with the release of significant parts of the defence estate, made redundant by the 'peace dividend' following the collapse of the Soviet bloc, and has opened up many development opportunities for the private sector.

Quangos

Example

> English Partnerships.

Nature of land holdings

The quango (quasi-autonomous non-government organisation) English Partnerships was formed by the merger of the Commission for the New Towns (CNT) and the Urban Regeneration Agency. They still have significant land ownership in the 'new towns' and planned expansion centres in the UK, although much has been developed or devolved back to local council ownership.

Comments

The CNT's traditional role was as a development initiator and coordinator in the new towns. Land was acquired by the state at the time of the town's inception and released for development in line with the development master plan for the town. This programme is still active, for example in Warrington, Cheshire, where a large block of new development land called Omega was released in January 2001.

Local government

Examples

> County councils
> city councils
> town councils, etc.

Nature of land holdings

Some county councils, in particular the urban city and town councils, have significant land ownership. In the past this was often due to post-war reconstruction programmes where large swathes of bomb-damaged land were acquired compulsorily to assist redevelopment. Another contributing factor to the large-scale land holdings was the comprehensive redevelopment programmes instigated, in the main, between the 1930s and 1960s. This left local councils with large land holdings, though often the remnants of these are in areas of economic deprivation.

Comments

Although local authorities have been criticised in the past for restricting development and economic growth by being slow to release land, this situation has largely changed. Many local authorities now take a more active role in the development process, either by identifying land that has development potential or by positively initiating development by entering into partnerships with private sector development. Some local authorities, acting on the encouragement and initiative of central government, have set up joint venture companies with the private sector to lead development in their localities (e.g. Liverpool Vision).

Ex public sector utilities

Examples

> Centrica
> Network Rail
> British Waterways
> electricity generation companies
> former Coal Board sites.

Nature of land holdings

Many of the old publicly-owned corporations set up in the post-1945 nationalised environment had acquired substantial land ownership through the widespread application of their compulsory purchase powers. Land holdings include rail lines and adjacent land, canals and tow paths but with the addition of large tracts of land adjacent to water plus significant amounts of land formerly held by other bodies.

Comments

A lot of the land held by these bodies is still used for the original purpose for which it was acquired; however, much is now surplus to requirement. This situation has existed for years and was exploited by many of these organisations while they were still in public ownership. British Rail had an active property arm that developed much of the valuable land adjacent to and sometimes over station sites in the major conurbations, particularly in central London. British Waterways acted in a similar fashion. The private sector successors to these bodies also have the potential to develop their land holdings. This may increase in future years as many of the traditional heavy industries in the UK continue to decline.

Institutional investors

Examples

> Life assurance companies (e.g. Prudential, Scottish Widows, etc.)
> pension funds (e.g. National Farmers' Union, PosTel, etc.).

Nature of land holdings

Institutional investors hold land as an investment, i.e. to receive income or to obtain growth in capital values, or both. Land holdings include large tracts of agricultural and forestry land.

Comments

Institutional investors are active players in the development market, as described below. The large-scale land holdings that are owned outside the major urban conurbations are not, however, often bought for development purposes.

Corporate and industrial landowners

Examples

> Various, but including steel, motor and chemical industries.

Nature of land holdings

In a similar manner to the former nationalised industries, the larger corporate concerns often build up significant land ownership as part of their operations.

Comments

Some of these companies have been directly active in the development market, setting up their own development companies. This is particularly true of companies whose core business was intrinsically linked to property, such as the major retailers (e.g. Boots and Asda). Others became involved but made heavy losses in the property crash of the early 1990s and withdrew. Other companies may become involved if and when their core industries contract.

Developers

Examples

> Larger house builders
> commercial developers in process of site assembly
> retailers holding strategic sites.

Nature of land holdings

In particular, the larger house builders build up substantial 'land banks' with the potential for development, although frequently without planning permission. Commercial developers preparing large schemes, particularly retail schemes, also sometimes build up land ownership in the area where their scheme is located as part of the process of site assembly.

Comments

The land here is intended for development. Sometimes individual developers are criticised by those with a vested interest in seeing development undertaken (e.g. local authorities who have their own economic goals for the area) for holding up schemes by retaining strategic land ownership while working up their own development ideas.

Other categories of landowners

Examples

> Various, ranging from the agricultural sector through the forestry commission to wealthy private individuals.

Nature of land holdings

This category encompasses quite varied land ownership.

Comments

These landowners can have widely varied goals and intentions.

FINANCIAL INSTITUTIONS

In property development, as with many other aspects of life, money makes the world go around. In fact, given the capital-intensive nature of property, finance and the institutions that control it are hugely influential on development. This section examines the key players using the following structure for each: example organisations, their role in the development process and comments.

Commercial banks

Example organisations

> Royal Bank of Scotland
> Barclays.

Role in the development process

> Providers of development funding for small to medium-sized commercial and residential schemes.
> Providers of long-term mortgage finance for commercial and residential property ownership.

Comments

Banks have traditionally been the main source of finance for the property company sector, both in terms of development and providing long-term finance for ownership. They tend to be at the heart of expansion of the development market; indeed, they have been criticised for fuelling development booms. Figures from the DTZ publication *Money into Property*[5] illustrate that the increase in development activity in the early 1970s, late 1980s and late 1990s coincided with a great increase in bank lending.

This may be a function of the behaviour of banks in lending to the property industry. The property market tends to run in cycles. Cycles are common in the general economy; indeed, contemporary thinking among government macro-economists is to dampen the swings in the general economy. Cycles in the property market tend to be bigger in amplitude, and this is partly due to how banks lend to the sector. They tend to lend when the property market is already healthy, with rises in rental and asset values well established.

Compared with other risky ventures, property lending is an attractive option for banks. The rates at which banks lend are relatively high, giving a good return with the added security of the underlying worth of the property asset to fall back on. This latter factor is not really available in lending to businesses. With businesses, the bulk of the value is usually in the ability to earn cash flow in the future; this can evaporate very quickly. Banks operate in a very competitive environment and are therefore keen to lend within sectors that will give them a good return. The tendency to lend when values rise is understandable but the rise in values is often a function of previous low levels of lending in the immediate past when the property market is poor and when development supply is low. Shortages in supply tend to fuel price rises, thus enabling both development and development lending. This is illustrated in greatly simplified form in Figure 1.8.

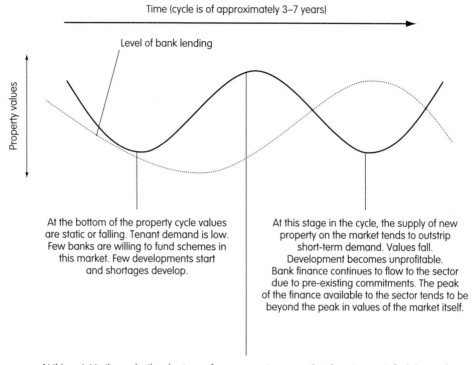

Time (cycle is of approximately 3–7 years)

Level of bank lending

Property values

At the bottom of the property cycle values are static or falling. Tenant demand is low. Few banks are willing to fund schemes in this market. Few developments start and shortages develop.

At this stage in the cycle, the supply of new property on the market tends to outstrip short-term demand. Values fall. Development becomes unprofitable. Bank finance continues to flow to the sector due to pre-existing commitments. The peak of the finance available to the sector tends to be beyond the peak in values of the market itself.

At this point in the cycle, the shortage of new property means that there is unsatisfied demand. Rents and/or property values rise. Developers bring forward schemes that start to show high levels of profitability. Some banks start to lend to developers. Slightly later in the cycle the majority of banks compete to lend.

FIGURE 1.8 The property cycle and bank lending

The result of this self-generating cycle is a series of 'feast and famine' events that is very difficult to break out of. Where the amplitude of the up cycle is large the consequent downturn is usually much larger. This occurred in the late 1980s and early 1990s, resulting in banks becoming large-scale property owners following the collapse in the commercial property markets where previous years of excessive supply coincided with a downturn in the general economy.

The banking sector is therefore very influential in the development market, being the primary source of finance for the small to medium-sized developer. They are not as dominant overall, however, as the outsider may believe. Developers also use other sources of funds.

Building societies

Example organisations

> Nationwide
> Yorkshire
> Skipton.

Role in the development process

Building societies are a traditional source of long-term mortgage finance for commercial and residential property ownership.

Comments

Building societies have always had a limited role in the development process. They were originally set up solely to allow regular savings to be made and for single purpose loans to be made against the purchase of houses. They were not allowed wider involvement until the deregulation that followed the Building Societies Act of 1986. The most common outcome of deregulation, however, has been the conversion of the (mutual) building societies into (corporate) banks. These new entities act exactly like the old banking sector, although often their commercial operations are not as well developed. Examples of converted societies include the Halifax, Abbey National and the Alliance and Leicester. Very few large building societies remain and fewer still will lend to development projects other than self-build housing schemes.

One other notable feature of the banking sector that is worth mentioning is that the sector has seen considerable consolidation over the period up to the time of writing. Many banks and other financial institutions have recognised the benefits of the economies of scale that come about through mergers and takeovers. This process seems likely to continue, perhaps on a global scale. This means that much more power and influence on the property and development market will be concentrated in fewer and fewer organisations. With fewer organisations making decisions it seems possible that the market may be even more volatile than it has been in the past.

Life assurance companies

Example organisations

> Standard Life
> Scottish Widows
> Prudential.

Role in the development process

These companies fund development of income-producing property, usually to receive long-term beneficial ownership rights, and initiate developments.

Comments

Together with the pension funds, these financial bodies are the ones termed the 'institutions'. Their influence on the development market is huge, being the biggest single market for the product of the development process. This is not as occupiers but rather as the owners of the freehold interests in property. It was calculated in

1998 that the total value of institutional ownership of property amounted to over £120 billion.

Institutional investors have strict criteria as to what an acceptable property development constitutes. These include being in the best locations, let to top-quality tenants who occupy the property on a long lease (usually of 15 years' duration) with periodic rent reviews that are adjusted only when the tenant is responsible for all the repair and maintenance of the property. This type of property investment does not require intensive management for the beneficial owner but should give the best long-term income growth and capital value appreciation. However, with the notable exception of retail property, the top performance allied to an ability to attract and keep the best quality tenant can only usually be maintained with 'young' property. Investors generally hold that the investment performance of offices, industrial and warehouse properties declines steeply when they get beyond about 10 years old. Many properties in the 10- to 15-year-old age bracket become classed as 'secondary' (i.e. not prime) and are sold off, mainly to property companies. This stock has to be replaced, hence the institutions' almost insatiable desire for newly developed property.

Although the institutions have a largely positive image, they have been accused of high levels of conservatism which leads to bland and unadventurous developments. They are also associated with the trend towards out-of-town developments and with encouraging developments that promote increased road vehicle use in most areas of their involvement. All of this is probably true, but also understandable. The institutions have a duty to invest their policyholders' funds wisely, in mediums that will give a good return but will not expose them to high degrees of risk. This is reflected in their property investment policies which favour low risk developments that appeal to the widest possible market in locations where there is occupier and/or consumer demand. There is no encouragement for institutions to take the lead in environmental protection, or build innovative structures or conserve energy in the current structure of the financial environment in which they work.

The influence of the institutions on all aspects of property development in the UK, both directly and indirectly, is still significant but the sector may be on the cusp of a major change. For about the past 20 years the relative importance of property as an investment to the institutions has greatly declined, although in both nominal and real terms the level of investment has increased. In the early 1980s property made up over 15 per cent of total investment portfolios. In 2001 this had fallen to around 6 per cent. This fall is due to a number of factors, not least of which has been the explosion in global equity markets allied to deregulation. Whatever the cause, the position of property as a part of portfolios is now questionable. The low percentage that property represents in many portfolios means that it no longer offers much in the way of multi-asset diversification for investors. Property is an odd asset that requires expensive specialist skills to make it perform well. It also has other disadvantages as an investment: it is illiquid, hard to dispose of and comes in big immobile quantities which means that large holdings are required to achieve intra-asset diversification. There may come a point when the difficulties of property as an investment outweigh its advantages. What this will mean for the development market is uncertain but an institutional withdrawal would certainly have a considerable impact.

Pension funds

Example organisations

> National Farmers' Union
> Hermes.

Role in the development process

These organisations fund development of income-producing property, usually to receive long-term beneficial ownership rights, and initiate developments.

Comments

Pension funds behave in very similar ways to the other institutions. Their behaviour can be influenced greatly by the underlying maturity of the fund. The older the contributors to the fund are, the shorter the time frame that exists for the maturity of the investments that are required. Less mature funds can invest in the long term for capital appreciation rather than high levels of income. These longer term requirements have tended to favour investment in property, including the purchase and funding of developments.

Other financial institutions

Example organisations

> Venture capitalists
> specialist property funders
> property companies
> unit trusts.

Role in the development process

These organisations are providers of development funding for commercial and residential schemes. They provide long-term mortgage finance for commercial and residential property ownership.

Comments

This is a diverse group of institutions encompassing a range of different motives, purposes and behaviour. At one end of the scale there are the high-risk takers, the venture capitalists and specialist funders who will put money into schemes rejected by more risk-averse organisations. Sometimes this is as a primary funder, sometimes as the provider of gap or mezzanine finance where the developer has a shortfall (see Chapter 3, which discusses finance in detail). At the other end of the scale, there are very conservative organisations providing traditional, property-backed debt finance. These groups' overall influence on the property market is relatively small, but can be considerable in certain locations, sectors and markets.

LOCAL AUTHORITIES

Local authorities have a key role in the development process. This role can be very complex given the range of functions, powers and goals they possess. Local authorities can possess the following range of – sometimes conflicting – powers, goals and functions:

> strategic planning
> detailed land use planning
> development control
> development initiator
> landowner
> economic stewardship of area of responsibility
> representative of the aims, wishes and welfare of all members of the local area.

For convenience we will refer to this list as the concerns of local authorities. Sometimes these concerns are held in a single body, sometimes they are distributed across a range of bodies.

The range of local authorities has always been complex, but it has become more so in recent years. Local authorities, assuming a very loose definition, might be taken to include the Scottish Parliament, the Welsh Assembly and the mayor of London, as well as the various metropolitan councils, county councils, unitary authorities and district councils. The various powers of these authorities are bewildering but a summary can be attempted by looking at the list of 'concerns' identified above.

Strategic planning

Strategic planning is concerned with the overall development of an area. The most clear cut example of this is the structure plans prepared at county council level. This is primarily a written (as opposed to a map or plan-based) document that sets out the overall objectives of the local authority concerned with economic development by way of land use. It sets targets for residential development numbers, for example, and also identifies broad areas where these units should be developed and where there could be concern about the development. It can identify objectives and policies regarding conservation. Its remit is very wide but its aim is to set strategic direction for authorities lower down the ladder of authority.

In England and Wales the original concept was that the larger county councils would set the 'big picture' for the development of the larger areas they controlled with the detail being implemented by the smaller and more numerous district councils below them. This division has been blurred by the development of different tiers and types of local government. In England, unitary and metropolitan authorities fulfil both the strategic and land use planning and development control functions. In Scotland and Wales, the parliament and assembly have, respectively, taken some of the strategic powers. This has also occurred in London and Northern Ireland.

Land use planning

The land use planning function is a map-based system that should execute the strategic plans laid down by the higher authorities. The UK planning system does not zone land use for particular activities, instead each site is considered on its merits. The local plan system, however, does record and classify both existing and established land uses and also identifies land suitable for development of various kinds. It might, for example, identify current agricultural land that is deemed suitable for residential development. The identification of this land should be in accordance with the strategic objectives laid down in the structure plan. The classification of land into categories of use does not either guarantee that developments of that type will be automatically given the go-ahead, or that non-compliant development proposals are completely barred from success. All development, apart from a few special categories and in special development areas, will require a planning application to be made under development control powers (see below). The plan does, however, give considerable guidance to developers as to what is or is not favoured in the locality. The document is of considerable importance and goes through a long process of preparation and consultation before it comes into use. The normal life of a local development plan is ten years, however even draft plans have considerable weight with the planning authorities, developers and the courts.

The local or town plan was traditionally prepared by the third tier of government: the district, borough or town council. This is still the case, although the power is part of the portfolio of powers of the unitary and metropolitan authorities.

Development control

This tier of government also has the responsibility of controlling existing development as well as planning future development in their area of responsibility. Most activities that require a material change of some kind require planning consent. This includes physical development including new build and refurbishment. It also includes many changes of use. There are exceptions; some minor development by householders including small extensions can be done under the General Development Order without additional permission being required. Activities are also classified under the Use Classes Order into different types of uses. Retailing, for example, is classified into: A1, general retail; A2, financial services; A3, Restaurants and Cafes; A4, Drinking Establishments; and A5, Hot Food and Drink. While consent is required to change from A1 to A2 or A3, for example, no additional consent is required to move from A2 (as long as a ground floor display window exists) or A3 to A1.[6]

Applications follow a formal procedure and usually an indicative timetable. They are submitted to officers of the local authority, the professional employees who negotiate with the applicant, carry out consultation and make reports to the planning committee, made up of elected members of the authority, who make the final decision. Usually this follows the recommendation of the officers, but this is not always the case.

As noted, development control powers are vested in the same authority that creates the development plan. Again, this sometimes means a single authority with the full range of powers, sometimes the last tier of separate local authorities.

Development initiator, landowner, economic stewardship of area of responsibility, representative of the aims, wishes and welfare of all members of the local area

These four concerns have been brought together because they are closely related and because they sometimes complement and sometimes contradict the other functions of the local authority.

We have seen that local authorities often have considerable land holdings. They are also highly concerned with the development of their area, its economic well-being, the maintenance of social and environmental balance and urban regeneration. This, today, often leads local authorities to be the promoter and initiator of developments, particularly of large, strategic sites.

This is often a difficult balancing act. Some local authorities act on both sides of the development fence. The modern trend is towards private sector type entrepreneurial behaviour, or partnerships with the private sector to achieve these ends. This can be seen with the development of the partnership urban regeneration companies such as Liverpool Vision. They can find themselves promoting and designing developments that they themselves have to judge via their development control system. To be fair, in the main, this seems to work reasonably well, the authorities balancing their ambitions with their responsibilities to the community, but there are dangers in excessive power and the possibility that private sector developers might be squeezed out.

Whatever the case, the role of the local authority in the development process is pivotal and, with devolution and changing structures of governance, this is likely to be even more true in the future.

Some of the systems of government and indicative diagrams showing areas of responsibility are outlined in Figures 1.9–1.12.

CENTRAL GOVERNMENT

In a democratic market economy such as the UK the role of government might be seen to be limited in the development market. In the past 20 years government has tended to retreat from direct involvement, i.e. initiating and conducting development itself. This is a reflection of the Thatcherite/monetarist/Reagonomic economic way of thinking which sought to re-establish the primacy of the market over state intervention

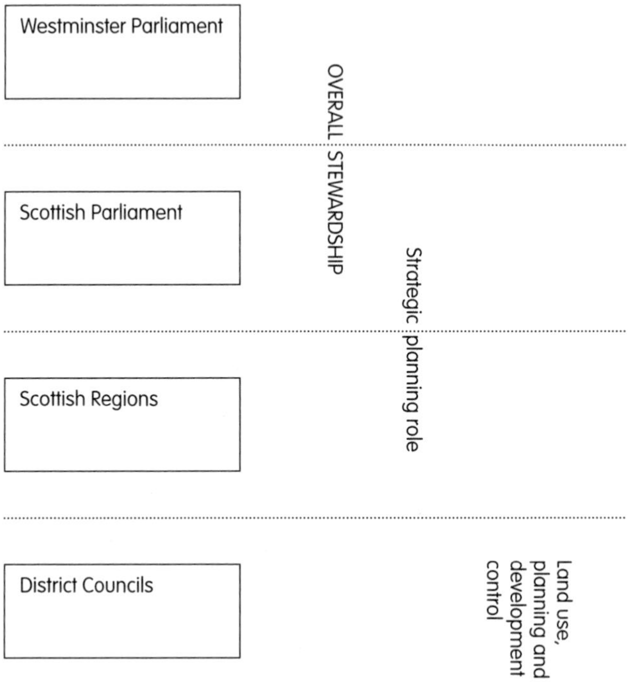

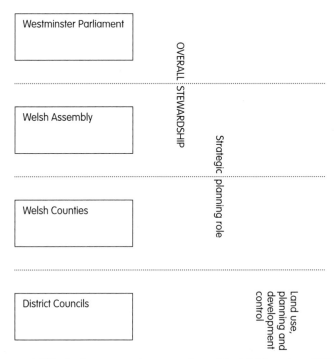

FIGURE 1.9 Responsibilities in development: an overview of the Scottish system, 2007

FIGURE 1.10 Responsibilities in development: an overview of the Welsh system, 2007

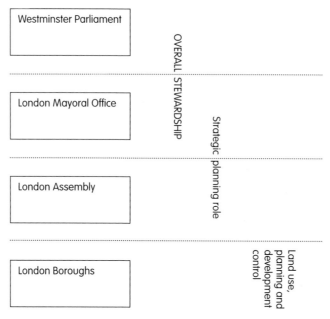

FIGURE 1.11 Responsibilities in development: an overview of the London system, 2007

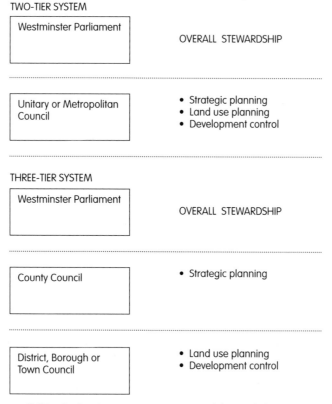

FIGURE 1.12 Responsibilities in development: an overview of the English systems, 2007

by encouraging private enterprise. Hand-in-hand with this has been successive governments' desire to control the Public Sector Borrowing Requirement, which has further restricted the scope for centralised development. Certainly the privatisation of the majority of the old state-owned industries has greatly reduced direct state involvement in the development markets.

Despite this, central government's influence over the development sector is still considerable and arises out of a number of areas, as described below.

Strategic economic direction

The Government's role as macro-economic manager of UK PLC is very influential. This is both indirect, in terms of the effects of general fiscal and monetary policy, and specific, in terms of policies on areas such as urban regeneration. Fundamentally, the demand for all types of property is one derived from the activity in the economy as a whole. The Government's policy on economic growth and inflation is very influential in determining the level of demand and the cost of finance. The monies, tax and grant regimes directed towards deprived areas are closely connected with development activity in these regions. Central government also almost completely controls the money flowing to local government.

Planning policy: strategic and detail

Although regional strategic planning, land use planning and development control are undertaken at local government level, all of these areas are strongly influenced and monitored by central government. The guiding legislation is obviously set centrally but the influence goes further. Structure plans must be approved by the Secretary of State for Communities and Local Government (CLG), who also has 'call in' powers for large controversial schemes, removing the power from the local authority to the centre. Any planning appeal for a refusal at local level is to the CLG. Government also issues Planning Policy Guidance (PPG) notes to the local authorities. These set out how local planning authorities should seek to deal with key issues in planning, such as transport, the location of retailing and whether development should be on brownfield or greenfield land. These PPGs have statutory effect and planning authorities must have regard to them in making decisions.

These powers mean that central government has a huge influence on what happens in the development market at the local level.

To these two areas can be added many other areas of influence. As we have noted, central government still has significant land holdings and constitutes a major occupier of property, even though substantial devolution to the private sector has taken place. There is a trend for the Government to move away from direct ownership to the PFI/PPP route (see page 7). Whatever the case, central government remains an important initiator and occupier of schemes and thus influential on the demand side of the development equation as well as in determining the shape of the supply side.

PROPERTY CONSULTANTS AND AGENTS

The vast majority of people reading this book will have had some involvement with agents, if only through dealings with residential estate agents. The role of agents is questioned by some, asking whether their function is really necessary. Certainly, it is possible to do without agents as houses, for example, can be sold privately. Furthermore, the advent of the Internet has greatly increased the ability of individuals to expose their properties to the wider market.

In fact, the role of the consultant and of the agent is essential in most property development as almost no development goes ahead without one or both being employed. The involvement of agents greatly improves the efficiency of the development disposal process. This is due to pre-development advice as to the form, design and marketing of the project and as a single point of contact and interaction between buyer and seller on disposal. This is usually more marked in the commercial rather than the residential market.

There is a schism between the residential and commercial property markets with relatively little cross-involvement between the agents of each in the respective markets. The exceptions are the country house market and development.

In the commercial market the fundamental nature of the property market is marked. There is no central observable market for property and an information gap exists between owners and occupiers, developers and investors. It is this void that agents and consultants fill. If there is one word that sums up the importance of the role of the commercial agent, it is 'knowledge'. Agents' specialist knowledge gives them the commercial advantage in many aspects of the development process. This is not only in acting as the catalyst between developer and tenant, owner and occupier but also in contacts with the planning authorities, funding bodies and central government.

The nature of the leading commercial consultants is relatively consistent. There are regional and local specialists based in all the UK's major cities but the leading operators are based in the West End of London. These include firms such as DTZ Debenham Thorpe, Jones Lang Lasalle, HB Hillier Parker and Insignia Richard Ellis. All of the above are notable for being UK firms who have gone global, normally with tie-ups with US investors, banks and advisors.

Sometimes these firms are accused of 'talking up the market'. There may be some truth in this, but there is no disputing the essential role that these agencies have in enabling development.

PRESSURE GROUPS

A larger number of special interest groups are involved in this category. They are also unique in that they have no direct involvement in initiating development. They do, however, have a significant effect on whether a development goes ahead and the form it takes if it does. The groups include:

> Country Land and Business Association

> conservation groups
> Campaign to Protect Rural England
> Friends of the Earth
> National Farmers' Union.

This is clearly a diverse group with diverse motives but they have common qualities. They are relatively small in number but large in influence and they are well organised, which means they can have a great effect in spite of the numbers involved and, possibly, in excess of the quality of the arguments they can put forward.

DEVELOPERS

The final group of key players in the market are the developers themselves. Developers are diverse in size, motives and areas of activity, making it difficult to provide a summary. One relatively easy division has traditionally been between the commercial and residential markets where players in one rarely operated in the other. To an extent this is still true. However, the division has become blurred in recent years. A number of commercial developers have become involved in the residential market, especially in city centres where the new trend for city living has seen traditional commercial buildings being converted for residential use.

Broadly, however, developers fall into three categories:

> residential developers (house builders)
> commercial developer traders
> commercial developer investors.

Residential developers are some of the most influential and active players in the market-place. The large house builders produce a great number of housing units each year and also acquire large tracts of land, as detailed in preceding sections. Although relatively few in number, the large house builders have huge influence on both the environment and the housing markets.

Commercial developer traders perhaps come closest to the general public's idea of a property developer. Developer traders are so called because they are largely concerned only with development. Their idea of development is short term; they are interested in producing a property, selling it on and realising the profit. Although these organisations can be large they generally have relatively few assets and instead trade on the track record of producing profits. They tend to be entrepreneurial risk takers, who make good profits in buoyant markets but who tend to disappear when the markets take a downturn. In the mid- to late 1980s, it was this type of developer who dominated the markets. In the early 1990s, when the market fell, many of these developers went out of business due to their inability to sell or let their schemes. Because they owned very little in the way of assets, they were unable to meet interest payments on loans from other sources and therefore the banks foreclosed. Many of these developers have since reappeared having taken a break for 3–5 years and have restarted new development businesses.

This type of developer can be contrasted with commercial developer investors who tend to be more risk averse. The main motive of these developers is to produce properties for retention in their investment portfolios. Example organisations include British Land and Slough Estates, two stalwart traditional UK property investment organisations who both have a stock market listing. As they are in development for the long term they take fewer risks and in many ways are more 'boring' than developer traders. Although they make less profit in good times, and are often criticised by market analysts because of this, they do tend to survive.

This is an admittedly superficial review of what is a very large and diverse sector of contemporary property development. Certainly there are organisations that carry out both residential and commercial development work. There are also commercial developers who move from being traders to investors and back again according to market conditions and opportunities. The divisions are, however, largely valid and very useful for understanding the workings of the market and the behaviour of developers within it. This book will return several times to developers, often examining how the different types of developer behave in different circumstances, for example in their dealings with financiers.

Section 3: the property markets – residential and commercial, occupier and investment

It is important to gain some understanding of the nature of the property market, or rather 'markets', as several exist, broken down into different types and sectors, locations and interests. These markets are complex and may not behave in the same way at the same point in time.

An example of how the overall market can be broken down can be illustrated in Figure 1.13. It represents a hypothetical decision-making process that might be followed by a fund manager deciding where to place funds, which culminates in a decision to place them in the office market in Edinburgh. To start with the fundamentals, money is put into the property market, followed by a sequence of decisions as to which sub-market to invest in. This forms a cascade of choices, which are not, in fact, exhaustive. Further choices include, for example, whether to put money into developments or standing investments. Similarly, the location decision in practice would be finer than the broad country/city choice illustrated.

All of the above can be considered to be separate and distinct markets that are related, in that they represent aspects of the property markets, but can behave independently.

One of the causes of the complexity of the property markets is related to the fundamental nature and characteristics of property as an asset. It is possible to create many sub-interests out of a single plot of land. It is helpful to consider a single site as an example, in this case a shopping centre in a metropolitan city that is owned by a local authority, developed by a financial institution and occupied by a series of

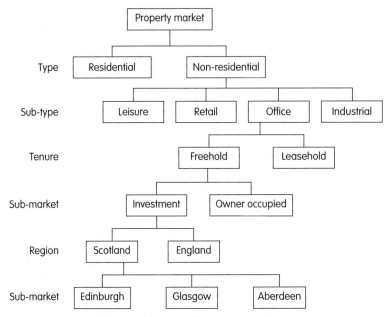

FIGURE 1.13 An example breakdown of the overall property market

national and local retailers. The tenure structure of a single part of the development may look something like Figure 1.14.

All of these interests represented in Figure 1.14 have value and can be tradable in the open market, subject to the terms of the various contracts between the parties. The point is that it is possible to create investment markets of several tiers from the same piece of property as well as an occupational market, which itself can involve several

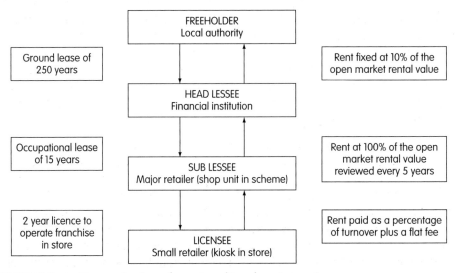

FIGURE 1.14 Typical tenure structure of a metropolitan shopping centre

parties. All of these markets are important; fundamentally, the property market would not exist without the demand from occupiers. Similarly, the commercial investment market is very influential in shaping the property market.

A complete book could be devoted to examining the property markets, far beyond the capacity of this publication. This book will concentrate on an examination of the basic structure and sub-types in the property markets, giving an indication of the most important sub-sections.

It would not be possible to examine each geographical sub-market as these vary from year to year. Up-to-date information on these markets can, however, be found in the specialist property press, particularly the weekly magazines *Estates Gazette* and *Property Week*, both of which include regular features on different parts of the country and different sectors of the market.

The biggest schism in the property markets is between the residential and commercial markets, and each of these will be examined separately. The other major division in the property markets lies between the investment and occupation markets, the balancing sides of the landlord and tenant equation. The occupation market is also diverse and difficult to summarise, and will thus be considered with the review of the commercial markets. The investment market is smaller and easier to split into investor groups and behaviours. As a result, the three areas that will be examined in detail are the residential, commercial and investment markets. The complexity of the markets, as reviewed in this preamble should, however, always be borne in mind.

A further important point for developers to be aware of is that the property markets constantly evolve and change. Because the market for property for occupation and use is a derived demand, it is the requirements of the market that shape the type and characteristics of the property provided by the development sector. Users of property do not generally adapt their needs or businesses to what is available on the market; the property market meets their requirements. This is constantly reflected in the markets, particularly the commercial markets, with new types or different specifications for existing types emerging very frequently. For example, if this book had been written in 1981 instead of 2007 there would have been no mention of retail warehousing, of regional shopping centres such as the MetroCentre or Meadowhall, of business parks or of high-bay distribution buildings, to select just four innovations of the past two decades.

There are a number of implications in this constant change for developers. First, developers must be very cautious about analysing past trends to determine future demand. The requirements of many users of property are likely to have changed. Second, there are always opportunities for the risk-taking developer to spot or to anticipate trends in the market. There is also the reassurance that the constant evolution of occupier requirements actually provides constant demand for the product of development. Whatever the case, it is essential for developers not only to have an understanding of the markets in which they operate but also to keep abreast of developments in those markets.

RESIDENTIAL MARKETS

Occupational markets

Perhaps the most stable of the property markets in terms of changing demand is the residential market, but even this statement requires severe qualification. There has been a constant demand for single-family dwellings in the UK over the past 40 years. As a result, although some aspects of the technology of the product in terms of some of the materials used have changed in this period, the product itself has not evolved very much. What has changed is the number of additional housing markets that have developed. These have come about, as with all changes in the property markets, due to changes in society as a whole. Over the recent past, society has changed to produce more single-person or childless households at both ends of the age spectrum, leading to markets developing aimed at the young urban professional and at the retirement sector. Smaller households, due to the trend to have fewer children or as the result of single-parent families, have led to an expansion of the market for smaller properties. These are just a few of the many changes that have affected the sector.

The residential markets are split between the owner occupation market and the investment or rental market. The investment section will be considered separately, because the characteristics of this are somewhat different from the owner occupation markets. In the main, however, the players in the market, the locations and the characteristics of the product are very similar and so the following comments relate both to the owner occupier and the leasing market. It should be noted, however, that the former is much larger than the latter, particularly when the private sector residential market alone is being considered.

The residential market is by far the largest of the property markets and in many ways it is the most accessible of the markets for the new developer. The product is generally low tech and demands of the potential user in terms of the specification and location required are fairly easy to establish or predict. There is also a whole range of sizes of development that are acceptable, requiring a fairly modest financial commitment from a new developer. These include the development of new single houses on vacant plots and also the refurbishment or conversion of existing stock. Many developers have become established by taking large single houses in established urban areas and converting them into flats. Another advantage is that there is a ready market of owner occupiers to buy the completed product and provide a lump sum to the developer to pay off the development costs. In the commercial markets, for example, there is simply a far smaller number of both potential occupiers and owners. All in all, it is relatively simple for a developer to become established and become knowledgeable enough to compete quite successfully.

Having said this, there are some areas of the market that are very difficult for a small developer to penetrate, mainly due to the sectors being dominated by a relatively small number of major players. One such area is large-scale private house building. This sector has long seen large house builders dominate but in the period up to 2001 a series of takeovers and mergers in the market has led to a further concentration of power.

There are a number of reasons for this domination. Land for large-scale housing development is in relatively short supply in a crowded island like Britain. Planning authorities are careful in their identification and release of such land because of the potential impact on services and other resources. The larger scale house builders are able to build up 'land banks' of prime development sites, either with or without planning consent, in order to safeguard future work. This is not a luxury within the scope of the resources of the smaller developer. In addition, profit margins have, in the past, been relatively low in this sector, meaning that each unit of housing has to be built to quite tight cost margins. This is easier to achieve within the larger organisations with economies of scale including their weight of buying power. The larger organisations also have an extensive stock of experience and data on the markets which greatly assists in decisions such as the timing and make up of developments.

It will be interesting to see whether this 'low margin' position will continue. One of the effects of the consolidation in the sector is likely to be to reduce the overall level of competition. The house builders may behave more like oligopolies, as in the car market. Here, on the surface, there appears to be price competition but in fact most of the competition is based on non-price issues such as customer service and brand image. This may occur in an unregulated housing market.

Another notable feature is that, although much attention is drawn to the sector, the new stock of houses developed each year is dwarfed by the existing stock. This means that there is some scope for redevelopment and refurbishment development. This scope is limited, however, because residential buildings in the UK tend to have a considerable lifespan and retain their value over time. The importance of this can be seen when an alternative market is compared with the pattern of values in the UK, as in Table 1.1, which compares a UK house with its Australian equivalent.

What we are observing is the effect of depreciation. In Australia, and in other markets, it is common for mass market houses to have a limited design life span. Often this is due to the environmental conditions of heat and insect attack, which mean that decay is inevitable. It is much more common for combined house and plot values to decline towards site value. It makes buying to refurbish, or clear and reconstruct far more common. This occurs in other markets as well, such as in parts of the USA. Interestingly, this characteristic is reflected in these countries' property valuation approaches where there is a requirement to value the land and the improvements to land separately – in the UK valuers value the land and the building as a single entity. The reason is that values of older and new houses are not markedly different. With good maintenance, houses in the UK can last almost indefinitely and maintain their value over time. This makes refurbishment, or demolition and reconstruction relatively rare.

TABLE 1.1 Retained values of UK and Australian housing

UK detached house		Australian detached house	
Value when new	Value at 50 years old (inflation adjusted)	Value when new	Value at 50 years old (inflation adjusted)
£100,000	£95,000	AUS$250,000	AUS$150,000

There are, however, development opportunities related to older stock. First, there are circumstances where housing stock has not been well maintained and where values have fallen to close, to or even below, site value (this can occur where the structure is a major maintenance liability or where the cost of demolition takes the value of the site to below cleared site values). This is common in inner city areas where the stock has been in public control or where social conditions have declined. There is the opportunity here for purchasing these properties at low values and carrying out a refurbishment programme.

There are also opportunities that arise out of changes in society and consumer demand. The case of the large single family house in inner city areas has been noted. These larger buildings are ripe for division into smaller units whose sum of values is greater than the value of the dwelling in single occupation. A similar situation occurs in suburbia. It was traditional for large family houses to have large gardens. Although these are still sought-after features, such large plots are not always a requirement. A common type of development in these areas is the creation of a new plot and house out of an existing garden (a good clue as to when this has occurred is when house numbers are suffixed by letters, for example 20, 20a, 21, etc.). All of this requires the cooperation of the planning authorities, of course, who can be very cautious about the growth of existing urban areas.

Investment sub-market

The residential investment sub-market in the UK saw a resurgence in the 1990s having been in almost total decline since the 1900s. The rise in the investment market, both in terms of individuals 'buying to let' and in private companies and financial institutions becoming involved, has been a major change in the UK market.

Until the 1990s the UK was almost unique among the world's countries in not having a significant private housing investment and, therefore, letting market. Other countries have long enjoyed the benefits of leased residential property, which include generally lower costs of occupation but particularly the benefits of occupier flexibility. A leased property is easy to dispose of and does not require any major capital commitment and risk. It is ideal for those with few savings or those who move jobs or locations frequently. Continental Europe, the major cities of the USA and Australia all see a substantial number of private sector letting properties often occupied by people who, in equivalent positions in the UK, would buy the properties. A mainstream private letting market, i.e. one that serves more than the extreme ends of the market (the low income and student market at one end and the luxury market at the other), provides occupiers with flexibility and options.

At the beginning of the 20th century, the UK did have a private letting market; indeed this was the most common means of occupying property. For a number of reasons this situation steadily changed during the first half of the century. First, legislation designed to protect tenants from unscrupulous landlords restricted the owners' ability to charge rents that would allow the properties to be adequately maintained while giving an adequate return on investment. Similarly, tenants were given greater security of tenure and rights of succession to relatives. This legislation was well meaning but caused private landlords to withdraw from owning property. Complementary developments in society encouraged the trend: the public sector became the provider of low-cost social housing to a large proportion of the population, the country became more affluent and wealth spread to the urban middle classes bringing home ownership within reach. The building society movement enabled further purchases to be made (see page 18). All of these factors in society led to the UK residential sector being dominated by owner occupation.

Although the advent of a 'property owning democracy' had a number of advantages in terms of giving people a stake in the country, it had disadvantages in terms of choice and restricted physical labour mobility. As a result, measures were put into place to rekindle the private rented sector. Fundamentally, this revolved around the introduction of assured short-hold tenancies in 1980 that allowed fixed-term lettings with limited security of tenure at market rents. Even then the change in the market came about very slowly. It was not until the mid- to late 1990s that a reasonable number of developments of residential investment properties commenced. Part of the reason for the slow change was the attitude of institutional investors and banks, neither of whom viewed residential investments positively. Institutional investors were put off by the high levels of management required to look after this type of investment. Banks were cautious because they doubted that buyers could be found for the completed developments.

Finally, it was market changes and cycles that seem to have triggered a change in attitude from the financial and development community. The property crash of the early 1990s had two complementary effects on the market: on the one hand, home owners who needed to move around the country often found it difficult to sell their properties at reasonable prices and were forced to let out their properties and rent elsewhere. This allowed a number of people to experience this form of tenure, boosting numbers in the market. On the other hand, the commercial sector found that there was a huge surplus of mainly secondary commercial space that seemed to have very little prospect of ever being let. The only economic possibility for many office and industrial buildings was to convert them to residential use. In addition, urban regeneration and the general desire of young professionals to live in city centres boosted the move back towards city living. All of this created the environment which sees residential development for rent being a very active sector in current UK markets.

In addition to these mainstream markets there are a number of other active residential letting markets. These include:

> *the student market* – this sector has grown considerably with the expansion of university-level education over the last 20 years of the 20th century. Some of the universities have entered into partnerships with developers and investors for the provision of privately run flats and halls of residence, but where there is a contract with the university to provide the service. These schemes have become an important element of urban regeneration programmes as a number of universities are located in these types of areas. The market has become much more sophisticated and the quality of development has greatly improved;

> *government-supported housing benefit schemes* – a large part of the remaining private rental market falls within this category. The market seems to be largely confined to the older existing stock and is not frequently associated with the development market.

It is important to complete the review of the residential property market by examining the public sector, social housing and low-cost housing sectors. Until the mid-1970s the public sector was dominated by major developers of residential property for let, i.e. council housing. The right-to-buy schemes and public sector spending constraints on local authorities have reduced new development by the public sector almost to zero. The stock of council housing has also been reduced by right-to-buy and by the transfer of some public sector estates to private sector landlords.

The provision and development of low-cost and social housing has been largely devolved to charitable private bodies, the housing associations. Using a combination of public grants and privately sourced funds, these bodies are major players in the residential property markets, particularly in inner urban areas. These non-profit-making bodies have proved very successful and efficient at providing good quality, new, affordable housing. They also offer a wide variety of choices of tenure including traditional tenure, low-cost purchase schemes and shared ownership. A substantial proportion of development in inner city areas is carried out by these bodies.

One of the big issues in all spheres of development at the start of the 21st century is the re-use of previously developed land – brownfield land – which is part of the sustainability debate. This debate is at its most sensitive when related to residential land.

COMMERCIAL MARKETS

Although the schism between the commercial and residential market has been noted, with few residential investors and developers also working in the commercial field and vice versa, this division has broken down somewhat over recent years. This is mainly due to the rise of the investment market in residential property.

Some of the disadvantages for the inexperienced new developer in breaking into the commercial markets are detailed below.

1. The 'entry level' size of commercial developments and thus the degree of financial commitment tends to be much larger than with residential property.
2. Successful development in the commercial markets requires specialist knowledge. Each market tends to be individual and distinct both in terms of product and local market requirements. The demands of the market change far more frequently than with the residential market. The supply and demand balance can change relatively rapidly. Markets therefore need to be monitored very carefully.
3. Opportunities for development are rarer than with residential markets and competition is keener. The reason for this is simply that there is less land ripe for commercial development than for residential use.

Despite this there are distinct advantages in operating in the commercial markets. Not least of these is that the potential returns from the sector are higher, although this is simply a reflection of the additional risk involved in commercial development.

The main sectors of the commercial market are relatively easy to define. They are:

> offices
> retail
> industrial and
> leisure.

Despite this ease of definition, in reality the divisions between the sectors can be blurred. The Government has, for planning purposes, allocated many urban land uses into use classes. The A class, for example, refers to retail use, the B class, business and so on. Illustrating the blurring that can occur, A2 uses refer to financial services including banks, building societies, estate agents, etc. trading out of shop-type premises. Many of the functions of the businesses in this use class resemble offices, which are normally classified under use class B1. This class, however, can also include hybrid types such as 'hi-tech' research and development buildings and light industrial uses. The development of new types of property use often blurs the basic distinctions further. Call centres, for example, are office-type functions but often they take place in industrial-type buildings. Similarly, the first generation retail warehouses occupied industrial buildings on industrial estates.

The basic market types can be divided into different sub-sections and sub-types. The basic characteristics of the main markets and the key sub-markets will be outlined below. However, these outlines can only be drawn very broadly. It should be noted that regional and local requirements and market characteristics show considerable diversity.

Offices

Offices tend to be among the most popular sectors for developers. The reasons for this tend to be the quantity of the product and its ubiquitous nature. The greatest sectoral growth in the economy of developed nations in the past century has been in the service industries – and service industries need offices. In any major town or city across the world, you will find offices, usually with the same basic characteristics, specifications and layouts. Another reason for the popularity of office development is that a wide range of qualities and sizes have market demand, making the sector very accessible.

Another attraction to developers is that the majority of businesses choose to lease rather than own their own office space. Although owner occupation in the office market has its attractions, including the ability to raise finance against the value of the asset and to obtain premises that can be exactly tailored to the requirements of the occupier, consideration of the costs of management and the degree of capital tied up in the 'bricks and mortar' rather than in the core business, tends to favour leasing. This means that there is an established market in most locations for leased office

37

space as well as the ability to create investment vehicles with the security of good quality tenants securing the income flow.

There are, of course, disadvantages for the developer as well. The office sector is prone to rapid changes in demand from occupiers as expansion or upgrading plans are made and then shelved by occupiers as the business climate waxes and wanes. Offices have considerable flexibility in terms of their intensity of occupation. A firm can delay the decision to move by simply packing more desks and work stations into an existing space. This demand elasticity is in contrast to the supply chain. Office schemes tend to take many years to reach fruition, largely because the components required to complete a scheme (the site, legal and planning issues, ownership, tenant identification and negotiation, design and specification, etc.) are numerous and complex. A moderately sized city centre office is likely to see a 3- to 5-year development period from idea through inception to completion by way of occupation, letting or sale. During this time market requirements, conditions and demand can have changed markedly several times.

A second major risk to developers is related to changing occupier requirements in terms of specification and location. Occupiers do tend to follow the herd, despite any protests that might be made to the contrary. There a number of examples in the UK where sudden changes in fashion can make locations and types of buildings almost obsolete overnight. This usually occurs when the traditional core office location where the best occupiers reside is characterised by older, period buildings, perhaps Victorian or older. These buildings have drawbacks for modern occupiers in terms of layout and ability to incorporate modern communication technology. Usually restrictions are imposed on redevelopment and refurbishment by the planning and heritage authorities. Occupiers tend to put up with these inconveniences because of the prestige and image that goes with the address. Developers and investors can pour money into these areas to maintain the stock and to go as far as they can to provide modern facilities to occupiers. This situation goes on for many years until a developer builds a modern, highly specified prestige building, usually in a hitherto fringe location. In these conditions it will only take one or two major tenants to move to the new location to make it acceptable and for a mass rush of movement to occur out of the traditional areas. These areas can be transformed overnight to wastelands of high vacancies and collapsing values. The author has observed this situation occurring to a lesser or greater extent in London (with the influence of Docklands), Edinburgh, Manchester and Birmingham.

There are a wide variety of types and sizes of offices as has already been noted. These include:

> single rooms
> offices above shops
> suites
> serviced offices
> city centre
  – Grade A
  – Grade B

- Grade C
> business parks
> call centres
> standalone headquarters buildings.

The key types will be reviewed below.

Single rooms and offices above shops

Although not a major development sector in their own right, these two sub-types of office provide the developer with useful ancillary income from a scheme. They are also sometimes popular with planning authorities as they provide mixed use elements to schemes. These key types tend to be occupied by smaller businesses and professionals such as solicitors, accountants and surveyors.

Developers have to be aware that the additional income may be countered by movements in investment yield by incorporating the additional use into the property. Some investors equate additional uses and tenants in investments as creating additional restrictions and management cost, and may require an additional initial return to compensate them. This impacts on capital values.

For example, consider a retail development that produces £50,000 p.a. in rent and for which investors are willing to accept an initial yield of 7 per cent. This equates to the following completed value:

Initial income		£50,000
Capitalised at a year's purchase in perpetuity		£714,250
@ 7%	14.285[7]	
Value of investment		£714,250
	Say	**£710,000**

Let us assume now that a developer incorporates a small office suite on the hitherto unused upper floors of the scheme. This mixed use scheme is less attractive to investors in the market at the time of development due to the additional management costs that are anticipated as the office will be let on a separate, shorter lease than the main shop. Investors require an additional 1 per cent return on additional income in compensation.

Initial income		£55,000
Capitalised at a year's purchase in perpetuity		
@ 8%	12.500	
Value of investment		£687,500
	Say	**£685,000**

The additional income of £5,000 has reduced the completed value of the development by £25,000. The attitude of investors can seem illogical but it is real and a very important factor for both developers and planners to consider.

Suites

One major attraction of office markets is that multiple occupation of buildings is an accepted part of the market. Many buildings lend themselves to sub-division into suites, although issues such as security, tenant mix and fire escapes must be considered. Division of a building into self-contained suites can be a low-cost development option for a building that has previously been in single occupation. The income flow from the divided building can often be significantly higher than for the single occupancy building, largely because the market for smaller suites is so much larger than the market for large single buildings. The initial yield effect for multi-let buildings as noted above, however, occurs here too and the value situation must be carefully monitored.

Serviced offices

Serviced offices is a sector that is very much in vogue, with a number of competing operators offering space in most UK cities as well as in other smaller or more rural locations. Serviced offices offer occupiers flexibility of occupation and the ability to set up in business quickly without the need to establish the infrastructure (support staff, office equipment, etc.). The office buildings are divided into a range of different sizes of suites and are staffed and equipped by the service office provider. Potential occupiers enter into short-term agreements with the provider to take office space in the facility as well as being provided with a range of back-up facilities at an additional charge. Although the occupation charges are high compared with traditional renting, as a short-term solution to many firms they are cost effective. They also do not require the occupier to take on the liability of taking out a traditional lease.

There are a number of major players in the service office market who own or lease space in a variety of locations ranging from traditional city centres to business parks. A number of smaller private investors and local authorities also offer schemes, the latter often as a service to assist small business development.

City centre offices

City centres were the traditional home of the office as they were convenient for transport routes, particularly public transport, and there was also the attraction of being close to complementary and competing offices for such things as the transfer of messages and documents. The rise in personal transport and the development of information and communication technology has largely freed office users of the physical reasons for their location choice but city centre locations are still very important. This is partly due to the continuation of the aforementioned factors but also for reasons such as prestige and the social elements of city centre environments.

The changes in information and communication technology and the rise of personal transportation have seen some diversion of office demand to the edge of built-up areas and onto business parks. These locations allow more space, far better car access and are usually much more cost effective with total occupation costs (including rent and property taxes) of, generally, between 50 and 70 per cent of the cost of city centre space. As a result of this, businesses have moved many of the more labour-intensive, lower grade office functions out to the fringe-of-town locations. Similarly, businesses that do not need to locate in prestige locations – perhaps those who do most of their business at a distance from their customers – have also moved to these locations. The city centre, however, continues to be very important and, generally, generates the highest rental values.

City centre offices are usually graded into A, B and C quality specifications. There is, however, no absolute definition of what these grades are from year to year. They approximate to the following:

A   Top-quality new, usually air-conditioned open plan space, let on institutionally acceptable leases, in the most sought-after locations, for which the highest rents are paid.
B   Lesser stock, usually second-hand, often – but not always – in inferior locations and possessing characteristics which limit their attractiveness to top quality occupiers.
C   Older, poor quality, poorly located offices, usually let at low rents on shorter leases.

The reasons for the doubts about the definitions are numerous. First, it is often a relative grading based on the characteristics of the local property market, i.e. Grade A space in one location may not be considered Grade A in another. Second, occupiers' requirements for top quality space vary over time. During the explosion of personal computer use in the early 1980s, space that could not provide underfloor raised access for data and communication runs was down-graded. Similarly, while new, well-located, well-specified office space may be provided within a city centre such as Manchester, it may not be graded as Grade A by occupiers if it fails to meet the modern requirement for large single floor plates.

Although some demand has been diverted away from city centres to business parks and the communication revolution has allowed such activities as home working and hot-desking, the prospects for the city centre office are still good. First, the concept of the office is remarkably durable. People do not need to work in offices but they choose to do so because of the human need for social interaction. Second, governments and pressure groups throughout the world are pressing for a sustainable use of resources. This implies long-term reduction of car use, the regeneration and re-population of city centres and the development of improved and more modern public transport systems. All of this suggests yet more use of and demand for city centre offices.

Business parks

Some of the attractions of business parks have already been discussed. The business park concept started, as with most things in the property markets, in the USA, in this case in the 1960s. The basic concept of the business park is low-density development of relatively low-rise buildings in landscaped, pleasant environments.

These locations are on the edge of major urban areas and need to have both good car access to the motorway network and extensive car parking.

There are a range of developments that are referred to as business parks but which, in fact, do not possess all of these characteristics. Indeed, the term has come to refer to virtually all edge-of-town or out-of-town office development. True business parks tend to have very low densities (below 30 per cent of site area) and high degrees of landscaping. The realities of development in a congested and competitive market such as the UK are that site densities tend to be rather higher and landscaping limited to planting around the car parks in order to make the schemes cost effective for developers.

Similarly, cost constraints limit the specification of decentralised offices. Lower rents in decentralised locations mean that construction costs of investment buildings tend to be about 30–50 per cent of the costs of top-quality city centre space. Part of the lower costs are due to the easier construction conditions found on decentralised sites as opposed to city centre locations but mainly they are due to limited specifications. These types of offices are invariably two- to three-storey steel-framed, brick-clad buildings with shallow-pitched concrete tiled roofs. They are double glazed but are often not air conditioned in the UK. Where air conditioning is fitted, the systems tend to be unsophisticated. There are usually raised access floors and suspended ceilings but this is generally the limit of specification. This is simply due to the limits imposed by the relatively low rental values generated.

Call centres

Call centres are a form of office use, although they do not specifically appear in the use classes order of 1987 as they were not even thought of at that time. They are populated by a rolling staff of workers who operate PC-linked telephone lines. Call centres occupy a range of building types from traditional offices (both in city centre locations and on business parks), converted warehouses and distribution buildings to purpose-built facilities.

Standalone headquarters-type buildings

The final type of office included in this brief review is the headquarters building of major organisations. These tend to be in decentralised or even rural locations, either in converted country houses or bespoke, modern buildings. These properties tend to be owner occupied and have very little interest for the private developer other than as potential future development sites.

Retail

The retail sector has been very resilient in the UK. In some respects the core activities of retailing – city centre and high street shops – have changed very little over the past 30–40 years. Having said this, there have been substantial changes over the period that can be summarised as the following trends.

1. The rise of the national multiple. In many ways, all high streets and shopping centres in the UK and, increasingly, major cities in Europe, have started to look very similar. The main reasons for this have been the consolidation of retail groups and also the result of the preferences of institutional investors who favour the larger retailers in their developments. These retailers themselves are very influential and many locations and shopping centre schemes need to be occupied by certain groups in order to achieve credibility with funders and, indeed, other retailers.

2. The rise of the supermarket. There has been a steady trend towards single-visit bulk shopping over the past 40 years. Supermarkets have grown in all ways: in size, in the number of ranges offered by each store and in influence on the retail sector. Again, the number of supermarket operators has fallen as groups consolidate. The current trend at the time of writing in the UK is for global players to develop. An important example is the growth of the Wal-Mart group which has entered the UK by the acquisition of Asda. In the USA Wal-Mart has a reputation as the 'Killer Big Box Store' and while the UK market is more diverse with stronger competition from local operators such as Tesco and Sainsbury, the trend for ever-larger stores and more pressure on the competition seems set to continue.

3. Both of the abovementioned trends and the influence of national multipliers has had a detrimental effect on smaller retailers and smaller retail centres which have seen steady decline over this 40-year period.

4. Shopping has become decentralised. The traditional town centre is still important to retailers; however, there has been considerable gravitation to the edge of town. This has been caused by the development of out-of-town shopping centres and retail warehousing, both of which will be covered below.

5. The rise of the covered shopping centre. People may not admit it, but by simple weight of numbers it is clear that shoppers prefer to carry out their purchases in a controlled, weather-tight environment.

6. The rise of leisure associated with retailing. Shopping has become a leisure activity and has sometimes become seamlessly associated with mainstream leisure activities such as cinemas, public houses, bars and restaurants.

7. The general increase in wealth of society has given people more disposable income and has fuelled a great increase in the volume of the sector.

The future of traditional retailing has been questioned in some quarters. E-commerce and e-tailing have been cited as being alternatives to physical shopping. The question is whether this is truly valid. There is no doubt that modern technology has already had an impact on certain sectors of conventional retailing and some forecast that the traditional high street may be badly hit by the diversion of spending. It seems more likely that e-tailing will tend to complement and expand the retail sector with only a few sectors seeing a diversion of trade. Technological changes tend to increase activity rather than provide alternatives, witness the 'paperless office' predicted in the computer age. Anyone working in an office knows that computers have vastly increased the ability and opportunity to create paper! Shopping is a leisure activity as well as a necessity. It is unlikely to be supplanted.

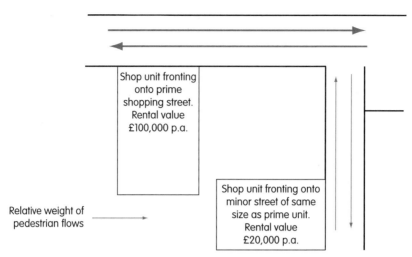

FIGURE 1.15 Effect of pedestrian flow on retail rental value

Retail investments come in many different types and sizes. This makes them popular with both investors and developers. Retail property is, however, extremely sensitive to location, making the acquisition of suitable sites difficult. The difference of a few metres can have a huge impact on the rental capital value of a property. Figure 1.15 illustrates how the weight of pedestrian flows determines this.

Strong retail locations tend to be very 'tight' markets. Retailers tend to try to hold onto properties in these locations. This means that vacancies are rare and development opportunities difficult to find in town and city centres. One exception to this in recent years has been the redevelopment of older department stores. Many traditional department stores occupy old, inefficient buildings that have often been acquired piecemeal over the trading life of the store. These operators now find either overall trading difficult or else find it more cost effective to move to newer, smaller but more

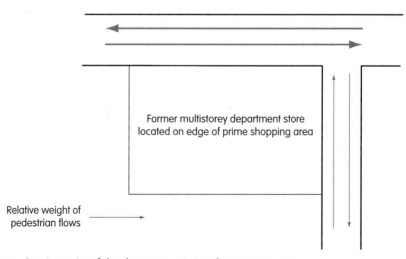

FIGURE 1.16 Starting point of development: existing department store

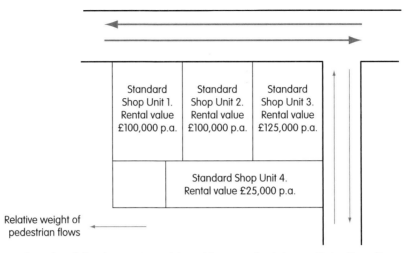

FIGURE 1.17 Completed development: provision of four standard shop units trading off ground and first floor. Ancillary storage area above with nominal value. Note that Unit 3 has a higher value due to its corner location increasing its visibility to shoppers and thus attractiveness to retailers

efficient premises, often as part of a shopping centre development. This opens the building up for conversion into smaller, standard shop units (SSUs; see Figures 1.16 and 1.17).

This type of development can realise considerable extra value. It should be noted that the majority of high street, supermarket and bulk retailing (as in retail warehouses) takes place on the ground floor only. Again, this is to do with the effect of the flow of people which tends to drop off considerably above ground level. The exception to this is in the busiest retail locations such as the absolute prime retail areas of major towns and cities where the expense of the locations forces retailers to maximise floor area utilisation.

Some of the key retail types are listed below and each will be considered in turn in brief thumb-nail sketches:

> kiosks
> standard shop units
    − comparison goods
    − financial services
    − hot food and drink
> local parades
> convenience stores
> supermarkets
> hypermarkets
> motor showrooms
> petrol stations
> shopping centres
    − in-town shopping centres

The trends in the market suggest that supermarkets may have merely delayed this competition and that the big players in the main market will also do the same in the convenience sector. The financial clout of the large players is such that there is little doubt about who will be the winners of this battle. Convenience stores tend to put even more pressure on local stores and traders and it seems inevitable that these traders will struggle to compete against the sector.

Supermarkets and hypermarkets

This sector marks perhaps the biggest change in world retailing behaviour, let alone that of the UK, over the past 50 years. From small beginnings they now dominate retailing in most countries. Their influence spreads even further as their presence and behaviour shapes the pattern of farming in the UK. Their business practices have led to the development of distribution networks including the motorway system and distribution warehouses. They have been a significant cause of the change to a car-dominant culture. They have both led, caused and reflected changes in society and the way we lead and organise our lives. This is a considerable burden to lay at the door of what is, after all, an overblown corner shop but the more thought that is given to the nature of society today, the clearer it becomes that the supermarket is central to it. This is not to lay any blame for the negative effects of these changes at the door of the supermarket operators; they are only giving us what we clearly want.

The ideal modern supermarket or hypermarket is a large (3,000m^2 plus and usually much larger than this) single-storey steel-framed box located on a large site where the building itself makes up only 20–30 per cent of the site area, the rest being devoted to car parking and, usually, a petrol filling station. It will be located within a few minutes' drive time of a substantial population centre and will have excellent road access. Preferably there will be no competing large supermarket within at least 2 miles. The best sites have high visibility so they will be easy to find for potential customers. The supermarket itself will carry thousands of product lines both in terms of fresh food and non-food goods such as clothes. They will usually include a newsagents, bakery, chemist and butchers. They are essentially town centres under a single roof.

The major operators, of which there are relatively few, have reached this point through evolution. There are still a high proportion of smaller, older stores who do not meet these specifications. In recent years the big players have been trying to move towards closing their older stores and moving to the larger, more efficient locations. The planning system has been tightened up to try to limit expansion of the sector, which may cause the operators to rethink their activities. For example, they may have to consider redeveloping older, smaller urban stores.

There are still considerable development opportunities in the sector, although most of the large operators tend to have their own development departments who carry through their own schemes. The best a private developer may be able to do is to locate possible sites for introduction to the major operators. Another possible development opportunity arises out of the trend for supermarket operators to take space on retail warehouse parks. These outlets tend to be smaller than the standalone schemes.

There are a number of segments in the market. The leading operators have tended to operate at the premium end of the market. These operators include Asda/Wal-Mart, Tesco, Safeway and Sainsbury, the giants of the sector. At the budget value end of the market are operatives such as Aldi and Lidl. The problem for the budget end of the market is that the giants of the sector seem set for a period of price competition as they vie for supremacy. This in itself will reduce the price advantage of the budget operators but this is not the least of their worries. The stores of the supermarkets are so large that the operatives can afford to compete in a number of sectors from the same store. The leading operators, for example, offer branded products, their slightly cheaper but good-quality own brand version and a budget 'no frills' version of the same product in the same aisles. It seems that the sector will see more consolidation in time, which will make the giants more dominant. This will, in some cases, make development in this sector more difficult for the independent developer, although securing a major operator in a mixed retail scheme will be an even greater guarantee of success.

Motor showrooms

This is a slightly odd sector in that it is not considered as being retail in many sectors (it is defined as being *sui generis*, i.e. a class on its own in the Use Classes Order), yet it clearly is a retail sector, albeit one that sells a specialist product from locations removed from mainstream retail. There have been development opportunities in the past but usually for owner occupation. This situation may change, however, hence the inclusion of this section in this review of property markets. There are changes afoot in the market that may push the operatives out of traditional patterns into different ways of operating. This may include a number of brands being offered from supermarket-type locations.

Petrol stations

This is another market that is dominated by major players, in this case the oil companies. There are relatively few successful independent operators in the market, mainly due to the ability of the large operators to secure the best sites and the low profit margins that are associated with petrol retailing. The market has seen a contraction in the number of outlets to concentrate on the best, most visible sites close to population centres. One effect of the low margins and the move to larger sites is that the operators have increasingly placed more emphasis on the ancillary retail parts of the business. Most filling stations now effectively operate as convenience stores or small supermarkets. While it is unlikely that a private development company would be able to break into this market, the effect of the competition of filling centre sites on convenience store development should not be overlooked.

Shopping centres

Along with the supermarket sector reviewed above, shopping centres – or shopping malls to employ the increasingly used US term – have represented the greatest change in the landscape of retailing throughout the world. Shopping centres tend to dominate the world markets, although the form they take in each country tends to reflect local requirements.

Shopping centres can take numerous different forms. The principal types are reviewed below.

In-town shopping centres   The development of covered centres in the middle of urban areas is the main way in which the retail capacity of these towns is increased. There are two main reasons for this. First, shoppers do seem to show a preference for shopping in controlled environments where a range of shops are joined together. The second reason is to do with the constraints that exist within established urban areas. The demand for retail products has increased with the rise in real gross domestic product (GDP) of the country. GDP growth leads to rises in spending and this normally gravitates to existing centres. This tends to lead to a rise in rents in these locations as expansion is difficult in most town centres. The development of a shopping centre is the normal way that this expansion takes place. How this is often achieved is illustrated in Figure 1.18.

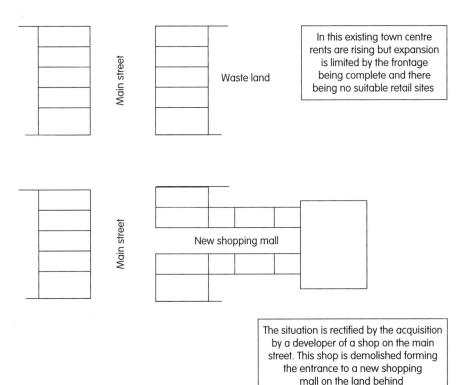

FIGURE 1.18 Typical shopping mall development

Within most town centres, situations like the one illustrated in Figure 1.18 are fairly common. There is usually some low-intensity, large-scale land use that can be exploited. Quite commonly this is surface car parking or service yards or sometimes an industrial-type use.

These types of town centre expansion schemes have to be carefully planned as they can have a considerable impact on the dynamics and economics of the existing town centres. The schemes themselves are also not guaranteed success, even when they are constructed in a town or city where there is clear retailer demand. There are a number of examples where centres have been constructed in such locations where, for various reasons, the schemes have been failures because they have not attracted sufficient pedestrian flows into the malls. Town centres and shopping centres have an organic quality that is sometimes hard to predict. Shopping centres have a difficult balancing act to achieve: they need to attract the right quality of tenant to attract shoppers but if those tenants find they have not generated sufficient business and withdraw, even fewer shoppers are attracted and a centre can enter a vicious cycle of closure and down-grading of tenants.

Trends in in-town shopping centres over the past few decades have included the move from simple, basic covered centres towards much more expensive environments with high-grade finishes and climate control. Most centres need an 'anchor', usually some large-scale space user that acts as a magnet to shoppers who then make complementary visits to the other shops in the scheme. Anchor tenants are crucially important to the success of a scheme and developers and funders spend considerable time in negotiation and selection of this key tenant. Schemes are frequently abandoned if a suitable anchor cannot be found, largely because the other retailers will not sign up to a scheme until this identity is known.

Out-of-town or suburban centres   Suburban centres tend to have a slightly different make up to city centres as they are designed to serve the local residential community, usually anchored by a supermarket or other food store, the rest of the centre being populated by a mixture of national multiples and local or regional traders. Rental values tend to be rather lower than in-town centres, although this does depend on the amount of turnover that the centres can support, which in turn depends on the catchment area of the centre.

Suburban centres tend to be unexciting but very lucrative and profitable investments. This is mainly due to the fact that they are usually in a local monopoly situation. There is insufficient demand for more than one suburban centre in a local area and the planning authorities, will, in any case, have planned for the development rather than allow it to be developed speculatively. The scope for future development is thus limited to circumstances where an area is expanding, i.e. substantial numbers of new houses are being built, or else an area that is underserved by existing retail centres can be identified.

Regional centres   These are the largest of the current breed of shopping centre and are likely to remain so with the current attitude of governments and planning authorities regarding sustainable development and being against car use. Regional centres are so named because they serve whole regions, their catchment covering a vast area. In the UK, the first example of such a centre was the Metrocentre on Tyneside. This pioneer has been followed by centres such as Meadowhall in Sheffield, Bluewater Park on the M25 and the Trafford Centre near Manchester. These centres need excellent road access with millions of potential shoppers within an hour's drive time. In time they will probably all need mass rapid transit systems to link to them as well. Inside, they contain two to three department stores to act as anchor tenants, with the remainder of the units occupied by national multiples. There is usually a range of local tenants or a market-type arrangement to give variety and character to the development. All the regional centres have a high leisure content as well as extensive food and drink outlets. Leisure and entertainment is essential to keep families coming and spending in the centres.

Regional centres are developed by some of the largest companies. It seems that the market in the UK may have reached its peak but it is probable that the existing schemes will be extended in time. The biggest impact that schemes such as this have on most smaller developers is on developments in the smaller centres close to the regional scheme. These centres tend to see considerable diversion of trade. Development in these centres should be considered very carefully, particularly if it contains a retail element.

Retail warehouses

This sector represents another major trend of the past 20 years, although it is part of the same trend to move out of town. It is also a sector that has evolved very rapidly over its relatively short life.

The principle behind retail warehousing is that it involves shop operators trading out of industrial-type buildings in industrial-type locations. The first generation retail warehouses were indeed developed with the idea that if the concept failed, the buildings could be converted back to light industrial or warehouse use.

The original users were traders of big bulk items such as furniture and DIY companies who found it difficult to trade cost effectively in traditional, small, in-town shops. The move out of town offered them large, cheap premises with good vehicular access. The success that these sectors enjoyed encouraged a large number of other retailers to adopt the format, including electrical goods, fashion and white goods.

The units themselves changed as the sector became more mature. The initial developments were of standalone units; later, terraces were built allowing the agglomeration of complementary uses. The later generations of retail warehouses tend to be in warehouse parks in prominent locations. The buildings have become further removed from their industrial roots with relatively high-quality clad frontages that involve extensive glazing and facing brickwork.

Rental values of the initial retail warehouse units were around 25–50 per cent above the equivalent industrial rents with investment yields in double figures. Rents have risen considerably, although they still are well below town centre rents. Rents are now about 2–3 times above industrial figures. Retail warehouse development is strictly controlled by planning authorities, which artificially controls supply and tends to fuel rental growth. There is still considerable scope for development, although at high rent levels some operators struggle to make the locations viable. In particular, the control of expansion of retail warehousing into new sites tends to support the redevelopment of older, first generation sites that have existing consent for retail use.

Industrial

The industrial sector is viewed by some as the least exciting of the mainstream property types. It attracts the lowest values in terms of rents and capital values. The buildings are the simplest in the whole property sector, the cheapest to construct and have the shortest economic life on average. Despite this view, industrials may be a little bit of a Cinderella underneath their mundane appearance.

The positive side of industrial properties includes the fact that demand tends to be steady. A large range of businesses can operate out of industrial premises; they are, after all, merely simple boxes in the main. A major attraction of the sector also lies in its lack of popularity with speculative developers. The balance between supply and demand rarely gets out of equilibrium because the sector rarely gets overbuilt.

Like all of the other property sectors considered to date, the industrial sector is divided into various sub-markets and sub-types. Some of these are listed below:

> lock-up workshops
> starter units
> standard industrial units
> hi-tech industrial units
> general industrial buildings
> warehouses
> distribution units
> specialist industrial buildings
> self-storage.

Again, some of the major types will be reviewed below.

Lock-up workshops

Lock-ups are the traditional heart of the small industrial market. They are generally older stock located within existing urban areas, occupied by small businesses. They generate relatively low rents and attract high yields, which equates to high value. They are, however, attractive to a number of businesses and to those who promote mixed-use schemes. A selection of sizes of lock-up workshops and warehouses can add vitality and important job opportunities in an inner city area. They can be useful, therefore, as both a magnet to attract other activities but also to ease the passage through the planning system of a scheme with more valuable mainstream commercial or residential elements.

Starter units

Starter units are the modern successors to the lock-up. These are small units (not often larger than 100m^2) that offer simple but modern facilities for smaller businesses. They are quite often provided by local authorities and regeneration companies to provide assistance and start-up premises for these small operations. Again, the rents are relatively low and the covenant of the businesses that take the leases is rarely very strong. As a result, values are low. It would be difficult for a developer to make sufficient development profit to justify the development of starter units alone.

Standard industrial units

In some respects this is a misnomer. There is no such thing as a standard industrial unit as they vary so much in size if not in specification. There are, however, some standard features that modern units possess.

They are usually, in the UK market at least, of steel portal frame construction with 6m eaves height with a relatively large, clear floor span unencumbered by columns. This gives the maximum flexibility in operation. The buildings are usually clad with profile insulated light metal sheeting with translucent panels on the roof. The lower parts of the walls are usually built of non-load-carrying concrete blocks. There is an increasing tendency in new units to face the front of the buildings in facing brickwork with high quality fenestration, to give them an office-like appearance. The main entry to the building is by way of a large roller shutter door at the front with, generally, a separate pedestrian access to the unit. Typically part of the unit, usually the front, is given over to office space, either at mezzanine level or over both stories. The office space forms between 5 and 15 per cent of the total floor area in a typical unit. Sizes of light industrial units range from around 100 to 2,500m^2 plus, in the main. The floors are of reinforced concrete, usually around 200mm thick, which gives a good load-bearing capacity.

The units can be standalone or else arranged in terraces. The former gives the tenant the highest visibility and identity and also the ability to expand the property easily. The latter usually offers the developer the most efficient utilisation of the site and also reduces overall construction costs by reducing the amount of steel and cladding required. An essential part of these units is the yard area around or in front of the units. There must be sufficient area to allow for staff and visitor parking as well as large vehicular servicing. The larger units require access room for large articulated vehicles and often incorporate dock levellers. These are ramps set into the yard areas that bring the tailgate of the vehicle level with the floor of the building, allowing for ease of unloading and loading. These features are also incorporated into distribution buildings (see below).

Hi-tech industrial units

Hi-tech industrial units at one point looked set to be a major component of the property market, being a brief feature of the technology revolution of the mid-1980s. The sector has, however, had a limited impact. Hi-tech units are essentially flexible structures that incorporate office, research and development and a manufacturing function within the same shell. They are essentially industrial buildings with a very high office content (up to about 50 per cent usually).

That the sector has failed to become distinct in its own right is due to a number of factors. Probably the most important was the change in the planning system and specifically the Use Classes Order (UCO) of 1987. The planning system had not kept pace with developments in the economy and, prior to the new UCO, industrial and office uses were considered separately. This caused real problems with the new electronic industries which required office-type facilities as part of their production and development activities. Some of the industrial units that were occupied at this time were fitted out accordingly but were probably illegal. There was, however, no option to move to office-type buildings because, first, the buildings were unsuitable in layout and facilities and, second, the office use class did not allow manufacturing to take place on the premises. The 1987 UCO accepted the facts of the situation and recognised that offices and light industrial activity could be incorporated together and would have a similar impact on the environment. The new business Class B brought offices and light industrial uses together in Class B1, general industrial into Class B2 and warehousing into Class B8.

These changes meant that occupiers have the flexibility to adapt most light industrial buildings to meet their needs as required. Hi-tech buildings have not so much disappeared but have been absorbed into a continuum of uses that has traditional light manufacturing at one end and pure offices at the other. The requirements of the major hi-tech units have also apparently changed over time. As their businesses have grown and matured it seems they have adopted the traditional separation of manufacturing and office functions as per other industries.

There is still a premium attached to hi-tech type units. Rents are higher than conventional industrial buildings but this is largely due to the higher office content of the units.

General industrial buildings

General industrial buildings fall into Class B2 of the 1987 UCO (The 'missing' Classes B3–B7 not mentioned in the review to date refer to specialist industrial activities). The B2 uses include activities that potentially conflict with public access and with neighbours due to the use of heavy plant and machinery or the production of noise or noxious fumes. The buildings tend to be similar to that described above for the standard light industrial uses, although they are on the larger end of the size spectrum. The sector tends to be dominated by owner occupation, although there are some investment properties and speculative development.

Warehouses and distribution units

These two categories of industrial building are considered together because they fall into the same category of use class, B8. They are essentially intended for the same use; however, while smaller warehouses are very similar to light industrial units (indeed many industrial buildings at the smaller end of the scale can be used for both B1 and B8 use and, frequently, for B2 (General Industrial) use as well) the larger distribution units have started to become distinctly different from 'normal' industrial buildings.

Strictly, warehouse buildings are distinct from B1 industrials. They tend to have a lower percentage of office space, they normally have an eaves height in excess of 6m and require additional circulation space externally to allow for articulated lorry movements. In fact, as noted, often flexibility is built into the design of smaller industrial units to allow for a range of uses including warehousing.

Distribution units, on the other hand, are distinct. They are another example of how the property market both reflects and enables change in society. Modern retailing in general, and supermarkets in particular, require excellent distribution systems. Most companies follow the 'just-in-time' principle of stock holding, storing very little material on the premises but ordering new stock as and when needed. This requires a system that is flexible and which is quick to react and service orders. The only way to achieve this is to set up a massive logistic system revolving around huge warehouses located within a few minutes' drive time of the major motorway intersections.

This means that the system revolves around road transport. The system is remarkably efficient but is also vulnerable, as the fuel protests of late 2000 illustrated. It also underlines how difficult it would be to change the system to an alternative. At present, clusters of warehouses owned or occupied by either the main distribution companies or directly by retailers are found at key motorway intersections.

The buildings tend to be vast. The typical distribution warehouse today has a floor area in excess of 10,000m^2 with eaves height of 8–10m. The units will have a large number of dock levellers allowing many vehicles to be serviced at once.

Rents of these units are relatively high but the operators tend to try to negotiate shorter leases than is the norm in the rest of the prime industrial market. This is because the contracts that logistic companies have with the main retailers and other customers also tend to be renewed regularly and the occupiers like to match their commitments to their income flow.

Self-storage

Self-storage is a relatively new industrial/warehousing type use for the UK, though it has been long established in the USA. The facilities are usually located in traditional industrial/warehousing type locations. They offer individuals and small companies the ability to store equipment and personal effects for the period when they are not required. This market is very big in the USA and is getting bigger in the UK. The first phase of expansion in the UK saw existing second-hand units being converted. There has now been a small amount of development of new units.

Leisure

Leisure property used to be a fairly marginal sector but in recent years has blossomed into one of the most active and popular for investors and developers alike. It may, indeed, be too popular at the time of writing with a tendency to overbuild.

Investors have long known that this sector would boom due to societies' increasing focus on leisure, the increase in leisure time, rise in disposable incomes and other changes. They had, however, traditionally avoided the sector for a number of reasons.

1. The sector is risky because it is the one that is most subject to fashions and fads. A development may be profitable for a short period of time but then may go out of fashion. Most property investment requires sustained income over a long period of time to repay the high levels of capital involved in its creation.
2. Leisure properties tend to suffer from high levels of depreciation. They need frequent refurbishment and alteration to keep them competitive and up to date.
3. Leisure spending tends to be the first affected by a slow-down in the economy. Downturns are therefore perceived as having a more marked effect on this sector of the property market than any other.

Despite these factors the trend and attitude in the market has turned around almost completely. Investors and financiers have fallen over themselves to pour money into the sector. The reasons are numerous:

a. The sheer weight of consumer spending and the durability of this spending has convinced investors and developers that the sector will continue to thrive.
b. Certain sectors, particularly cinemas and restaurants, have proved particularly durable and consistent, producing excellent returns over a long period of time.
c. The UK economy has enjoyed a near unbroken period of growth since the last major downturn in the early 1990s, meaning that leisure spending has continued to grow.
d. Investors have gained experience of the sector, making it less of an unknown quantity. In particular, investors found that large retail schemes worked best when an element of leisure was included. This encouraged them to form a working relationship with the leisure operators where none had previously existed.
e. Investors recognised that the large leisure operators offered high-quality covenants as tenants.
f. The effect of the herd instinct should never be overlooked in the property markets. Although the players in the market are increasingly sophisticated they do not like to be exposed as individuals going a different way from the crowd or to miss out on any potential gains that others are making in a sector. When a number of larger players put money into a sector the others will invariably follow. This actually has the effect of driving up values and thus returns in these sectors, as the demand for investments causes competition just as in any other market. The drive for higher returns tends to be self-generating, at least in the short term.

There are a number of leisure vehicles that have been developed. Some of these are listed below:

> cafés

TABLE 1.2 Players in the UK investment market

	Pension funds	Life assurance companies	Overseas investors	Real estate investment trusts	Banks and other similar institutions	Large property companies: stock market listed	Large private property companies	Small to medium-sized property companies	Individuals and others
Investor motive	To provide long-term pension products for pension holders of the organisation	To provide life assurance, investment and pension products to investors competitively in the open market	Varied, but usually part of investment portfolio for pension and life products as per the UK financial institutions. The UK offers an investor-friendly market and diversification options	US tax-efficient investment vehicle	Usually two motives: (1) for general profit on banking activities (2) for pension and investment products	To increase the value of investment portfolio and thus shareholders' funds	To increase the value of investment portfolio and thus shareholders' funds not offered on open market	As per large private companies, left	Various motives
Source of funding	Equity funded. Contributions from workers and employers into pension funds	Equity funded. Contributions from investors and policy holders	Mainly equity funded. Contributions from investors and policy holders	Mainly equity funded. Contributions from investors and policy holders	Mainly equity funded. Contributions from investors and policy holders	Part equity (shareholders' funds) and part debt (usually debenture stock)	Part equity (shareholders' funds) and part debt (usually debenture stock)	Part equity (shareholders' funds) and part debt. Debt is usually conventionally sourced through bank lending	Usually investment of personal wealth but some debt financing
Tax status	Largely exempt from taxation on investments	Beneficial tax status. Pay tax but at low rates	Depends on how investment vehicle is set up but usually taxed as offshore investor	Offshore tax status. Limited tax payable in USA if majority of income and gains distributed	Mixed, some beneficial status but pay corporation tax in UK	Pay corporation and income tax	Pay corporation and income tax	Pay corporation and income tax	Pay corporation and income tax
Behaviour in the property market	Generally invest in low-yielding prime property that enjoys high levels of capital appreciation. Tax status means most funds can be retained. May forward fund development schemes but rarely directly carry out developments	As per pension funds but are slightly more risk taking due to need to outperform competition in order to attract investors. May forward fund development schemes and sometimes directly carry out developments	Similar to the previous two but with some differences. First, they will rarely invest outside London or the southeast. Second, some have an appetite for 'trophy buildings', high status landmarks obtained at high cost. Finally, they concentrate on covenant above growth consideration	Invest aggressively in overseas markets to meet unsatisfied demand for property investment from the US home market. Tend to go for higher risk, higher yielding products	Some direct investment but usually is connected with own occupational requirements. Also involved with joint venture developments for profit share	Tax status means that they cannot outbid the institutions for the lowest yielding properties. Tend to operate mainly in the office and industrial market, plus some secondary retail. Risk taking, therefore will undertake development	Tax status means that they cannot outbid the institutions for the lowest yielding properties. Tend to operate mainly in the office and industrial market, plus some secondary retail. Risk taking, therefore will undertake development	Tax status and cost of funds restricts activity largely to secondary (i.e. poorer quality) investments that are high yielding and thus self-funding. Many developers in this sector	Tax status and cost of funds restricts activity largely to secondary (i.e. poorer quality) investments that are high yielding and thus self-funding

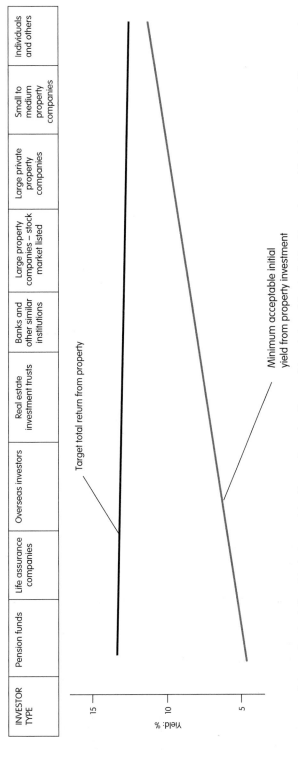

FIGURE 1.19 Schematic of relationship between identity, motives, funding and tax status of the individual investor and their behaviour in the property market. The equity funded, risk averse, beneficial tax status of the institutions allows them to bid to the lowest yields

potential due to occupiers competing for space. Having said that, not all locations will have institutional grade property of all types. London has a number of such locations in each category, for example institutional grade office locations exist in the West End, the City, 'Mid-Town' (a term imported from the USA which in London covers the area between the city and the West End and including areas such as Holborn and Fleet Street) and Docklands. A small provincial town may have no institutional quality locations at all, the one possible exception being in the retail sector where top-quality tenants may take space on longer lease terms.

It can be seen that it is not simply the location that defines institutional investment but a combination of all the factors.

Institutional grade specifications

Again, to generalise, institutional grade specifications are those that have the greatest demand from occupiers. These are usually the most modern, newest type of buildings. The importance of the specification is greater in some property types than in others. The most notable example of this is the office sector which is strongly specification-led. We have already seen that the office sector is more footloose than, say, the retail sector. The highest value offices are in good locations but are usually specification-led and brand new. Older property suffers from physical depreciation and functional obsolescence so will, by definition, not be prime. Retail property is often an exception to this, being simple concrete boxes that retailers fit out themselves. Even in this sector the environment and layout of retail units tend to deteriorate over time.

Institutional grade leases

The terms under which the top-quality property is occupied is one of the most vital components of the institutional property. These terms have varied over time, for example the average lease term has come down since the property crash of 1990. The terms can be summarised as in Table 1.3.

These lease clauses are among the most investor-friendly in the whole world, which explains why the UK is popular with overseas investors. They make property investment as clean and as 'hands off' as it possibly can be. The terms may seem onerous but one of the key points to remember is that tenants agree to these terms in the open market. They only agree to do this due to the qualities of the properties that they wish to occupy.

Impact on the development market

The importance of covering this section on investors and investment grade property is twofold. First, it is vital for people who intend to operate in the development market to have an understanding of the investment market and investment vehicles. Second, the relationship with the development market must be appreciated. Prime property of investment grade is the best quality property that appeals to the best quality occupiers, thus producing the highest quality income stream. These, almost

TABLE 1.3 Terms of property occupation

Length of term	10–15 years	This has come down from the traditional 25 years. The new length of term guarantees a secure income flow to the investor, particularly valuable when tied to a good quality corporate tenant
Repairs and maintenance	Full repairing and insuring	Tenants are responsible for all aspects of maintaining the property including the structure. Tenants are expected to give the building back in the same order as they acquired it. The landlord will be able to recover all outgoings from the tenant
Rent reviews	Normally the rent is reviewed every 5 years to the rental value that similar properties let on new but similar lease terms are achieving on the open market, such reviews being 'upward only'	This clause enables the value of the property to be maintained by periodically adjusting the lease rent. Perhaps the most controversial part of this clause is the 'upward only' component, although strictly this means that the rent cannot fall even if market values have gone down. It does act to maintain the quality of the income flow to the investor
Other terms	Open user clause, open alienation clause, open alteration clause	These clauses are open in that they require the landlord's consent but that consent is 'not to be unreasonably withheld'. This helps to maintain rental values. A recent change is the introduction of authorised guarantee agreements that help maintain the value of the property if the original, good quality tenant leaves

invariably, are qualities that are associated with the newest properties. As property ages it loses these institutional qualities, indeed it becomes secondary. Institutional investors thus have an insatiable demand for the products of the development process. Lesser quality, older properties are sold on to investors seeking higher yields and lower capital growth. In time these properties require refurbishment and, sometimes, redevelopment at which point they often transfer back to the institutions. Whatever the case, the institutions are the financial engines that drive the market.

Conclusions

The preceding sections have provided the context to property development. They have hopefully illustrated the breadth of the subject, although no single work can hope to cover all of the potential development scenarios. The property markets are rich and diverse in character and scope. The players within the development market are very varied in type and character and interact with each other in many complex ways. Development can be done for many reasons and parties directly involved with development can come together in many different ways. Essentially, the whole process involves a highly complex set of interactions which result in development. Anyone involved in the industry must understand and get a feel for this complex environment in which development is undertaken.

Development inception: an introduction

As noted already, this book is intended to be a practical guide to development rather than one that concentrates on theory. Property development is, after all, a hard, practical world where there is little room for pure academic thought. There is one area, however, where it is difficult to avoid taking a theoretical approach because the reality is that the subject is so diverse. This area is development inception. In practice, there are a huge number of reasons as to why a development commences. Almost every development case is individual, making summary very difficult. It is useful, therefore, to take a step back into the theory, albeit briefly, as there are certain fundamentals that explain why particular sites get developed.

The fundamental questions that this section will attempt to answer are:

> What makes a site ripe for development?
> How is one use of the site chosen over other competing uses?
> How and why are decisions taken to start the development process?

It is not possible to answer these questions separately as they are all part of the development inception process.

It is best to go right back to first principle fundamentals. Land is one of the factors of production identified in economic theory by economists, along with labour and capital. To produce any goods or service, land, labour and capital need to be combined. Whereas people's wants are unlimited, factors of production are scarce. Productive activities compete for use of the factors of production but not all demand can be accommodated. This competition leads to all factors of production having value, the extent of which depends on the degree of demand and the relative scarcity of the factor.

Land, the basic raw material of development, therefore does not have intrinsic value. In fact, land itself usually has no cost of production in its own right (the exception being reclaimed or man-made land). The value of land is derived from the demand for the goods and services that can be produced on it and from it. In principle, the more valuable the goods and services that can be produced from the land, the more valuable the land itself, particularly if that land is scarce. Each piece of land is unique, even if only in terms of location. Each piece of land can be used for different purposes and at different intensities due to factors such as topography, soil quality and, in particular, location. Some of these factors appear to be intrinsic, such as soil quality and topography with agricultural land, but essentially the same principles apply whether it is rural or urban land; it is the value of the product that can be produced from the land that gives it its value. Grade A agricultural land is more valuable than rough grazing because more income can be earned from it. It is also not ubiquitous; in fact, top-quality land is scarce, adding to its value. Land in the central business district (CBD) of cities is more valuable, in general, than industrial land on the edge of town because it is (a) scarcer and (b) more able to generate income from business activity.

Having established the economic principles of land value, let us now turn to individual sites. Essentially, the same principles apply.

As an example we will examine the case of a site in an established urban area. As noted above, each piece of land will have a value based on the most valuable use for the site. This is related to the earnings that can be generated from the site less the cost of improving the site, i.e. constructing a structure and providing all services to the site (power, water, drainage and road access, for example). Let us assume that the current use of the site is as an industrial site, perhaps for light manufacturing. The value of the site is dependent on the bid a potential user would make for it. In the market-place only the prices bid are observable, but the economics that underlie these prices are approximately as follows. (Note that issues such as taxation are ignored for this calculation. Negative figures are given in brackets.)

Company turnover	£500,000 p.a.
Operating costs	(£420,000) p.a.
Gross profit	£80,000 p.a.
Less: reasonable net profit to operator	
(15 per cent of turnover)	£75,000 p.a.
Surplus (rent)	£5,000 p.a.

Taking a reasonable return of 10 per cent on initial income to the freeholder of the land would give a value of £50,000 to the right to receive the income stream of £5,000 (£5,000/10 per cent=£50,000). This is the current full value of the site.

It should be stressed that valuers and agents assessing the value of land do not start with a calculation of the surplus that firms can make and thus pay in rent when looking at individual sites. The problem with doing this is that each potential user of the site will have different cost and profit structures. Some will be efficient, well run, profit-maximising enterprises; others may have quite different motives for being in business, or may run the business in an inept, inefficient way. The amalgam of bid prices for rent and land acquisition is taken as a better signal of land prices as a whole across all potential users, efficient and inefficient. It is, however, a useful tool for our purposes.

The value of the land in its current use, at the point of time being considered here, is thus £50,000. This will not remain static. It will change according to the general business cycle in the economy with inflation and with the specific attractions of the site for its current use. While land values trend up they can fluctuate and, for specific uses in specific locations, can certainly fall.

The pattern of values over various periods is illustrated in Figure 2.1(a) for agricultural land and Figure 2.1(b) for industrial land for development in London.

Land value will also not be universal throughout the country. There are considerable variations, as can be observed from Figure 2.1(c).

Returning to the plot of land we were looking at earlier, let us consider alternative uses for the land. The land could, for example, be redeveloped for residential use. Let us assume that five houses could be built on the land. There are constraints, however, which may prevent the site being developed. One is the existing occupier

67

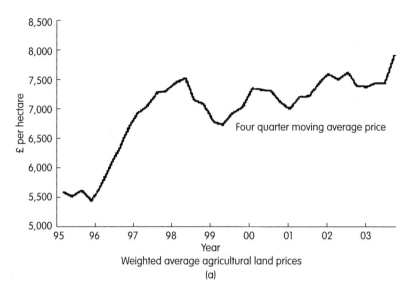

Weighted average agricultural land prices

(a)

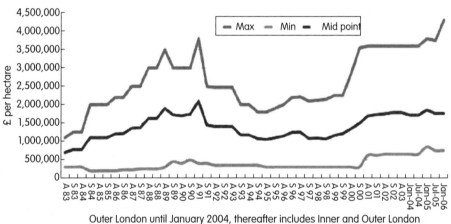

Outer London until January 2004, thereafter includes Inner and Outer London

(b)

FIGURE 2.1 Variations in land values: (a) agricultural land (England and Wales) 1996–2003, (b) land for industrial development in London 1983–2006

who may have a long lease on the site. They would have to be willing to sell that lease or to extinguish it in some way. If the site is leased, there will also be the freeholder to consider. The freeholder is the ultimate beneficial owner of the site who would either have to sell their interest or grant a developer a long lease (in excess of 100 years if development is to be considered). There are also the legal aspects of development; land can have rights over it (access, rights of way and service easements), restrictions on its use (covenants) and will also, of course, require planning consent. The final constraint is the market and the cost and value equation. It is this aspect that we will concentrate on for the moment. The other constraints mentioned illustrate the complexity of the problem of site development that has to be addressed before development can commence, and will be considered again, later.

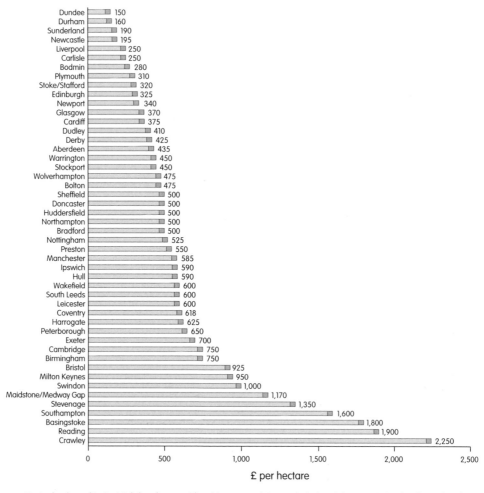

Typical value of industrial development land in some of the main industrial areas in England, Scotland and Wales (excluding London)

FIGURE 2.1 (c) land for factories and warehouse development as at 1 January 2006 in some of the main industrial areas (excluding London). Source: *Property Market Report January 2006*, Valuation Office Agency (2006). Reproduced under the terms of the Click-Use Licence

For the moment we will assume that vacant possession of the site can be obtained, that the freeholder is willing to sell, that no legal obstructions exist and that planning consent can be obtained.

Let us now deal with the land value equation. What we are considering is the value of the site for its alternative use. The equation to calculate this value is very similar to the calculation that we made above, and we will assume that it is being done at the same time as the previous calculation. The land is in industrial use. We will assume that the area surrounding the site is of similar character to the site in question, i.e. it is in light industrial/manufacturing use. This will reduce the attractiveness to house buyers and thus will reduce demand for the product, and consequently the price.

CONTEMPORARY PROPERTY DEVELOPMENT

The calculation of land value for the alternative use is therefore as follows:

Value of completed houses	
(£50,000 each × 5 units)	£250,000 p.a.
Less: construction costs (inc. fees and finance)	
(£35,000 per unit)	(£175,000)
Less: demolition and site clearance	(£10,000)
Less: reasonable profit to developer	
(20% of development costs)	(£37,000)
Surplus (land value)	£28,000

It can be seen that it is possible to develop the land – the houses can be constructed profitably and can be sold to end users – but only if the land can be bought for £28,000. At the time of the calculation this is below the existing use value. The highest and best use (HBU) is as an industrial site.

The HBU is an important concept. The HBU of land is defined as being the highest value use the land can be put to subject to the constraints that:

> this use must be legal;
> there is a reasonable chance that it could be used for that purpose; and
> demand exists for that use.

Given this, land use should naturally move to the highest and best use over time, although there are several qualifications to this, which will be considered below.

In this case the use of the site will not change until the most valuable alternative use produces a land value that exceeds the value of the existing use. Again, this picture will not be static. Areas change in character and the value of alternative uses changes in the wider economy making development of the alternative viable in situations where it would not otherwise be.

In the case of our site we will assume that the demand for its current industrial use declines over time as manufacturers either find that they cannot continue their businesses profitably or else find that they need to move, perhaps to more modern premises elsewhere. This is a process that continuously happens in urban areas, albeit at a slow, sometimes almost unnoticeable pace; a transition from one dominant use to another. Hence, as the value of industrial use declines (Figure 2.2), so the value of the best alternative use increases. In this case, when one residential development takes place, the area will tend to improve in terms of attractiveness to other residential users. A process of appreciation in value for the alternative residential use takes place (Figure 2.3).

Let us revisit our calculations of land value for the alternative use, considering the situation ten years after the original appraisal (and ignoring the influence of inflation). The effect of the change in land use and the environment has boosted the potential sale prices of the houses that can be built from £50,000 to £70,000. The developer can afford to spend slightly more in terms of construction cost to produce a higher quality product to capture these higher values.

70

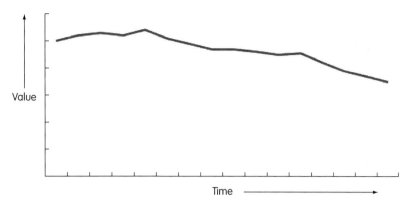

FIGURE 2.2 Progressive value of land for current use over 15-year period

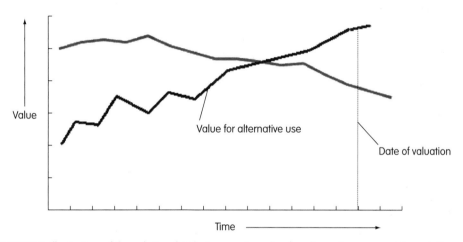

FIGURE 2.3 Illustration of the relationship between site value for alternative use and the existing use value over time

Value of completed houses	£350,000 p.a.
(£70,000 each × 5 units)	
Less: construction costs (inc. fees and finance)	
(£40,000 per unit)	(£200,000)
Less: demolition and site clearance	(£10,000)
Less: reasonable profit to developer	
(20% of development costs)	(£42,000)
Surplus (land value)	£98,000

This is clearly a much higher value than that of the existing use and thus this is the new HBU and, indeed, scrutiny of Figure 2.2 illustrates that this had been the case for some years.

In our individual case it was somewhere between years five and six that the transition occurred. It was at this point that development could have taken place. However, it may not have done so for a number of reasons.

TABLE 2.1 Difference between manufactured goods and office property

	Confectionery product	Office property
Unit cost of production	Low	Very high
Product production lifespan	Usually long	Relatively short
Investment in production infrastructure	High	Low
Numbers in target market	Very high	Very low
Geographical spread of target market	Universal	Usually limited
Entry qualification for purchase	Very low	Very high

This in many ways is an unfair comparison. Economists would argue against comparing such dissimilar goods but this is done for a purpose, namely to illustrate the problems faced by market researchers in property. Market research for most manufacturing concerns is recognised as that business's lifeblood. It is also relatively easy to carry out by way of consumer surveys, blind trials and tastings and focus groups among many other techniques. This process is sophisticated and works with everything from Mars Bars to Mercedes Benz cars.

The property market is different and much more difficult to research. The products tend to be individual, often one-offs. The client or consumer of the product in some sectors is not obvious. The product takes a long time to produce, during which time the market for the product may have changed entirely. Manufacturers of other products can change the production focus relatively quickly, for example confectioners can switch volumes of production from chocolate bars to ice cream products over a few weeks to react to warmer than average seasons. Production of property takes many years and, like a super tanker, it requires a lot of warning to change direction, by which time conditions may have changed yet again!

This situation makes good market analysis even more essential despite the difficulties of carrying it out. Certainly one of the most notable trends in property consulting over the past 20 years has been the rise in research departments. All the major UK firms have such departments. Often these are major fee earners for the firms involved. Quite a high proportion of these fees are earned from the development sector. From being data collection centres and chart producers of dubious quality, these research departments have employed extremely bright people – many from the academic community – and the quality of the techniques employed has greatly improved.

This last statement is made largely in preparation of a defence against the likely reaction to the next! If the quality of the research done in property development at the dawn of the third millennium can be summed up in one word it would probably be 'patchy' or 'mediocre'. Ten years ago, the word would have been either 'poor' or 'awful', so things have improved. Some research is very sophisticated and thorough, particularly when carried out by the research departments of the major firms, in other cases it is so superficial as to be almost non-existent.

To generalise, good research tends to be carried out in the larger development projects where the product is relatively ubiquitous and where the market (both in terms of the occupier and the occupier's business market) can be well defined. The two markets that this description fits best are the retail and large-scale private residential market. It is no surprise to learn that it is in these two markets that the most sophisticated research is carried out.

Even in these cases, however, the nature of the property market is such that a lot of the research requires subjective assumptions to be made. These assumptions can be manipulated either deliberately or unconsciously to produce the result that the commissioner desires. For example, retail impact studies used in planning disputes are often prepared by consultants employed by both sides. Using the same facts and looking at the same development, the respective reports usually support the stance taken by their commissioners. This process applies to market research in property, therefore the results can be misleading.

WHO CARRIES OUT RESEARCH FOR DEVELOPMENT PROJECTS?

Before looking in detail at market research for development, it may be useful to establish who plays what role in the process (Table 2.2). Research for development is not confined to being carried out by a single external party. Many parties involved in the development also carry out research related to development.

AN EXAMPLE OF GOOD PRACTICE IN MARKET RESEARCH FOR PROPERTY DEVELOPMENT: RETAIL IMPACT ANALYSIS

To examine examples of how research is actually undertaken, we will look at research for a retail project. As has been noted, retailing is often the most sophisticated of the

TABLE 2.2 Parties carrying out research for development

Party	Research role
Developer	• Initiating force but often do their own market research • For small schemes the majority if not all research carried out by the individual developer
Property consultant/agent	• Occupier research (requirements, trends) • Research into investor requirements • Market monitoring generally • Economic base and market analysis
Specialist research consultant	• Economic base and market analysis • Occupier research (requirements, trends) • Research into investor requirements • Market monitoring generally
Architect	• Planning concept • Site analysis • Physical form
Planning consultant	• Planning history • Planning viability • Economic base and market analysis
Environmental consultant	• Historical use of site • Identification of possible sources of contamination

markets for which research is undertaken. However, before this is examined in detail, we will look at some general principles of market research for property development.

Preliminary investigations

Fundamentally, before major expenditure is made on market research, some basic investigation will be carried out to establish whether there is evidence of demand for the property type envisaged. This is generally undertaken by talking to people in the market, usually the agents who are vitally important in making the market in the first place. Whatever the market, residential or commercial, they will have a 'feel' for what occupiers and potential owners require. Developers look for markets where there either are unfulfilled enquiries or known requirements that remain unfulfilled.

Other signs are more apparent in the actual environment where the development is proposed. In an established commercial environment, a prospective developer should drive around looking for marketing boards and vacant premises. If these are few on the ground and if most premises are occupied, this is a very good indication that there is unfulfilled demand in the market.

Sadly, many developers do not research beyond this level. To be fair, often talking to the market makers and looking at the visible signs of the state of the market is sufficient but these signs can mask the true state of the market or current occupation trends that could lead developers into making expensive mistakes (and careful scrutiny of every UK city will throw up examples of developers' 'expensive mistakes'!). More in-depth investigations can reveal these trends.

In-depth investigations

In general, there are two types of market research that are relevant to property development:

1. area research; and
2. consumer demand analysis.

Area research

Area research usually consists of some form of market analysis. This is carried out to determine the best size and nature of the development and can be used to provide the information for the financial appraisal.

The research can be carried out at several levels. At the top level, equivalent to the strategic level of decision-making, the research assists the developer in deciding where to carry out a development. The largest investor developers may be working through a gradual process of narrowing down where to carry out the development. Once the fundamental decisions about location have been made, the research can be viewed as occurring at the tactical level, aiding decisions about the detail of the scheme and leading up to the decisions made about which site to develop and the final design of the scheme.

Whichever level the developer is working at, the process and data collected is essentially the same. Fundamentally, the developer is looking for the location that will give them the best return for the type of development envisaged. The data will also aid the planning of the project, including decisions about timing and phasing of the scheme, as well as providing information for planning applications and development impact studies.

In general, the market analysis process consists of four stages:

1. data collection
2. data analysis
3. analysis of the effect of introducing the scheme into the market
4. conclusions and recommendations.

Each stage is examined in turn below.

Data collection. At the strategic decision level the following data should be collected:

> past, present and future population trends within the chosen area or areas;
> social characteristics of the area – per capita income, social structure, employment structure and trends, etc.

These two sets of data can be obtained from a number of official and commercial sources, including census data and the Office of National Statistics (ONS), and may include family expenditure surveys, HM Revenue and Customs' survey of personal incomes and the ONS' Annual Survey of Hours and Earnings (formerly the New Earnings Survey), among others. Some of this data is sold commercially via market research firms and delivered through GIS technology. Much of the data is available free, as is illustrated in Table 2.3 and Figures 2.4–2.6.

Your Location

WA34LL is in Culcheth, Glazebury and Croft ward in the Warrington local authority in the North West region.

For statistical purposes the country has been divided into small blocks of land called Output Areas. These allow us to look in more detail at smaller local areas. Output Areas have been combined to form two layers of Super Output Areas known as Lower Layer Super Output Areas (LSOAs) and Middle Layer Super Output Areas (MSOAs). This profile includes data from LSOA level upwards, reflecting LSOA Warrington 002A. The respective MSOA is Warrington 002.

A selection of statistics for LSOA Warrington 002A

- As at the 2001 Census, Warrington 002A had 1,485 residents. By mid-2003 this was estimated to have changed to 1,466 residents.

- Also from the 2001 Census, the LSOA had:

  • 622 households;
  • 72 per cent of residents describing their health as 'good';
  • 19 per cent of 16-74 year olds having no qualifications; and
  • an unemployment rate of 1.3 per cent of all people aged 16-74.

- In the Index of Multiple Deprivation 2004, the area was ranked at 29,837 out of 32,482 LSOAs in England, where 1 was the most deprived LSOA and 32,482 the least deprived.

Map of Warrington 002A LSOA

FIGURE 2.4 Location data for a sample location in England using Office of National Statistics data. Source: National Statistics Website: www.statistics.gov.uk. Reproduced under the terms of the Click-Use Licence

TABLE 2.3 General population data and forecasts for England and Wales. Percentage of the England and Wales population by English Government Office Region and by broad age group, mid-1985, mid-2005 and mid-2025

Area	Mid-1985				Mid-2005				Mid-2025[a]			
	All ages	Children	Working age	Pensionable age	All ages	Children	Working age	Pensionable age	All ages	Children	Working age	Pensionable age
England and Wales	100.0	20.5	61.2	18.3	100.0	19.3	62.0	18.7	100.0	17.5	58.6	23.9
England	94.4	19.3	57.8	17.2	94.5	18.2	58.7	17.6	94.5	16.6	55.5	22.4
North East	5.2	1.1	3.2	0.9	4.8	0.9	3.0	0.9	4.5	0.8	2.6	1.2
North West	13.7	2.9	8.3	2.5	12.8	2.5	7.9	2.4	12.4	2.2	7.2	3.0
Yorkshire and The Humber	9.8	2.1	6.0	1.8	9.5	1.8	5.9	1.8	9.6	1.7	5.6	2.3
East Midlands	7.8	1.6	4.8	1.4	8.1	1.5	5.0	1.5	8.2	1.4	4.7	2.1
West Midlands	10.4	2.2	6.4	1.8	10.0	2.0	6.1	1.9	9.7	1.8	5.6	2.4
East	10.0	2.1	6.1	1.8	10.4	2.0	6.3	2.0	10.5	1.8	6.0	2.7
London	13.6	2.6	8.6	2.4	14.1	2.7	9.4	1.9	14.7	2.7	9.8	2.2
South East	14.9	3.0	9.1	2.8	15.3	3.0	9.4	2.9	15.3	2.7	8.8	3.8
South West	9.0	1.8	5.4	1.9	9.5	1.7	5.7	2.1	9.8	1.6	5.4	2.8
Wales	5.6	1.2	3.4	1.1	5.5	1.1	3.3	1.1	5.5	0.9	3.1	1.5

[a]Pensionable age will rise to 65 for women by 2025 but for ease of comparison, working and pensionable ages have been kept on the same basis as for 1985 and 2005.

Notes: Children are aged 0–15. Working age is 16–59 for females and 16–64 for males. Pensionable age is 60 and above for females and 65 and above for males.
All the statistical data in the UK can be accessed through www.statistics.gov.uk/
Source: National Statistics Website: www.statistics.gov.uk. Reproduced under the terms of the Click-Use Licence.

Economic activity

This profile relates to the Lower Layer Super Output Area Warrington 002A, which is located in Warrington local authority in the North West region.

Business premises

On 1 April 2005 Warrington had 1,453 retail premises (includes shops, financial and professional services and food and drink outlets, but excluding public houses and hotels). There were also 1,399 office premises, 786 factories and 977 warehouses. [Note that these totals exclude leisure and sports premises, as well as public facilities such as schools, hospitals and libraries. Note too that the figures cannot be compared directly with the 1 April 2004 statistics previously quoted on this page. This is because some of the premises assigned to these categories in 2004 were re-assigned to an unquoted 'Other' category as a result of the 2005 revaluation process.]

Employment rates

Of the people in Warrington who were of working age (i.e. those aged 16 to 64 for men or 16 to 59 for women) the employment rate was 81 per cent during the Summer of 2004 (June to August), compared with an average for Great Britain of 75 per cent. Over the same three months in 1999, the number of people in employment in Warrington as a proportion of those of working age was 77 per cent and the rate for Great Britain was 75 per cent.

The 2001 Census provided the following breakdown of employment status in the area:

Percentage of resident population aged 16 to 74 in each group, April 2001

	Warrington 002A	Culcheth, Glazebury and Croft	Warrington	North West	England and Wales
People aged 16-74: Economically active: Employee Full-time[1]	35.8	37.3	44.0	38.8	40.6
People aged 16-74: Economically active: Employee Part-time[1]	11.6	11.6	13.3	11.9	11.8
People aged 16-74: Economically active: Self-employed[1]	6.2	9.0	6.6	7.1	8.3
People aged 16-74: Economically active: Unemployed[1]	1.3	2.2	2.9	3.6	3.4
People aged 16-74: Economically active: Full-time student[1]	1.9	1.8	2.4	2.5	2.6
People aged 16-74: Economically inactive: Retired[1]	29.7	17.7	13.5	14.3	13.6
People aged 16-74: Economically inactive: Student[1]	3.9	2.8	3.0	4.6	4.7
People aged 16-74: Economically inactive: Looking after home / family[1]	5.9	4.9	5.5	6.1	6.5
People aged 16-74: Economically inactive: Permanently sick / disabled[1]	3.2	5.0	6.2	7.8	5.5
People aged 16-74: Economically inactive: Other[1]	0.7	7.7	2.9	3.3	3.1

[1] National Statistics

Of the people in LSOA Warrington 002A who were unemployed in 2001, 29 per cent were aged 50 and over, 21 per cent had never worked and 43 per cent were long-term unemployed. This compares with England and Wales as a whole, where 19 per cent of unemployed people were aged 50 or over, 9 per cent had never worked and 30 per cent were long-term unemployed.

More detailed information on unemployment can be obtained by analysing work-related benefits.

Benefits data

Claimants of work-related benefits, September 1999 and 2004

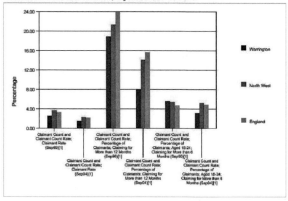

FIGURE 2.5 Economic data for a sample location in England using Office of National Statistics data. Source: National Statistics Website: www.statistics.gov.uk. Reproduced under the terms of the Click-Use Licence

In September 2004, 8 per cent of people claiming work-related benefits in Warrington had been doing so for more than 12 months; this compared with 19 per cent in September 1999.

Between September 1999 and September 2004 the number of young people aged 18 to 24 years who were claiming work-related benefits reduced by 67 per cent in Warrington, compared with a reduction of 31 per cent in Great Britain overall.

In August 2005, there were 15 claimants of Jobseeker's Allowance (JSA) in Lower Layer Super Output Area Warrington 002A. The Jobseeker's Allowance (JSA) is payable to people under pensionable age who are available for, and actively seeking work.

At the same time there were 35 people in Warrington 002A claiming Incapacity Benefit or Severe Disablement Allowance. These benefits are paid to people aged 16 to 64 who have been assessed as incapable of work due to sickness or disability.

Also in August 2005, Warrington 002A had 15 claimants of Income Support. This is paid to people aged 16 and over, who are working for fewer than 16 hours a week, and who have less money coming in than the law says they need to live on. In general Income Support is only paid to those not required to be available for work, such as carers, lone parents, and the sick and disabled. Unemployed people get Jobseeker's Allowance, and less well off pensioners get Pension Credit instead.

New Deal

The New Deal is a Government programme to get unemployed people back to work. There are three New Deal schemes:

New Deal for Young People. This is designed for 18- to 24-year-olds. In 2004 there were 6 starters on this scheme in Middle Layer Super Output Area (MSOA) Warrington 002.
New Deal 25plus. This is designed for people aged 25 and over. In 2004 there were 6 starters on this scheme in MSOA Warrington 002.
New Deal for Lone Parents. In 2004 there were 9 starters on this scheme in MSOA Warrington 002.

Datasets referenced

Dataset	Source	National Statistics?
Commercial and Industrial Floorspace and Rateable Value Statistics (2005 Revaluation), 2005 - (for business premises data)	Valuation Office Agency (VOA)	Yes
Employment Rate (1999 and 2004 datasets)	Office for National Statistics (ONS)	Yes
Economic Activity - All people (KS09A) - (for employment status & % of over 50s and long-term unemployed)	Census 2001, Office for National Statistics (ONS)	Yes
Claimant Count and Claimant Count Rate (1999 and 2004 datasets)	Office for National Statistics (ONS)	Yes
Benefits Data: Summary Statistics, 2005	Department for Work and Pensions (DWP)	Yes
Starts to New Deal for Young People, New Deal 25plus and New Deal for Lone Parents, 2004	Department for Work and Pensions (DWP)	No

FIGURE 2.5 Continued

The developer appraiser can quickly produce an accurate picture of the characteristics of the area which they are considering for development, to see how it compares with national data and also with competing locations. The size, quality and characteristics of the existing property market and proposed developments that will compete with the project under consideration will all be taken into consideration.

Data on this issue are becoming easier to obtain although detailed field studies may be required. Sources of information include Estates Gazette Interactive (EGi), the subscription website of *Estates Gazette*, the industry's weekly property magazine. Other sources include the planning department of the local authority.

Detailed appraisal of the current situation should be carried out for all levels of decision-making. As the fundamental or strategic decisions are taken, more detailed information can be gathered. This may include an economic base study which is carried out to establish or understand many factors that relate to the detailed execution of the scheme. The data collected may include:

> the geographical extent of metropolitan area
> road patterns
> population levels
> employment levels and bases
> catchments or trade analysis
> per capita incomes by geographical sector.

Housing and households

This profile relates to the Lower Layer Super Output Area **Warrington 002A**, which is located in **Warrington** local authority in the **North West** region.

Dwelling stock data

In Warrington there were a total of 82,185 dwellings in April 2004 of which 1,611 (2.0 per cent) were vacant and 2,055 (2.5 per cent) were classed as unfit. This compares with 'unfitness' levels of 6.1 per cent in the North West region and 4.8 per cent in England as a whole.

Dwellings by tenure in Warrington, April 2004

	Total number of dwellings	% classed as unfit
Owner occupied / private rented	68254	3
Local authority	9342	0
Registered social landlord	4589	1
Other public sector	0	-

Housing register

Most local authorities maintain a register of households that have applied for social rented housing. In Warrington there were 4,430 households on the Housing Register as at 1 April 2004. In terms of number of homeless, the authority had 1,048 households accepted as such (these are included on the Housing Register, in local authorities where one exists).

Property prices

Between 2002 and 2003 the average price for a home in North West region increased by 21 per cent, compared with England where the average rise was 12 per cent.

Average dwelling prices £s, 2002

	Culcheth, Glazebury and Croft	Warrington	North West	England and Wales
Changes of Ownership by Dwelling Price, Price Indicators by Dwelling Type: Detached - Mean[2,3]	195,079	201,340	168,376	208,435
Changes of Ownership by Dwelling Price, Price Indicators by Dwelling Type: Semi-detached - Mean[2,3]	109,900	98,532	85,877	119,748
Changes of Ownership by Dwelling Price, Price Indicators by Dwelling Type: Terraced - Mean[2,3]	90,900	69,948	52,663	103,351
Changes of Ownership by Dwelling Price, Price Indicators by Dwelling Type: Flat - Mean[2,3]	-	84,421	90,176	130,962
Changes of Ownership by Dwelling Price, Price Indicators for All Dwellings: Mean[2,3]	145,177	117,636	88,382	138,370
Social Housing Rents, All Dwellings: LA Net Rent[1,2]	-	44	44	

[1] All of the rent values quoted are weekly rents and are in UK Pounds.

[2] Due to a policy requirement, the 2001 dataset was originally referenced to 1998 geographic boundaries. In accordance with the agreed policy for Neighbourhood Statistics, this dataset has now been referenced to the 2003 Census Area Statistics wards, local/unitary authorities, GORs and countries.

[3] Not National Statistics

2001 Census data

In Lower Layer Super Output Area (LSOA) Warrington 002A there were 622 households in April 2001. 100 per cent of the resident population lived in households and 0 per cent lived in communal establishments. [A communal establishment is one providing managed residential accommodation, for example in supervised hostels, hotels, large hospitals and prisons.]

The average size of households in LSOA Warrington 002A was 2.4 people, compared with an average of 2.4 people for England and Wales.

Type of Household: percentage of each type, April 2001

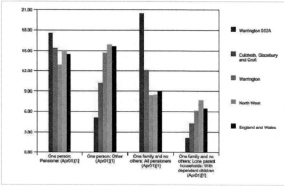

[1] National Statistics

Note: this graph only shows a selection of household types, so the columns for each area will not add up to 100 per cent. To obtain a full breakdown of household types for any area, please use the 'Find Statistics for An Area' option, available via the Neighbourhood Statistics homepage.

FIGURE 2.6 Housing and household data for a sample location in England using Office of National Statistics data. Source: National Statistics Website: www.statistics.gov.uk. Reproduced under the terms of the Click-Use Licence

Tenure: percentage of households, April 2001

	Warrington 002A	Culcheth, Glazebury and Croft	Warrington	North West	England and Wales
Owner occupied: Owns outright[1]	55.5	30.9	29.7	29.8	29.5
Owner occupied: Owns with a mortgage or loan[1]	37.1	44.6	45.6	38.9	38.8
Rented from: Council (local authority)[1]	5.0	9.8	12.2	13.6	13.2
Rented from: Housing Association / Registered Social Landlord[1]	0.5	0.9	5.6	6.5	6.0
Rented from: Private landlord or letting agency[1]	0.8	2.6	4.2	7.3	8.7
Rented from: Other[1]	1.1	2.1	2.2	3.0	3.2

[1] National Statistics

Percentage of households living in type of accommodation, April 2001

	Warrington 002A	Culcheth, Glazebury and Croft	Warrington	North West	England and Wales
Accommodation type: Whole house or bungalow: Detached[1]	73.5	45.1	24.3	17.6	22.8
Accommodation type: Whole house or bungalow: Semi-detached[1]	20.6	38.0	42.7	36.6	31.6
Accommodation type: Whole house or bungalow: Terraced (including end terrace)[1]	5.6	11.2	24.4	31.7	26.0

[1] National Statistics

In April 2001, 0 per cent of households in LSOA Warrington 002A were accommodated in flats or maisonettes, compared with 19 per cent for England and Wales as a whole. In addition 0.0 per cent lived in caravans or other mobile or temporary structures, compared with 0.4 per cent for England and Wales.

According to the Indices of Deprivation 2004, 0 per cent of households in the Warrington 002A at the time of the 2001 Census were living in overcrowded conditions, and 1 per cent did not have central heating.

Also in April 2001, 12 per cent of households in LSOA Warrington 002A did not have a car or van, compared with 27 per cent in England and Wales overall. Households with access to two or more cars or vans accounted for 50 per cent of all households in the LSOA, compared with 29 per cent of households in England and Wales.

FIGURE 2.6 Continued

Where specific sites have been identified, other, more detailed data related to these factors may be collected:

> site analysis
>   − size
>   − configuration
>   − environment
>   − relationship to existing residential/commercial areas
> access analysis
>   − road system
>   − rail transport routes
>   − identifying traffic problems
> trade/catchment areas.

Defining a trade or catchment area depends on:

> the size and nature of the scheme
> natural, man-made or psychological factors
> existing or proposed access conditions
> size and location of existing and proposed competition.

There might seem to be a large degree of repetition in these lists; however, this has been done to underline the fact that market research in property development does not take place at a single point in the process but instead at many stages as different decisions are taken. As the scheme becomes more certain and closer to fruition, the type of data collected changes. Market research is a continuous process that should be ongoing throughout the life of a scheme.

Data analysis The next step following the collection of the data is the difficult process of analysis. This is undertaken to provide an understanding of current and possible future conditions in the market where the development is proposed. This analysis can take many forms and can be done at many levels. At the lowest level this may be no more than a detailed description of the market. At the higher levels some kind of regression-based modelling may be undertaken. Modelling attempts to identify key associations with the variables that can be used to forecast future trends.

In many types of developments – hotels, residential, retail and offices – one of the key areas of analysis will be related to the catchment area or trade analysis. It is from this that the market for guests, occupiers and customers can be estimated. The extent of the area will be determined by many of the factors on which data have already been collected. These include the presence of physical or psychological barriers to potential users, access conditions and the availability of transport links, and the size and location of existing and proposed developments.

Part of the ability to capture a share of the specific market which the property is intending to serve is related to the site itself. The micro location of the proposed development can be critical. This is particularly true of retail schemes. A location may, on paper, appear to be very attractive in terms of all other criteria but may not be able to capture sufficient market share to make it viable. In retail, being a few metres off the 'prime pitch' can greatly reduce the ability to attract shoppers and, thus, rents. This point will be discussed further below; however, it should be stressed that the analysis of a development's market potential should be carried out at the detailed level as well as at the broad aggregate level.

Analysis of the effect of introducing the scheme into the market This is perhaps the most difficult of the four steps. Collecting the data is usually straightforward, although access to some data can be difficult. Analysing how the existing situation works is a process of careful deliberation but one that is based on current facts and relationships in the main, although the effects of planned developments such as new roads or significant new developments can create problems. (An example of the latter was faced by those responsible for redeveloping the retail heart of Manchester following the IRA bomb in 1996. An imponderable at the time was the effect that the regional shopping centre being built on the outskirts of the city would have, which was due to open as the Trafford Centre within the next 18 months.) The problems tend to be even greater when trying to predict the effect that the scheme itself will have on the market.

Markets are dynamic, almost organic structures that can be quite sensitive to change. Some are more sensitive than others, but most large schemes can have a major effect. Office markets are usually not so footloose but single schemes or sometimes single lettings can cause the entire office core to move. An example of this occurred in Manchester where the development of two large offices close to the GMEX exhibition centre and their subsequent letting to some of the larger solicitors' practices in the city caused a substantial shift away from the traditional centres close to the retail heart of the city.

The effects in retailing, where location is more sensitive, can be even more striking. In Aberdeen, the development of a large in-town shopping mall, the Bon Accord Centre, saw a substantial realignment of the prime shopping area from the traditional area along Union Street.

What the impact will be depends on many of the factors already discussed above, including the nature and micro location of the site itself.

Conclusions and recommendations   The final stage in the process is the decision and recommendation about the scheme itself. The market analysis can tell the developer whether there is a fundamentally unfulfilled demand for the type of property proposed. It should also give the developer valuable information about the form, size and timing of the scheme among many other things.

Consumer demand analysis

Consumer demand analysis is quite different in character to area research. Area research tends to concentrate directly on the potential customers of the companies or organisations who will operate out of the property to be developed. This type of research involves talking to the potential occupiers themselves, either by way of general surveys of the type of occupier who might take the premises, in order to clarify the sector's general requirements and future expansion intentions, or else by contact with specific potential occupiers who might subsequently buy or lease the scheme.

Due to its direct nature, this is actually the most common form of property development research. It is an efficient way of establishing market demand for the proposed product and it is often carried out on an informal basis, usually by the developer's property consultant or agent, although more formal research programmes are sometimes carried out on behalf of developers for larger development proposals.

The section below outlines the sort of analysis that might be carried out for a major retail scheme at the broad aggregate level, i.e. that would be done above the site-specific level of decision-making. Here the developer is examining the opportunity to build a new department store in a large market town in the UK.

PROPERTY MARKET RESEARCH CASE STUDY: RETAIL SCHEME

The first step is to establish the population levels from census data for the area served by the existing retail centre. This involves establishing the catchment and trade areas for the town. Usually up to three zones are determined. The most important is the primary trade area, where the population almost invariably shops in the retail area considered. Secondary and tertiary catchments are also defined, where progressively less of the population make shopping trips to the retail centre where the development is proposed. The definition of these trade areas varies. Sometimes they are defined from actual surveys of shopping destinations carried out by market

TABLE 2.4 Historic population of trade areas

Trading area zone	1981	1991	2001	Annual change 1981–91: %	Annual change 1991–01: %
Primary	100,000	110,000	115,000	1.00	0.45
Secondary	130,000	132,000	135,000	0.15	0.23
Tertiary	50,000	55,000	60,000	1.00	0.9

research on shoppers. The cut-off points tend to be determined by the proportion of trips made. Sometimes the division is made purely on travel times or distances, e.g. 15-, 30- or 45-minute isotimes.

In our example, the trading area zones have been established by survey, and the defined areas of population history (Table 2.4) have been researched.

The next step is to forecast the change in population in the zones over the development period (Table 2.5). For this exercise the development is due to start in 2001 and take one year. The development is expected to be fully established in the year 2004. ('Fully established' means trading to full potential. It takes a number of years for a new shop to build up to its maximum turnover, as the clientele increases.)

These projections may be based on past trends, such as the previous census records or local planning projections, or they may be modelled using regression models.

The next step is to calculate the retail area's retention levels (Table 2.6) over the development period. The retention level is the area's ability to capture spending from the trade areas. From this the total effective catchment for the centre can be calculated.

The income and buying power of this population now needs to be established. This is where the socioeconomic data collected, including the CSO National Income and Expenditure tables, can be used. Two important targets of this analysis are to calculate annual disposable incomes (Table 2.7) and the amount the target

TABLE 2.5 Projected population of trade areas

Trading area zone	2002	2004	2006	Change 2002–06: %
Primary	117,638	119,249	120,882	0.46
Secondary	136,541	137,474	138,414	0.23
Tertiary	62,777	64,505	66,280	0.93

TABLE 2.6 Retention levels

Trading area zone		2002	2004	2006
Primary	90%	105,874	107,324	108,794
Secondary	50%	68,271	68,737	69,207
Tertiary	25%	15,694	16,126	16,570
Total	Catchment	189,839	192,187	194,571

TABLE 2.7 Disposable incomes

	2001	2004	2006	Annual change 2001–06: %
Primary	4,300	4,563	4,842	2.00
Secondary	4,500	4,846	5,219	2.50
Tertiary	5,000	5,464	5,970	3.00
Mean	4,600	4,958	5,344	
Per capita expenditure	2001	2004	2006	
75% expended	3,450	3,718	4,008	
25% saved				
Food	1,553	1,673	1,804	
Hardware	69	74	80	
Chemist	86	93	100	
White goods	259	279	301	
Large area stores	259	279	301	
Clothing	518	558	601	
Furniture	276	297	321	
Other comparison goods	431	465	501	
	3,450	3,718	4,008	

population spends on different types of goods. In this case the most relevant statistic is the amount spent in large area stores, i.e. department stores.

It should be noted that, similar to the population analysis, this is normally carried out in two steps: first, an establishment of historical patterns of expenditure, then a projection of future trends. In the example below, just the current year and appropriate future projections are illustrated.

The next step carried out is called a competition survey. This entails establishing the current spend and capture of market share by the existing competition. Following this it is necessary to estimate the capture of market share by the competition after scheme completion. After this the sales potential of the proposed department store can be estimated. This is a process of residual analysis and is illustrated in Table 2.8.

TABLE 2.8 Competition survey

	2001	2004	2006
Population attracted to town centre	189,839	192,187	194,571
Expenditure in large stores	£259	£279	£301
Total town centre large store spend	£49,168,301	£53,620,173	£58,565,871
Less			
Effective competition (50%)	£24,584,151	£26,810,087	£29,282,936
Unsatisfied potential	£24,584,151	£26,810,087	£29,282,936
Project share (50%)	£12,292,075	£13,405,043	£14,641,468

From these data a recommended scheme size can be determined. This is calculated by dividing the expected income of the store by market-derived trading figures per metre square based on industry experience:

	2001	2004	2006
Recommended size of unit (m^2)	4,097	4,468	4,880

(based on £3,000/m^2 sales per floor area)

Our analysis therefore suggests that a store of approximately 4,000m^2 could be supported on a suitable site in the town centre.

It should be noted that many aspects of this process require assumptions to be made which can greatly affect the outcome of the process. Some caution should be used when acting on the results.

RESEARCH FOR OTHER TYPES OF PROPERTY

Market research for other property types is done in a similar way, although it is in retail that most of the effort is focused, given the direct relationship between retail rents and retail expenditure patterns. The links between economic factors and other types of properties are less straightforward and the results of the analysis are therefore less conclusive. This is only really a problem where property is built speculatively, i.e. not for a specific end user. Where an occupier or purchaser is identified prior to construction, few problems arise. Unfortunately, a high proportion of development is carried out on a speculative basis.

Residential property

Perhaps the next most sophisticated and extensive market research carried out in other property markets is concerned with the residential sector, particularly the volume house building market.

Residential developers can closely identify their target markets, enabling them to balance the supply and demand equation with a fair degree of accuracy. The goal of a residential developer is to supply the product at a rate just below the equilibrium level demanded in the market. This will ensure that prices rise steadily – but not at such a high level as to attract too much competition – and that all their units sell within the target period. This means that market research is worthwhile for the sector. Data are usually gathered on the following areas.

Site and access data as per retail schemes:

Market area	Catchment (who is the scheme going to serve?)
	Employment generators (who are the main employers? What are the prospects for the future, etc.?)
	How good are the transport routes/links to the site/suburb?
Population	Trends/structure (is the population rising or falling? Is it aging? Are there lots of young families?)
	Family size

Population	Employment levels
	Income levels
	Rate of family formation
Competition	What other schemes have been built or planned for the area?
Take-up/sale levels	Have the units sold quickly or have some similar dwellings remained unsold for long periods?
Price trends in the region	Have prices risen?
	Is this a sudden rise indicating a shortfall of supply?
	Is this a long-term trend?
	How do prices compare with similar areas in other parts of the region or country?

There has been a period of consolidation in the residential development sector with many mergers and takeovers. This reduction in competition will increase the ability of house builders both to analyse the market and to predict the level of demand and therefore the level that needs to be supplied. It is likely that the methods employed to do this will become even more sophisticated in the future.

With smaller scale residential developments it is hard to carry out such detailed analysis, nor will it be likely to be cost effective to do so. In these cases, the developer must rely heavily on the market knowledge and experience of a residential agent. The discussions with, and subsequent appointment of, an agent who possesses this information is a vital part of the market research process for smaller schemes.

Market research for offices and industrial property

With the other sectors, market research is more difficult and rarely carried out effectively because of more indirect links between aspects of the economy.

The office sector is perhaps the most problematic due to inadequate data about the supply and demand factors in the market. It is very hard to access adequate and reliable data about future take-up rates from occupiers. Offices can be used more or less intensely, according to the occupiers' requirements. Acquisition of additional space can be postponed by an occupier who is uncertain about future trading conditions. Businesses in the UK can also shed and take on staff more quickly than in many places in the world. On the supply side, developers can postpone decisions to take up planning consent for many years, often by re-letting a secondary office building bought for redevelopment on short-term leases. This means that although the analysis outlined for retail schemes above can be carried out, it is often a waste of time and money.

Office developers rely on a handful of key indicators to make their decision. These are:

> number of years' supply in market – this is calculated by dividing the annual area of space let by the vacant space of the appropriate quality in the market

> outstanding unfulfilled requirements for office space – many businesses register future or current requirements with property agents. High levels of unfulfilled demand are a key sign for developers to proceed
> rental trends – when rents start to increase this usually indicates unfulfilled demand
> vacancy rates in each class of office – a key factor for developers is the quantity of Grade A, i.e. top quality, space on the market (see the section on the property markets in Chapter 1, page 29).

Although this low level of research in the office market is understandable, one word can be used to sum it up: 'inadequate'. Essentially, as with small-scale residential development, the appointment of an agent who knows the market really acts as a proxy for conducting formal research. These agents will provide a depth of knowledge about market trends and occupier requirements, both general and specific.

Essentially the same situation exists with the industrial markets. Knowing occupier intentions and requirements tends to be the key to successful developments. This information can be gathered by contacting key occupier firms but it is easier and more cost effective to use the services of a good industrial agent.

Site assembly and land acquisition

INTRODUCTION

It is a straightforward fact that a site is a basic requirement of property development. The developer must acquire an interest over, or the rights to develop on, a piece of land. The actual purchase of this land must, however, follow a complex path of investigations that are carried out in order to ensure that the development is viable on the site chosen. Many problems and heartaches can be avoided if this preliminary work is carried out properly.

Before we examine the process of acquisition we must consider the question of site identification. How this is done depends on how the idea of the development came about. In some cases the idea comes first. The developer is either working to fulfil a known requirement, or has been commissioned to supply a building to a known client, or a gap has been identified in the market that the developer is seeking to fill. In this case, the developer seeks a site that can fulfil these requirements. The alternative scenario is where a site that is ripe for development is brought to the attention of a developer. This happens in the course of normal business activity in the property market but also where local authorities identify key sites for development and issue a brief to the market. In this case, the developer knows the nature and characteristics of the site and attempts to find a suitable development that can be successfully built on it. This is a subtle distinction but it does affect both the behaviour of the developer and the process of investigation that has to be carried out.

Some development sites are made known to the development sector by being marketed. This is the normal case where existing users of the land have completed their activities and wish to dispose of their interests or, again, where a local authority wishes to promote a development site. Here, some of the preliminary work on bringing the site to development will have been carried out, although the developer will still have a substantial amount of work to do. There are a number of advantages in dealing with a site that is on the market; not least of which is that the owner of the site is known and that some appraisal of the site and some idea of value will have been determined.

There are some potential disadvantages to developers buying a site 'on the market'. First, the price that will be paid for the site is likely to be 'full'. Exposing the site to the market means that all interested parties will have had time to weigh up its qualities and submit bids before it is (generally) sold to the highest bidder. This is very good for the vendor but can make life difficult for a developer trying to make a profit out of the site. The second disadvantage is related to timing and competition. A development is often time sensitive and the developer needs to have all the components in place before proceeding. Being forced to bid for a site forces their hand and the developer may have to proceed before being completely ready. The bidding process also allows the market to have information about the developer's scheme; rival developers can either bring forward their own schemes or else put in 'spoiling' bids to drive up the price of the land. It is not uncommon for the owner of a key piece of land to hold out for a high price once development plans have been released. These 'ransom strips' can be acquired compulsorily if one of the promoters of the scheme has compulsory acquisition powers (such as local authorities or public utilities) or if the development is viewed as being in the public interest. However, such problems can seriously delay a development.

Developers are therefore often very sensitive about revealing details of their plans. As a result, many developers prefer to deal 'off the market'. This refers to the acquisition of sites that are either not for sale or else are being marketed discreetly, an approach that allows for confidentiality. It also offers the potential for the site to be acquired at a price below the value that could be obtained in the open market. It should be remembered that where development potential exists, the value of the site for alternative use exceeds the existing use value but that it requires someone to identify this as values are not easily observed.

There are, of course, distinct disadvantages in following this approach; for example in England and Wales it has traditionally been difficult to identify the owner of land (although the Land Registry has now been reorganised, allowing easier access to information like this). The other obvious disadvantage is that the landowner may not be willing to sell.

This position applies to the acquisition of all sites but the 'off market' approach is particularly pertinent where a large development is planned that requires the acquisition of a number of sites that are joined together to make the main site. This can be done in one step where the developer has access to compulsory acquisition powers. Where these do not exist, however, it is common for developers to acquire individual sites slowly and quietly over time as they come on the market, without revealing the purpose of the acquisition to the vendors. These properties can be held on short-term leases as investments until the time comes to commence the development. Developers assembling sites in this way have to show extreme patience and maintain good security for this approach to be successful.

BASICS OF SITE ACQUISITION: USEFUL MEMBERS OF THE DEVELOPMENT TEAM

The roles and duties of the development team will be considered elsewhere; however, it seems appropriate here to identify the key members who should be employed by a developer at the site acquisition stage.

The pivotal member of the team at this stage is the solicitor. A good solicitor, experienced in development is indispensable, as he or she can carry out the checking of titles, covenants, easements and rights of way. Other advisors who can be used include planning consultants who can save valuable time and effort in identifying possible development avenues and in consultation and negotiations with the planning authorities. Similarly, an experienced chartered surveyor specialising in the field of land acquisition and/or development can assist in site identification, pricing and in negotiations with landowners, occupiers and vendors. Finally, environmental consultants and engineers may be required in some circumstances to work on some aspects of the site appraisal process.

PRELIMINARY INVESTIGATIONS PRIOR TO PURCHASE

In this section the main areas of preliminary investigation required to be carried out before acquisition will be reviewed. In following this procedure it is assumed that the developer has identified a site and is carrying out investigations as to the feasibility of developing it.

Planning

This is one of the fundamental areas of investigation as the planning status of the site is critical to the success of a development. The developer needs to establish whether the site can be used for the most valuable appraised development and also needs to establish what restrictions the planning authority will place on this use. Planning clauses such as height restrictions, the building line, the degree of car parking allowed and the total area permitted to be built on the site are the principal determinants of completed value and, thus, the economic viability of the site.

Information on these areas can be determined from a number of sources and at a number of levels of investigation. Again, the developer's attitude to how much information can be released about the development determines the type of approach followed.

Development plan documents (DPDs)

A considerable amount of information can be gleaned from the DPDs. The DPDs are planning documents prepared by the local authority to assist in the physical and economic development of the area under their jurisdiction. A local development framework includes a core strategy, site-specific allocations of land, a proposals map and may also contain additional optional development documents such as area action plans. DPDs are subject to rigorous procedures of community involvement, consultation and independent examination. Once adopted, development control decisions must be made in accordance with the DPDs unless material considerations indicate otherwise. DPDs are also subject to a sustainability appraisal to ensure that the economic, environmental and social effects of the plan are in line with sustainable development targets. The core strategy sets out the general spatial vision and objectives for delivery in the local development framework. The core strategy plays a key part in the delivery of the council's community strategy by setting out its spatial aspects and providing a long-term spatial vision strategy relating to the development and use of land and outlining the council's strategy for delivering strategic development needs, including housing, leisure and retail. The allocation of land for specific uses must be set out in a development plan document of site-specific allocations, which is separate from the core strategy. This allows the local authority to update allocations in the light of changes to other local development documents or implementation on the ground. The adopted proposals map illustrates all site-specific policies in all the adopted development plan documents in map form and should also identify areas of protection such as nationally protected landscape and local nature conservation areas, green belt land and conservation areas.

Planning history

Following the consultation of the DPDs, the next level of investigation to be carried out by the developer or their agents regarding planning issues is the investigation of the planning history of the site. All planning authorities keep records of each site under their jurisdiction. These records are in the public domain and available for public scrutiny. Normally this requires a visit to the local authority to inspect the records but some authorities will supply written information.

The site's planning history will provide a range of information. This includes:

> the history of planning applications made on the site – this is very useful in determining whether other developers have shown, or are currently showing, an interest in the site;

> a record of approved applications and the conditions attached to the consent – this can be used to establish the existing planning status, i.e. the current established use, the size of building approved for the site and the form of building allowed, as well as whether there are any outstanding consents that can be utilised to develop the site. Historical, as well as current, consents can be useful in that old uses may be cited as evidence in planning negotiations to argue for a reversion to a more valuable use;

> a record of rejected applications and the reasons for rejection – this gives a good picture of the planning authority's attitude to development on the site. A history of rejections for the use proposed illustrates that a developer is unlikely to succeed unless the reasons for the rejections can be addressed in the new scheme;

> whether any building or element of a building on the site is listed – listing illustrates that the building is of historical or architectural importance. It means that another tier of consent will be required before planning permission can be granted and that some aspects of the development may be restricted. There are three tiers of listing: Grade I, the highest tier applied to exceptional and outstanding buildings and structure; Grade II* applied to very significant buildings and structures; and Grade II, the remainder. Listing can apply to whole buildings or just elements. Listing a building does not mean that development is completely barred but that the developer will be restricted and may need to conserve elements;

> whether the building is in a conservation area – planning authorities often wish to preserve the character of key areas within their areas of responsibility, such as areas characterised by particular architectural styles or dominated by buildings of a particular period. The buildings within the area may or may not be listed. Development is normally allowed but must be sympathetic to the character of the area in terms of material or design.

Discussions with the planning officer

The above investigations can be done quietly, without attracting much attention. Sometimes, however, more in-depth discussions are required to test the attitude of the planning authorities. These will certainly be required at a later stage of the acquisition process. One issue that may be material to the development is whether the planning authorities will be seeking any 'planning gain' through section 106 of the Town and Country Planning (1990) Act. Meeting with a planning officer may clarify this issue.

Meeting a planning officer is very useful as general planning policy can be articulated as well as the authority's position regarding particular sites, which may not appear in the written documentation. The outline of the development can also be discussed with the planning authority directly, prior to an application being made. This allows a developer to gauge whether a development would be allowed or resisted. Other details that can be discussed include the scale of the development and what features and characteristics would have to be incorporated to give the application the best chance of success.

Success in a planning application cannot be guaranteed. Planning officers can only make recommendations that go in front of the elected members of the planning committee. However, building up a relationship and discussing proposals in detail with officers can allow the developer to gain a good understanding of the situation pertaining to particular sites. This is useful both in terms of deciding whether the acquisition should be made and also later, when the detailed design of the scheme is being prepared.

TITLE

To succeed, a developer needs, as far as is practicable, to acquire an unencumbered clear title to a site, be it freehold or leasehold. Clear ownership of the site needs to be obtained and all legal restrictions to the title that may restrict or even prevent development must be identified and extinguished. One of the key aspects that must be examined with regard to title is clear ownership of the interest to be acquired. It is not always possible to identify who owns land. Despite the Land Registry, some landowners have never been registered or cannot be traced. Particularly with freehold interests, the rights of ownership of the land are passed to the rightful heirs of the previous owners who may have to be traced. Another problem that should be recognised is in relation to the establishment of ownership rights. Land ownership can be acquired by occupation for a prescribed period without protest by the rightful owner (similarly, rights of way over land can be established by use without protest or objection). Even when ownership of the land is clear there can be problems with the establishment of boundaries. It is not always easy to establish the extent of a site.

As well as these questions over title and extent, there are a number of rights that can be established over, or in connection with, land that can significantly affect the development viability. These include:

> rights of way to third parties and neighbours over land;
> existing leases, whether or not the tenant is in occupation;
> easements for the passage of cables of pipes over, under or through the site;
> restrictive covenants that prevent certain activities or uses of land;
> mortgages on the land – land and property are often used as security for loans, thus a charge may exist that needs to be discharged;
> offers to sell – there may be a requirement in the title or the lease on the property to sell to a named party;
> other rights to the land, such as grazing rights, rights to mineral extraction or rights to hold a market on the land, are all historic rights that can exist even on urban land.

All of these rights are defensible against third parties, i.e. they are real rights recognised in courts of law that cannot simply be arbitrarily extinguished by the owner of a superior interest. They can only be extinguished or modified by negotiation and agreement with the beneficiary. If that party cannot be identified – and with historic titles this is quite common – these rights can be extinguished or modified by application to the Lands Tribunal. This can be a time-consuming process and a site with a number of title problems may not be a viable prospect for development.

RELATIONSHIP WITH NEIGHBOURING SITES

Connected with the questions of the title and rights over the site itself is the relationship with the site's neighbouring owners. A building does not exist in isolation; the relationship with its neighbours is regulated by law. Some issues that need to be considered are the following.

Easements and rights of way benefiting the site

To make a development economically viable it is sometimes necessary to establish rights over neighbouring land. This may include simple access to the site over neighbouring property, but there is no automatic right of way over land in law. If the site being considered is an isolated pocket of land remote from, say, road access, a right of way needs to be established. Other similar factors include easements to allow services onto a site and also rights of egress and escape to meet fire regulations.

Rights to light

There are complex rules dealing with neighbours' rights to daylight and views. This must be taken into account in designing schemes as well as in negotiating compensation to neighbours adversely affected by new buildings.

Party walls and support of neighbouring structures

Similarly, there is statutory protection for the rights and responsibilities of neighbours and site owners in questions of shared walls and rights of support. These need to be negotiated and agreed before development can proceed, although neighbours cannot prevent development on these grounds.

Craneage and oversailing rights

Finally, on tight urban sites, the possibility of crane jibs used in the construction of the new building passing over neighbours' sites must be considered. Properties have rights to the airspace over land, so there is no automatic right for a crane to pass over the site.

Other issues that might be considered are road closures and the effect of neighbouring businesses on the construction work. All these issues have to be investigated and this is best done as early as is feasible.

SITE SERVICING

The utilities have a statutory duty to service developed land but there are practical issues that must be considered which can have significant effects on the development planned, in particular an assessment of the capacity of the services to meet the requirements of the development. If there is a shortfall in some areas of supply it may take considerable time for adequate facilities to be supplied – if at all. If it were not practical to raise the capacity of supply then the service supplier would use this as an argument to the planning authority against the scheme being given consent. The services to the site that should be investigated are:

> gas
> electricity
> telecommunications
> water
> sewerage and rainwater run-off.

A further factor to consider is whether pipes and service runs interfere with the physical development of the site. High-pressure gas pipelines, for example, have exclusion zones around them where no development is allowed.

HIGHWAYS AND ACCESS

Virtually all developments will involve some generation of traffic and need servicing by roads. As a result, one of the most important issues to resolve will be the highways situation. Like the services connection, consultation with the highways authorities is one of the key components of consideration by the planning authorities, therefore consultation at the pre-acquisition stage is important both in assessing whether the scheme is acceptable on the site and in shaping the form of an acceptable scheme.

The highways authorities will first consider whether the scheme is acceptable in terms of the potential increase in car use generated by the development. They, and the planning authorities, will take into account whether the scheme is in line with central government guidelines on transport and car journey generation. They will also assess whether the scheme is in conflict with any proposed road schemes in the area.

If the scheme is acceptable, consideration will then be given to the degree of road alterations required, if any, to accommodate the scheme. New junctions or roundabouts may be required. If they are directly connected with the scheme, the developer may have to contribute to their development or pay for the alterations in their entirety. Ascertaining, at least in principle, what is required, gives the developer the opportunity to cost the commitment and set it against the completed value of the scheme. The developer may also be able to gain information about future schemes that may affect the development, either positively or adversely.

GROUND CONDITIONS AND BEARING CAPACITIES

Key physical characteristics that affect the building that goes onto the site are the ground conditions. These include the frequency of flooding that the site suffers (for example, is it located on a floodplain?) and the groundwater height. The type of soil, geology and the bearing capacity of the site are also key issues, each having a strong influence on the design of the building and, in particular, the foundations. All these factors can have an influence on both the cost of construction and the end value of the development. Spending a relatively small amount of money on site investigations can help to save the commitment of considerable sums.

CONTAMINATION

The final main issue to consider about the site has been one of the most important ones of the recent past. Contamination is likely to become increasingly important in the future as the Government acts to encourage more development on previously used brownfield sites. It is also likely to be an issue affecting developers as occupiers of property have shown a trend to become increasingly litigious.

It is therefore very important to carry out investigations on the previous users of the site. If processes had been employed which used harmful chemicals then there is a strong risk that the site is contaminated with chemicals potentially harmful to human or animal life, one of the main definitions of contamination under the legislation of the Environment Act 1995. Some of the potentially harmful uses are obvious, such as chemical works and gas works, but some are less obvious: dry cleaners, petrol stations, and animal rendering and abattoirs are associated with contamination.

The principle followed in dealing with contamination is that the 'polluter pays' for making the land safe. Although this is reassuring to the developer, it is not an absolute panacea. First, with historical contamination the polluter may not be identifiable or may no longer be in business. There will almost certainly be timing issues. It may take time for the site to be treated by the polluter, which may cause the project to miss the window of economic viability. It may be advisable, under most circumstances, for the developer to control and thus carry out the work on the site. Developers should therefore employ environmental consultants to carry out a survey for contamination and to assess the potential cost of cleaning up the site before making the commitment to purchase.

Remediation is a complex area, outside the scope of this book; however, it should be noted that most sites can be remediated. It is the cost and time issues that are important to consider, as well as any potential stigma associated with the contamination which may have an impact on the end value of the scheme.

CONCLUSIONS

Acquiring the site is perhaps the most important point of the whole development process. It usually marks the point of the start of the development proper and certainly the point where the major financial commitments begin. It is therefore imperative to carry out investigations into the site diligently and thoroughly. This will pay dividends later on.

Obtaining planning consent and other legal issues

INTRODUCTION: PLANNING AND DEVELOPMENT

In the preceding section we have covered some ground dealing with planning and other statutory authorities. Because planning requirements are so important to development, however, we will look in more detail at the systems and processes involved.

Planning and development go hand in hand. Most countries have planning systems in place; some are restrictive and prescriptive, some are liberal and largely market-led. Whatever the case, the planning system represents state intervention in the land markets.

There are a number of reasons why the state chooses to intervene but they all revolve around the importance of the built environment to the economy, to society and to the individual. In a market economy there is the need to balance the requirements of the state and the business community in the economic development and growth of the economy, with the requirements of the population for a safe and healthy environment. There is the need to ensure that resources are used as efficiently as possible. In an unregulated economy there would be a tendency for developers to follow trends that would give short-term profits only, developing only those properties for which there was the highest demand and ignoring the rest, leading to a boom and bust cycle in individual markets. The planning system works best when a balance is achieved between the needs of the state, business and society, ensuring balanced development and an efficient use of resources, smoothing out short-term trends in the market.

Some parties view planners as the enemy of development and developers. This is, in fact, not the case. In fact, the planning system, although restrictive in many cases, assists developers and investors by creating certainty and, sometimes, artificial construction of supply of the type of property most in demand. Where demand exceeds supply of any commodity the price of that commodity invariably rises, as is certainly the case with property.

An effective planning system on land values can be observed in many ways. One classic way is by taking a profile of land values across any major city. The highest values tend to be in the centre where demand is greatest, falling towards the suburbs. There is usually a point at which values drop close to agricultural values and then pick up again. This is usually an indication of the position of the 'green belt', an artificial constraint on development introduced to prevent urban sprawl.

This can also be seen in individual cases. In the mid-1990s there was a clamp-down on out-of-town retailing in the UK by a tightening up of the planning system. It was felt by many commentators that the dynamism of traditional town centres was being undermined by the growth of hypermarkets and retail warehousing on the edge of towns. The growth in these markets also led to an increase in road traffic, another factor that is becoming a key issue in politics and planning. A sequential test was devised that required developers to consider sites closer to the centre of urban areas first, and there was a presumption against giving consent to new out-of-town schemes. The result of this was a significant rise in value of both developed and undeveloped retail sites with planning consent on edge-of-town locations, as investors and operators realised that an artificial constraint on supply had been imposed. This rise in value actually increased the impetus for both the development of new sites and for the redevelopment of existing locations. Planning can be a crude instrument but it is one that is also essential.

The land use planning system is an integral part of the national planning system. Other elements of planning include transport and highways. It is the land use planning system which lies at the interface between the state and the development market, and hence this is the area on which this chapter will concentrate.

THE UK LAND USE PLANNING SYSTEM

It is not the purpose of this book to give a history of the development of the planning system; nor is this book intended to provide a comprehensive analysis of all aspects of the planning system as it affects the developer. The UK has a mature, extensive and complex land use planning system with almost 100 years of legislation from the first true planning act in 1909 (The Housing, Town Planning, etc. Act 1909). Much of the system is embodied in a huge range of statutes, rules, regulations, directions, policy statements, circulars and such like. The whole system cannot be discussed here; only key features can be examined. It should be noted that there is a crucial difference between the 'framework' and the way in which the system actually operates. There are a number of political, social and economic factors that can significantly alter the way the system actually works from time to time.

A major change in the operative legislation came about in the 1990–01 period with the passing of the Town and Country Planning Act 1990 and the Planning and Compensation Act 1991, and it is these acts which were in operation at the time of writing the first edition of this book. In 2004, the Government introduced a new planning system to manage how development takes place in towns and the countryside. The earlier Acts were supplanted by the Planning and Compulsory Purchase Act 2004. The legislation was designed to pave the way for a more flexible and responsive planning system for England and Wales. The Act made a number of changes and had a number of objectives:

> it introduced what the Government believed was a simpler and more flexible plan-making system at regional and local level;
> it increased the effectiveness and quality of community involvement at regional and local level and enabled the provision of financial assistance to Planning Aid;
> it improved the development control process by introducing powers for standard application forms and new provisions which change the duration of planning permissions and consents as well as allowing local planning authorities (LPAs) to bring in local permitted development rights via so-called local development orders;
> it speeded up the handling of major infrastructure projects (i.e. airports, power stations, major new energy transmission networks) by allowing the different elements of inquiries to be heard concurrently rather than consecutively;
> it removed the Crown's immunity from planning processes; and
> it made the compulsory purchase regime simpler, fairer and quicker to support policies on investment in major infrastructure and on regeneration.

The Planning and Compulsory Purchase Act 2004 introduced a new 'two-tiered' plan system, comprised of:

> *regional spatial strategies (RSSs)* – prepared by the regional planning bodies (or, in London, the spatial development strategy prepared by the mayor of London). These set out a broad spatial planning strategy for how a region should look in 15 to 20 years' time and possibly longer;
> *local development frameworks (LDFs)* – a folder of local development documents prepared by district councils, unitary authorities or national park authorities outlining the spatial planning strategy for the local area.

Local development framework (LDF) components

Development plan documents (DPDs)

A local development framework includes a core strategy, site-specific allocations of land, a proposals map and may also contain additional optional development documents such as area action plans. DPDs are subject to rigorous procedures of community involvement, consultation and independent examination. Once adopted, development control decisions must be made in accordance with the DPDs unless material considerations indicate otherwise. DPDs are also subject to a sustainability appraisal to ensure that the economic, environmental and social effects of the plan are in line with sustainable development targets.

Core strategy (required)

The core strategy sets out the general spatial vision and objectives for delivery in the LDF. The core strategy plays a key part in the delivery of the council's community strategy by setting out its spatial aspects and providing a long-term spatial vision strategy relating to the development and use of land and outlining the council's strategy for delivering strategic development needs, including housing, leisure and retail.

The core strategy must be kept up to date and all other development plan documents must be in conformity with it and the RSS (or the spatial development strategy in London).

Site-specific allocations (required)

The allocation of land for specific uses must be set out in a development plan document of site-specific allocations, which is separate from the core strategy. This allows the local authority to update allocations in the light of changes to other local development documents or implementation on the ground.

Adopted proposals map (required)

The adopted proposals map illustrates all site-specific policies in all the adopted development plan documents in map form and should also identify areas of protection such as nationally protected landscape and local nature conservation areas, green belt land and conservation areas.

Area action plans (optional)

An area action plan (AAP) is a development plan document focused on a specific location or an area subject to conservation or significant change. This could include a major regeneration project or a growth area and focuses on implementation providing an important mechanism for ensuring development of an appropriate scale, mix and quality for key areas of opportunity, change or conservation. An AAP should outline protection for areas sensitive to change and aim to resolve conflicting objectives in areas subject to development pressures.

Other development plan documents (optional)

These can include thematic documents concerned with housing, employment, retail development, etc. and can also include generic development control policies.

Local development scheme (required)

The local development scheme is a public 'project plan' identifying which local development documents will be produced, in what order and when. The local development scheme acts as the starting point for the community and stakeholders to find out about the authority's planning policies with respect to a particular place or issue, and the status of those policies. It also outlines the details of and timetable for the production of all documents that make up the LDF over a three-year period.

Statement of community involvement (required)

The statement of community involvement (SCI) shows how and when planning authorities intend to consult local communities and other stakeholders when preparing documents. Every SCI must provide open access to information, actively encourage the contribution of ideas and representations from the community and provide regular and timely feedback on progress.

Annual monitoring report (required)

This is a report submitted to the Government by a local planning authority to establish the progress and the effectiveness of an LDF in assessing the following issues:

> Are policies achieving their objectives and is sustainable development being delivered?
> Have policies had the intended consequences?
> Are the assumptions and objectives behind policies still relevant?
> Are the targets set in the LDF being achieved?

To achieve this goal, the annual monitoring report includes a range of local and standard (core output) indicators. It should also highlight if any adjustments to the local development scheme are required.

Supplementary planning documents (optional)

Supplementary planning documents (SPDs) expand or add details to policies laid out in development plan documents, or a saved policy in an existing development plan. These may take the form of design guides, area development briefs, a master plan or issue-based documents.

These documents can use illustrations, text and practical examples to expand on how the authority's policies can be taken forward.

Local Development Orders and Simplified Planning Zones (optional)

The LDF may also contain Local Development Orders and Simplified Planning Zones.

> A Local Development Order is made by a planning authority in order to extend permitted rights for certain forms of development, with regard to a relevant local development document.
> A Simplified Planning Zone is an area in which a local planning authority wishes to stimulate development and encourage investment. It operates by granting a specified planning permission in the zone without the need for a formal application or the payment of planning fees.

CONTROL OF DEVELOPMENT

Most forms of development require prior approval from the local planning authority, which has considerable powers of discretion in considering applications. Decisions must have regard to the development and structure plans but they can take into account any other material considerations and arguments.

Applications must be made in a proper form to the local planning authority which employs 'officers' – professional planners who consider the applications, advise applicants and make recommendations to the authority's planning committee, which is made up of elected members. A fee is charged for the submission of an application.

The local planning authority has three choices when an application is made. It can:

> give unconditional planning consent – this is actually quite rare; normally conditions are attached to consents;
> give planning consent subject to conditions – these can be just about anything as long as they are material and reasonable. Consent is not open-ended: a time limit is imposed requiring the development to start within three years. Another requirement is related to the materials and design of the building. In England and Wales the consent may be given subject to an agreement under section 106 of the Town and Country Planning Act 1990. This allows the authority to obtain what is commonly termed 'planning gain', usually some community facility to be provided by the developer at their cost or by way of a major contribution to the overall cost in exchange for consent being given. Although this may sound like bribery, the effect of this section is moderated by the Government and the courts, requiring the article gained under the agreement to be related in some way to the development;
> refuse consent.

Applicants for planning consent have the option of applying for detailed or outline consent. The latter is often used to establish, in the eyes of the market and the planning authority, what size and type of buildings would be allowed on a site that is ripe for development. Obtaining outline consent can be useful if, for example, the site is to be marketed prior to development, as it shows the potential for the site. It also may be useful for a developer in obtaining finance or development partners for a site. The outline consent granted will not be sufficient to allow immediate development and usually the conditions applied are that the detailed application will follow.

The most obvious reason for applying for outline consent in the early stages of the development, however, is related to design. At the inception phase of a development the design of the scheme is not usually finalised. A full planning application requires the inclusion of detailed plans. It is normal, therefore, in a development project to obtain outline consent at the land acquisition stage to prove that the broad development planned will be allowed. A full, detailed application then follows as the scheme design is finalised.

If an application is rejected, the applicants have the right to appeal to the appropriate secretary of state. This right also exists against conditional approval where the applicant feels the conditions applied are inappropriate or unusually onerous. In addition, the applicant can resort to the courts if the local planning authority is considered to have acted *ultra vires*, i.e. outside its powers. Where an appeal is made to the secretary of state, an experienced planning inspector is appointed to consider the case and hear representations.

The appropriate secretary of state has wide powers on appeal. An inspector may reverse decisions, impose new conditions, or refuse consent altogether where it has previously been given. About one-third of appeals tend to be allowed. Most decisions are made by the inspectors employed by the ministry with a very few, larger schemes going to a public inquiry.

It is important to define what development actually is. It is defined in the 1990 Town and Country Planning Act as 'the carrying out of building, engineering, mining or other operations in, on, over or under land, or the making of a new material change in the use of buildings or other land'. This is clearly an extensive definition that also includes demolition in some cases. It should be noted that it includes not only physical operations or alteration to a building but also the changes of use of a building. For example, if a developer wanted to change a building currently used as an office to, say, an estate agency, planning consent would be required, as an estate agency is considered a retail use and, therefore, a change of use.

The definition is so broad that it could include almost any aspect of development. This would imply that all activity would require consent from the planning authority. In fact, some leeway is given to reduce the burden of bureaucracy:

> Some activities are specifically stated not to be a development, for example internal alterations to many buildings are not classified as such.
> Other items may constitute development but are specifically declared not to require consent by government instruments.
> There are a number of instruments which would allow development to take place without specific application to local planning authorities:

- General Development Order (GDO)
- Use Classes Order (UCO)
- Special Development Order (SDO).

These are discussed in more detail below.

The General Development Order (GDO)

The GDO is a statutory instrument which is intended to save time and effort for both the community and the planning authorities. The GDO lists activities which are defined as permitted development. These are essentially activities either of a very minor level or else which have a minor impact on the local community or area. Examples include minor alterations to residential buildings and small extensions within certain size limits. Similarly, the erection of certain agricultural buildings is deemed not to require additional permission under the GDO. This also applies to certain changes of use. For example, in the retail Class A it is possible to move from Class A3 (food and drink) to a Class A2 or A1 without the need for a planning application to be made. This is because the change represents a reduction in intensity and impact of use. A move in the opposite direction from Class A1 to Class A2 or A3 does have an additional impact on the location of the shop and, consequently, consent is required (see Chapter 1).

Although most of the GDO deals with minor matters which are not of concern to most developers, it is worth checking in some cases whether consent is actually required, especially where change of use is concerned.

The Use Classes Order (UCO)

The UCO is an important element of the planning system. It defines 16 classes of activity in the built environment. Class A is the retail class, Class B is a broader business class and includes office, light industrial and warehousing activities, and so on. Classes are subdivided, for example Class A is broken down into five separate subsections. The UCO is used by planning authorities to define activities suitable for individual sites and/or areas. It also allows, as we have seen above, some changes in use to take place without the need to go through the planning application process. In this, the UCO and the GDO work in tandem.

It should be noted that not all uses in the built environment are included within the UCO. Some users are *sui generis*, i.e. they are in a class on their own. Car showrooms fall into this category.

The UCO was revised in 2005. The changes are reviewed in Table 2.9.

The Special Development Order (SDO)

The GDO is applicable everywhere. SDOs are more limited and apply only in specific cases. They relate to particular areas or types of development. For example, the Urban

TABLE 2.9 Summary guide to Use Classes Order and permitted changes of use

The Town and Country Planning (Use Classes) Order 1987 including 2005 amendment	Description	General Permitted Development (Amendment) Order 2005[1]
A1 Shops	Shops, retail warehouses, hairdressers, undertakers, travel and ticket agencies, post offices, dry cleaners, Internet cafes, pet shops, cat-meat shops, tripe shops, sandwich bars, showrooms, domestic hire shops, funeral directors	No permitted changes
A2 Financial and professional services	Banks, building societies, estate and employment agencies, professional and financial services, betting offices	Permitted change to A1 where a ground floor display window exists
A3 Restaurants and cafes	Restaurants, snack bars, cafes	Permitted change to A1 or A2
A4 Drinking establishments	Pubs and bars	Permitted change to A1, A2, A3
A5 Hot food takeaways	Hot food takeaway	Permitted change to A1, A2, A3
Sui generis[2]	Shops selling and/or displaying motor vehicles, retail warehouse clubs, launderettes, taxi or vehicle hire businesses, amusement centres, petrol filling stations	No permitted changes
B1 Business (a)(b)(c)	(a) Offices, not within A2 (b) Research and development, studios, laboratories, high technology (c) Light industry	Permitted change to B8 where no more than 235m^2
B2 General industry	General industry	Permitted change to B1 or B8 B8 limited to no more than 235m^2
B8 Storage or distribution	Wholesale warehouses, distribution centres, repositories	Permitted change to B1 where no more than 235m^2
Sui generis	Any works registrable under the Alkali, etc. Works Regulation Act 1906	No permitted changes
C1 Hotels	Hotels, boarding houses and guesthouses	No permitted changes
C2 Residential institutions	Residential schools and colleges, hospitals and convalescent/nursing homes	No permitted changes

105

TABLE 2.9 Continued

C3 Dwelling houses	No permitted changes
Sui generis	Hostel
D1 Non-residential institutions	Places of worship, church halls, clinics, health centres, crèches, day nurseries, consulting rooms, museums, public halls, libraries, art galleries, exhibition halls, non-residential education and training centres
D2 Assembly and leisure	Cinemas, music and concert halls, dance halls, sports halls, swimming baths, skating rinks, gymnasiums, other indoor and outdoor sports and leisure uses, bingo halls, casinos
Sui generis	Theatres, nightclubs

No permitted changes
No permitted changes
No permitted changes
No permitted changes

[1] The permitted development rights under the GDO shown here do not require planning permission as long as all the criteria set out in the Order are met and no restrictive conditions apply.

[2] '*Sui generis*' means 'of its own kind'. Any planning use that does not fall within a class within the Use Classes Order will come under this category.

106

Development Corporations, a feature of urban regeneration in the UK in the 1980s and 1990s, had SDOs granted in their favour to speed up the development process in the areas of their authority. SDOs have to be debated in Parliament and can be revoked. They can be used for specific developments, for example if a local authority is opposed to a plan which the Government wants to carry out or see developed. The Government can override the local planning authority by issuing an SDO, thus bypassing the normal planning system.

CERTIFICATE OF LAWFULNESS

In certain circumstances it is difficult to determine whether planning consent for a development is required. In these circumstances an application can be made to the local planning authority for a certificate of lawfulness which confirms whether planning consent is or is not required. A certificate of lawfulness is not in itself consent but it can remove uncertainty.

OTHER PLANNING ISSUES

What are the chances of success on applications?

This varies from area to area but on average some 80–90 per cent of applications are successful. This increases with the level of consultation undertaken by the developer.

The powers of the local authority

Local planning authorities also have powers of enforcement related to development. They can:

> require the developer to consult with the local planning authority if development has been carried out without permission;
> invoke their powers to demolish or remove structures constructed without consent or in breach of consent;
> issue stop notices to prevent development proceeding.

What is the situation if development has taken place without permission?

This is a difficult position. As detailed above, local authorities have powers of enforcement up to and including the removal or demolition of the development concerned. Where development has taken place in good faith or in ignorance, it is possible, however, for the local planning authority to issue retrospective planning consent. This can legalise the situation; however, it should not be relied on as a matter of course.

What other official permission may be required in development?

A number of other applications may be required to execute the development. These include the following.

> An environmental assessment – this is a European Union requirement, arising out of concerns about protecting the environment. It requires a qualitative and quantitative review of the proposed project and its potential impact on the local environment, and the preparation of an environmental statement and also information on the environmental effects of the development by the local planning authority and the developer. The project must be of more than local significance or importance. It will usually be required where the project is in, or near, a vulnerable location. These types of locations include sites of special scientific interest (SSSI) or nature protection sites (NPS). Finally, environmental assessment will be required where the project is unusually complex or where the potentially adverse effects of the project are unusual or high.

> Listed building consent – as can be seen from the above, a number of historical or architecturally interesting buildings are what is termed 'listed'. This means that their details are contained within a document highlighting their importance. There are three grades of listing (see page 93) which means that, in addition to the planning application, application must be made to the heritage authorities – for example in England this would be to English Heritage. Any alterations require listed building consent in addition to the planning consent. Having a listing does not entirely protect the building. It is relatively easy to gain consent for working with a Grade II building but almost impossible for a Grade I listed building.

Other related considerations

> Conservation areas – as we have seen from the site acquisition section, local planning authorities can declare whole areas as conservation areas to protect some special characteristic. Although no specific additional consent is usually required for work in these areas (other than if a listed building is involved), consultation with the planning authorities, the local civic society or the national heritage bodies will usually be necessary prior to the making of an application.

> Archaeology – many historic towns and cities in the UK can claim centuries of continuous occupation. Consultation with the county archaeologists, university departments and the heritage bodies may be required at the planning application stage.

> Sustainability – in addition to the environmental issues, it is likely that future developments may see energy audits and sustainability statements becoming a requirement of many applications.

CONCLUSION TO THE PLANNING SECTION

Obtaining the necessary legal consents is a vital requirement of the development process. Without consent development cannot take place. This section can only give an introduction to the issue. Anyone involved in a development of significant size is advised to research the area in detail and to obtain advice from a planning and development specialist in order to avoid expensive delays or even failure of the scheme.

Conclusions

A developer reaching this stage will have four of the important pieces of the jigsaw in place. Initially, an opportunity will have been identified. This apparently simple step is surprisingly complex; the identification of latent development potential requires a number of components to come together at the same time. A fundamental part of this process is establishing whether the demand for the proposed product actually exists. After this has been done at a superficial level, more in-depth analysis of the market adds detail to the nature of the demand, leading to the form of the scheme becoming crystallised in the mind of the developer. Next, a site will have been identified and, after a process of due diligence, will have been acquired. Planning and other consents will finally have been applied for and obtained. The scheme can now proceed.

All of these key pieces need to be in place. Without any one of them the development puzzle cannot be completed. The developer now needs to assemble the remaining pieces in order to see the development to its conclusion. These components are examined in the following chapters.

THE FINANCE AND ECONOMICS OF DEVELOPMENT
CHAPTER 3

Fundamentals of development finance

In order to understand the way that developments are financed it is important to first review the characteristics of development. It is these characteristic that shape the behaviour of both developers and financiers.

To explain this we will take the example of the development of an investment property by a private sector developer. This is, in any case, one of the most common circumstances where funders need to be involved.

Phases in development funding

As can be seen from Figure 3.1, the development breaks down into distinct phases.

Developments of this sort usually commence with the purchase of the land, a major capital outlay. There is then, typically, a period of negative cash flows, i.e. payments, as the development is planned, constructed and while an occupier is sought. Once a letting is achieved the property settles down, hopefully, into a long, stable life as an investment. Once it is fully let it becomes a valuable, saleable asset. Until fully let, a development property can only be sold at a substantial discount to full value.

This illustrates that two distinct phases, with different cash flow and risk characteristics, exist. In the development phase, the project is high risk. There are large negative cash flows, there is little or no income and the asset is largely unsaleable. After completion and letting, the asset is a relatively low-risk investment, with a high underlying value, a steady, but relatively low income stream and low, sometimes negligible, outgoings.

RELATIONSHIP BETWEEN PROJECT CHARACTERISTICS AND FUNDING

These differing characteristics usually force developers to consider finance in two phases and often to obtain the finance from more than one source. The first of these is the project or development finance phase. This tends to be short-term finance bearing a high risk and is therefore usually expensive. The second phase of finance is that concerned with the long-term ownership: the investment finance. This tends to be long-term finance and bears a low risk.

This need to consider the two phases separately is illustrated in Figure 3.2.

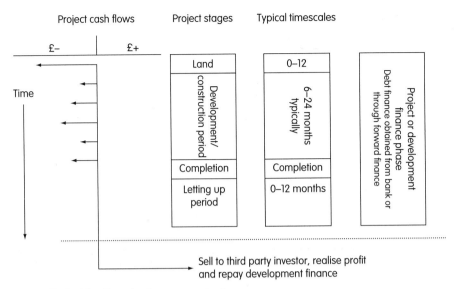

FIGURE 3.3 Project funding structure: non-retention

purchase it. This involves the investor in a greater degree of risk in that they become involved in the development phase of the scheme. Money is drawn down from the investor as the project proceeds. The final payment, including the developer's profit, will not be made until all the conditions are met by the developer, hence the risk is limited. The developer normally would need to provide a rental guarantee to the investor for a period of years. A wise investor would seek to ensure that the development funding agreement is tightly written to ensure that the quality of the tenant and the terms of the lease granted by the developer are acceptable to them.

RETAINING THE BUILDING: FUNDING OPTIONS

The second option – the retention of the scheme by the investor – is rather more complex with more options available. Usually they involve splitting up the two phases of finance as before; however, in this instance with project finance being arranged for the development phase as above and longer term finance found for the investment part.

One traditional method for financing the investment phase is by mortgage, i.e. a property-secured loan. The income from the property services the debt and the principal is paid off by way of entering into a repayment mortgage, as per house purchase, or by way of an interest-only loan, where the principal is paid off by the sale of the asset. Alternative ways of financing the long-term ownership include corporate debt, equity-raising ventures and joint ventures with financial bodies, especially banks.

Retention is illustrated in Figure 3.4. An alternative way of achieving retention is to finance both phases of the project in a single step. This is rarer for the smaller developer as the cost of lending overall would tend to be higher than with conventional debt. It is much more common with the larger developer investors who

Project cash flows Project stages Typical timescales

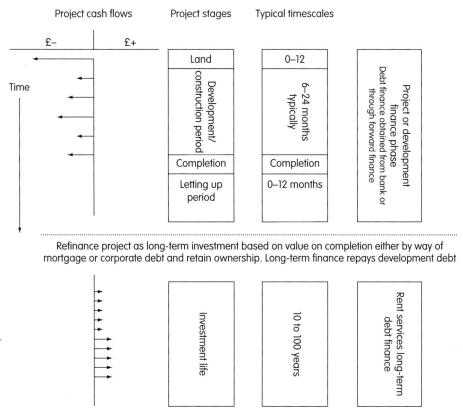

Refinance project as long-term investment based on value on completion either by way of mortgage or corporate debt and retain ownership. Long-term finance repays development debt

FIGURE 3.4 Project funding structure: retention

raise debt finance via the stock and money markets. Large companies such as these raise medium- to long-term finance by offering corporate debt on the market against their track record or, more rarely, contracting to carry out a specific project or projects (Figure 3.5). This debt, usually a debenture, pays the investor a guaranteed coupon or rate of interest and will be repaid at a fixed date. This gives the developer a pool of money with a known cost to use in general development projects.

More rarely these funds are raised via equity issues, i.e. the sale of new shares in the company. This is usually a more expensive option than raising debt but is advantageous under certain market conditions.

The final factor affecting development finance is the attitude of the person or body that is the source of the finance. This is largely dependent on market conditions and market sentiment. There are times when development finance is virtually unobtainable from any source. This was the case in the early 1990s when the over-building in some sectors coupled with the contraction in the general economy bankrupted many developers and left the banking sector with many uncompleted projects as developers defaulted on loans. The state of the market, allied to the losses made by the banks, meant that obtaining development loans was all but impossible. It was many years before banks would lend on anything that was not 100 per cent pre-let or

115

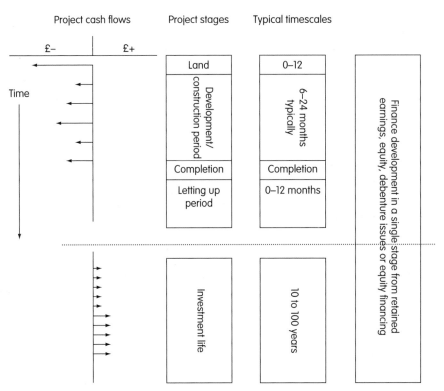

FIGURE 3.5 Project funding structure: retention variant

pre-sold. Similarly, there are periods where falling markets, high levels of gearing and poor sentiment closes the avenue of the stock market to the sector. The attitude of the financial community is critical to obtaining finance at all times.

Where does the finance come from for development?

Before some of these aspects of development finance are examined in more detail, we need to explore where the finance comes from for development. This requires an understanding of the workings of the financial system, which is illustrated in Figure 3.6. Basically, money flows from the top of diagram to the bottom, although there are, of course, flows back as investors, hopefully, get a return on money invested. These have been omitted for clarity. Savers and individuals, and parties from abroad, outside of the system, place funds, usually through the second tier – financial intermediaries – into the system. These financial intermediaries[1] invest these funds on behalf of the investors, usually in the stock market and money markets but also directly in property, which is not shown on this diagram. These funds are then available for the corporate sector and government.

This is very much the traditional economist view of the financial system. In a second diagram (Figure 3.7) the development sector is represented as being an additional

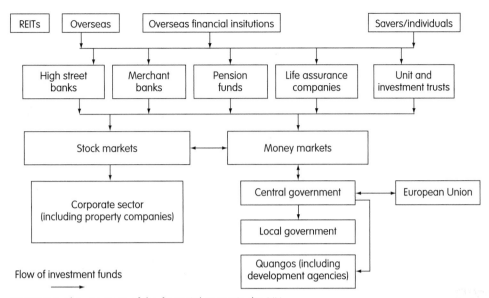

FIGURE 3.6 The structure of the financial sector in the UK

part of the system for the purposes of our understanding as to the sources from which the funds flow.

Three types of funding are distinguished. First, there is debt funding, which is defined as money that must be specifically repaid to the lending body. The second

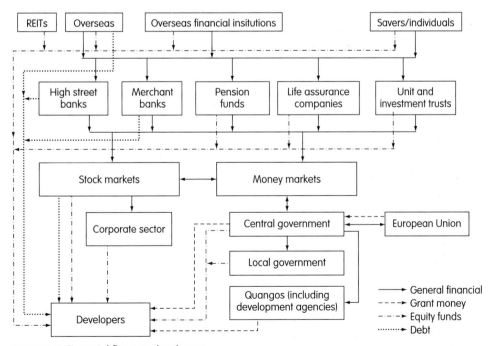

FIGURE 3.7 Financial flows to developers

type is equity funding. This includes corporate funding of the development sector (e.g. money raised by share issues) as well as moneys flowing for the purchase of completed developments (which can be loosely viewed as long-term finance). The final source of funds, which has not been mentioned to date, is grant funding. This generally flows from the public sector (central and local government, quangos and the European Union). These funds usually flow to support development in deprived areas to encourage private sector participation.

Figure 3.7 will give an idea of the sources of the bulk of the funds that flow to the development sector. Further reference will be made to this later in the chapter.

A NOTE ABOUT DEBT

There is an old saying about property development finance. The most important factor to take into account when financing a development is the OPM principle: use Other People's Money!

Although this rather jocular phrase might underline some people's opinions of property developers as fly-by-night shysters, in fact there are some very sound principles that underlie the statement. Better returns to the developer can be obtained by using OPM. The reason is gearing or, to use the American term, leverage.

Let us use a simple illustrative example, a development that gives a 20 per cent return on cost:

100% equity finance

Total development costs	£1,000,000
Completed development value	£1,200,000
Return on equity	**20.00%**

The following example considers the return on equity, i.e. the developer's own money, if 50 per cent of the money is now borrowed:

50% equity finance/50% debt finance

Total development costs	£1,000,000
Made up of:	
Debt	£500,000
Equity	£500,000
Completed development value	£1,200,000
Repayment of debt	£500,000
Surplus to repay equity and give profit	£700,000
Return on equity	**40.00%**

The developer has invested £500,000 to get £700,000 back, a £200,000 profit which is a 40 per cent return.

Borrowing or gearing up increases the return further:

25% equity finance/75% debt finance

Total development costs	£1,000,000
Made up of:	
Debt	£750,000
Equity	£250,000
Completed development value	£1,200,000
Repayment of debt	£750,000
Surplus to repay equity and give profit	£450,000
Return on equity	**80.00%**

The question might be raised as to the validity of this calculation. Is it not true that borrowed money has a cost, an interest charge, while equity is free, i.e. you would not charge yourself interest? Does not this therefore increase the cost of debt over equity? The answer is no, not if the developer is accounting for costs correctly. All money used in projects has an opportunity cost, a cost equal to the highest opportunity with similar characteristics forsaken in order to put the money into this project. Simplistically, the opportunity cost of all funds used in a project should be similar to the cost of money borrowed to do the project.

So, debt in projects tends, in theory, to be good. There are downsides, however, to gearing up. First, debt does have to be serviced. Equity returns do not have an immediate charge, the owner of the equity has to wait. Lenders will not wait, they expect the debt to be serviced. Excessive debt over a large development portfolio can drag a company down, particularly when interest rates rise. Also, gearing works in reverse. If the project does not do as well as expected then equity destruction takes place much more rapidly with gearing. This is illustrated below:

100% equity finance

Total development costs	£1,000,000
Completed development value	£800,000
Return on equity	**−20.00%**

50% equity finance/50% debt finance

Total development costs	£1,000,000
Made up of:	
Debt	£500,000
Equity	£500,000
Completed development value	£800,000
Repayment of debt	£500,000
Surplus to repay equity and give profit	£300,000
Return on equity	**−40.00%**

25% equity finance/75% debt finance

Total development costs	£1,000,000
Made up of:	
Debt	£750,000
Equity	£250,000
Completed development value	£800,000
Repayment of debt	£750,000
Surplus to repay equity and give profit	£50,000
Return on equity	**−80.00%**

So, gearing (borrowing) has its dangers. As a result, there are usually limits, determined by lenders, to the amount that developers can borrow. Lenders prefer developers to have some equity stake in a scheme for obvious reasons. If a scheme goes wrong, a developer with no equity can walk away with no loss except the loss of an opportunity to make a profit. Developers with equity are much more likely to work hard to protect it.

There is a further attraction with long-term debt: this is tax relief on interest.

Development finance in detail

PROJECT FINANCE: PROJECT-SPECIFIC LENDING

This is the most common type of finance used by property companies of all sizes, although it is particularly commonly used for individual projects and occasional or new developers. It is provided by a number of different sources including banks and specialist property financiers.

Features

Project-specific lending has many variants but there are some common characteristics as detailed below.

> The finance is short term, for the period of the project only or sometimes until the first rent review. This means that most loans of this type are for a 2- to 3-year period, extending to 7–8 years if funding continues to the first rent review. These latter, longer arrangements usually occur when there is an option with the lender to convert the loan from a development to an investment loan. As noted, there is usually the need to renegotiate the loans due to the very different risk characteristics of development projects and standing investments.
> There are several options regarding the security required by lenders. Many loans are on a non-recourse or a limited recourse basis. In the former, the only security for the loans is the value of the development itself. This is particularly attractive to smaller developers who rarely have other assets sufficient to provide security for lenders. It is also attractive to larger developers who have stock market listings. Excessive borrowing that appears on the balance sheet of these firms reduces the net asset value and thus the share price. Such developers try to achieve

TABLE 3.1 Rolling up of interest

Total finance required			£316,649.57							
Interest rate per month			1%							
Month	1	2	3	4	5	6	7	8	9	Totals
Expenditure	£100,000	£20,000	£30,000	£40,000	£40,000	£30,000	£20,000	£10,000	£10,000	£300,000
Interest		£1,000	£1,210	£1,522	£1,937	£2,357	£2,680	£2,907	£3,036	£16,650
Total balance owed	£100,000	£121,000	£152,210	£193,732	£235,669	£268,026	£290,706	£303,613	£316,650	£316,650

lending 'off balance sheet' by carrying out developments in subsidiary companies, sometimes in partnership with their financiers.

> Lending is limited to a proportion of the value of either the completed development or the predicted development costs. With project finance this is usually the latter. Loans are available up to around 70–80 per cent of the development cost.

> Interest can be charged on any interest calculation period, for example, daily, weekly or monthly, although the latter is the most common.

> The sum borrowed is usually not taken as a lump sum but is drawn down from the lender as required. Most frequently this is on a monthly basis to coincide with the stage payments made to the construction team.

> Interest can be payable on a regular basis but it is much more common for interest to be 'rolled-up', i.e. added to the principal of the loan as the project proceeds. This is a common pattern because most developments do not produce any income to service debt as the project proceeds. If the project is phased with disposals during the course of the development then the loan may be structured to see partial repayment of interest and/or principal as cash is received. The rolling up of interest is illustrated in Table 3.1.

> The interest rate charged on the loan depends on a number of factors. Fundamentally, it is the Bank of England base rate that determines all domestic interest rates. In practice, the banks obtain their own money based on LIBOR, the London Interbank Offered Rate. The individual lenders will then add a premium to LIBOR when lending, dependent on their assessment of the loan risk. This will itself depend on factors such as the status of the borrower, their experience, track record and financial stability as well as the characteristics of the property, the state of the property market and, crucially, the availability of a buyer or tenant for the completed project. Other factors include the competitiveness of the lending market; banks are often keen to lend to property development because the level of returns available tends to be higher than from other commercial loans.

> The lender will need to satisfy themselves about the viability of the project before lending at all. The lender will require the developer to provide much of the evidence to convince them of this and may require evidence of market research, as well as recent lettings, market trends and movements. The financial appraisal will be scrutinised very carefully. This will include an examination of the rents and yields used, an analysis of the void allowances and whether the profit margin allowed is sufficient. They may well carry out a due diligence process into aspects such as title, planning consent and contamination issues, etc. References from

firms and persons of standing who have had experience of working with the developers may be required.

> Although it is most common for the site itself to act as security, lenders may require additional security from the developer. This may include personal guarantees and bonds. As additional security, banks are quite frequently requiring developers to pay for the bank's own team of project experts to sit in on the progress meetings of the development. This team monitors progress and acts to safeguard the lender's investment. This enables early steps to be taken to rescue projects that are running into difficulty.
> Where the project is very large, the loan may be syndicated, i.e. spread over a number of lenders by a lead bank or lender.

Variations

In some cases developers will seek and be able to cover all of the costs of the development from borrowing. Normally this will require market conditions to be buoyant to be achieved. There are three main ways of achieving in excess of the normal funding levels.

1. *Mezzanine finance (Figure 3.8)*. This is where a lender agrees to close the gap in funding by taking a higher level of risk. In return they get a higher rate of interest on the loan. The mezzanine finance is usually subservient to the senior debt, i.e. the senior debt will have first call on any funds if, say, the developer defaults.
2. *Insurance (Figure 3.9)*. The additional money loaned is covered by an insurance policy, the premium of which is paid by the developer.
3. *Equity sharing arrangements (Figure 3.10)*. Here, the lender becomes the partner of the developer to share in the profits made by the scheme. The lender frequently charges the market rate for the senior debt but lends 100 per cent of the predicted cost of the scheme in exchange for a percentage of the developer's profit. The actual detail of the arrangement depends on the status and bargaining strength of each party in each individual case but normally one would expect the lender's

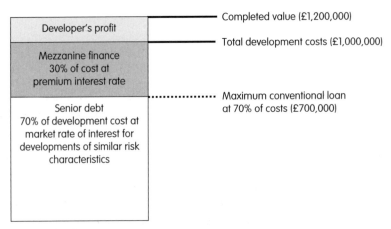

FIGURE 3.8 Mezzanine finance

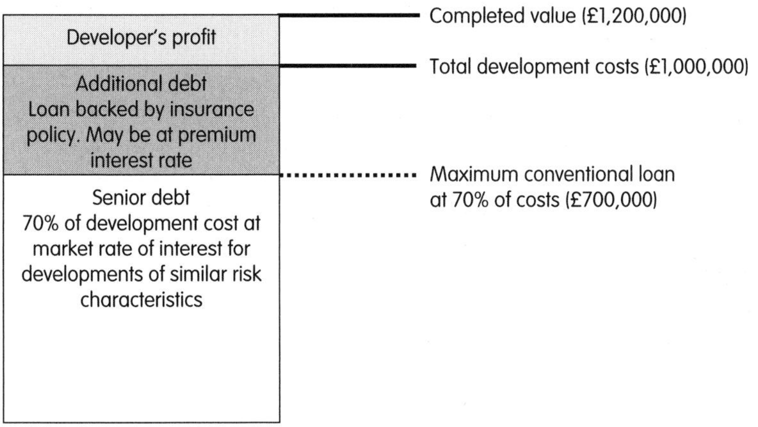

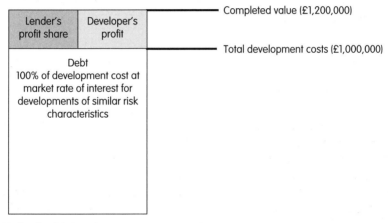

FIGURE 3.9 Insurance

FIGURE 3.10 Equity sharing

profit share to have a degree of guarantee with the developer still taking the risk of failure.

PROJECT FINANCE: SELL ON

A further option for short-term finance is connected with forward selling. A variation of forward selling is forward funding where the long-term investment owner, usually an institution, also provides development finance.

In these cases the development finance is provided at a lower rate than that which can be obtained in the open lending market, at least if the developer is forced to seek retail sources of debt. It is therefore a cheaper source of finance to the developer. The developer also gets the security of an exit from the scheme. The attraction to the investor is that they can usually negotiate a lower price for the project. When these types of arrangements work well they are advantageous for all parties. However,

TABLE 3.2 Forward funding: initial appraisal

Building dimensions	
Net area	4,000m^2
Built area	5,000m^2
Car spaces	15

Costs	
Land cost	£3,000,000
Building cost	£946.50m^2
Contingency	5.00%
Demolition	£100,000
Architect	4% cost
Project Manager	2% cost
Engineer	2% cost
Quantity surveyor	2% cost
Marketing	1% value
Letting fees	10% ERV
Sale fees	2% sale price

Finance and value factors	
Rental value	£235.00
Investment yield	**7.00%**
Rental incentive	12 months
Interest rate	**10%**
Car spaces	£2,500.00

Time	
Planning period	6 months
Construction	12 months
Letting	6 months

Expected realisation

ERV

Net office area 4,000m^2		
×	£235.00	£940,000
Car parking spaces 15 nr		
×	£2,5000.00	£37,500
Total income		£977,500
Capitalised @ 7.00%	14.28571429	
		£13,964,286
Less		
Purchaser's costs (5%)		−£664,965.99
Gross realisation		**£13,299,319.73**
Less		
Incentive		−£940,000
Net realisation		£12,359,320

Less: development costs

Demolition			£100,000
Construction	5,000m^2 × £946.50		£4,732,500

Finance on construction and demolition

£4,732,500 ×

0.5

£2,366,250 ×

| | 10% for 12 months | £236,625 |

Professional fees: construction

Architect	4%	£193,500
Project Manager	2%	£96,650
Engineer	2%	£96,650
Quantity surveyor	2%	£96,650

Finance on professional fees

£483,250

0.66

£318,945 ×

| | 10% for 18 months | £49,019 |

Finance on void period

£5,601,394 @

| | 10% for 6 months | 273,398 |

Professional fees: letting and sale

| Letting fees | 10% | £97,750 |
| Sale fees | 2% | £265,986 |

| **Marketing** | | £132,993 |

| **Contingency** | 5.00% | £236,625 |

Land cost

Purchase	£2,578,435	
Acquisition costs	£128,922	
Total	£2,707,357	
Finance	10% for 24 months	
Total finance cost	£568,545	£568,545

| | | £9,884,048 |

Profit in 24 months' time	**£2,475,272**
Discounted at 10%	0.826446281
Profit (today)	**£2,045,679**

Non-discounted profit on cost	25.04%
Non-discounted profit on value	20.03%
Rent cover	2.09 years

this type of arrangement is only really suitable for institutional quality investment properties, which form a relatively small part of the market.

Over the next few pages an illustrative example is shown, using a traditional development appraisal (covered in Chapter 4). The first calculation is the initial market appraisal for the scheme. This is carried out by the developer to test the viability of the project and to prepare the case for forward funding from the institution. The appraisal (Table 3.2) illustrates a surplus equivalent to a 20 per cent profit on cost.

The second appraisal (Table 3.3) shows the variations as agreed in the funding agreement.

TABLE 3.3 Forward funding: agreed purchase

Building dimensions

Net area	4,000m^2
Built area	5,000m^2
Car spaces	15

Costs

Land cost	£3,000,000
Building cost	£946.50m^2
Contingency	5.00%
Demolition	£100,000
Architect	4% cost
Project Manager	2% cost
Engineer	2% cost
Quantity Surveyor	2% cost
Marketing	1% value
Letting fees	10% ERV
Sale fees	2% sale price

Finance and value factors

Rental value	£235.00
Investment yield	**7.25%**
Rental incentive	12 months
Interest rate	**8%**
Car spaces	£2,500.00

Time

Planning period	6 months
Construction	12 months
Letting	6 months

Expected realisation

ERV

Net office area 4,000m^2			
	×	£235.00	£940,000
Car parking spaces 15 nr			
	×	£2,5000.00	£37,500
		Total income	£977,500
Capitalised @ 7.25%		13.79310345	
			£13,482,759
		Less	
		Purchaser's costs (5%)	−£642,036.12
		Gross realisation	**£12,840,722.50**
		Less	
		Incentive	−£940,000
		Net realisation	£11,900,722

Less: development costs

Demolition				£100,000
Construction	5,000m^2	×	£946.50	£4,732,500

Finance on construction and demolition

£4,732,500 ×

0.5

$\overline{£2,366,250}$ ×

	8% for 12 months	£189,300

Professional fees: construction

Architect	4%	£193,500
Project Manager	2%	£96,650
Engineer	2%	£96,650
Quantity surveyor	2%	£96,650

Finance on professional fees

£483,250

0.66

$\overline{£318,945}$ ×

	8% for 18 months	£39,029

Finance on void period

£5,544,079 @

	8% for 6 months	£217,497

Professional fees: letting and sale

Letting fees	10%	£97,750
Sale fees	2%	£256,814

Marketing		£128,407
Contingency	5.00%	£236,625

Land cost

Purchase	£2,578,435	
Acquisition costs	£128,922	
Total	£2,707,357	
Finance	8% for 24 months	
Total finance cost	£450,504	£450,504

		£9,639,034
Profit in 24 months' time		**£2,261,689**
Discounted at 8%		0.85733882
Profit (today)		**£1,939,033**
Non-discounted profit on cost		23.46%
Non-discounted profit on value		19.00%
Rent cover		1.98 years

The fund has agreed to purchase the investment based on a yield of 7.25 per cent, i.e. 0.25 per cent above the market rate of interest. The development funding is then provided by the fund at a rate of 8 per cent based on the opportunity cost of money to the fund. In comparison with the base appraisal this is considerably under the market rate of funds.

The funds are drawn down from the fund as if it were a traditional bank-type lender. The balancing payment, reflecting the profit, is not paid until the building is let. The risk is usually transferred to the developer either by requiring the developer to guarantee the rent until letting is achieved or else by the erosion of the balancing payment by the continual accumulation of interest on the drawn-down funds.

These arrangements are carefully documented in a development funding agreement. In particular, the funding institution is usually very careful regarding who or what constitutes an acceptable tenant to whom the developer can lease the building. It is normal practice to attach a draft lease to the funding document. This forms the basis of the final lease document agreed with the new tenant.

One major issue regarding with these types of arrangements is overage. This is additional value over and above the base value in the agreement. This can occur in rising markets where upward movements in rents and improving investor sentiment can drive prices up.

In some circumstances all of the overage passes to the investor. This will occur naturally where the agreement is silent as to overage. The payments stay the same and any increase in value is enjoyed by the investor who acquires the asset at a deeper discount than expected. It is, however, usual to address this issue mainly to provide an incentive for the developer to try to maximise the value of the scheme. It is, after all, usually the responsibility of the developer to find the tenants and agree the lease terms for the scheme. Some reward for maximising the overage should exist.

The procedure normally followed is illustrated in Table 3.4. This is based on the example above but here a rent of £250/m^2 has been achieved on the letting, i.e. £15 above the originally appraised figure. The parties have agreed to split any overage 50/50. The balancing payment is calculated as shown. Although the additional £15 adds £60,000 to the actual rent roll, only half, £30,000, is included in the calculation

TABLE 3.4 Procedure for maximising overage

Expected realisation				
ERV		Achieved rent	£250.00	
	Net office area 4,000m^2			
		× base rent	£235.00	£940,000.00
		Overage £15.00		
		50% £7.50		
	Car parking spaces 15 nr			
		×	£2,500.00	£37,500.00
		Total income		£1,007,500
Capitalised @ 7.25%			13.79310345	
				£13,896,552
		Less		
		Purchaser's costs (5%)		−£661,740.56
		Agreed purchase price		**£13,234,811.17**
		Less		
		Incentive		−£940,000
		Net realisation		£12,294,811
	Less			
	Total costs	Total development costs		£9,639,033.92
		Payment to developer		**£2,655,777.24**

of value to work out the final balancing payment to the developer. The developer thus obtains an extra payment of around £400,000 for achieving the higher rent. The investor receives the full benefit of the increase in value of the asset.

FORWARD SALE AGREEMENTS

Forward sale agreements are very similar to forward funding arrangements except, of course, for the provision of development finance. The purchaser agrees to purchase the completed development at some point in the future at an agreed figure, once the developer has met certain conditions. These conditions include the satisfactory completion of the building and the leasing of the building to an acceptable tenant on lease terms that are acceptable to the funder. The investor usually has control over the choice of tenant to whom the building can be let.

There are numerous alternatives to this arrangement, including where the developer guarantees the rent for a period after completion, thereby obtaining the full sale receipts from the investor on completion of the building. The developer, however, has the burden of meeting the rental payments over the period of the rental guarantee until a suitable tenant is found.

These two alternatives are illustrated in Figures 3.11 and 3.12. The basics of the deal, predicated on agreed rental and investment yield figures, are agreed at the time of

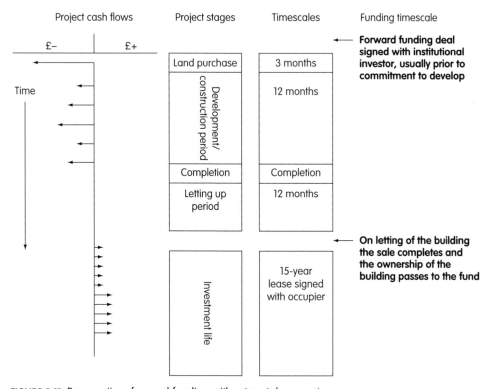

FIGURE 3.11 Base option: forward funding without rental guarantee

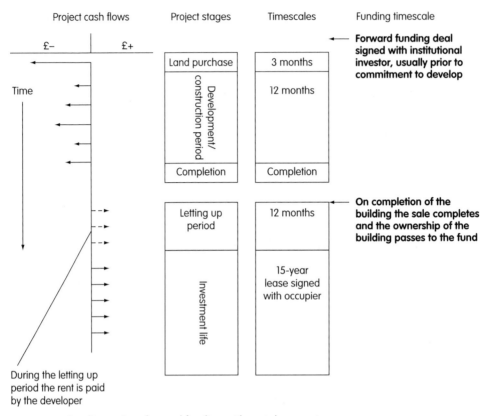

FIGURE 3.12 Funding option: forward funding with rental guarantee

the original funding deal. Any overage on rents is treated as per the forward funding arrangement detailed above.

RETENTION FINANCING

Chapter 4, which examines finance in detail, covers the ways in which developers can arrange funding to retain developments. We are therefore examining the point where development funding moves from the project finance stage to the long-term investment finance stage for smaller developers. This section will also look at 'whole life' funding, as occurs most commonly with larger investment. This requires corporate finance to be introduced in addition to project finance. Several options are available.

Mortgage finance

Mortgage finance, i.e. property-backed loans, is the traditional way of obtaining finance to fund property, both in the residential and commercial markets. These types of instruments are mainly confined to the funding of the completed standing investment but they can, with some funders, be used for 'whole life' funding of the project.

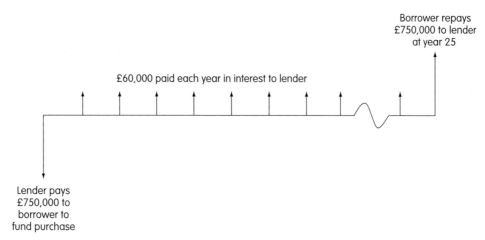

FIGURE 3.13 Interest-only mortgage: 25 years @ 8 per cent (fixed or variable)

There are two main types of mortgage, interest-only and repayment or amortised. These vary according to the way in which the capital is repaid.

Example
Property value   £1,000,000
Development costs   £750,000
Rent produced   £60,000 p.a.

With the interest-only mortgage (Figure 3.13), no principal is repaid on the loan during its course. The borrower merely pays interest on the loan, either at a fixed or variable rate of interest, at regular intervals and then repays the loan at one step at the completion of the loan.

With the repayment mortgage (Figure 3.14), both interest and the principal repayments are made on the loan during its course. The borrower pays a single payment, either at a fixed or variable rate of interest, at regular intervals. The loan is repaid by completion of the loan's term and therefore there is no balancing payment at the end.

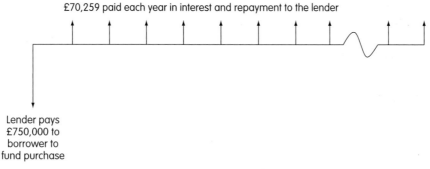

FIGURE 3.14 Repayment mortgage: 25 years @ 8 per cent (fixed or variable). Repayment on £750,000 mortgage at 8 per cent over 25 years works out at £70,259 p.a.

A repayment mortgage works in the following way:

Year 1

Balance owed		£750,000
Interest at 8% on balance	£60,000	
Capital repayment	£10,259	
Total payment	£70,259	

Year 2

Balance owed		£739,741
Interest at 8% on balance	£59,179	
Capital repayment	£11,080	
Total payment	£70,259	

Year 3

Balance owed		£728,661

and so on.

This pattern of reducing the balance of the principal as the loan proceeds means that in the early years of a mortgage very little principal is paid off. The pattern is illustrated in Figure 3.15.

Repayment mortgages are more expensive on an annual basis than interest-only mortgages.

Mortgages come in and out of fashion as means of funding property. The main reason for this is the characteristics of property as an investment. Property yields, i.e. the relationship between income return and capital value, are relatively low. This is particularly true at times of high inflation, as property rents, and therefore capital values, tend to rise in line with inflation making the asset a good inflation hedge. The potential for future growth tends to be factored in by investors who pay higher prices to acquire the investments, thus driving immediate income returns even lower. This produces a strange paradox: property is generally a good inflation hedge yet it is difficult to finance a purchase during inflationary times.

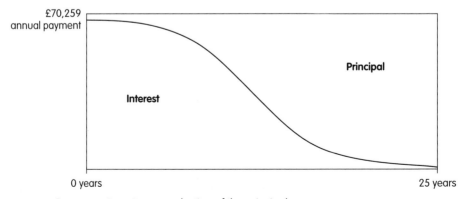

FIGURE 3.15 Repayment mortgage: reduction of the principal

The example below illustrates this situation.

Example investment 1: high street shop, inflation running at around 10 per cent p.a.

Development costs	£800,000
Property value at completion	£1,000,000
Rent	£60,000 p.a.
Yield	Income yield 6% on value
	(7.5% on development costs)

With inflation running at these levels, bank lending rates will be high. Bank interest rates reflect inflation rates, the banks trying to ensure that they get a 'real' return after inflation has been stripped out. In this sort of environment interest rates are likely to be in the 12–15 per cent range.

With a 70 per cent loan to value (LTV) ratio the loan advanced will be £700,000. This, of course, already indicates a shortfall on development costs. The annual debt service on the loan, on interest-only and repayment basis respectively, at 14 per cent would be: interest-only loan, £98,000 p.a.; repayment loan, £101,849 p.a.

This would create huge problems for securing the loan. Lenders usually require that the income from the investment covers the annual repayment. In these circumstances there is a very large shortfall.

The next example examines the situation that exists in a low inflationary environment.

Example investment 2: high street shop, inflation running at around 2.5 per cent p.a.

Development costs	£800,000
Property value at completion	£1,000,000
Rent	£60,000 p.a.
Yield	Income yield 6% on value
	(7.5% on development costs)

With inflation running at these levels, bank lending interest rates will be low. In this sort of environment interest rates are likely to be in the 5–6 per cent range, a level that will give the lender a similar 'real' interest rate to the first situation after allowances have been made for inflation.

With a 70 per cent LTV ratio the loan advanced will again be £700,000. It is more likely in this environment that lenders would be prepared to extend this LTV ratio. The annual debt service on the loan, on an interest-only and repayment basis respectively, at 6 per cent would be: interest-only loan, £49,000 p.a.; repayment loan, £60,067 p.a.

The situation has changed significantly. The interest-only loan annual payment is easily serviced out of the rent. The deal is what is termed 'self-financing'. This is almost true of the repayment loan too; indeed this very slight shortfall would probably be acceptable to a lender.

Given this pattern, it will be no surprise to learn that mortgage finance was the king of property deals in the 1950s and 1960s, which was the last era of low inflation prior to the current situation. This completely changed in the 1970s onwards when inflation made such financing much more difficult. It was also in this era that the institutions and pension funds became major players in the property markets, thus providing alternative sources of financing. Mortgage finance was marginalised to the higher yielding end of the property spectrum, particularly in the financing of secondary office and industrial investments. It is possible that the situation may have come full circle again. In the USA and Europe a low inflationary environment was established in the early 1990s and appears to have the power to be maintained in the long term. Interest rates are low, therefore many more deals are self-financing. Mortgage finance may be the once and future king.

There are, in any case, ways around both the shortfall in funding due to the LTV limitations and the low yield problem. As we have seen from the project finance section, mezzanine finance and insurance-backed extensions to the primary loan can close the gap. The low yields of property can be offset by clever structuring of the loans to take into account the capital growth potential of the asset.

There are numerous ways of achieving this. One way is to cap the initial payment at or below the initial income, rolling up the debt shortfall and adding it to the loan once the income level of the property has risen.

Let us use the same base example as we have considered above, but now we will assume that we have an 80 per cent LTV ratio and the interest rate is 7 per cent. We are assuming a slightly higher inflationary environment. On a repayment basis, the annual debt service would be £68,648 p.a. on a 25-year term. With the income at £60,000 p.a. as before there would be a shortfall of £8,648 p.a.

Most modern institutional quality leases have rent review clauses. This allows a periodic increase in rents to the current market rental value. The intervals between rent reviews vary, but most institutional leases have rent reviews every 5 years. If rental growth in shop rents is at 5 per cent p.a. then the £60,000 initial rent will rise to around £76,500 p.a. at the start of year 6. The lending pattern would then appear as in the following example.

Example investment 3: high street shop, inflation running at around 5 per cent p.a.

Development costs	£800,000
Property value at completion	£1,000,000
Rent	£60,000 p.a.
Yield	Income yield 6% on value
	(7.5% on development costs)
Repayment loan @ 7%	£68,648 p.a.
Repayment capped for 5 years to	£60,000
Shortfall	£8,648
Rolled up value of shortfall over 5 years	£49,732

Adjustment after rent review

New rental income (assuming 5% p.a. growth)	£76,500

Amount of loan still outstanding at end of year 5 (assuming full payment)	£727,258
Add: rolled up shortfall	£49,732
Actual amount of loan outstanding	£776,989
Repayment on this total @ 7% on a mortgage with 20 years of term left	**£73,342**

This now becomes the annual payment on the remainder of the loan. It should be noted that this is easily covered by the new annual income. There is obviously a measure of risk to both parties in this situation, particularly as the success of this arrangement is dependent on property rents rising in line with expectations. These rises in income are not guaranteed, they are determined by market factors, but historically property rents have grown.

There are many other ways of tackling the low-yield problem; in fact the ways of achieving a satisfactory outcome are limited only by the ingenuity of developers, surveyors, brokers and financiers. Other options include loans that are generally interest-only but have periodic repayments of capital, loans with capital repayment holidays, balloon payments and loans with initially low rates of interest at the start balanced by rates that are above the market rate later in the term. All achieve the same balancing act that matches properties' investment characteristics against the lending requirements of the financial community.

VARIATIONS ON LENDING

The financial markets have, naturally, become more sophisticated over time. Many different types of instruments have become available. One area of increasing sophistication concerns the removal of some of the uncertainty about future interest rates. Most shorter term loans are likely to be at a floating or variable rate of interest. This exposes the borrower to the risk of interest rate movements eroding the profit margin or creating cash-flow problems. A solution to this is to 'cap' the loan, i.e. set a maximum limit to the interest rate on the loan. This is achieved by taking out an insurance-type policy. There is a cost to this, but uncertainty can be greatly reduced. There are several variations on this, some aimed at reducing the cost of the instrument such as limited or flexible caps, others aimed at providing alternatives (hedging or 'swaps'). A developer concerned about future interest rate movements should explore the options available with their financial advisors.

CORPORATE FINANCE

So far this chapter has concentrated on the project- or property-specific type of debt. There are, of course, options that allow funding of development projects via corporate funding, i.e. the funding of the company itself. This tends to be limited to larger organisations with an established track record in development and, often, but not always, substantial assets to act as security for loans. Smaller developers tend to be restricted to project finance. Whatever the case, there is no doubt that a substantial proportion of development in the UK is financed via corporate sources of funds.

Financing of companies falls into the same two types that we have considered before, debt and equity. In practice, companies will attempt to balance the two to achieve financial efficiency and it is therefore hard to consider them in isolation in reality. The following section will look at debt and equity sources of corporate finance separately, starting with debt.

Corporate debt

Retail debt

Retail debt refers to those sources of finance that arise from borrowings through financial intermediaries. The most obvious source of this is via the company's own overdraft facilities through its own bank, or banks. This is 'normal' lending to the company and the banks will make decisions as to the level of credit to be advanced, based on their scrutiny of the quality of the company itself. Banks lend against the security of the business, its ability to earn profits and/or produce cash flow as well as against the value of the company's assets. These arrangements can be with the company's main bank or else a syndicated loan facility arranged across a range of organisations. Many large organisations have multi-option facilities, allowing them to draw down funds as required. The loans may be open but are often for a fixed period of time (1 month, 3 months or perhaps up to 5 years). Rather than being repaid on the date, the debt is continually serviced then rolled over into a new loan.

The actual arrangements and operations of corporate debt finance are complex and tend to spill over into the realms of corporate accountancy. The detail is thus largely beyond the scope of this book.

Stock market debt

Stock market debt refers to instruments issued by companies that raise finance, can be traded on by the originator of the debt finance, but, unlike shares, do not give ownership rights to the holder. These instruments are debenture stock and loan stock issues. The distinction between the two is that the former is secured on specific assets of the company. By definition, this sort of finance is limited to larger companies which have a stock market listing and a sufficiently good track record to attract investors seeking a secure return. This source of finance can provide property developers with a low-cost source of long-term money, dependent on market conditions, of course.

Debenture stock is like a company loan. The company borrows money from investors, usually for a fixed period of time, for example 10 years. The company pays the bond-holder a coupon, an annual interest rate guaranteed in the debenture certificate. At the end of the term of the loan, the entire sum is repaid to the investor. The stock is often unsecured on any assets of the company, although some floating charge can be made.

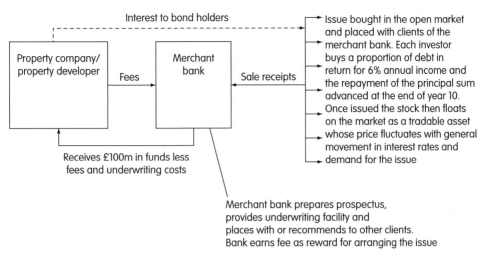

FIGURE 3.16 Example: £100 million conventional debenture issue for 10 years paying a coupon of 6 per cent

The parties involved in debenture issue are outlined in Figure 3.16.

A number of variants on these instruments exist. One of the most common is the convertible bond or debenture. This starts off the same as the above but there is an option, which can be operated by either the company or the debenture holder or one of the parties only, to convert the debt to ordinary shares. This is normally done at a stated price or price range and can be at a fixed date or at a floating point in the future.

The attraction to the borrower of this arrangement is that it saves the company the need to repay cash. The share conversion is a paper transaction without the need for a flow of funds out of the company. The investor also gains the potential for sharing in the future growth in asset value or profits of the firm, i.e. they move from a fixed interest security to a growth stock. It should be noted that a convertible bond or debenture is only really acceptable to the market where the company has a good track record and has good long-term growth potential.

Debenture stock or loan stock has many factors in its favour, but things can also go wrong. Money can be borrowed in the long term at rates which appear cheap at the time. Market movements in interest rates, such as occurred in the last decade of the 20th century, can make the money look expensive and damage the returns of the company. Michael Brett, *Estates Gazette* finance guru, illustrated the effects when examining the accounts of the property company Land Securities in 1999:

> The trouble comes when you look at the true value of Land Securities' £1.59 billion of gross debt. It includes various debentures which are not due for repayment for more than 25 years, and were raised at a time when a 10 per cent coupon seemed to offer cheap long-term funding. Judging by their price in the stock market, Land Securities could raise the same money today at a cost of little over 6 per cent. But it is committed to that 10 per cent for the next 25 years and more. Thus the market price of those debentures is way, way

above their face value. With the continuing fall in long-term bond yields, the 'fair value' of Land Securities' non-convertible debt has risen by a further £217 million (an almost 11 per cent increase) to £1.98 billion against a face value virtually unchanged at £1.3 billion. Offset this £217 million rise in the market value of debt against the £333 million revaluation surplus on its property assets, and it is clear that much of the year's gain has, in reality, been wiped out by events on the liabilities side.

M. Brett, *Estates Gazette*, 5 June 1999

Variations on the corporate debt type of finance include commercial paper and eurobonds. Commercial paper are short-term IOUs issued by large companies in return for loans from investors. They are usually issued at a discount to their true value. The borrower pays no interest during the term of the loan, which is generally for periods of less than 1 year. At the end of the loan period the borrower pays to the lender the full face value of the loan, thus giving the borrower a return on their funds.

For example, a borrower issues £100 million of commercial paper for 364 days. They receive £93 million from the lender. At the end of the term they pay the full value of the loan, £100 million back to the lender. This gives a return of 7.526 per cent to the lender.

Although this paper is short term, it can be used for long-term financing by rolling over the loans into new ones at the end of the term.

The bond and eurobond market is another form of unsecured lending. They are confined to being used by companies with excellent credit ratings and are used to raise large amounts of capital. Eurobonds are usually sold outside the borrower's own country. They are similar to debentures and loan stock in that they are certificates that promise to repay a debt of a fixed amount at a date in the future. They rely on the trading and credit record of the underlying company to reassure lenders that the loan will be repaid.

Equity funding

In this context equity funding refers to the moneys raised by the company itself that are part of the assets of the corporation. It is effectively the company's own money as opposed to borrowed money. People who own shares in a company are sharing in the ownership of the company, they are not lending it money. This is why shares are referred to as equities. The fundamental value of the company arises out of its share capital. Hopefully, this value will grow as the company trades and makes profits. Shareholders share in that growth.

Essentially, there are two types of organisation involved in the corporate side of development in the UK: private limited companies and public limited companies (PLCs). Private companies cannot sell their shares to the general public. PLCs have the option to make public share issues and thus raise considerable funds. Not all PLCs choose to follow this route but certainly many of the larger firms do so. We will examine this route in slightly more detail.

A company can have its shares traded on the stock market in one of three ways. An 'introduction' is when it already has a large number of shareholders and is not seeking to raise fresh capital. It simply seeks permission for the shares to be dealt in on the market. The second method is a 'placing'. Shares are sold privately to a range of investors and permission for them to be traded on the market is obtained at the same time. Only investors who are existing clients of the proposer, a broker or merchant bank, are likely to be involved. The third method, which gives the public at large an opportunity to apply for shares, is the 'offer for sale'. A prospectus and application form (or an invitation to apply for them) are publicised by brokers or banks. Normally the shares are offered for sale at a fixed price, which is calculated by the sponsoring broker or bank by reference to the prices for shares of comparable companies that are already traded on the market.

Companies can launch either on the Stock Exchange itself (the 'main market', in which case they are described as being 'listed'), or on the Unlisted Securities Market or USM (in which case the shares are generally described as being 'quoted' on the USM). Trading procedures are much the same in the two markets, both of which are run under the Stock Exchange aegis. The main difference is that a lower level of trading record and listing requirements is acceptable for the USM. It is also possible to float a smaller amount of the capital on the USM than the main market, and flotation costs may be somewhat lower.

An initial flotation can thus raise considerable funds for a developer. The developer can issue shares representing a proportion of the company to the market while retaining control of the remainder of the equity. Further funds can be obtained by further issues of stock, for example by way of a rights issue to current shareholders. Stock market listing is, however, relatively expensive and requires a good trading record over a long period before it can be even entertained. A public company also has less freedom in its actions as it is being monitored constantly by both analysts and its shareholders. Ultimately, the management of the firm may be changed by action of the shareholders. Listing does, however, open up many more opportunities for funding, for example the issue of debenture stock as outlined at page 136.

Shares come in a number of different types, the most common being ordinary shares and preference shares, the latter receiving preference for the receipt of dividends but having limited, if any, voting rights in the company.

Other options

Other corporate-type funding routes which have been explored include securitisation. Securitisation has been a holy grail for property financing over the past 25 years or so but, in the UK at least, has largely failed to be achieved. Property has a number of disadvantages as an asset, particularly in that it comes in large lumps and is illiquid. Also there are tax disadvantages in holding property indirectly. Securitisation is viewed as a solution to this. Securitisation or unitisation involves the dividing up of the underlying property asset into tradable shares which would be floated on the market and which would be treated like any other share for tax purposes. An alternative approach is to create a unit trust approach but based around a single investment.

Various vehicles have been tried (property income certificates (PINCs), single property ownerships trusts (SPOTs) and single asset property companies (SAPCOs)) but all have run into problems regarding taxation transparency and/or legal problems. In contrast, in the USA, real estate investment trusts (REITS), a tax efficient vehicle that largely achieves the goals of securitisation, have been very successful. To date, securitisation in the UK remains a holy grail, and one that the market is not sure whether it really wants.

Part disposal options

It may seem odd that this section includes what is, in many ways, a procurement option for development rather than a financing route per se. However, one of the main motives for entering into an equity sharing deal or partnership is, often, financial. It is inevitable that there should be some blurring of the division between financing the development and how it is executed.

There are a number of different ways of either achieving part disposal or involving shared ownership of the benefits that flow from the scheme. These are as follows.

> 'True' joint ventures – these are situations where the parties genuinely enter into the scheme together to carry it out. Risk and expertise are shared between the parties in some respect (not necessarily equally).
> Ground rents or building leases – in this situation, which is common where a local authority is involved, one party brings only the land to the deal. The developer takes on the risk of completing the scheme, usually receiving a long lease on the property (99–150 years for example). The local authority shares in the investment performance in the long term via a ground rent.
> Lending with participation – equity-sharing loans, as discussed in the section above and detailed below.
> Sale and leasebacks – sale and leasebacks exploit the fact that a number of different interests can be created out of property. Developers can retain an interest in a scheme by selling on the freehold interest in a property but taking a lease from the freeholder at a rent that is a proportion of the market rental value. There are numerous ways of setting up these arrangements, some of which will be reviewed below.
> Forward funding arrangements with leaseback – a combination of forward funding and sale and leasebacks.

Developers are quite frequently in situations where they need a partner to complete a scheme successfully. The reasons why these situations occur are manifold. They include where the partner possesses a key component for the development, such as the ownership of part or all of the site, or where they possess specialist expertise either in a technical aspect or in a particular sector of the market, or in the case that the financial resources of the developer are insufficient to undertake the development

This agreement must detail a number of different aspects of the progression of the development including:

> the functions of each member of the partnership or company
> the responsibilities of the day-to-day management of the project
> how strategic decisions should be reached
> consultation arrangements
> rights of veto
> arbitration procedures
> the timescales of the development
> the exit strategies of the parties, including whether the long-term ownership of the development should pass to one or more of the parties to the agreement and under what terms.

OTHER FINANCING OPTIONS

There are numerous other options for raising the finance for property development. These tend to be used in special procurement arrangements, such as PFI and PPP procurement, or to provide top-up funding for schemes, such as that provided by grant funds.

These are major topic areas in their own right and will only be explored in outline here.

PFI

PFI is not strictly a source of finance for developers. It is a procurement route of governments, chosen for its potential ability to save money but in particular to avoid making large-scale public expenditure and thus increasing the public-sector borrowing requirement (PSBR).

The private finance initiative was launched by the Conservative government in the early 1990s. Its principal feature is that facilities such as government buildings, hospitals and prisons among others would no longer be procured, built and financed by the Government directly but, instead, the private sector would provide the facility. The provision would include the design, construction and financing of the facility and often the management of the facility and provision of services over a fixed period, frequently between 15 and 25 years. The public body requiring the space would then pay an annual fee to the provider for the provision of the specified service over this period, thus saving the need to pay for the capital provision and maintenance of the asset.

PFI and PPP projects have continued under the Labour administration, indeed have increased apace. They now form a significant proportion of public projects and expenditure and this trend seems set to continue. This type of procurement is of limited relevance to the consideration of finance in mainstream development.

Grants

Public sector grants have been available to developers in certain areas for many years. They are an important tool of governments for regeneration and the encouragement of economic growth. For around 20 years in the UK, regeneration of economically disadvantaged areas has been property- and infrastructure-led, thus grants have been specifically targeted at development and widely used by both developers and development agencies to complete projects. The current trend is to move away from the support of physical projects towards the support of the community concerned itself. This is achieved by programmes of education and training and small enterprise support. Notwithstanding this change of emphasis, grants are likely to remain significant to developers in disadvantaged areas for the foreseeable future.

The principle followed by the grant regime is that public sector money should be used efficiently to 'lever' private sector money and to enable development. Public sector bodies administrating programmes often had, and have, lending criteria that require them to achieve a certain ratio of private to public money before aid can be approved. This may be four units of private money to one unit of public grant aid. Usually these criteria go hand in hand with other requirements, such as employment creation.

The basic problem with development in disadvantaged areas such as inner cities is that the revenues produced are often not high enough to make development profitable. An example is shown below using a simplified development appraisal.

An inner city project of a mixed-use commercial building is planned for an economically disadvantaged area. The initial appraisal, below, shows that the project is just profitable, but that the profit margin is too small to give an adequate return to the developer, who can obtain a 20 per cent return by developing elsewhere.

The reason for the shortfall is the combination of income (rent) and investment yield. The tenants in this area cannot pay high rents and still trade profitably. Investors recognise that the traders are not of a high quality, therefore there is an increased risk of tenant default. In addition, the investment growth potential is limited.

Inner city commercial project: no grant funding

Income		£100,000	
Year's purchase @ investment yield	10%	10	
Completed value		£1,000,000	
Less			
Development costs			
Construction			
Area 1000m²			
Unit cost £600		£600,000	
Fees, etc.		£150,000	
Finance		£75,000	
Land cost		£100,000	£925,000
		Surplus	£75,000.00
Profit on cost			8.11%
Profit on value			7.50%

Without some kind of intervention the project will not go ahead and economic regeneration will be restricted. However, with a grant of £110,000 paid to the developer, the profit margin is increased to an acceptable level and the scheme can proceed.

Inner city commercial project: with grant funding

Income		£100,000
Year's purchase @ investment yield	10%	10
Completed value		£1,000,000
Add: public sector grant		£110,000
		£1,110,000

Less
Development costs
Construction

Area 1000m^2		
Unit cost £600	£600,000	
Fees, etc.	£150,000	
Finance	£75,000	
Land cost	£100,000	£925,000
	Surplus	£185,000.00

Profit on cost	20.00%
Profit on value	18.50%
Private/public sector finance ratio	8.4090909

In this case, the granting body has achieved £925,000 of private sector investment for only £110,000 of public funds. It is this efficient use of funds that most bodies try to achieve.

There is a large number of granting authorities and sources of public grant aid. In the UK a first port of call is the Department for Communities and Local Government (CLG) which administers many of the grants. The European Union is also a major source of grant aid. Both the UK and European Union identify certain areas for assistance. In the EU case this is based on target regions that fall at a certain level of average GDP of the EU as a whole. The highest level of assistance is given to regions that fall into 'Objective 1' status, meaning that they are identified as having a very low per capita GDP. The objective set by the EU is to raise per capita GDP towards the EU average. The UK Government also identifies towns and regions requiring special assistance. A notable recent example is the former coalfields which received assistance under the 'Coalfields Challenge' programme. Another programme is the 'City Challenge' consisting of competitive bidding programmes, usually involving public private partnerships, to obtain a five-year rolling programme of central government funds for regeneration programmes.

The funding regime is rather complex and frequently changes. Recent initiatives include the Regional Development Agencies for England (RDAs) which have taken over many of the roles of the former agency for regeneration, English Partnerships (EP). Rather confusingly, EP has continued to act, but in a rather changed role. In Wales, the Welsh Development Agency controls some grant funding, while in Scotland the Scottish Development Agency and the Highlands and Islands Development Board fulfil similar roles, and have done for many years. Regeneration and economic development have many political aspects and new initiatives are very common. Developers are well advised to keep up to date with the current situation.

Risk reduction and finance

It seems appropriate at this point to consider risk and financing decisions. A number of aspects of risk in development exist but the one that is the most common concern of developers is financial risk. One source of this risk is connected with the cost of finance.

The major risks concerned with finance are as follows:

> interest rate fluctuations
> project over-runs
> withdrawal of support by lender
> incorrect forecasting of future values or cash flows.

Of the above list, it is only in the consideration of interest rates where much can be done at the beginning of the loan to mitigate the risks involved. The other three areas of risk tend to arise either out of changing market conditions over the life of a project or from a failure to carry out the project appraisal correctly or to be realistic in the assumptions made. With the latter three, some precautions can be taken when setting up the finance, at least by the larger developers. This basically involves engineering flexibility into the financing facility, both in terms of the length of time over which the finance is required and also the sources of finance. Usually, however, problems such as these require a measure of renegotiation, refinancing and rescheduling of debt, as well as flexibility of the financiers involved.

The sheer scale of large projects tends to give them a big advantage over their financiers, who simply cannot countenance failure. Examination of projects such as the Channel Tunnel, the Millennium Dome and Euro Disney (all of which suffered from grossly over-optimistic assessments of cash flow and underestimates of operating costs) would show that the projects were all in such serious trouble that they should have failed and the financiers foreclosed. Instead, the consequences of failure led to each of these projects being refinanced on very generous terms. This generosity on the part of banks does not usually extend to the small developer which defaults on its loan, so the fundamental financial risk mitigation measure for this type of body is to ensure that the appraisal is realistic!

Interest rate fluctuations are a feature of finance. Interest rates are not constant. Fundamentally, market interest rates vary in the financial markets on a minute-by-minute basis although the Bank of England minimum lending rate (MLR) is more stable. Even so, over the space of only a few months interest rates can change quite

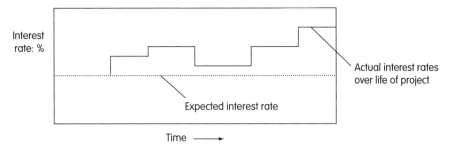

FIGURE 3.18 Unexpected interest rate changes

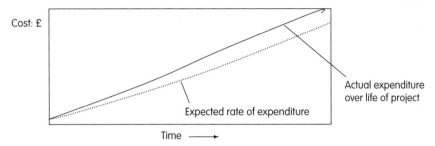

FIGURE 3.19 Increased expenditure due to interest rate changes

markedly, particularly as many governments use interest rates as the principal tool of macroeconomic management and manipulation.

Interest rate changes lead to unbudgeted cost increases. This is illustrated in Figure 3.18.

The effect on the project depends on a number of factors, including the relative level of debt and timing issues. Some projects are highly sensitive to interest rate changes, others are less severely affected (see the section on financial appraisal which discusses project sensitivity, page 218). Effectively, in this case, it would seem obvious that expenditure on the project as a whole would be higher than initially anticipated (Figure 3.19).

Measures to mitigate both the risk and the effect of fluctuations in interest rates can be put in place when the project finance is set up. A number of ways of achieving this are outlined below.

FIXED RATE LOANS

This is the simplest way of avoiding interest rate movements and a good route if either the project's profitability is rather sensitive to interest rate movements or if certainty as to this element of future cash-flows is required. It is also one of the only hedging routes available to the smaller developer.

There are, however, a few problems with regard to fixed interest loans. First, they are not always available. Financiers have to cover their own commitments and the cost of money to customers is closely related to the cost of money to the bank or lender. In times of financial volatility, where there is a risk of general interest rates moving upwards, lenders will be reluctant to lend at low rates of interest. They will, however, be more than willing to fix rates if there is a risk of rates moving down! It must be remembered that banks and financiers are in the business of making profits and will lend on the terms that are most advantageous to them not to the borrower.

The problem is guessing which way market rates are going to move. The borrower can end up fixing rates at the wrong time. The author is aware of a university which financed stage one of a conference centre development using variable rate finance. Interest rates then proceeded to move from around 9 to 14 per cent very quickly and maintained those levels over the next 18 months. Having suffered this painful lesson, for phase two the university secured fixed rate finance at around 13 per cent. Market interest rates promptly fell to 6 per cent! Although this looks like dreadful decision-making they were really just desperately unlucky, but these things can and do happen.

Derivative-backed hedging

One way of avoiding this risk is to use derivative-backed hedging. Derivatives are financial instruments that allow the borrower to take the alternative financial position to that which will cost them the most. The return from this alternative position balances the increased cost. Derivatives are based on futures and options. If the future is uncertain, people in the market-place will have differing views about the future. For every person who thinks that interest rates will be higher in a year's time than today there will be someone who thinks that they will be lower. In simplistic terms, futures markets bring those two sides together with one party effectively betting against the other, buying and selling contracts that give the opposite view.

In the context of interest rate hedging, if, for example, a borrower was concerned about the possibility of interest rate rises, the borrower could arrange a loan that would include, for a fee, a derivative that would pay out a sum that would give a payment equivalent to the cost of the interest rate rise. This would be achieved by the lender taking out a contract or giving an option to a third party in the derivative markets that would pay out on the contrary situation occurring.

These types of derivative-backed loans include:

> swaps – these fix the interest rate as per a fixed interest loan. They have the attraction of fixed interests with, usually, no upfront premium, but the borrower sees no benefit from falling rates;
> collar – here the loan interest rate is restricted to a known maximum and minimum cost;
> caps – these give a known maximum cost.

There are many other options including captions, caplets, limited caps and flexible caps.

Taxation

INTRODUCTION: TAX AND DEVELOPMENT

Finally, in this chapter on money and finance it is important to consider government intervention by way of the tax system. In the past, governments have gone so far as to nationalise development land, taking all but a reasonable return in tax (this was done in 1947 under the original post-war Town and Country Planning Act and again under the Community Land Act of 1975). The Government now contents itself with using the general tax system to deal with the property markets.

As is well known, tax is one of the two certainties in life. It is also one of the most complex of subjects. The system in the UK is somewhat labyrinthine. The rates, rules and regulations are subject to regular changes. Although the basic taxes have remained the same in the UK since 1973, tax regulations regularly change. These changes can cause a complete alteration in the character of taxes even though the name and the basic method of calculation stays the same. An illustration of this is capital gains tax, which was a significant factor to developers and investors in the 1970s and early 1980s. The basic principles of the tax remain the same but changes in the rates levied and in allowances given reduced its impact and completely altered the tax strategy followed by investors and developers.

The topic has been introduced in this way to illustrate some of the problems in dealing with taxation through the medium of a book. The topic is very complex. A comprehensive review would require a considerable amount of detail and there is a risk that the resulting section would be rather inaccessible to the reader. There is also a risk that changes in the regulations and rules would rapidly cause the information to be out of date.

What has been attempted here instead is a simple and hopefully understandable review of the major taxes in the UK and illustrations of how would they could affect investors and developers. This basic information should form the basis of future investigations by developers into the detail of the system operating at the time and also an evaluation of how the specific development is impacted by tax. All parties involved in the development process are urged to take professional tax advice as part of the due diligence process followed prior to the commencement of the project and also during the financial appraisal.

A further point to note is that tax is not just about payment, there are gains to be made in certain aspects of work. Essentially, these are not repayments to the recipient but they are reductions in tax liability allowed by the Government. This is not down to an act of charity on the part of the Government but rather it is an illustration of how tax can be used to achieve certain aims. For example, capital allowances for industrial buildings allow their owners and developers to offset tax by way of a depreciation allowance. This is done to encourage the development of industrial buildings, which are often the least attractive of the property development mediums. Similarly, 100 per cent of capital allowances were allowed against the construction of buildings in enterprise zones. This was designed to encourage the regeneration of deprived urban areas. In this respect, HM Treasury uses the tax regime far less firmly than other nations, for example the USA and Australia, to achieve its desired ends; however, the tax benefits from these initiatives are worth having and are usually worth investigating by developers.

TAXES THAT MAY BE ENCOUNTERED BY DEVELOPERS

A large number of taxes may be encountered by developers. These fall into two main categories (although there is an overlap between the two).

The first category comprises taxes on the developer or investor as an individual or company. These include income tax, corporation tax, inheritance tax and capital gains tax (although this is also strongly related to the second category). The development can contribute to the earnings taxed under the systems either by way of profit (corporation tax and capital gains) or income (corporation tax and income tax).

The second category includes those taxes which are more closely related to the development itself, i.e. the property. These include stamp duty, value added tax (VAT) and business rates or council tax.

Each will be briefly outlined below.

Capital gains tax

Capital gains tax (CGT) is a tax on the change in value of capital assets. It therefore has a potentially great effect on property – a major capital asset subject to increases in value over time (property is usually taken as a good hedge against inflation as the value of the asset moves at least in line with general inflation) as well as being subject to development and thus the release of latent value. In fact, the way that the tax is calculated greatly reduces its impact.

The amount of CGT due is based on the gains made on disposals of assets and capital sums that are received from assets in the tax year. The amount chargeable to CGT is calculated as summarised in Tables 3.5 and 3.6, extracted from the Government's own guidance documents.

A few notes are required to explain the calculation of the tax. Capital gains tax is only charged on realised gains – the difference between what an asset was bought at and what it was sold at. However, allowable expenses may be taken into account; these include development expenditure. The effect of inflation may also be taken into account using the indexation allowance. This utilises a table of inflation covering the period from March 1982 to April 1998 (see Table 3.7). This has the effect of stripping out the effect of general inflation on the change in asset values in the tax calculation, at least up to April 1998. The Government stopped indexation after this date to increase the tax take from CGT. Although inflation is low at present this could significantly change tax strategies in the future. Whatever the prevailing situation, only 'real' growth in the asset value is taxed. Additionally, gains made in one area can be offset against losses made in another part of the business. The taxpayer is also allowed 'taper relief', which encourages assets to be held over a long period by progressively reducing the tax paid over time. At the time of writing, the Chancellor in

TABLE 3.5 Capital gains tax

	Disposal proceeds or sum received from assets	After allowing for reliefs which reduce the figure to be treated as proceeds Sometimes market value is used instead of the actual proceeds
Less	Allowable costs	
	Gain before indexation	If this is a negative number, then a loss has been made, which may be an allowable loss
Less	Indexation allowance	For inflation, up to April 1998; may not create or increase a loss
	Indexed gain	
Less	Other reliefs	Reliefs other than taper relief which reduce or defer a gain
	Chargeable gain	For each asset individually
Sum	**Total chargeable gains**	Total of all the chargeable gains in the tax year
Less	Allowable losses	Losses in the tax year and unused losses carried forward from earlier years
	Chargeable gains after losses	
Less	Taper relief	A relief that reduces a chargeable gain after losses according to how long the asset was held. Taper relief is applied separately to each chargeable gain
	Tapered chargeable gains	
Less	Annual exempt amount	£9,200 for the tax year 2007–08
	Amount chargeable to CGT	

Source: HMRC website: www.hmrc.gov.uk. Reproduced under the terms of the Click-Use Licence.

TABLE 3.6 Annual exempt amounts for capital gains tax 2008

Annual exempt amount	Capital gains tax: individuals and trustees		
	2005–06 (£)	2006–07 (£)	2007–08 (£)
Individuals, etc.[a]	8,500	8,800	9,200
Other trustees	4,250	4,400	4,600

[a] Individuals, trustees of settlements for the disabled and personal representatives of the estate of a deceased person. Source: HMRC website: www.hmrc.gov.uk. Reproduced under the terms of the Click-Use Licence.

the 2007 Budget indicated plans to delete taper relief from 2008. The rules as they exist for the 2007–08 tax year are outlined in Table 3.6 and below.

The amount chargeable to CGT is added on top of income liable to income tax for individuals and is charged to CGT at these rates:

> below the starting rate limit at 10 per cent
> between the starting rate and basic rate limits at 20 per cent
> above the basic rate limit at 40 per cent.

Indexation allowance

The indexation allowance for corporation tax on chargeable gains is published monthly in the form of press releases.

TABLE 3.7 Index allowance for disposals after 31 March 1998

Year	Month											
	Jan.	**Feb.**	**Mar.**	**Apr.**	**May**	**Jun.**	**Jul.**	**Aug.**	**Sep.**	**Oct.**	**Nov.**	**Dec.**
1982			1.047	1.006	0.992	0.987	0.986	0.985	0.987	0.977	0.967	0.971
1983	0.968	0.960	0.956	0.929	0.921	0.917	0.906	0.898	0.889	0.883	0.876	0.871
1984	0.872	0.865	0.859	0.834	0.828	0.823	0.825	0.808	0.804	0.793	0.788	0.789
1985	0.783	0.769	0.752	0.716	0.708	0.704	0.707	0.703	0.704	0.701	0.695	0.693
1986	0.689	0.683	0.681	0.665	0.662	0.663	0.667	0.662	0.654	0.652	0.638	0.632
1987	0.626	0.620	0.616	0.597	0.596	0.596	0.597	0.593	0.588	0.580	0.573	0.574
1988	0.574	0.568	0.562	0.537	0.531	0.525	0.524	0.507	0.500	0.485	0.478	0.474
1989	0.465	0.454	0.448	0.423	0.414	0.409	0.408	0.404	0.395	0.384	0.372	0.369
1990	0.361	0.353	0.339	0.300	0.288	0.283	0.282	0.269	0.258	0.248	0.251	0.252
1991	0.249	0.242	0.237	0.222	0.218	0.213	0.215	0.213	0.208	0.204	0.199	0.198
1992	0.199	0.193	0.189	0.171	0.167	0.167	0.171	0.171	0.166	0.162	0.164	0.168
1993	0.179	0.171	0.167	0.156	0.152	0.153	0.156	0.151	0.146	0.147	0.148	0.146
1994	0.151	0.144	0.141	0.128	0.124	0.124	0.129	0.124	0.121	0.120	0.119	0.114
1995	0.114	0.107	0.102	0.091	0.087	0.085	0.091	0.085	0.080	0.085	0.085	0.079
1996	0.083	0.078	0.073	0.066	0.063	0.063	0.067	0.062	0.057	0.057	0.057	0.053
1997	0.053	0.049	0.046	0.040	0.036	0.032	0.032	0.026	0.021	0.019	0.019	0.016
1998	0.019	0.014	0.011									

Source: HMRC website: www.hmrc.gov.uk. Reproduced under the terms of the Click-Use Licence.

Individuals and others within the charge to capital gains tax are not entitled to indexation allowance for any period after April 1998. Table 3.7 can be used to calculate indexation allowance up to April 1998 on disposals on or after 6 April 1998.

The indexation allowance is calculated by multiplying the amount spent by the indexation factor.

The net effect of this is to greatly reduce the tax consequences of CGT. This may change in future and the tax may revert to being more significant to developers and investors.

Income tax

Income tax is a tax with which most individuals are familiar. It is a tax on income (as opposed to capital) received during the tax year by individuals. Income from property such as rents to an individual are taxable as are profits on trading properties (i.e. on properties that were bought to trade on) so a developed property owned by an individual would produce a tax liability. The distinction between trading and investment properties used to be significant when CGT was taxed at a higher rate than income but there is no such distinction now. There are fairly complex rules about allowances and the treatment of various sorts of income (for example, income from overseas properties and the treatment of rental incentives and service charges) that an investor/developer should investigate for the current rules. The 2007 allowances and rates are presented in Table 3.8.

TABLE 3.8 UK income tax allowances 2008

Income tax allowances	2007–08 (£)	2008–09 (£)
Personal allowance	5,225	5,435
Personal allowance for people aged 65–74	7,550	9,030
Personal allowance for people aged 75 and over	7,690	9,180
Married couple's allowance[a] (born before 6 April 1935 but aged less than 75)	6,285	6,535
Married couple's allowance – aged 75 and over[a]	6,355	6,625
Income limit for age-related allowances	20,900	21,800
Minimum amount of married couple's allowance	2,440	2,540
Blind person's allowance	1,730	1,800

[a]Tax relief for the married couple's allowance is given at the rate of 10 per cent.

Taxable bands allowances	2006–07 (£)	2007–08 (£)
Starting rate 10%	0–2,150	0–2,230
Basic rate 22%	2,151–33,300	2,231–34,600
Higher rate 40%	Over 33,300	Over 34,600

Source: HMRC website: www.hmrc.gov.uk. Reproduced under the terms of the Click-Use Licence.

Corporation tax

Corporation tax is the equivalent tax to income tax applicable to companies. If the company is resident in the UK, it is generally chargeable to corporation tax on its total profits. If it is a club or charity, different rules may apply. The company's total profits are found by adding together the profits from all its activities, including any capital gains. This can therefore include investment income, profits arising from the release of development activity and the rise in value of assets and also on the sale of assets. The starting point for working this out will be the company's accounts, but there are some special rules which must be followed for tax purposes.

Companies make a self-assessment and pay tax for an accounting period. Corporation tax is different from the charge on individuals, and also on companies that are not resident in the UK and who do not trade in the UK. Individuals and these types of company pay tax for the year that runs from 6 April in one year to 5 April in the next year. With corporation tax the key period is the company's own accounting period not the Government's tax year. The company must assess its own liability to tax and pay the tax that is due. It must pay this tax no later than 9 months and 1 day after the end of the accounting period (the normal due date). HM Revenue and Customs (HMRC, previously Inland Revenue) will not send the company an assessment, or work out the tax that it must pay.

'Large' companies must pay most of their tax earlier than this date, by quarterly instalment payments.

The 2007 allowances and rates are presented in Table 3.9.

TABLE 3.9 Corporation tax rates 2007

Corporation tax on profits – £ per year (unless stated)

Rate	2005–06	2006–07
Starting rate: 0%	£0–£10,000	N/A[a]
Marginal relief	£10,001–£50,000	N/A[a]
Small companies' rate: 19%	£50,001–£300,000	£0–£300,000
Marginal relief	£300,001–£1,500,000	£300,001–£1,500,000
Main rate: 30%	£1,500,001 or more	£1,500,001 or more
Non-corporate distribution rate	19%	N/A[a]

[a]The 2005 Pre-Budget Report announced that the starting rate and non-corporate distribution rate would be replaced with a single banding for small companies set at the existing small companies' rate.
Source: HMRC website: www.hmrc.gov.uk. Reproduced under the terms of the Click-Use Licence.

Value added tax

VAT is a tax that has significance to developers although in most respects its effect is marginal in that a VAT-registered developer can reclaim all VAT charged on inputs to the development (construction work, etc.) if VAT is charged to the end user. The repayment is usually made 3 months after the expense has been incurred and this can be factored into the cash flow appraisal. There are circumstances where VAT is significant, however. The explanation is rather complex.

VAT is the newest major tax in existence in the UK. It is essentially a 'European tax' being introduced as part of the UK's entry in 1973. This legislation introduced then was essentially concerned with levying a turnover tax in connection with the supply of goods and services as set down in the first EC Council Directive of 11 April 1967, the tax being defined to 'cover all stages of production and the provision of services', and as 'achieving the highest degree of simplicity'. In fact, VAT is one of the most confusing and complex taxes in existence. The tax would be levied at each stage of the supply of goods and services, eventually falling on the consumer/end user.

VAT was introduced into the UK on 1 April 1973 at a standard rate of 10 per cent and replaced purchase tax and selective employment tax. VAT is a tax on the final consumption of certain goods and services in the home market but it is collected at every stage of production and distribution. It is currently levied at three rates: standard (17.5 per cent), lower (5 per cent) and zero (0 per cent). Most items attracting VAT are standard rated but some, such as domestic fuel (lower rated) and books (zero rated), are at a lower rate for political or social reasons. Residential property is a zero-rated supply.

It was not until the Sixth Directive of 17 May 1977 that the rules for property were clarified. Property in general was exempt from VAT. The Sixth Directive (Article 13 para B) provided that the letting and leasing of property (with certain exclusions), and the supply of buildings or parts of buildings, other than partly and newly constructed buildings, were to be exempt from VAT, i.e. no VAT was to be charged on the supply. This created a potential problem for developers and investors: it was fundamental to the concept of the tax that, at each stage, the VAT charged on the outputs, i.e. the supplies made by the supplying party, was available to offset any input VAT, i.e. on supplies made to the supplier. This ensured, in the chain of goods or services, that the VAT liability was passed down the chain, ultimately to the consumer/end user. But this could not happen with exempt supplies.

Because of this problem, the concept of the option to tax (Article 13 para C of the Sixth Directive) was introduced, giving the supplier the option to charge VAT in certain situations. This came into effect in England in 1989, when it became known officially as the 'election to waive exemption'. The VAT liability has then been transferred to the developer, who then has to make taxable supplies to recover their input VAT. The VAT charged to the developer will be based on the price of the freehold together with the stamp duty. The developer's solicitor must always ask whether an election has been made, see a certified copy of it and ensure that it relates precisely to the description of the development being sold. The investor will normally make the election if it would otherwise incur irrecoverable input VAT, thus avoiding, or reducing, a VAT cost on its sale.

The basic rules have evolved considerably since their introduction. Once the election is made, all future supplies in respect of the 'elected' property are chargeable to tax. By making the election, a liability to be registered will usually arise. In the case of an existing lease or licence, the lessor or licensor has a right to add VAT to the agreed rent following an election, unless the lease or licence specifically provides otherwise. If an election has been made, but, under the terms of the lease, VAT cannot be added, the rent is regarded as VAT inclusive.

The election is a personal decision of the elector; a purchaser of an interest in land may pay VAT on the acquisition but is not bound to make standard-related supplies itself.

Buildings, or parts of buildings, that are intended for use as dwellings, or solely for residential purposes, are excluded. Other exclusions include: the sale of land (or land with buildings to be demolished) to a registered housing association that provides the seller with a certificate stating that the land is to be used to construct dwellings or residential buildings; buildings, or parts of buildings, for charitable purposes (other than offices); pitches for residential caravans; facilities for the mooring of a residential houseboat; do-it-yourself builders in certain cases; and sales under the capital goods scheme.

This is complex but straightforward so far. However, like other areas of tax law, the rules relating to property have anti-avoidance provisions, which often hit quite innocent transactions. VAT is particularly problematic. Property developers cannot recover the input VAT of a development if it is a bank, an insurance company or other VAT-exempt body that intends to occupy the building. The key word is 'exempt'. These bodies are exempt from VAT, therefore they cannot recover VAT charged to them. This includes VAT on the sale of buildings and on rent. If a developer elects to charge VAT, the building automatically becomes 17.5 per cent more expensive than a non-elected building to these types of organisations ('normal' companies if VAT registered can also recover input VAT, including that charged on rents or sale of buildings). In some markets these companies form a significant proportion of the market. The developer must, therefore, choose to either reduce the competitiveness of the building or not recover their own input VAT. In addition, if the prospective tenant pays for so much as a small variation to the building, the developer may be prevented from recovering all their VAT.

There are other complexities to VAT regarding the supply of land and converting buildings. A developer should take competent advice on VAT issues and be up to date on the regulations current at the time that the development takes place.

Stamp duty

Stamp duty used to be what the name implied: a tax on the 'stamping' of legal documents including the conveyancing of freeholds and the grant of leases. Stamp duty on property transactions was reformed in 2003.

Stamp duty land tax (SDLT) is a new tax in land transactions that was introduced by the Finance Act 2003 and largely replaces stamp duty with effect from 1 December 2003. SDLT is not a stamp duty, but a form of self-assessed transfer tax. SDLT is charged on 'land transactions' and for typical transactions in land, such as the buying and selling of a residential house, there is little change from stamp duty, except that a tax return is required to be made to HMRC and documents no longer need to be given a physical stamp.

In addition to SDLT on the purchase price for land, SDLT is also charged when a lease is granted. Any premium for the grant is charged to SDLT at the same rates as for the purchase price for a sale of land; SDLT is also charged on the rent payable under the lease, at the rate of 1 per cent of the net present value of rent passing under the whole term of the lease. The amount of SDLT due on the grant of a typical commercial lease generally amounts to a substantial increase above the amount of stamp duty that would have been due previously.

SDLT is also charged on certain transactions involving the transfer of land involving partnerships (transfers of land from or to the partners, or changes in the partners' partnership interests where the partnership owns land – see Table 3.10).

Stamp duty is the perennial bugbear of the property industry. Governments have used it as a useful cash-cow alternative to income tax, which is now politically difficult for them to raise. As stamp duty increases so property must perform better to justify an investor selling it on. Stamp duty has increased from just 1 per cent on most transactions since May 1997.

The Budget of 2001 introduced an exemption for stamp duty on all property transactions in the most disadvantaged parts of the UK. This was aimed at promoting urban regeneration through the refurbishment and return to use of existing properties and aiding new development. In the Government's own words 'This will encourage businesses and families to locate in these areas, reviving depressed property markets and providing employment'. However, since property values are usually rather low in these areas anyway, it is doubtful whether the actual impact of the changes will be

TABLE 3.10 Rates of stamp duty land tax from 2006

Land transactions with an effective date on or after 23 March 2006
Transfers of land and buildings (consideration paid)

Rate	Land in disadvantaged areas – residential	Land in disadvantaged areas – non-residential	All other land in the UK – residential	All other land in the UK – non-residential
0%	£0–£150,000	£0–£150,000	£0–£125,000	£0–£150,000
1%	Over £150,000–£250,000	Over £150,000–£250,000	Over £125,000–£250,000	Over £150,000–£250,000
3%	Over £250,000–£500,000	Over £250,000–£500,000	Over £250,000–£500,000	Over £250,000–£500,000
4%	Over £500,000	Over £500,000	Over £500,000	Over £500,000

Note: disadvantaged area relief for non-residential land transactions is not available for non-residential land transactions with an effective date on or after 17 March 2005.

However the relief is preserved for:

> the completion of contracts entered into and substantially performed on or before 16 March 2005
> the completion or substantial performance of other contracts entered into on or before 16 March 2005, provided that there is no variation or assignment of the contract or sub-sale of the property after 16 March 2005 and that the transaction is not in consequence of the exercise after 16 March 2005 of an option or right of pre-emption.

New leases (lease duty) – duty on rent

Rate	Net present value of rent – residential	Net present value of rent – non-residential
0%	£0–£125,000	£0–£150,000
1%	Over £125,000	Over £150,000

Note: when calculating duty payable on the net present value (NPV) of leases, the NPV calculation must be reduced by the following *before* applying the 1% rate:

> residential – £125,000
> non-residential – £150,000.

Duty on *premium* is the same as for transfers of land (except that special rules apply for premium where rent exceeds £600 annually).

Source: HMRC website: www.hmrc.gov.uk. Reproduced under the terms of the Click-Use Licence.

significant. The exemption is targeted at the areas most in need of regeneration, at the level of particular wards. This use has been continued under the SDLT regime.

Inheritance tax

Inheritance tax (or more strictly capital transfer tax, CTT) is tax charged on the transfer of assets such as passing on property to relatives, for example in a will. It can also be charged on the transfer of assets between companies. Good tax planning can reduce the burden of CTT almost to zero. CTT is a tax for a developer or investor to be aware of in order to avoid incurring a liability but it is one that is not of particular significance.

Business rates

Business rates are a UK-wide and nationally collected tax on business premises, used to contribute to the funding of local councils but completely under the control of central government. They impact on property development and investment in two ways. First, rates become due on the product of development once the construction works have been completed. There is 'empty rates relief', whereby the tax payable is reduced by 50 per cent but the cost of the business rate has to be factored into the holding costs of completed but vacant premises as the owner is liable to pay it until an occupier is found. The second impact of rates is on the general competitiveness of the product of development; rates are a significant proportion of occupation costs even if they are normally paid by the occupier of the building, and decisions by firms as to location are determined partly by an assessment of the *total* costs of occupation.

Rates are based on the annual rental value for the property as assessed by the district valuer employed by the Government. Rateable values are a key factor in the calculation of business rates. They are not the rates bill. In broad terms, the rateable value is a professional view of the annual rent for a property if it were available on the open market. A rateable value is a notional rent calculated solely for rating purposes. It may, therefore, differ from the actual rent on the property agreed or set in the open market. Occupiers of identical rented properties will each negotiate the terms of their own leases and the circumstances of the actual landlords and tenants and the rents they pay may differ widely from each other for many reasons. The valuation officer has regard to this evidence in making a judgement as to what the reasonably expected rent might be. All properties' rateable values are valued at a single date.

The Valuation Office Agency has a legal duty to review all rateable values for non-domestic rates every 5 years. The valuation officers assess the rateable values of all non-domestic properties in England and Wales and compile these into a rating list. The Valuation Office Agency then maintains the lists until the next revaluation. The latest lists came into force on 1 April 2005 and the lists run for 5 years.

The uniform business rate (UBR, sometimes known as the multiplier) is an amount set by the Government each year. There is a UBR for England and one for Wales. It is set to ensure that the overall amount collected in rates only ever increases by the rate of inflation. The rate for 2007–08 is 44.4p (and 44.1p for small businesses as they receive a small amount of relief from the Government). An example of the tax due on a property is given in Table 3.11.

As can be seen from Table 3.11, the tax can be quite a significant amount and one that developers should budget for if it is anticipated that the property will stay empty for some time.

TABLE 3.11 Example of the tax due on a property

Open market rental value of property	£50,000 p.a.
Valuation Office Agency assessment of rateable value (1 April 1998 valuation)	£48,000 p.a.
Applicable universal business rate	£0.441
Tax due	£21,168

Appeals against rating assessments are allowed but there are restrictions as to when these can be made.

Council tax

Council tax is the equivalent tax to business rates for residential property. It is based on property values but uses a much simpler system of banding. Rather than assessing a value for each premises as is done with commercial property, each domestic property is placed into an appropriate value band based on its market value. There are eight bands, each increasing in value. Each band pays a progressively higher level of council tax. The setting of the bands and the valuation of the properties is done nationally by the Valuation Office Agency. The setting of the rate of council tax is largely a responsibility of the rating authority, the local council. This causes the tax rates to vary markedly across the country.

Tax relief

As noted above, the Government makes use of its discretionary powers in the tax system to give some relief to stimulate activity in certain sections of the market or to achieve certain aims. An investor or developer can take advantage of these concessions to boost the return from property. Recent examples not covered below include Business Expansion Schemes and Housing Action Trusts both of which gave tax concessions to investors to ease the supply of affordable housing in inner city areas for rent or purchase.

Relief on interest payments

The effect of tax relief on interest payments has been covered in the finance section above (see page 118). It remains one of the most significant tax concessions to investors and developers.

Capital allowances

Capital allowances allow the cost of capital assets to be written off against taxable profits. They replaced the charge for depreciation in the business accounts, which is not allowable for tax relief. The UK has no allowance for the depreciation of buildings and property generally, unlike other countries, other than capital allowances. The reliefs given are limited (see below) but can still be significant particularly if, in general buildings, significant amounts of plant and machinery are included. Owners of commercial property can make considerable corporation tax savings if they take full advantage of allowances available on expenditure on machinery and plant.

Industrials, hotels and enterprise zones

An annual allowance of 4 per cent on the cost of agricultural land and forestry land, new industrial buildings and structures, and qualifying hotels is allowed by the tax authorities.

161

Plant and machinery elements of other buildings

Capital allowances may be obtained in respect of machinery and plant in a building. These items attract a written down allowance of 25 per cent on a reducing balance basis against the original expenditure. Sometimes the Government gives a larger first-year allowance for small and medium-sized businesses. The allowances are deducted in the company's corporation tax computation.

For example, if a company spends £100,000 on a new air-conditioning system for a property it owns, in year 1, 25 per cent of the purchase price (i.e. £25,000) can be deducted in the company's corporation tax computation. In year 2, the allowance is 25 per cent of the written-down value (£75,000). This equals an allowance of £18,750. In year 3, the allowance will be £14,062.50 (25% × (£75,000 – £18,750)), and so on, until there is no more written-down value against which to set allowances.

In an investment situation it is important for the investment owner to retain ownership of the plant and machinery and not pass it on to the tenant in order to claim the sums due.

Brownfield development and remediation

In an effort to regenerate inner cities and increase the use of previously used land, the Government has placed tax relief provisions within the Finance Act 2006 for investors and developers of contaminated land. This effectively creates a tax shelter for companies developing contaminated land. Corporate investors will be able to claim an upfront super-deduction of 150 per cent of remediation expenditure, even where the costs are entirely capital and not normally qualifying for a deduction. Developers benefit from an additional 50 per cent deduction in calculating their development profit. Companies that cannot utilise the additional relief may be able to claim a tax credit from HMRC.

Listed buildings

It is a popular misconception that listed buildings attract copious amounts of grant aid. The system of securing grants is, in fact, complex and grant aid is only a possibility for a small number of projects. Where it is granted, conditions are often attached which may, in some cases, negate or reduce the grant benefit. VAT applies, in general terms, to all listed buildings and the developer will need to take account of this, particularly where substantial building costs are involved. In certain cases, zero business rating relief is possible, but this depends on individual circumstances.

TAX STRATEGIES

It is difficult to generalise about tax strategies as each development and each developer investor tends to have different tax status and goals. Sensible tax planning at the feasibility stage can, however, increase or even create a profit margin for property development that might not otherwise exist. It is often rewarding to keep abreast of government policy and investigate HMRC tax concessions in order to be able to react to any changes in direction and policy. Getting good tax advice is sensible for all businesses but can be especially important in the property markets.

CONCLUSIONS

Tax is an important and complex issue. It can make or break some developments. A wise developer should seek good tax advice early in a development project to minimise the impact of tax and engineer the maximum benefits from tax concessions.

Conclusions

Financial matters are often the lifeblood of development. It is very important to secure the right amount of finance, at the right cost and with the right flexibility and risk profile for the development. This is easy to write but often hard to achieve. Finance is one area where the weight of advantage is strongly with the bigger organisations. The options available to these bodies are much wider than those available to a small developer with a short track record. There is a 'Catch 22' situation operating here, but this will probably always be the case. A small developer can, however, have some flexibility in finance and this area will always reward good preparation, diligent research and intelligent strategies.

FINANCIAL APPRAISAL OF
DEVELOPMENT PROJECTS
CHAPTER 4

Introduction: the importance of development appraisal

Financial appraisal is one of the key aspects of assessing the viability of a development project. Development appraisal, to give the alternative name to the process, is used throughout the development process to fulfil a number of key tasks.

First, development appraisals are used to determine the price that should be bid for a piece of land. Land for development has no intrinsic or set value, as we have seen from Chapter 2 (Development inception). Development land has a value derived from the use it can be put to. Each scheme proposed for any plot of land will generate a different land value. A landowner will generally sell to the developer who submits the highest viable bid. The appraisal process, when used to determine land value, determines the highest bid that a potential developer can make and still meet their target return.

Second, they are used to determine the profit (or loss) that a scheme will make. This is vitally important, not only to show the developer whether the scheme is viable but also as a tool to obtain finance. Potential financial backers, be they commercial lenders or potential purchasers of the final development, are not primarily interested in the aesthetics of the scheme or the cleverness of its technical solution. They are concerned with its financial viability.

Commercial lenders will scrutinise the financial appraisal very carefully before advancing money. They will essentially be looking at two things:

1. Whether the assumptions and the programme underlying the development are sound. They will ask a number of questions. For example, are the assumptions made about the value of the scheme sound? Is the selling or leasing programme realistic? Are the construction costs valid? The developer will have to prove that the components of the appraisal are soundly based.
2. If this is established, then the financier will look closely at the profit margin predicted by the appraisal. Financiers want to be satisfied that the developer will achieve a sufficient profit margin. This is not out of concern for the developer's wealth as such, but rather because the profit margin reflects a risk margin for a development. Effectively, the larger the profit margin is, the less the risk that the borrower will default because there is less chance that the scheme will go into deficit if things go wrong. There is no set scale as to the margin that

TABLE 4.1 Approximation of what lenders have historically looked for

Type of scheme	Normal return on cost required by lenders (%)
Speculative commercial	20
Commercial with pre-lettings	10–20
Residential	10–15

lenders require; however, Table 4.1 gives an approximation of what lenders have historically looked for.[1]

Both the development appraisal and financial appraisal are carried out early in the lifespan of the project, essentially at the feasibility stage. Later in the project other uses of appraisals are common.

a. They are also used by developers to explore the effect of altering, reworking or re-timing a scheme. Projects often require rethinking during their lives. The appraisal is used to see what the effect of proposed changes will be.
b. Sophisticated versions of the basic development appraisals are also used during the course of a development as monitoring tools.

This chapter will cover all of these potential uses of appraisal in turn.

HOW THIS CHAPTER IS LAID OUT

This chapter starts by looking at the basics of appraisal and concentrates initially on the appraisals which developers need to carry out to assess the bid they should submit when considering purchasing a piece of land. Rather than just illustrate the calculation, the approach followed is to take a detailed analysis of the appraisal, illustrating how a developer needs to build a set of assumptions about the development envisaged. The type of assumptions required and the way values are ascribed to them are considered in detail.

Once all the assumptions have been made, then the calculation can be carried out. Again, how the calculations are done is examined in detail.

This approach means that this chapter is rather long and, on the surface, complex. In justification, it is intended to provide a comprehensive introduction to appraisal. Developers should have a good grasp of appraisal in order to be able to make sound decisions in the development process. This chapter should provide this.

The book also accepts that appraisals are increasingly being carried out using specialist software and less frequently by manual means or using spreadsheets such as Excel. An illustrative example using the most widely used software, ARGUS Developer (formerly CircleDeveloper) is included at the end of this chapter.

BASIC TYPES AND FEATURES OF DEVELOPMENT APPRAISALS

The vital role of financial appraisals is unarguable. Constructors and users must, however, be aware of the basic characteristics of these appraisals. The outcome is often extraordinarily sensitive to change in some of the key constructional variables and the appraiser is required to make assumptions about uncertain factors when building the appraisal model. This is inevitable as the appraisal looks ahead into an often uncertain future, dealing with factors that may change. The appraiser must make assumptions about rental levels, investor sentiment, occupier requirements and demand, interest rate levels, the timing of several factors such as how long the scheme will take to get through planning, to build, to let, to sell – the list is almost infinite. It is also inevitable that some of the assumptions made in the model will be wrong, and that appraisers will allow themselves to be too optimistic about the end result. Developers are naturally optimistic people, risk takers who need to see the up side to actually take the risk. Development appraisals can, with very minor differences in assumptions, be made to show just about anything from a given set of facts. They are easily manipulated and easy to mislead, either deliberately or unconsciously.

A personal anecdote may illustrate this point. As a young surveyor, the author worked for a private practice firm in the southeast of England. Part of the job involved assessing developments put forward by development clients or as part of loan security assessments for bank clients. My main role in the firm was preparing formal valuations and valuation reports, a role which required a degree of conservatism to produce a realistic valuation figure that the user could rely on. When I carried out development appraisals on projects submitted, almost all my appraisals suggested that the projects would make a loss, or that the purchase figure for the site could not be supported. The developers were, however, keen to proceed with either the development or the land purchase at the agreed figures. Their own appraisals clearly told them a different story even though they dealt with the same sites, in the same market and the same proposed scheme as my own appraisal.

So who was right and who was wrong? The answer was we were probably both wrong. And both right! I was too cautious, the developers too bullish. Only time would tell how wrong or right we both were. It is too easy to look on the black side, to always take the downside risk, or to be too risk seeking, too optimistic. The former would lead to never carrying out a development, the latter to financial ruin. Clearly, one must find the middle ground but this area is never clearly labelled! The only sensible course of action is to become aware of the frailties and failures of both development appraisals and human nature. It is absolutely essential that the characteristics of each financial appraisal are fully explored. In particular, it is vitally important that some degree of risk assessment is undertaken with development appraisal. This is usually referred to as 'sensitivity analysis' within the development world, although, strictly speaking, sensitivity analysis is just one of a family of risk appraisal techniques that can be applied.

Development appraisals can be carried out to answer one of three basic questions, although in reality only two of the three are common. They are:

1. What is the land worth?
2. What profit will be made from the development?
3. What is the construction budget for the proposed scheme?

The answer to these three questions represents the factor that is unknown at the time of the appraisal. This can be illustrated by looking at the basic components of a development appraisal to assess land value:

VALUE OF SCHEME ON COMPLETION
less
COSTS OF DEVELOPMENT
less
DEVELOPER'S PROFIT
equals
VALUE OF LAND (the unknown part of the equation)

Here, the appraiser knows the top three items. The balancing sum, the unknown, the residual, is the land value for the purpose proposed by the developer.

Compare this with the developer wanting to know what profit can be made on a development. Is it sufficient to go ahead with this scheme, or to purchase a piece of land at the asked price? In this case, the developer must know the price of the land and must form a judgement about the other items. The one piece that is left, the residual in this case, is the profit (or loss) figure to balance the equation:

VALUE OF SCHEME ON COMPLETION
less
COSTS OF DEVELOPMENT
less
PRICE OF LAND
equals
DEVELOPER'S PROFIT (the unknown part of the equation)

By a process of elimination, the third alternative considered is where both the profit figure and the price of the land are known. This may occur when the land or the building being redeveloped is already owned but it can also occur in other circumstances. Here, the unknown is the budget figure for doing the development work, i.e. the total construction budget.

The equation is as follows:

VALUE OF SCHEME ON COMPLETION
less
VALUE OF LAND
less
DEVELOPER'S PROFIT
equals
BUDGET FOR DEVELOPMENT (the unknown part of the equation)

Although there are many different models for development, these are the fundamental equations that underlie them all. Certainly, the two most common are the first two and it is these that we will concentrate on.

We will start with the basic model, the residual or hypothetical development model.

The basic development appraisal model

There is a fair amount of debate within the property profession about the merits of traditional methods of valuation and those where the assumptions underlying the valuation are made more explicit. This occurs with approaches such as discounted cash flow (DCF) models. The debate also takes place with regard to development appraisals. Here, there is a traditional model where many of the assumptions made are implicit but there are also more explicit, complex, cash flow models. In the UK property market DCF is most widely applied in development appraisals. In fact, as in other areas of valuation, the truth about the two models is that they are essentially two versions of the same thing. Both the traditional and DCF approaches are, in fact, discounted cash flow approaches. The former is, however, a greatly simplified DCF. This simplification has both disadvantages and advantages, a disadvantage being that simplification leads to inaccuracies that can be serious. The advantages include speed of construction and ease of interpretation.

Rather than one being superior to the other in all circumstances, each has their use and a developer needs to be familiar with both types of approach. As a rule of thumb, the traditional approach is best applied in the early stages of a project, such as the initial appraisal, where the details of the proposed scheme are not certain, while the time and effort required to construct a DCF are best rewarded where the scheme's details are at a more advanced stage.

Having said that, much of this division is artificial, reflecting a historical fact that, before the advent of personal computers, appraisal was restricted by calculation difficulties. Some calculations were too problematical or too time consuming for accurate estimation and as a result the traditional residual appraisal approach contains substantial simplifications. These simplifications lead to inaccuracies. Other approaches are superior and the commercial development software available, although often presenting results in a traditional format, carry out the calculations in a sophisticated way (usually using a cash flow). The traditional presentation has advantages in terms of clarity of presentation but the layout is retained for similar reasons to the retention of the QWERTY keyboards for computers – tradition.

We will first examine the traditional approach. The starting point will be the calculation of a bid price for the land. To do this we need a site to appraise.

BASE SITE FOR APPRAISAL

The base scenario we will use for the appraisals is a medium-sized commercial development, an office, proposed for a site in a provincial city in the UK. This is a purely hypothetical development but is based roughly on what might happen in reality in current market conditions correct at the time of writing.

The site we are considering is one of 1,000m^2, close to the city centre in the established business area of the city. We will assume it is of regular dimensions. It currently has an obsolete 40-year-old office building on the site that is both derelict and vacant. The ground conditions are good, with good bearing capacity ground but with no hard rock to create problems in excavation. There is no contamination on the site. There is clear title to the site with no legal encumbrances. The site is fully serviced. No cables, pipes or sewers cross the site. It is not in a conservation area. There is outline planning consent for the site to be developed for offices up to a total built area of 5,000m^2. It is envisaged that a modern, concrete-framed office building will be constructed on the site. The specification will be typical of a high-specification office building in such a location.

The office letting market has been good over the past three years with indications that there is sufficient demand for a development of this size. The development will be speculative, i.e. the building will be marketed to the occupational market as it nears completion and will not be built for any specific client, and the developer intends to find an occupational tenant to take a lease on the building. Once the building is let, the developer intends to sell the freehold with the benefit of the lease as an investment to an investor.

Some of the assumptions in this scenario give an indication of the areas where complexity can creep into the development appraisal and process. A development value is derived from a combination of physical factors, the legal and planning environment and market conditions. Although property development is not rocket science, as an experienced developer once remarked, the context in which it takes place is often amazingly complex, and the appraiser must be aware of this and consider all these factors.

From this list of assumptions, or the facts that the appraiser must gather in real life, the assumptions specifically related to the development must be made. This stage is like an accounting exercise with all the key factors being considered. These factors and this process are common to whichever appraisal method is applied.

The specific areas where assumptions are required to be made can be broken down into four broad areas:

> the building dimensions
> the timing of the development and its stages
> the costs related to the development and
> the factors related to its value.

Each of these broad categories will be considered in turn. It should be noted that the ARGUS Developer V3.0 software is used in the construction of this appraisal.

THE SPECIFIC ASSUMPTIONS

In summary, the specific assumptions that are fed into the financial appraisal pertinent to this site are listed below. How each is derived will be considered in turn.

Building dimensions

One of the key factors that will influence the value of the site is clearly what can be built on the site. A number of factors will affect this:

> the physical and spatial characteristics of the site
> the planning and legal situation pertaining to the site and
> the requirements of the market.

Each of these will now be considered in turn.

The physical and spatial characteristics of the site

Clearly, this is a very important factor with a number of interrelated issues which affect individual sites. The physical size of the site is important but the shape of the site is very influential in terms of the size and number of buildings that can be built. Narrow sites or those which are irregularly shaped can lead to problems with access and spacing of individual buildings. In city centre locations where 100 per cent site coverage is to be expected, these factors can lead to problems with layout and uneconomic remnants of sites and access.

Other factors to consider include the bearing capacity of the ground and topography, i.e. the shape of the ground surface (slopes, etc.). These can be negated by the design or engineering of the building. An example is poor ground-bearing capacity which can be corrected by piled foundations. The main impact of these factors is therefore on cost and only indirectly on the quantum of built area that can be constructed by way of reducing the profitability of development.

In this case, as noted, the city centre location implies 100 per cent coverage. The site is regularly shaped so there is no loss of space. The building-on plan will maximise the site area and so will therefore be 1,000m^2 on plan.

The planning and legal situation pertaining to the site

The planning system   This has a major influence on the quantum of buildings produced as well as the type of development allowed in particular areas. Planning authorities can impose density regulations on sites, allowing only a certain number of dwellings per hectare or a certain percentage of site coverage or, as in this case, a restriction on total built area according to a multiple of site area. They can also have requirements for certain types of development to be included on sites such as a requirement for low-cost housing or starter industrial units where the developer, if unrestricted, would develop a higher proportion of the most valuable use. Other ways that the quantum developed can be restricted is by height restrictions and by requirements for set backs (allowing a gap between the building and the street) and building lines.

For many years, car parking has been a major concern to planning authorities, particular within cities. Urban authorities have been preoccupied with the increase in congestion, parking problems and pollution caused by the increase in car use. In an attempt to counter this, they have tended to impose maximum limits on the number of car spaces that can be provided. This has not restricted built area but has, of course, influenced it greatly. An alternative approach is for planning authorities to impose a car parking requirement per unit of built floor area, for example a requirement to provide one space per 200m^2 of built area. This happens when the authorities want developers to provide spaces so that public or on-street spaces in the locality are not placed under pressure, or when the authorities are trying to restrict the amount of useable space developed.

Planning authorities work within the framework of the Town and Country Planning Acts and within the rules laid down by legal precedents. Their ability to impose restrictions on development is not, therefore, infinite and there are some things that they cannot do legally, even if they want to. One way in which planning authorities can get around this is by entering development agreements under section 106^2 of the Town and Country Planning Act 1990 (now covered under the revised Planning and Compulsory Purchase Act 2004), which can influence the shape and form of development. For example, recently in Warrington a development site existed within an established retail park area which was suffering from excess traffic problems. The purchasers of the site were required to enter into a section 106 agreement which

1. restricted the site to non-retail development and
2. allowed for a development that would accommodate no more than 100 employees in the buildings.

This naturally has a direct effect on the built area.

The legal situation The legal characteristics of the site also have similar influence. Development sites can be either freehold or long (in excess of 50 years) leasehold tenure. In the latter case, the detail of the lease contract can determine what is built on the site; indeed, that is often the reason that bodies such as local authorities retain the freehold ownership of a site while granting a long lease to an occupier or developer. The lease allows control, either specifically in the construction of clauses or simply by requiring the landlord's permission to carry out developments or make alterations. This extra element of control is one of the key reasons why the value of sites held on leasehold tenure is always lower than that of sites held freehold.

Freehold sites are not, however, unrestricted. It is quite common for owners to place covenants on the title that will run with the land and bind future owners to abide by their requirements. These restrictive covenants are often related to future development by the type, size or, in some cases, the materials to be used. Other covenants include giving certain rights to third parties, such as the right to extract particular minerals, or to graze animals or hold markets. Some of these restrictions on the title on land can have a major influence on the building that may be constructed on the site. Historic or unreasonable covenants can be altered or extinguished by application to the Lands Tribunal in England and Wales or by agreement with the relevant beneficiary of the covenant but the process can be time consuming and is by no means certain.

Other legal issues that can affect the form and size of the development include easements, wayleaves, rights of way and rights of light. Easements and wayleaves give rights over land to things such as pipes, cables and electrical transmission lines. Rights of way allow access over the land. Rights of light are enjoyed by neighbours to the site. All these issues need to be fully investigated because they can often have quite major influences on what can be built on a site and where.

In a historical and densely developed country such as the UK, it is very rare indeed for a site to be unaffected by some of these legal factors.

The requirements of the market

The final set of factors that influence the built dimensions of the development are more indirect but cannot be ignored. In most for-profit developments the requirements of the market are paramount in determining the built form:

> households have requirements for certain features in residential developments; retailers from particular sectors will only occupy units of a certain size, shape and layout;
> industrial and warehouse users need units of specific sizes, heights and with sufficient yard or service areas to meet their needs;
> office users require buildings of particular specifications and size, not only in terms of area but also in particulars – such as sizes and shapes of floor plates, etc.

All these factors must be taken into account when the size and form of the building being developed is considered.

The three factors listed above have been considered in the dimensions of the building as laid down in the assumptions. This has led to the decision that the site can support the development of a 5,000m² building with 15 car spaces (Figure 4.1).

Questions may be raised regarding the separate statement of the net floor area of the building. This is a requirement related to the valuation of commercial buildings, particularly shops and offices. Occupiers of these types of buildings will only pay for the space they can actually use for their business. In an office, for example, space lost to columns, lifts, staircases, circulation space, internal walls, toilets and kitchens is, in most cases, excluded for the purposes of calculating rent. How a building should be measured is laid down in the Code of Measurement Practice produced by the Royal Institution of Chartered Surveyors (RICS). Whatever the case, just as we need to calculate the built area in order to determine the cost of construction, so we need to ascertain the net area of the building in order to assess its value.

Detail					
Heading	Office	Gross Unit Area m²	5,000.00	Alternate Area	0
Unit Number	1	Gross Area m²	5,000.00	ITZA Area m²	0.00
Use Type	Offices	Net Unit Area m²	4,000.00	Gross:Net Ratio	80.00%
Number of Units	1	Net Area m²	4,000.00	Locked	

FIGURE 4.1 Commercial floor area schedule for the example property as displayed in ARGUS Developer

Assumptions related to time

Time is often critical to the success of a development. It is very important in the appraisal, and it is related closely to money – the longer a development takes, the more interest is charged or the greater the costs incurred through giving up the right to use the money. The longer a development takes to complete, the longer the developer has to wait to recoup the capital expenditure. Money receivable in the future is worth less than money receivable today. The time value of money needs to be carefully taken into account in the appraisal.

A development can usually be broken down into three broad phases. The first is referred to as the planning phase. It is the period that may start with the initial expenditure on the development, such as the purchase of land. However, it is more accurate to consider it as commencing from the point where the decision is made to begin development or the actual time of the initial appraisal. It is during this period that the development is designed or the detailed design is finalised. All necessary consents are obtained in this period – planning, listed building, fire and safety and building regulation consents are just some of the things that need to be put into place. The contract documentation for the construction works is prepared and any title problems can also be resolved during this time period.

There is no easy formula for determining the length of this period. Obviously, the rough rule of thumb is that it will be shortest in simple developments and will lengthen as complex issues increase but beyond this it is hard to generalise. If there are major planning issues, such as the development proposal being in conflict with the local authority development plan or where consent has been refused, the planning phase may be lengthy. This is a situation where there is no substitute for experience, particularly within the development team. Some guidance can be obtained by looking at what has happened in the past with similar schemes. In our example, the planning period has been assessed as being 6 months long.

The timing of the second phase of development is easier to assess in most cases, although there can still be major problems. The construction phase is the period that commences with the start of site works and usually ends at practical completion, when the building is handed over from the contractor to the developer or building owner. In a traditional development the developer places the development in the hands of a single building contractor who undertakes to complete the project in the agreed time period and at an agreed cost (see the section on procurement, page 265, for a more complete discussion on this issue).

The timing of this phase can be assessed in a number of ways. The most reliable way is to consult a construction professional who has experience of the type of scheme planned. One of the functions of a quantity surveyor (QS), as we have seen, is to assess the timing of a scheme as well as the cost implications. In larger schemes it will be the QS in tandem with the other professional team members (particularly the architect, structural engineer, service engineer and project manager) who will assess the timing issues. On smaller scale projects, direct discussions with contractors may assist the assessment. Some guidance may also be found in building price books but these can only be considered to be approximate guides.

A number of issues can affect the timing of the construction phase and the ease of its assessment. Where a greenfield site is being developed and a straightforward type of building is planned, the timing is relatively easy to assess and the estimate is likely to be accurate. The process becomes more difficult and the accuracy of the prediction less certain when the site is in an existing urban centre, where there is substantial excavation in unknown ground, where demolition is involved or, particularly, where the work involves the alteration of an existing structure. The difficulties arise where there are unknown or unusual aspects to consider and to make assumptions about. Consider a developer working on the redevelopment of a nondescript 1950s shop in the centre of a British city such as York. York has been occupied for well over 1,000 years. Many of the buildings are historic with substantial archaeology under the ground surface. There are considerable potential problems with getting access to the site due to the presence of tourists and shoppers. In this case, assessing how long the construction will take once work has commenced on site is not straightforward. It is not easy for the appraiser to find the balance between being too cautious and being overly optimistic. It is here that the importance of sensitivity analysis, considered below, becomes apparent in our example; we are assuming that there are few of these problems. Twelve months has been allowed for the development, which is about par for the course for a city centre office scheme of this size and specification.

The timing of the third broad phase is more problematical. It is the time required for the development to be leased and become income producing (or the time to sell the individual units in a residential scheme). This is highly dependent on the state of the market. It is a very sensitive part of the development process as it is the time when interest charges are accumulating on the full total of the amounts physically expended on the project and the total rolled-up interest to date. The debt charge can rapidly accumulate at this stage. The letting period is, therefore, an opportunity for the appraiser to be realistic about when the scheme will let or be in a position to be sold. It is also a very important risk allowance. The longer the letting period allowed, the more the risk is being offset, i.e. the more cautious the developer is being (Figure 4.2[3]).

Assumptions related to costs

There are ten cost items to consider in our particular appraisal but this list could be longer if items such as planning fees, a planning consultant and an environmental consultant were to be included. As noted above, an appraisal consists partly of an accounting exercise. For the purposes of our example these items will suffice, particularly as they are the most typical of the cost items involved in a development. Each will be considered in turn.

Building costs

Building costs are dependent on many factors. These include the specification of the building, its size and shape, the method of construction used, the nature of the site

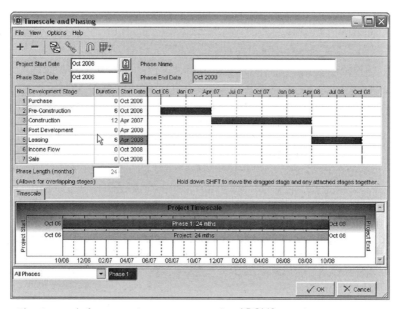

FIGURE 4.2 The timescale for our project as generated in ARGUS Developer

and its surroundings, its location within the country and the time period required to construct it. An example of how costs can vary can be seen from the gross cost per square metre of office construction in the UK, which can vary from £300 to £2,500 per square metre.

Building costs in an appraisal can be determined in a number of ways and the cost data derived from a number of sources.

The methods of estimating building costs break down into three main categories:

> superficial area
> elemental cost
> quantity surveyor's approach.

The superficial area approach simply involves calculating an appropriate all-in cost that will approximate to the total cost of the development of all components of the building. For example, if we know that a 1,000m² building costs £1,000,000 to construct then we can say that the construction cost was £1,000/m². This figure can then be used to calculate the construction costs of similar buildings. For example, if we are appraising the development of a similar specification building of 800m² in the same city which is going to be built in a year's time, this figure may give us a good guide. Our estimate of building costs may be as follows:

Built area	800m²
Multiplied by	
Construction cost (£1,000/m²	
+ 5% inflation allowance) =	£1,050
Estimated construction costs	£840,000

Nothing could be simpler; indeed, this is the method that is used in the vast majority of initial appraisals and is usually perfectly adequate. However, there are considerable problems with the approach that the appraiser should be aware of.

The fundamental problem is one of comparability that this simplistic approach requires. Every construction project is different, buildings are not mass-produced, they are hand built and tailored to meet the differing requirements of the procurer and the differing conditions and characteristics of the site. This is particularly true of commercial properties, each of which tends to be unique. Two ostensibly similar properties can have quite different construction costs because of differences in ground conditions, or problems with access during normal working hours that forces weekend or evening working, or work that has to be carried out by hand instead of machine, the former being highly expensive. One particular source of variance is market conditions: at times when there is little work available, firms may build at cost price or below, simply to maintain cash flow and keep head office staff employed. At other times when there is a glut of work, firms may work with very high profit margins which greatly inflate construction costs. All these factors can be incorporated in the superficial area approach by adjusting the rate upwards or downwards as they are taken into account. It is, however, always going to be an approximation and is likely to be an inaccurate predictor of actual costs, particularly in complex situations.

The problems with this approach do not bar its use. It is still, and will continue to be, the most widely used of methods at the initial appraisal stage. Like many things in appraisal it is, however, best to be aware of the method's shortcomings so as to avoid being misled into making an incorrect decision based on the costs indicated.

The source of cost data used in this model will be considered below.

The elemental cost approach

The elemental cost approach to the estimation of building cost is not one approach but a family of approaches that attempts to provide more detail regarding the development, thus achieving greater accuracy. The approach requires the built elements of the building to be divided into elemental components for more accurate cost estimation. These components can be technical – for example, substructure, structural frame, structural walls, etc. – or else functional – such as parking, office space, etc. This allows a more accurate estimation of cost to be made than with the superficial area method.

The Building Cost Information Service (BCIS) cost element breakdown is as follows:

Element
1 – Substructure
2 – Superstructure
2A Frame
2B Upper floors
2C Roof
2D Stairs

2E External walls
2F Windows and external doors
2G Internal walls and partitions
2H Internal doors

3 – Internal finishes

3A Wall finishes
3B Floor finishes
3C Ceiling finishes

4 – Fittings and furnishings

5 – Services
5A Sanitary appliances
5B Services equipment
5C Disposal installations
5D Water installations
5E Heat source
5F Space heating and air treatment
5G Ventilating system
5H Electrical installations
5I Gas installations
5J Lift and conveyor installations
5K Protective installations
5L Communication installations
5M Special installations
5N Builder's work in connection with services
5O Builder's profit and attendance on services

Building sub-total (excluding external works, preliminaries and contingencies)

6 – External works
6A Site works
6B Drainage
6C External services
6D Minor building works

7 – Preliminaries

8 – Contingencies

Total

Source and acknowledgement: BCIS Publications.

The quantity surveyor's approach

The final approach used in cost estimating is the quantity surveyor's method. This is the most accurate but also most detailed and time consuming to produce. It requires the building to be broken down into its building components, each being accurately measured or estimated, with accurate costs per unit attached to each. For example, the quantity of concrete used in the foundations would be calculated and a price to supply and fix that component per cubic metre would be assessed for the individual case concerned. This would be done for each component of the building, the sum of the total costs being the total construction costs less overheads and (usually) profit.

Although this is the most accurate method of cost estimation, it is often not practical in the early stages of a development project's financial appraisal. It requires access to detailed information about the project to justify its use, but this information is often simply not available in the early stages of a development.

Sources of cost information

A variety of sources of cost information exist, which can be used with the models discussed above. Which is ultimately employed depends on a number of factors including which model is used, the nature of the development scheme, the point at which the appraisal is being carried out and the speed with which the cost information is required or, more likely, a combination of all of the above factors. The sources of the data vary markedly in terms of speed, ease of use, accessibility and accuracy. Those which are the quickest, cheapest and easiest to access are also usually the least accurate (this statement also applies to the methods of cost estimation). There is a trade-off between these factors that the person constructing the appraisal should be aware of.

Some of the basic sources of data that may be available are detailed below.

Building price books

These include those books published by Spon,[4] Laxtons[5] and BCIS Wessex.[6] They are commercially available and are compiled from information furnished by contractors and quantity surveyors. The books contain pricing data suitable for use in all three basic methods of price estimation detailed above. They also include information useful for calculating the regional variation in construction costs and for assessing other items related to building cost, such as professional fees.

This source of data is relatively cheap, highly accessible, comparatively easy to use and provides a swift estimation of construction cost. However, it loses out in terms of accuracy as it provides general, non-site-specific information, which may not reflect the circumstances of the development being addressed. Quite often a reasonably accurate estimate of building costs may be made using this method but there is also a danger that the assessment may be inaccurate and even misleading in certain circumstances.

Computerised databases and estimation systems

One of the main sources of information is produced by BCIS (the Building Cost Information Service). This organisation monitors construction contracts of all types throughout the UK. It collates and analyses data submitted by its members and incorporates material from other relevant sources. Information is made available through several publications and an online service. BCIS is a subsidiary company of the RICS and was established in 1962. Subscribers are provided with data in an accessible form on the current, historic and probable costs of building maintenance and property occupancy, and can access cost information for a wide range of commercial, industrial, residential and public sector buildings. BCIS provides capital cost information while the Building Maintenance Index (BMI) covers maintenance management information and building maintenance, property occupancy and refurbishment costs.

Quantity surveyors

Quantity surveyors are the cost experts of the development team. If a QS is part of the team he or she should be the normal source of cost information. If a previous relationship exists with a QS, this might still be a viable source of the requisite information.

Contractors

Contractors are often themselves valuable sources of cost information. Not only do they have hard information on project costs, they also employ professional estimators to price the construction work prior to bidding. If the developer has worked closely with contractors on previous projects it may be wise to consult them in order to obtain current market cost information.

Previous development/construction projects

The final source of information on construction cost may come from the developer's own experience of costs on previous projects. Experienced developers hold a valuable well of information from previous schemes.

Contingency

It is normal to allow for some degree of contingency in the calculation of construction costs. Contingency is effectively an allowance for risk in the construction element. There will always be some items that will be difficult to assess in a construction project prior to the commencement of work. Similarly, when work is underway things can occur which cause construction costs to rise, including unforeseen ground conditions, the effects of adverse weather and the impact of design changes during the construction programme. The contingency is a realistic acceptance that this will occur. This is one area where a degree of pessimism – anticipating future problems – allows a realistic appraisal to be made, rather than one that paints a misleading picture of future profits. It may be that the contingency is not used. In this case, a higher level of profit will be made on the completion of the development. This is always more welcome than the reduction in profit that will result from failing to allow for uncertainty.

The level of contingency allowance will vary from development to development. As a rough rule of thumb, lower levels of contingency allowance will be appropriate in simple developments of conventional buildings on greenfield sites, i.e. situations where the risk levels are low. A higher contingency level is appropriate where the development is complex. Particular caution should be taken where the development involves the conversion of an older structure and/or where there is a potential risk of contamination on site.

In this case, a contingency allowance of 5 per cent is applied to the construction costs only. Some appraisers apply the contingency percentage to all costs of development including professional fees. There are no hard and fast rules concerning this, it is down to the personal preference of the appraiser (or sometimes to the way that the software package used by the appraiser is constructed).

Professional fees

Most of the normal cost estimation approaches and sources of cost information reviewed above do not include the cost of employing the professional team. These costs are not fixed and are open to negotiation. The relative levels of fees will vary according to the size and complexity of the work involved and, often, the length of the developer's previous relationship with the team. The fees can be a fixed amount agreed between the parties but it is more usual for the team to work for a fee calculated as a percentage of the construction costs. The total fee percentage depends on the number of different professional disciplines required for the project, which naturally depends on the underlying project's complexity. Here, the total percentage is around 10 per cent, which is relatively low. A range of between 8 and 15 per cent of construction costs should be expected.

This is the situation with a traditionally procured project where the design and production phases of the project are separated. In alternative procurement regimes such as 'design and build' the design costs are integrated into the construction costs and the total fees will probably, although not certainly, be lower.

It should be noted that recent lending practices of financial institutions have increased the percentage of professional fees that need to be allowed for in the initial appraisal. Banks, in particular, have increasingly insisted on placing their own professional team in the project to monitor progress and safeguard the financial outlay. The cost of this 'shadow' team is borne by the developer. This is strictly a cost of arranging finance and may, more appropriately, be included in the finance section of the appraisal, but it may be allowed for in the 'professional fees' section in some appraisals, depending on the preference of the person constructing it.

Marketing

With projects other than those where there is a contract with an occupier in place or where one is expected to be in place at the commencement of the scheme, an allowance for marketing the property will have to be incorporated. This sum covers all advertising, publicity fliers, web page generation, etc. It is a separate sum from the allowance for selling or leasing the property, which is covered below. As with most things, the sum allowed for marketing depends very much on the nature of the development. The larger and more unusual the development, the larger the budget needs to be. Residential developments often require an on-site presence during the period in which the units are being sold. It is normal to allow for this in the marketing sum.

The marketing allowance built into the appraisal is normally an appropriate lump sum budget.

Letting and sale fees

These are the fees paid to the agent who finds, and negotiates with, tenants and occupiers for the scheme. Sale fees apply where owner occupation is the result of the development, as in many residential schemes. With commercial schemes, it is likely that the occupier will lease space in the development. Agents are paid a fee once leases have been signed. This fee is usually based on a percentage of the annual rental value of the space let, although minimum charges may apply or the agent may work to a lump sum fee. This is rarer as it removes the agent's incentive to achieve the best possible rent for the client.

If the investment is to be sold on letting, and this is a common way for developers to recoup the development costs of a project and crystallise the profit, then a second tranche of fees is usually payable. This is for the agreement of the investment sale of the project to an investor with a requirement for this type of investment. This sale fee is usually calculated as a percentage of the sale price of the property, typically between 0.5 and 2 per cent of this price, although again a lump sum fee can be agreed. It is possible that two different firms may be appointed to deal respectively with the letting and sale of the property. This occurs typically where the development is located in a provincial town or city and where the likely occupiers are locally based companies in contact with a locally based agent. In contrast, the investment market tends to be dominated by organisations that deal nationally, usually through a limited number of London-based consultancy firms. These firms have greater access to the investment customers for the product and thus it is usually sensible to appoint one of these agents, even though the overall fee may be higher.

Developer's profit

Developer's profit is a cost which must be accounted for in appraisals. Just as contractors will not carry out construction work without being paid, professional fees accrue to the advisors to the development and interest is paid to the banks for the loan of funds, so developers need a 'payment' to recompense them for the time, effort and risk expended. Banks look very closely at this figure as it is an important measure of the security of their investment. They will expect a developer to receive at least a 15 per cent return on cost and usually more in the appraisal given to them. These funds represent extra security if things go wrong. If a building is not let quickly enough, interest charges will rise and start to eat into the developer's profit. A relatively high profit will ensure that this erosion can be covered for a fairly long time period before the developer goes into the red on the project and, thus, potentially into bankruptcy.

Developer's profit is usually calculated as a percentage of the development cost or as a percentage of development value. Each has its advantages and disadvantages, which will be discussed in the section covering development appraisal for profit estimation, below.

Finance and value factor assumptions

Finance and value factors:

Rental value	£235.00
Investment yield	6.50%
Rental incentive	12 months
Interest rate	10%
Car spaces	£2,500.00

This is the series of factors that determines the value of the development and also the cost of financing the development (or the opportunity cost of the developer's own money invested in the project – see below).

An introductory note on property values

The objective of this section is to give an insight into the way commercial property values are determined. It will not enable you to value your own commercial property but it should give you a good idea of the principles.

The first thing to understand is that there is no magical formula for working out property values. Property does not have an inherent value like most marketable goods; it is worth what somebody will pay for it in the open market, i.e. in competition with everybody else. If you commission a valuation of your property this is essentially how the valuer will work out the figure to report to you: they will look at what similar properties have been sold for or the rent at which they have been let and use this evidence to value your property.

Valuers work to a set of rules when carrying out a valuation to ensure that the figure they produce is reliable and would hopefully be reproduced if a property were offered on the open market. These rules are laid down by the professional body dealing with valuation, the Royal Institution of Chartered Surveyors, in a publication popularly known as the Red Book (RICS Appraisal and Valuation Standards). Among other things, the Red Book lays down the basis of valuations to be adopted under certain circumstances, clear assumptions that must be made by the valuer in preparing the valuation. There are several valuation bases, the most commonly used is market value (MV) which can be found in the Red Book, an extract from which is quoted below:

PS3.2 Market Value

Valuations based on Market Value (MV) shall adopt the definition, and the conceptual framework, settled by the International Valuation Standards Committee.

Definition

'The estimated amount for which a property should exchange on the date of valuation between a willing buyer and a willing seller in an arm's-length transaction after proper marketing wherein the parties had each acted knowledgeably, prudently and without compulsion.'

Conceptual Framework, as published in International Valuation Standard 1.

The Red Book explains at length that all valuations for a certain purpose are produced using common assumptions and are thus not widely at variance with other valuations.

If this is the technical rule that a valuer follows when preparing a valuation, what influences the value of the actual property holding?

Most people have heard the old adage, 'What are the three most important factors in determining the value of property? Location, Location and Location.' This is, of course, essentially true but the detail of what makes up the value of a property is more complex.

With business premises, usually two components or types of value are involved: rental value and investment, or capital value.

Rental value is essentially determined by how useful the premises are to the tenant. How good is the property for the tenant's business? What else is on the market? At what point or at what level of rent would the tenant choose to take an alternative set of premises? The answers to these questions depend, of course, on the nature of the tenant's business and the nature of the property.

At a less fundamental level, rent (or in actual fact, the usefulness of the property to the business) is determined by a combination of the physical make-up of the building, its size, location, quality, etc., and the nature of the legal contract under which it is occupied. These issues are covered briefly below.

Rent provides the income from property. The capital value of income-producing properties is determined by finding the current value of the future expected income to be earned (or potentially earned in the case of an owner occupied property). This is done by applying a discount factor to the future expected flows of income. This discount factor is referred to as a yield in property and is a reflection of investors' desired return for that type of investment, given its relative risk, quality and growth potential compared with other investments in the market. This may sound complex but, in practice, both the choice of yield and the mechanics of valuation are relatively simple.

For a start, there is generally no need to try to forecast explicitly the future cash flows from the property if it is a freehold. Freeholds are perpetual interests so therefore it is assumed that the ability to earn income from the property will also continue perpetually. The effect of this is to make the valuation formula for freeholds:

INCOME × 1/i

where i is the required yield. The formula 1/i is the mathematical formula for the present value of a perpetual income. For example, if a property produced a rent of £10,000 p.a. and this represented the current market rent for this type of property, and investors were seeking a return of 9 per cent, the value of this investment would be:

£10,000 × 1/9%
= £10,000 × 11.111
= £111,111

Where does this yield come from? Essentially, it comes from the market. Valuers look at the yields achieved on similar transactions and apply them to the subject, with alterations for any differences between the property being valued and that on which the transaction took place.

One point to note is that as the yield comes down the value goes up. This may seem illogical but it is not. Investors accepting lower income yields are paying more for a higher quality investment, either in terms of the quality of the existing income flow or in terms of higher growth potential, or usually both.

This is fundamentally how values of market-rented freehold income-producing properties are arrived at. The situation does become more complex where the property is let below or above the current market rent (with UK lease structures this can frequently happen) and with leasehold properties. Both these situations are really beyond the scope of this section but, in short, are valued using adaptations of the above model to reflect the uneven income flows of the former and the terminable nature of the latter.

Rental value

Rental value is the price per unit of lettable floor area that an occupational tenant will pay per annum as part of the lease contract. In most countries this is market-determined by the interaction of the forces of supply and demand for the specification of the floor space available.

Information on rental values for the type of floor space developed may come from a variety of sources. In some countries there is a statutory requirement to report property transactions and this information is available in the public domain. This does not occur in the UK, although technically the information is available, at a cost, through the Land Registry. The prime source of information on property transactions, and thus rental values, is through the market makers, the commercial agents. The one way to ensure that a reliable estimate of rental value is made is to employ the services of one of these agents either by way of a formal valuation or, more likely, by bringing the agent into the project as the letting agent.

Rental value varies markedly from one location to another and from one property type to another. For example, within Manchester, current retail rents are around £3,000/m² p.a. in the best areas, while the best office rent is at around £300/m² and the best industrial rents around £75–80/m². The rental values are location- and specification-specific: a shop located outside the prime shopping street, perhaps only 100 metres from the highest value shop, may attract a rent of less than one-tenth of its more favourably located competitor. A 30-year-old office in the prime office core of Manchester may attract a rent of perhaps half that of a modern building located nearby. This is simply an effect of image and user flexibility, which is so important to current office occupiers. Other factors that may influence rental value include the terms under which the property is leased, including the lease clauses themselves, and the length of the lease. Maintenance costs are a good example of such a factor: UK leases are usually on what is called full repairing and insuring (FRI) terms. This means that tenants are responsible for maintaining all aspects of the building, including its structure and fabric, throughout their tenure. The rent received by the building owner is therefore not open to any deductions to spend on building maintenance. If the building is maintained by the landlord, the rent will have to be higher than an equivalent building on FRI terms to allow for these costs.

The value factors that influence the main property types have been considered in Chapter 1.

In our case study a rental value of £235/m² per annum seems appropriate, given the specification of the building, its location and current market conditions. The building is assumed to have a net to gross floor area ratio of 80 per cent, which is conservative for a modern building.

Rental value ascribed to car parking

Other elements of a commercial building may provide income and thus value to the property. These include advertising hoardings, aerial sites, 'naming rights' (the ability of the lead tenant to attach their name to the building, e.g. 'BigCo Tower') and car parking among others. In this case the only additional item with this particular development is car parking.

Car parking does not always yield income; indeed, if the current trend of attitudes as regards car use continues it may be that car spaces will be heavily taxed and, thus, become a liability. A rent can only be charged when tenants are willing to pay for it. This is usually in cases where parking is in short supply, such as in city centres. Parking is not usually rented out separately in business park type locations; here tenants expect the provision of parking spaces as a reason for selecting such a location and do not expect to pay an additional rent.

Investment yield

As we have seen, the investment yield is important in determining the present value of the income flow that an income-producing property generates. The yield is determined by market forces representing the requirements of investors in terms of return for this class of property. This in itself is a very complex issue; a number of factors intertwine to determine it. These include the following.

> *The rate of return on other investments.* For major investors these include all potential alternative investments including the rate of return on cash deposits, government loan stocks of differing length of term, home and overseas equities, etc. These in themselves are determined by the spectrum of interest rates in the economy as a whole, including the bank base rate.

> *The cost of finance.* For smaller investors who finance a purchase partly with loaned money, it is often the lending rate that will determine the minimum yield that an investor can pay. For example, if a property is being purchased for £1 million, a bank or other financial institution would lend around 70 per cent of that sum, i.e. around £700,000. If the money is loaned at 10 per cent this means that the property must produce at least £70,000 (i.e. a yield of 7 per cent) to just cover the interest payments on an interest-only loan.

> *The risk characteristics of the investment.* Factors that affect the risk of the property (i.e. the danger of an interruption of the income flow or a significant fall in value of the property over time) include the location of the property, the property type and specification, the lease terms and the lease length, and the quality of the tenant who occupies the space. To illustrate what this means, consider the relative merits of the investments in Table 4.2. From the table, clearly the investment with the lowest risk of default is Investment A. Any investor buying Investment B would need to be compensated for the extra risk by paying less for the investment and receiving a higher annual return. In today's market, Investment A might command a yield of 5–6 per cent, dependent on the type of city in which it is located, while Investment B would see an investment yield in the range of 9 to approximately 12 per cent.

> *Growth potential.* Investments that have the greatest potential for growth in value also attract the lowest yields. The argument is that investors seeking growth are willing to accept lower returns in the short term in exchange for this growth which will, if realised, give them a higher overall return. For example, a shop investment bought for a yield of 5 per cent might expect to see annual growth rates of 10 per cent per annum over the long term, giving a total return of 15 per cent. A shop bought for a yield of 9 per cent might see growth at 3 per cent per annum, giving a total return of 12 per cent.

> *Supply of the type of investment in the market-place.* Investor sentiment and requirements can be very influential. Sometimes a particular type of investment is

TABLE 4.2 Relative merits of two investments

	Investment A	Investment B
Tenant	Boots PLC	Local chemist
Type of location	Large city centre	Small market town
Lease length	25 years	5 years
Type of property	Modern shop unit in modern shopping centre development	Traditional shop unit in parade of local shops

in short supply but is one that investors have targeted because of its longer term potential. This happened in the early 1990s with retail warehousing, where yields were driven down by the weight of competition between investors for an asset class that was felt to have huge growth potential but likely to have a restricted future supply because of changing government planning policy.

The result of the interactions of these factors is reflected in what investors pay for property investments in the market-place. These transaction prices are the best place to determine property yields. For example, if an office property has been sold for £10,000,000 and produces a rental income of £840,000, then it is relatively easy to calculate the investment yield the investor receives:

Purchase price	£10,000,000
Add: purchaser's acquisition costs	
(stamp duty, legal fees and surveyor's fees)	£500,000
Total sum expended	£10,500,000

$$\frac{\text{Rental income } £840,000}{\text{Sum expended } £10,500,000} = 0.08 \text{ or } \underline{8\%}$$

This yield can then be applied to the valuation of similar offices in the vicinity, with appropriate adjustments where required for differences such as in the specification and quality of the location.

It should be noted that this analysis becomes more complex when the rental value of the property being valued has not been set recently. Property markets have a degree of volatility, rental values can move up and down. Commercial property leases only allow for periodic adjustment of rent, usually every five years (although this period is sometimes shorter). Rents actually being paid under the lease contract on properties can frequently not be representative of what the property would let for if vacant and available for letting on the open market. Investors factor this into their decisions about what to pay for investments. For example, if the office example given above had been let three years prior to the sale and rental values had risen since letting, investors would probably accept a lower initial income return in return for the expected rise of rents at the rent review in two years. Let us assume that the rental value of the property has risen to £1,000,000 per annum.

Purchase price	£11,750,000
Add: purchaser's acquisition costs	
(stamp duty, legal fees and surveyor's fees)	£587,500
Total sum expended	£12,337,500

$$\frac{\text{Rental income } £840,000}{\text{Sum expended } £12,337,500} = 0.068 \text{ or } \underline{6.8\%}$$

The growth potential is reflected in the greater price paid for the investment (£11,750,000 is based on a valuation of the long-term income stream based on the 8 per cent yield suggested in the first analysis). The figure of 6.8 per cent is not a good indication of what newly let properties would exchange for in the open market but what this type of growth investment – called a reversionary investment – is producing for investors. This example is used as a cautionary indicator to the unwary as to how they can be misled by market evidence. When appraising a new income-producing investment it is important, where possible, that the evidence should be derived from similar, newly developed and newly let properties.

In our example, market evidence suggests that a 6.5 per cent yield is appropriate for this type of investment.

Rental incentive

Strictly speaking, this item should be included in the development costs section. It is, however, an item that is directly related to the negotiations connected with the leasing of the completed buildings and thus with the income flow, so there is some argument that it should be grouped with these items.

A rental incentive is a concession given to a tenant as an inducement to sign a lease on the property. Some sort of incentive has always been given to a tenant, although historically this amounted only to a few rent-free months granted to allow the tenant time to fit out the premises before occupation. In the market of the early 1990s, where supply of space greatly exceeded demand, the size and value of incentives grew enormously as developers fell over themselves to attract the few tenants that were available to the empty developments. These incentives included long rent-free periods, cash contributions, free fitting out and rental caps. In the more 'normal' market conditions that have followed this period, incentives did not completely disappear.

The question might be asked as to why developers gave incentives rather than lowering the rent. There are, in fact, many reasons, although three predominate. First, property owners are keen to protect the values of existing properties they own: lowering rents in new developments would have provided evidence of lower rents that could have been used in rent review negotiations. Second, lowering rents damages the long-term cash flows and, therefore, values of developments. The argument was that once, say, the two-year rent-free period on a development had expired, the high rent would kick in and the property would be valued according to that high-income stream. If a lower rent had been granted, it would have affected the property over at least the first 5 years of the rental cycle and possibly longer. Finally, tenants tended to prefer the incentives offered as they give them short-term relief from cash flow problems suffered during the economic downturn.

Rental incentives actually created huge problems for the property market, particularly for valuers and investors. The first two arguments used may also be seen as being both over-simplistic and inaccurate. Whatever the case, incentives are still a feature of many markets. Here, a 12-month rent-free period has been granted. This is counted as a cash deduction from the receipts. It may be necessary to make a deduction from the value of the completed property as an alternative to this approach. Deducting cash rent-free and adjusting the valuation would be double counting.

Interest

The final assumption that must be made in the appraisal is to do with the finance charges connected to the development.

Most developers borrow money in some way to carry out a development. This money will have a cost, i.e. an interest rate. However, even where developers are using internal sources of funds to carry out a scheme, the cost of money should still be allowed for. This is because all funds have an 'opportunity cost', money expended on a development scheme is money that could have been used elsewhere to gain return. The opportunity cost is the highest return that has been given up by not investing in alternative investment mediums. Some large firms using their own funds to carry out developments use their own internally assumed interest rate which is often quite low. Although this is legitimate in accounting terms there is a strong argument that the interest rate used should be one that reflects the rate that would apply to a project with a similar risk profile to the development scheme, i.e. that the rate should be that which the firm would require if loaning it to another developer to carry out a similar scheme.

This philosophical argument about interest rates can be set aside in the majority of cases where money is borrowed. Interest rates are set competitively by lenders. The rate set will depend on factors such as the track record of the developer, the risk characteristics of the scheme and, of course, the general tone of interest rates in the market-place. Bank base rates (which varied between 4 and 8 per cent between 1997 and 2002 and then stepped up to 5 per cent by the end of 2006 (Figure 4.3)) form the basis of the lender's calculation.

In a strong letting market, with a developer with a good track record of completing developments and where there are at least some tenants in place, and where the bank has the development (including the land), as security in case of default, the

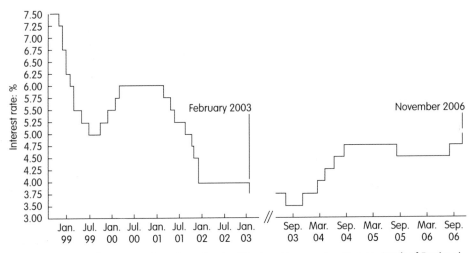

FIGURE 4.3 Historical interest rate pattern: Bank of England base rates. Source: Bank of England: www.bankofengland.co.uk

interest rate will be 2 to 4 per cent above base. This may rise considerably if any of these characteristics are weakened.

Financing developments is covered in Chapter 3 but some factors should be noted. First, there may be more than one loan in place, at different rates of interest. For example, the land may have been purchased at a lower rate of interest than the funds used to pay for the actual development costs themselves. Similarly, developers sometimes find that they have a funding shortfall and need to acquire additional sources of finance, or mezzanine finance. This is usually available at much higher costs of interest. Finally, banks are more frequently seeking to secure their money by requiring the developer to pay for the bank's own professionals to be in place as additional overseers of the development progress.

In our case study we are considering a simple loan to a developer with a reasonable track record and a moderate level of assessed risk. At the time of writing this would equate to an interest rate of between 6.5 and 7.5 per cent. *For ease of demonstration of the calculation and to produce appraisals in line with previous editions of this book, an interest rate of 10 per cent will be used.*

This completes the assumptions required to carry out the appraisal. The next section lays out a simple residual approach to the calculation of land value, then shows how each of the components is derived.

Worked example: traditional residual approach – land value

Development project
Contemporary Property Development Edition 2

Appraisal summary for Part 1 Commercial

REVENUE

Rental area summary	m²	Rate m²	Gross ERV		
Office	4,000.00	£235.00	940,000		
Car parking	15.00	£2,500.00	37,500		
Totals	4,015.00		977,500		

Investment valuation					
Office					
Market rent	940,000	YP @	7.0000%	14.2857	
(6 months rent free)		PV 6mths @	7.0000%	0.9667	
Car parking					
Market rent	37,500	YP @	7.0000%	14.2857	
(6 months rent free)		PV 6mths @	7.0000%	0.9667	
GROSS DEVELOPMENT VALUE					13,499,785
Purchaser's costs		5.75%	(776,238)		
NET DEVELOPMENT VALUE					12,723,547
NET REALISATION					**12,723,547**

advisors (solicitors and surveyors). This is in order to get their stated return on the money they expend. In this case, to get a 7 per cent return with their acquisition costs assumed to be 5.75 per cent, they need to pay the sum of £12.724 million.

THE NEXT STEP: CALCULATING THE DEVELOPMENT COSTS

From the sum calculated for the realisation, the development costs need to be deducted. This becomes an accounting exercise, ticking off the value of each. Some of these costs are relatively straightforward to calculate, others less so. The traditional residual model also incorporates peculiarities in the calculation of certain elements, particularly finance charges. These peculiarities are essentially short cuts or simplifications in calculation, dating from less technically advanced times when calculation aids available to the appraiser were primitive. There is very little justification for the continued use of these short cuts in the development appraisal model, other than that of familiarity, as they do not accurately calculate elements of the appraisal but give generally reasonable approximations of the true values. Most proprietary development appraisal software on the market gives the option of calculating these elements more accurately.

Construction costs

Construction costs are one of the simpler elements to calculate. The basic principles have already been discussed in the assumptions section (page 175). A lump sum has been calculated for demolition works and site preparation. The cost of the new build element has been calculated by applying an overall cost per square metre to the gross area of the building.

Finance on construction and demolition

While the construction cost element is a straightforward calculation, the calculation of finance charges on this element is rather less so. This represents the main area of simplification in calculation in the traditional residual model.

It should be noted that in the simplest of residual calculations interest charges on a development may be calculated as a single, gross element rather than being calculated on a number of individual elements. Here the interest calculation element has been divided into three: construction cost, professional fees and on the void period. Each element has different cost/time profiles and this separation allows a more accurate assessment of interest charges to be made.

Another point to be noted is that this calculation of interest charges should always be made, even when internal and not borrowed funds are used, in order that the true costs of development are assessed. Where borrowed money is used in the development the cost is reflected in the interest charged by the lender. Even when internal sources of finance are used, this money has a cost, known as an opportunity cost. The money spent on the development could have been used elsewhere in order to obtain a return. The logic of this has been discussed above, but it is worth underlining at this point. There is no such thing as 'free' money. Some appraisals see own funds and borrowed funds dealt with separately, often at different rates. This is acceptable; however, the author would stress the point that all money used in development has the same opportunity cost and should be valued at the same rate. For simplicity, in this and in the majority of other appraisals, it is best to assume that all money used is borrowed.

When money is borrowed for a development scheme it is normally executed by arranging a loan facility which is then drawn down in tranches as the project proceeds and expenditure is made. It is only when the money is drawn down that the interest accrues.

In the construction phase, with traditional methods of procurement, the building contractor is paid in stages, usually on a monthly basis. The contractor carries out a valuation as to the value of works completed each month which the client pays, normally after agreeing the sum using their own professional team to certify that the work has been carried out. The amount expended each month accumulates to the final contract sum, plus or minus any variations in work that have been agreed during the course of the work. This process means that the construction cost is only finally expended at the end of the contract and the average balance drawn down from the loan facility is typically rather less than the total. If finance were calculated at our rate of 10 per cent on the entire balance, then there would be a gross over-calculation of the amount of interest accruing.

This is where an allowance needs to be made and where the residual model's simplifying assumption is normally made. The traditional pattern of expenditure on a construction project follows an s-shaped curve (see Figure 4.4).

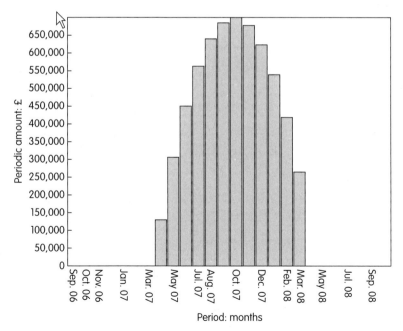

FIGURE 4.4 The s-curve

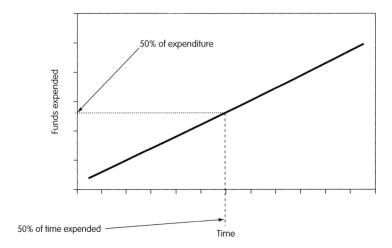

FIGURE 4.5 Simplifying assumption on balance owed

This shape reflects the fact that expenditure on site tends to be low at first. The initial work, ground preparation, excavation, foundations, etc. tend to be low-value/low-speed functions. The rate of expenditure increases greatly as the expensive high-value components (frames, walls, etc.) are installed. Towards the end of the construction period the pace falls off again as finishing trades become involved. This work tends to be slow and often only one trade at a time can work (e.g. electricians must finish before plasterers can complete the walls, which then have to dry before the decorating can start).

The normal assumption made in a *simple* residual appraisal is to simulate this process, albeit in a much simplified way in the traditional models. The normal assumption is that the average balance drawn down will equate to 50 per cent of the time period when 50 per cent of the expenditure has been made (see Figure 4.5).

The calculation thus assumes that 50 per cent of the money has been drawn down on average over the construction period. In our example this would be £4,732,500 + £473,250 + £100,000 + £236.625^7/2 = £2,771,187.50. Using the interest rate of 10 per cent p.a. this would equate to an interest charge of £277,118.75 for the construction period funding.

An alternative approach is to do the calculation based on the full cost of construction but for only 50 per cent of the elapsed time (i.e. £5,542,375 × [(1.10$^{0.5}$) − 1]). This produces exactly the same answer, although strictly speaking the logic behind taking this approach is rather suspect.

This assumption about 50 per cent of the expenditure is the biggest single source of inaccuracy in the traditional appraisal model. Ways of improving this problem are explored below, but it should be noted that the calculation in the appraisal reproduced above assumed level monthly expenditure and produced a finance cost of £271,364.

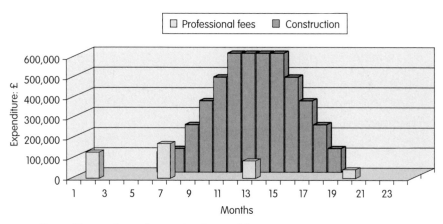

FIGURE 4.6 Expenditure patterns for construction and fees

Professional fees: construction

The derivation of the professional fees was discussed above. The calculation is simple as it is calculated normally as a percentage of construction costs.

Finance on professional fees

The calculation of the finance charges on professional fees is similar to that of the calculation of the charges on construction expenditure (as has been done above). The majority of development appraisals carried out at the early stage of development tend to see these two elements of finance calculated together. It is preferable to separate the calculation in most cases as the expenditure profile and thus the calculation of interest tends to be different between the two. The difference in the final appraisal is marginal as fees tend to be a relatively small proportion of expenditure but the sums involved can be significant.

The differences can be seen from Figure 4.6. Construction professionals receive payment earlier than the contractor, indeed the bulk of professional fees may be paid before construction work has advanced very far.

This should be reflected in the finance charge calculation.

Finance on void period

The third element of finance included in the calculation is the void period.[8] This is the period from the end of construction (or practical completion) to the point where the development becomes a saleable investment (usually when the building is fully let in the UK). It is virtually impossible to find a buyer for an empty investment building except at 'fire sale'[9] prices. One that is partly let may be saleable but at a sizeable discount to the full value. The sum obtainable is usually not sufficient to cover development costs so this is usually a last resort for a desperate developer intent on a damage limitation or time-buying exercise. As a result of this, most developer

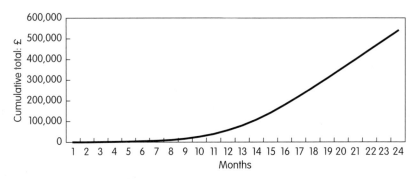

FIGURE 4.7 Cumulative interest charges

traders tend to hold buildings until fully let and this must be accounted for in the calculation.

Similarly, an allowance for a void period should be included not just where a sale is involved. The letting up process reflects the transition of the building from development to mature standing investment, often from short-term debt finance secured on the site to longer term mortgage finance secured on the building.

The void period on a speculative development is absolutely critical to the success or failure of the scheme. Finance charges quickly accumulate in this period because they are calculated on the full development costs. The effect of this can be seen from Figure 4.7. Interest charges accumulate on the development from day one, greatly increasing when construction starts. However, around half of the interest charge on our development takes place after month 18, i.e. when construction has been completed. The effect of compound interest is to give an exponential shape to the curve.

Unless some of the principal debt can be paid off – which is unlikely – this phase has a critical effect on most developers, as this is where the greatest concentration exists on risk mitigation in development (see page 307). The longer this void period exists, the greater the interest charge will be.

In an appraisal, the void period is the safety net and a financier will need to ascertain whether a sufficient allowance has been made.

Professional fees: letting and sale

The costs we have dealt with to date have in common the feature that they are assumed to occur at various times up to the end of the letting up period, and are therefore time-critical. The timing and extent of expenditure on these items affects the calculation of the cost of finance. The remaining items in the basic residual model usually take place at the end of the development period and thus have no effect on the interest calculation.

This deserves a note of explanation. The traditional residual is an accumulative exercise. For the most part it works forward, accumulating all the costs together,

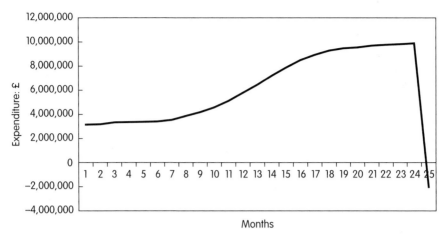

FIGURE 4.8 Pattern of expenditure over development period (negative figures represent receipts)

particularly the accumulated interest charges. This is represented in Figure 4.8. The items that occur at the end of the period have no additional effect on the interest accumulated.

These are items such as marketing, letting and disposal fees and the developer's profit. These items are usually paid at the end of the development or may even occur after the sale of the building.

Marketing

One of the exceptions to this is marketing, although the same basic assumption is made. In fact, common sense tells us that the marketing budget will tend to be expended earlier and indeed will need to be to have any effect. In both residential and commercial schemes it is not uncommon for advertising to take place before construction has commenced. Despite this, it is usually felt that it is not worth taking this early payment into account in a simple residual appraisal as the sums involved are relatively small when compared with the development budget as a whole and, consequently, the impact on the appraisal of this inaccurate assumption is negligible.

Developer's profit

Developer's profit is also, effectively, a final stage payment. It is the hoped-for surplus after the sale and when all the costs have been accounted for. Normally this is taken as a percentage of development cost or development value.

RESIDUAL IN 24 MONTHS' TIME

Once all of the development expenditure has been accounted for, the total sums expended can be calculated and then deducted from the net realisation. In our example we have the following values:

NET REALISATION		£12,723,547
TOTAL COSTS	£10,602,955	
Less		
TOTAL LAND COST	£3,163,606	£12,723,547
INTEREST	£474,035	
Sub-total	£6,965,314	
Add		
PROFIT	£2,120,592	
ADJUSTED COSTS		£9,085,906
RESIDUAL SUM		£3,637,641

This is the sum that we will have as a surplus in 24 months' time, if all our assumptions come to accurately represent the final course of the development.

This is not what we should pay for the land, however. It is the surplus that will be available at the end of the development period. It includes an allowance for holding the land over the two years of the development period and, particularly, an allowance for the cost of finance over this period. To calculate the sum we should actually pay for the land we need to make an adjustment to allow for this finance cost. This is covered in the next section.

SUM AVAILABLE TO BUY LAND TODAY

What we are seeking is the sum to be paid to the landowner to purchase the interest in the land at the beginning of the development.[10] This sum, L, will attract acquisition costs to the purchaser, i.e. stamp duty, solicitor's costs and surveyor's fees. The land will then need to be held for two years. We need to be able to calculate backwards to solve L.

A diagram may help in the understanding of what has just been done (Figure 4.9). The appraisal prior to the end adjustment has calculated the surplus money at the end of the scheme which will cover purchasing the land, the cost of paying solicitors' fees, stamp duty and any agents' fees, and then the cost of finance for holding the land over 24 months.

The residual at 24 months is a sum that will cover the land purchase, the acquisition costs and the finance charges over the period. The following equation solves the unknown, the land price:

If land is bought for £3,486,458, acquisition costs of 5% will be added making a total cost of £3,660,781	+	Interest charges at 10% per annum compounded over the 2 years. This equates to £768,764	=	Land price £3,486,458 Plus Acquisition costs £173,423 Plus Finance charge £768,764 Equals £4,429,545

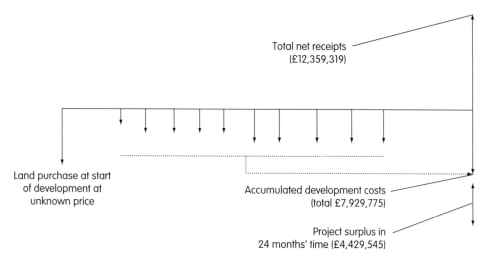

FIGURE 4.9 Scheme to accumulate funds for land purchase

TRADITIONAL RESIDUAL APPROACH: ASSESSING THE PROFITABILITY OF DEVELOPMENT

Contemporary Property Development Edition 2

Appraisal Summary for Part 1 Commercial

REVENUE

Rental area summary	m²	Rate m²	Gross ERV	
Office	4,000.00	£235.00	940,000	

Investment valuation				
Office				
Market rent	940,000	YP @	7.0000%	14.2857
(6 months rent free)		PV 6mths @	7.0000%	0.9667

GROSS DEVELOPMENT VALUE				12,981,890
Purchaser's costs		5.75%	(746,459)	
NET DEVELOPMENT VALUE				12,235,431

NET REALISATION				**12,235,431**

OUTLAY
ACQUISITION COSTS

Fixed price			3,150,000	
Stamp duty		4.00%	126,000	
Town planning			25,000	
Survey			10,000	
				3,311,000

CONSTRUCTION COSTS

Construction	m²	Rate m²	Cost	
Office	5,000.00	£946.50	4,732,500	4,732,500
Contingency		5.00%	236,625	
				236,625

PROFESSIONAL FEES

Architect	4.00%	189,300
Quantity surveyor	2.00%	94,650
Structural engineer	1.50%	70,988
Mech./elec. engineer	1.00%	47,325
Project manager	1.00%	47,325
C.D. manager	0.50%	23,662
		473,250

MARKETING AND LETTING

Marketing	135,000
Letting agent fee	94,000
Letting legal fee	47,000
	276,000

DISPOSAL FEES

Sales agent fee	1.50%	183,531
Sales legal fee	2.00%	244,709
		428,240

FINANCE

Timescale	Duration	Commences
Planning	6	Oct. 2006
Construction	12	Apr. 2007
Leasing	6	Apr. 2008
Total duration	**24**	

Finance

Land	289,882
Construction	146,718
Letting void	282,577
Total finance cost	719,177

TOTAL COSTS   **10,176,793**

PROFIT   **2,058,639**

The basic approach used in the calculation of land bid can be applied to the calculation of the potential profitability of the development. As noted in the introduction to this chapter, this is the second most common reason for carrying out a development appraisal.

The full appraisal is shown on the previous pages. The casual observer would find it difficult to distinguish between this and the earlier appraisal. Indeed, the appraisals only differ towards the end, which is logical as we are making the same basic assumptions about the same property development project. All we are seeking is the answer to a different question: What profit, or loss, will the development show?

To be able to calculate profitability we will need an additional piece of information – the price of the land. In this case we will assume that the land is to cost £3.15 million, roughly what we calculated in the original land appraisal.

The land and associated costs are added to the other development costs and summed as before to calculate the total development costs.

The residual, after the costs are subtracted from the net realisation are the profits (or losses if this figure is negative).

There is some argument as to how this sum should be treated. Strictly, these are the profits receivable at the end of the development period, i.e. at least 24 months in the future. There is an argument for discounting these profit figures back to the present using the finance rate as a discount rate. This is illustrated in the appraisal. Many developers prefer to use the raw profit figures and, as the section below illustrates, this produces figures that are in line with those produced by DCF calculations.

The profit figures can be presented in a number of ways. Some of these are presented below.

While the raw sum of money that the project returns is important, it is often essential to present the figure as a percentage of costs expended, or of value or in terms of the income return. This is done to ensure that the return is sufficient to justify the development. Property development is risky; anyone embarking on it should ensure that they are sufficiently rewarded for taking this risk. If an investor could get a return of say, 10 per cent from investing in, for example, an industrial building let to a 'blue chip' manufacturer, they should seek at least 15 per cent and probably 20 per cent to invest in a development project to produce a new industrial building of the same specification. Why? Consider the risks inherent in each option. There is risk with the existing investment, property values may decline, although they do tend to recover, and the tenant may go out of business. However, even in this case the building is still there, it can be re-let in time. The risk inherent is much, much lower than with a development where even a minor change in market conditions can cause a loss to be made, as we will see below. In order to assess whether the return is adequate then it is normal to see if certain benchmark figures are met. The most common figure is 20 per cent of costs, but this does vary from sector to sector (for example, development of houses in the UK does seem to work to lower profit figures).

Five of the alternative measures used to measure profitability are given below. Other measures exist. The calculation method for each is as follows:

$$\text{Profit on cost (D)} = \frac{\text{Residual profit figure (discounted)}}{\text{All development costs}}$$

$$\text{Profit on value (D)} = \frac{\text{Residual profit figure (discounted)}}{\text{Net realisation}}$$

$$\text{Profit on cost} = \frac{\text{Residual profit figure}}{\text{All development costs}}$$

$$\text{Profit on net development value (D)} = \frac{\text{Residual profit figure}}{\text{Net realisation}}$$

$$\text{Profit on gross development value (D)} = \frac{\text{Residual profit figure}}{\text{Gross sales receipt}}$$

The above measures are simple expressions of profit as a percentage of something. Sometimes developers and lenders wish to know how much time is available to let the building after completion. Two measures are often used, rent cover and interest cover. The formulas for their calculation are given below. Both of these are essentially benchmark measures, e.g. a lender may seek at least 2 years' rent cover as an indicator that the developer has plenty of surplus funds to cover outgoings before a risk of failure occurs. In fact, neither calculation accurately predicts the duration of their respective period due to the compounding nature of the interest rate appreciation on the debt.

$$\text{Rent cover} = \frac{\text{Residual profit figure}}{\text{Annual rental value}}$$

$$\text{Profit erosion} = \frac{\text{Residual profit figure}}{\text{Initial monthly interest payments}}$$

FLAWS IN THE TRADITIONAL MODEL

The traditional model does, in fact, have a considerable number of 'real' flaws. Some of these have already been mentioned. They can be classified into two different classes of flaw, those that are inherent in all development appraisal and those that are peculiar to the traditional model alone.

The inherent flaws are connected with the extreme sensitivity of all development appraisal models to the value of the assumptions made in their construction. Even some very small changes in the values of some of the key variables can make enormous differences to the outcome being calculated, whether this be land value or profitability. These flaws exist whatever you do, but can be accounted for in the sensitivity analysis, which is covered below.

The flaws in the traditional models are related to the simplifications included in order to make calculation easier. To be fair to the proprietary software available, most calculate the variable values in a sophisticated way but present them in the familiar appraisal model, so these criticisms are largely negated. However, anyone carrying out development appraisals needs to be aware of the problems that exist and this is particularly true where the appraiser calculates the appraisal manually or by their own spreadsheets.

The main problem with the residual models relates to the timing and extent of cash flows. These factors in turn affect the calculation of interest or finance. Let us look at the assumptions made in relation to construction expenditure. We assumed that the average balance owing was 50 per cent of the total budget and this was the figure used in the interest rate calculation. This equated to a total interest rate calculation of £236,625 based on the 10 per cent effective rate.

Let us now carry out the calculation making alternative assumptions as to how the money is expended in the construction period. We can assume that the same amount of money is expended each month. This is not, in fact, a realistic assumption

TABLE 4.3 Straight line expenditure assumption

Month 0	Expenditure per month	Interest 10%	Balance owed
1	£394,375	–	£394,375.00
2	£394,375	£3,144.80	£791,894.80
3	£394,375	£6,314.68	£1,192,584.48
4	£394,375	£9,509.84	£1,596,469.32
5	£394,375	£12,730.47	£2,003,574.79
6	£394,375	£15,976.79	£2,413,926.58
7	£394,375	£19,248.99	£2,827,550.56
8	£394,375	£22,547.29	£3,244,472.85
9	£394,375	£25,871.88	£3,664,719.73
10	£394,375	£29,222.99	£4,088,317.72
11	£394,375	£32,600.82	£4,515,293.54
12	£394,375	£36,005.58	£4,945,674.13
Total	£4,732,500	£213,174.00	

in terms of how monies are actually expended during a development. However, this approach tends to produce a more accurate estimate of interest accrual than the rather crude traditional model (Table 4.3, Figure 4.10).

Another approach is to assume a more realistic model of development expenditure, i.e. one following an s-shaped curve (Table 4.4). Expenditure in the early months of a construction project tends to be slow as site preparation and lower value ground works are completed. In the middle period expenditure tends to speed up as working conditions ease and higher value elements are installed. In later months the rate of expenditure slows as finishing trades move in. Often this involves inefficient work, as one trade needs to finish (for example plastering) before another can start (painting), slowing down the pace of the scheme and reducing the level of expenditure. This can be observed in the calculation and cumulative expenditure diagram (Figure 4.11).

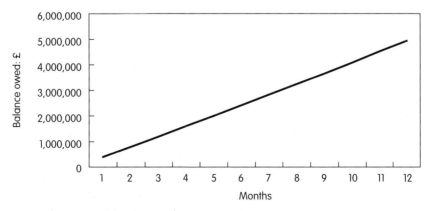

FIGURE 4.10 Balance owed: level expenditure assumption

TABLE 4.4 S-shaped expenditure curve assumption

Month 0	Percentage expenditure	Expenditure per month	Interest 10%	Balance owed
1	2.50%	£118,313	–	£118,313.00
2	5.00%	£236,625	£943.44	£355,880.94
3	7.50%	£354,938	£2,837.84	£713,656.29
4	10.00%	£473,250	£5,690.80	£1,192,597.08
5	12.50%	£591,563	£9,509.94	£1,793,669.52
6	12.50%	£591,563	£14,302.97	£2,399,534.99
7	12.50%	£591,563	£19,134.23	£3,010,231.72
8	12.50%	£591,563	£24,004.01	£3,625,798.23
9	10.00%	£473,250	£28,912.62	£4,127,960.85
10	7.50%	£354,938	£32,916.94	£4,515,815.29
11	5.00%	£236,625	£36,009.75	£4,788,450.04
12	2.50%	£118,313	£38,183.77	£4,944,946.31
Total	100.00%	£4,732,500	£212,446.00	

Summarising, we have now three different calculations for the finance charges on this section:

Calculation method	Finance calculation	Difference
50% average expenditure	£236,625	–
Straight line expenditure	£213,174	–£23,451
S-shaped curve expenditure	£212,446	–£24,179

Although these differences are relatively insignificant in the greater order of things, they are in themselves substantial sums. They may make a difference between a successful site bid and one that fails, or in achieving or not achieving a benchmark return. They also represent only one area where the assumptions about timing and extent of cash flows in the basic model lead to inaccurate estimation: any aspect of the project with timing issues is affected, including demolition, construction, professional fees, letting and sale fees and marketing.

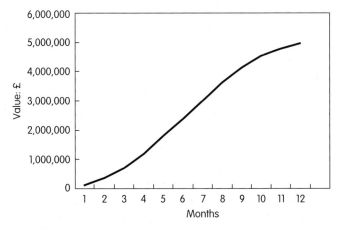

FIGURE 4.11 Typical s-shaped curve of construction projects

All of these factors suggest alternative approaches, namely cash flow based models. These will be reviewed in the next section.

Improving the breed: steps towards greater accuracy

INTRODUCTION

To improve the accuracy of the appraisal models there is a need to step away from the simplicity of the residual model.

This does not mean that the residual approach should not be used. In fact, the speed and simplicity of the model is a huge advantage in the early stages of a development, i.e. in the initial feasibility stage simply to determine whether the project should go ahead before any real details about the development are known.

There is scope for improving the calculation accuracy of the residual model, although this does add to the complexity of the model, increasing the time needed to construct it. The key improvement is to move towards more explicit assumptions, as has been done with the construction expenditure in the previous section. As noted, most of the proprietary models have seen a shift towards more explicit calculation.

These changes can be seen as move towards cash flow approaches to appraisal.

CASH FLOW APPROACHES TO DEVELOPMENT APPRAISAL

To move to a complete cash flow approach for the appraisal of a development project is a major step. It requires both more time and more information, and the appraiser must make more explicit assumptions. The resulting appraisal model is harder to interpret at first glance. These models can be difficult to alter and it is quite easy to incorporate errors. In moving from a traditional approach to a cash flow approach, it is very easy for the same appraiser to make very different assumptions about the project. Given these huge drawbacks, why use the method?

The answer is that some of these flaws are also virtues. The need to be more explicit requires the appraiser to consider the project much more carefully. The goal and major benefit is accuracy. If the assumptions made are correct then the appraisal will much more accurately reflect the actual financial outcome of the project. There are additional benefits to a cash flow approach, the main one being project financial control and monitoring when the project actually goes ahead. Each projected cash flow period can be checked against actual expenditure that can give valuable warnings of the development's progress and possible problems.

Cash flow approaches require the assumptions made to be more 'explicit'. The traditional approach is a 'lumping' approach that, as we have seen, requires a number of approximations to be made in the calculation. Cash flows require not only an estimation of the value of the individual variables but also an assessment of when the cash flows occur.

Although this addresses the weaknesses in the traditional model, using a cash flow approach also requires a much greater degree of information to exist about the development. Consequently, although cash flow appraisals can be done at the early feasibility stage, the value of doing so is questionable. The very nature of this stage is that details of the development are not finalised. The level of information available is low, likely to be sketchy, approximate and incomplete. This logically points to an approach that is quick, flexible and easy to apply and that itself relies on approximation rather than accuracy. This suggests that the traditional residual approach is best suited to application at this point. Using a cash flow approach would give the appearance of greater accuracy but the assumptions made would be based on such tenuous facts that it is unlikely that the figure produced would be as reliable as that produced by the traditional approach, which also has the benefit of being produced in a fraction of the time.

Cash flows should, therefore, only be used later in the appraisal stage when the data is more widely available and more reliable and when the scheme has started to crystallise. From this point on the benefits of greater accuracy will accrue and, later, provide the tool for managing and monitoring the development.

There are two main forms of cash flow models used in development appraisal: full discounted cash flows and what can be termed residual cash flows.

This is a distinction at which some academics and valuers would raise an eyebrow. It is true that the two approaches represent alternative ways of working the calculation to produce the same end result. In fact, the author would argue that in practical terms the two approaches are distinct, particularly in that they are generally used for different purposes by developers.

Both cash flow approaches are similar in that they require the project to be broken down into a framework based on a time structure and require that all expenditure and receipts are identified, quantified and placed within this time structure. The residual cash flow is an accumulative cash flow, rolling forward the expenditure and receipts as the development proceeds. The DCF is, by contrast, a discounting approach, in that the present-day value of each cash flow is calculated.

To explain what is meant by this we will convert our example project into a cash flow, the only exception to the original appraisal being the adoption of a land purchase price of £3 million before costs, this being a reasonable 'mid range' bid figure.

One of the first things that is required is to choose a time interval to form the framework for the cash flow. We can choose any time interval that we see fit or that is most appropriate for the project or the appraisal purpose. On very long projects this may be annual or half-yearly cash flows. However, more accuracy is gained by using shorter and shorter time periods. Theoretically, the greatest accuracy may be found by adopting daily cash flow periods but this would be very time consuming and cumbersome to produce. It would also be of doubtful benefit, considering that we are dealing with forecasts of questionable accuracy. Most developers find the best compromise between accuracy and practicality is to adopt a monthly cash flow period.

With our project we will adopt this monthly cash flow period. With a projected life of two years, this would give us 25 individual cash flows, as the project starts at time zero (usually the point when the land purchase takes place) with 24 months of the project ahead of us. The normal assumption is that expenditure is assumed to occur at the end of each period for the sake of consistency and simplicity. It is possible, however, to assume any point of expenditure or receipt, for example, at the beginning of the period. This makes the calculation slightly more difficult but not excessively so.

The next task in the construction of our cash flow is to forecast when the expenditure or receipts will be made or received. This rather blunt statement conceals what is actually a very difficult process. Some items are straightforward to forecast; for example, it is most common for the land purchase to take place at the beginning of the development, normally at time zero. If a quantity surveyor is employed and the project is well advanced then it may be possible to obtain a forecast of building cost expenditure. Other items are more difficult, requiring assumptions or forecasts to be made. An example of this is the modelling of construction expenditure against the s-shaped curve we saw previously. Using a combination of forecasts and models all items are logically placed into the time framework. This is illustrated in Table 4.5.

TABLE 4.5 Modelling of construction expenditure against the s-shaped curve

Month 0	Construction costs	Fees	Land	Marketing	Income	Expenditure per month
0			£3,150,000			£3,150,000
1						£0
2		£129,675				£129,675
3						£0
4						£0
5						£0
6	£100,000					£100,000
7	£118,313	£172,900				£291,213
8	£236,625			£33,564		£270,189
9	£354,938					£354,938
10	£473,250					£473,250
11	£591,563					£591,563
12	£591,563					£591,563
13	£591,563	£86,450				£678,013
14	£591,563					£591,563
15	£473,250			£53,702		£526,952
16	£354,938					£354,938
17	£236,625			£26,851		£263,476
18	£118,313					£118,313
19						£0
20		£43,225		£20,138		£63,363
21						£0
22					-£36,656	-£36,656
23						£0
24						£0
Total	**£4,832,500**	**£432,250**	**£3,150,000**	**£134,256**	**-£36,656**	**£8,512,350**

Table 4.5 represents a relatively simple cash flow (many 'real life' cash flows are extremely complex). This basic expenditure/receipts framework is used in both the cumulative (residual) model and the DCF models.

One of the major items that is required to complete the cash flow is the choice of an interest or discount rate, two alternative expressions of the same factor. Which is used depends on a number of things; for example whether it is a cumulative or discounting approach that has been taken. This will be outlined in the sections below.

It may be that finance rates are being used for the interest or discount rate or else that an internal target rate of return is being applied. In development projects there is a strong case for using the rate charged by lenders as the interest or discount rate. This is because the rates are market derived, being expressions of an adequate return that lenders seek given the risk and return profile of the project. It may well, however, be appropriate to use other rates. Government and public bodies, for example, that do not borrow funds often have internal rates of return or adopt a common rate for the cost of capital. Similarly, commercial organisations often adopt interest rates that reflect the overall cost of capital within the organisation for accounting purposes.

For the purposes of this exercise we will adopt the market cost of finance that lenders require for lending on the project. This is a rate of 10 per cent p.a. This equates to a rate of 0.7974 per cent per month.[11]

We will now examine each of the two main cash flow models used in practice for development appraisal.

Accumulative cash flows or residual cash flows

With the residual model the individual monthly cash flows (CFs) are found by the following formula:

CF + interest (the cost of finance) = total expenditure in the period

And to calculate the land value for profit, the following equation is used:

Total proceeds of project at time N (the end of the project) – Sum of the total expenditure (including interest) at time N = residual at time N

This can be represented as in Figures 4.12–4.14.

A number of observations can be made from Figures 4.12–4.14. First, the accumulative nature of the process can be seen; second, it can be observed that the surplus occurs in the future and must therefore be discounted back to the present day in order to produce a similar result to the traditional residual approach.[12]

The cumulative calculation in the residual cash flow sees each period being calculated separately. The full residual cash flow is illustrated later but in the meantime, the individual calculation needs to be explained. We will take the basic cash flow framework as illustrated above and step through the first few months to

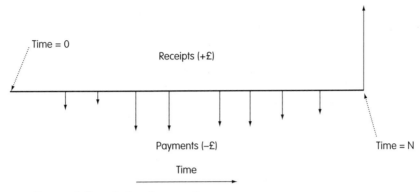

FIGURE 4.12 Raw cash flows in time framework

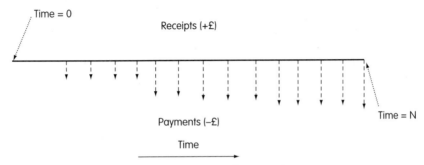

FIGURE 4.13 Cumulative interest (not to scale) in time framework

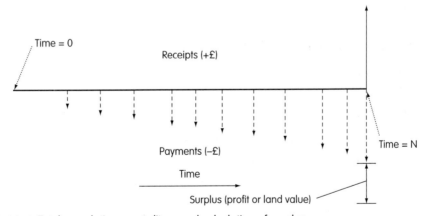

FIGURE 4.14 Total cumulative expenditure and calculation of surplus

illustrate the calculation process:

Month	Expenditure (receipts) during period	Interest @ 0.79741% per month	Total balance owed
0	£3,150,000	–	£3,150,000

At the end of the first period in the cash flow there is no interest accrued. This is because the expenditure is assumed to have taken place at the end of the period, so no time has elapsed following the finance draw-down (note that this draw-down may be from the lender or from the internal funds of the developer. As we have noted, all finance has a time value whether it is borrowed or not and thus, to be evaluated properly, requires the time value of money to be calculated).

By the end of the following month, however, interest charges on the amount owing become due. In our example there is no additional expenditure during the first month of the project so the change in the balance owed is merely due to the interest charge in the period, which is rolled up and added to the total amount owed:

Month	Expenditure (receipts) during period	Interest @ 0.79741% per month	Total balance owed
1	£0	£25,118.54	£3,175,118.54

The balance owed at the end of this month is thus the £3.15 million for the land plus £25,118.54 interest charge, giving £3,175,118.54 in total.

Interest again accrues on this sum over the next month, during which further expenditure takes place, in our case the payment of professional fees. Again, these are assumed to occur at the end of the month, the interest only being charged on the balance outstanding from the end of the previous period:

Month	Expenditure (receipts) during period	Interest @ 0.79741% per month	Total balance owed
2	£129,675	£25,318.84	£3,330,112.38

The new balance is made up of £3,175,118.54 (the old balance) + £129,675 (the spend during the month) + £25,318.84 (the interest for one month on £3,175,118.54). This accumulative process then continues until the end of the development. Although these calculations seem cumbersome they are, in fact, very easy to set up on a spreadsheet.

The results of the total calculation are illustrated in Table 4.6.

It is possible to calculate the value of the whole project using the cash flow, incorporating all the expenditure and receipt items into the time framework. An alternative is to do what is illustrated in the cash flow and the final calculation, which is to use the cash flow for the time-sensitive elements of the project but to use the output of the cash flow as an input into a traditional residual framework. Many proprietary development appraisal software packages use this approach, running the cash flow in the background but expressing the results in a traditional way. This has the advantage of easing the interpretation of the results and is illustrated in Table 4.7.

The residual cash flow solves many of the problems that exist with the model. It also has distinct advantages for development management in that the exact sum owing on the development is predicted for all stages of the project. This is helpful for both financial planning and for progress monitoring, the latter by comparing actual expenditure with that predicted in the cash flow.

TABLE 4.6 Results of the total calculation

Month 0	Construction costs	Fees	Land	Marketing	Income	Expenditure per month	Interest 0.7974% per month	Balance owed
0			£3,150,000			£3,150,000	–	£3,150,000.00
1						£0	£25,118.54	£3,175,118.54
2		£129,675				£129,675	£25,318.84	£3,330,112.38
3						£0	£26,554.78	£3,356,667.17
4						£0	£26,766.54	£3,383,433.70
5						£0	£26,979.98	£3,410,413.68
6	£100,000					£100,000	£27,195.12	£3,537,608.80
7	£118,313	£172,900				£291,213	£28,209.39	£3,857,030.69
8	£236,625			£33,564		£270,189	£30,756.50	£4,157,976.19
9	£354,938					£354,938	£33,156.29	£4,546,069.98
10	£473,250					£473,250	£36,251.00	£5,055,570.98
11	£591,563					£591,563	£40,313.83	£5,687,447.31
12	£591,563					£591,563	£45,352.50	£6,324,362.31
13	£591,563	£86,450				£678,013	£50,431.35	£7,052,806.17
14	£591,563					£591,563	£56,240.07	£7,700,608.73
15	£473,250			£53,702		£526,952	£61,405.74	£8,288,966.87
16	£354,938					£354,938	£66,097.39	£8,710,001.75
17	£236,625			£26,851		£263,476	£69,454.78	£9,042,932.73
18	£118,313					£118,313	£72,109.62	£9,233,354.85
19						£0	£73,628.07	£9,306,982.91
20		£43,225		£20,138		£63,363	£74,215.19	£9,444,561.50
21						£0	£75,312.26	£9,519,873.76
22					–£36,656	–£36,656	£75,912.81	£9,559,130.32
23						£0	£76,225.85	£9,635,356.17
24						£0	£76,833.68	£9,712,189.85
Total	**£4,832,500**	**£432,250**	**£3,150,000**	**£134,256**	**–£36,656**	**£8,512,350**	**£1,199,840**	

Discounted cash flow (DCF) approaches

DCF works in a slightly different way. The interest rate for the project is taken as the opportunity cost of the finance invested in the project. The calculation is based around the 'time value of money' in a slightly more explicit way than with the accumulative, residual model, although they use the same principles.

If you had a choice about receiving £1 today or £1 in a year's time it is logical to choose the £1 today, as long as the interest rate achievable in the market is greater than zero per cent, which usually it is.[13] If the interest rate was 10 per cent, you could theoretically invest the £1 receivable today at this rate and accumulate 10p over the year, having a year end balance of £1.10. Formulaically, this can be expressed as:

$$£1 \times (1 + i)^n$$
$$£1 \times (1.10)^1$$
$$= £1.10$$

We can also estimate what the £1 receivable in one year's time is actually worth today, using an adaptation of the formula. Either

$$£1 \times 1/(1 + i)^n$$

TABLE 4.7 Cash flow calculation but expressing the results in a traditional way
Part one: value on completion

Expected realisation					
ERV					
	Net office area		4000		
		×		£235.00	£940,000.00
	Car parking spaces		15		
		×		£2,500.00	£37,500.00
				Total income	£977,500.00
Capitalised @			7.00%	14.28571429	
					£13,964,286.00
				LESS	
				Purchaser's costs (5%)	−£664,965.99
				3%	£13,299,319.73
				LESS	
				Incentive	−£940,000.00
				Net realisation	£12,359,319.73

Part two: development costs

As per residual cash flow					−£9,712,189.85
Developer's profit					
Less					
Professional fees: letting and sale					
Letting fees	10%	£94,000			
Sale fees	2%	£268,571		£362,571	
Contingency	5.00%			£236,625	−£599,196.00
				PROFIT	£2,047,933.87
				Profit on cost	19.861%
				Profit on value	16.570%

or

$£1 \times (1 + i)^{-n}$

Using the latter we find that:

$£1 \times (1.10)^{-1}$
$£1 \times 0.090909$
or 91p

This is basically what is done in the DCF approach in development appraisal. Each individual cash flow has a nominal value, the actual monetary value at the time of the expenditure (or projected time). This is then discounted back to find the current or effective value of the cash flow. The general formula is:

Cash flow × discount factor appropriate for the time period
= Present value of expenditure

The land value or profit as appropriate is then the sum of these present values. This can be expressed diagrammatically as in Figure 4.15.

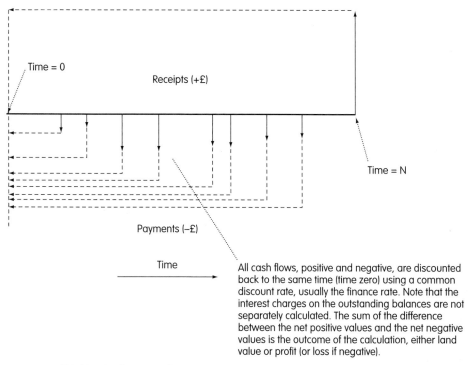

Time = 0

Receipts (+£)

Time = N

Payments (−£)

Time

All cash flows, positive and negative, are discounted back to the same time (time zero) using a common discount rate, usually the finance rate. Note that the interest charges on the outstanding balances are not separately calculated. The sum of the difference between the net positive values and the net negative values is the outcome of the calculation, either land value or profit (or loss if negative).

FIGURE 4.15 Total land value or profits

Using this principle we can see how the first few cash flows of our appraisal are constructed:

Month	Expenditure (receipts) during period	Discount rate @ 0.79741% per month $(1 + i)^{-n}$	Net cash flow (effective value at time=0)
0	£3,150,000	1.000	£3,150,000
1	0	0.99209	£0
2	£129,675	0.98424	£127,631.42

The full calculation using a DCF approach is displayed in Table 4.8.

The final figure sought, be it profit or land value, is simply found by summing the DCF column of Table 4.8. The figure produced is the net present value (NPV). This is one of the beauties of the DCF approach in that no additional step is required to calculate the figure in today's terms. The figure produced is automatically at the present value. A second major advantage is that the approach allows the easy calculation of the internal rate of return (IRR). IRR is a widely used measure of return in the investment world. Using a DCF approach therefore gives an additional measure of return that makes the development easily comparable with other investment mediums.

It may be sensible to review what IRR is at this stage, and also discuss how it relates to NPV, the other main measure of return used in the financial world. IRR is simply the discount rate that produces an NPV of £0. NPV varies according to the discount

TABLE 4.8 Discounted cash flow development appraisal

Month 0	Construction costs	Contingency 5%	Fees	Land	Marketing	Income	Sale	Letting and sale fees	Expenditure per month	Discount factor	DCF
0				-£3,150,000					-£3,150,000	1.000	-£3,150,000
1									£0	0.992	£0
2			-£129,675						-£129,675	0.984	-£127,631
3									£0	0.976	£0
4									£0	0.969	£0
5									£0	0.961	£0
6	-£100,000								-£100,000	0.953	-£95,346
7	-£118,313	-£5,916	-£172,900						-£297,128	0.946	-£281,059
8	-£236,625	-£11,831			-£33,564				-£282,020	0.938	-£264,658
9	-£354,938	-£17,747							-£372,684	0.931	-£346,974
10	-£473,250	-£23,663							-£496,913	0.924	-£458,972
11	-£591,563	-£29,578							-£621,141	0.916	-£569,176
12	-£591,563	-£29,578							-£621,141	0.909	-£564,673
13	-£591,563	-£29,578	-£86,450						-£707,591	0.902	-£638,175
14	-£591,563	-£29,578							-£621,141	0.895	-£555,774
15	-£473,250	-£23,663			-£53,702				-£550,615	0.888	-£488,773
16	-£354,938	-£17,747							-£372,684	0.881	-£328,209
17	-£236,625	-£11,831			-£26,851				-£275,307	0.874	-£240,535
18	-£118,313	-£5,916							-£124,228	0.867	-£107,679
19									£0	0.860	£0
20			-£43,225		-£20,138				-£63,363	0.853	-£54,057
21									£0	0.846	£0
22						-£36,656			£36,656	0.840	£30,779
23									£0	0.833	£0
24							£11,849,115	-£362,571	£11,486,544	0.826	£9,493,012
Total	-£4,832,500		-£432,250	-£3,150,000	-£134,256	-£36,656	£11,849,115	-£362,571	£2,737,569		-£1,252,099

NPV	£1,252,099
IRR month	1.650%
IRR	19.797%

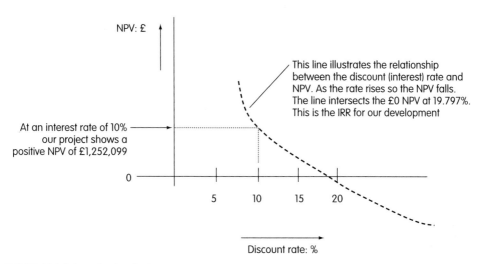

FIGURE 4.16 Internal rate of return

rate (interest rate) applied; as the rate increases, the NPV falls. This represents the surplus cash flow in the investment. Eventually, if the discount rate gets high enough, the NPV will actually turn negative, i.e. a loss will be made (or insufficient funds exist to purchase the land). The point where the crossover takes place is the IRR. In reality, although the interest rate charged on finance can theoretically go high enough to cause loss (though contrary to the layperson's expectations this is rare – it is not usually interest rates alone that cause this to occur), this exercise is carried out not to find the maximum lending rate a project can stand but instead to find the true project rate of return. The IRR percentage measures the rate of return that is peculiar to the cash flows of the project and is not affected by any factors external to the project such as changes in interest rate. The relationship is explained graphically in Figure 4.16.

It should be noted that the IRR figure is usually calculated on the nominal rather than the discounted cash flows. If the discounted figures were used, what would be measured would be the IRR surplus above the 10 per cent discount rate, i.e. it would be around 9.7 per cent. This measure is sometimes used but it is more conventional to take the true IRR figure, as this rate will not alter with any changes in the rate charged on finance that may occur, as will happen with the alternative approach.

SUMMARY OF THE TRADITIONAL AND CASH FLOW APPROACHES TO DEVELOPMENT APPRAISAL

The ability to calculate IRR gives a useful additional measure, and it is the main benefit in adopting a full DCF approach. Many of the more sophisticated investors and financiers require IRR figures from any project being proposed to them. DCF is less useful for project management than the residual cash flow presentation. The respective merits of the two approaches can thus be assessed:

> both cash flow approaches are more time consuming to construct than the traditional approaches and require a high level of information and transparency in the assumptions made;
> both offer a higher level of accuracy as long as the information is accurate and the assumptions made are sound;
> the true DCF approach gives the greatest benefit in analysis of returns, particularly in the provision of the IRR figure,
> the residual or accumulative cash flow is best suited to development management in that it provides true forecasts of cash flows, including accrued interest.

All methods therefore have their role for developers, including the traditional residual approach, which is best applied in the early appraisal stages.

Sensitivity analysis

INTRODUCTION

The basic appraisal models are not the full story concerning carrying out the financial appraisal of development projects. Development appraisals are extraordinarily sensitive to the inputs used to construct them, or, to be more accurate, to some of these variables.

Any development appraisal, be it calculated traditionally or by way of cash flows, is just one set of assumptions that leads to a single output, the land valuation or profitability figure. It is just one view of how the future is going to pan out. It may be the developer's best estimate of what may happen but it is just a forecast. The assumptions made about the scheme may be wrong: the ground conditions may be different to those expected; building costs may rise; market conditions and tenants' requirements may change; and the economy may stall or boom. It should be remembered just how long most developments take. A typical commercial scheme will take between two and five years. The reader is invited to think back to what the economy was like two years ago. Whenever this book is being read it can be certain that conditions today will always vary in some way from the past and will differ, even if only in small ways, from the future.

The question is, does this matter? The answer with development appraisals is almost invariably 'yes'. This is because of their sensitivity, which can be illustrated by turning once again to our base example. We take the calculation of Table 4.7 – the calculation of profitability produced by the residual cash flow. We will now look at the effect of changing just one figure, the rent achieved on letting. Let us assume that the rent achieved by the time the building came to the market was only £220 per square metre. This is a drop of just £15 per metre, or a 6.38 per cent fall in values. This is not a major fall, it may just represent a mild slow-down in the economy. The effect on the appraisal, however, is quite striking, as shown in Table 4.9. A 6.38 per cent drop in rent has seen a drop in profits of nearly 40 per cent. This degree of sensitivity is not unusual. Because of this, it is essential that some sort of sensitivity analysis is carried

TABLE 4.9 Calculation of Table 4.7, but with a different rent achieved
Part one: value on completion

Expected realisation					
ERV					
	Net office area	4,000			
		×		£220.00	£880,000.00
	Car parking spaces	15			
		×		£2,500.00	£37,500.00
			Total income		£917,500.00
Capitalised @		7.00%	14.28571429		
					£13,107,143.00
			LESS		
			Purchaser's costs (5%)		−£624,149.66
				3%	£12,482,993.20
			LESS		
			Incentive		−£940,000.00
			Net realisation		£11,542,993.20

Part two: development costs

As per residual cash flow					−£9,712,189.85
Developer's profit					
Less					
Professional fees: letting and sale					
Letting fees	10%	£94,000			
Sale fees	2%	£268,571		£362,571	
Contingency	5.00%			£236,625	−£599,196.00
			PROFIT		£1,231,607.34
			Profit on cost		11.944%
			Profit on value		10.670%

out on any development appraisal. This final section of the appraisal review requires an examination of the methods that can be used.

TYPES OF SENSITIVITY ANALYSIS

Sensitivity analysis can be carried out in a number of different ways with each method having different utilities and uses. Each form of sensitivity analysis also has a number of sub-types. The basic categories are:

1. simple sensitivity analysis
   > single variable analysis – changing the variables by fixed amounts
   > single variable – break-even analysis
2. scenarios
   > basic scenario analysis
   > probability-linked scenario analysis
3. simulation.

The categories of sensitivity analysis represent steps towards increasing complexity and sophistication. Simple sensitivity analysis is most useful in identifying areas of vulnerability. This is both in terms of the appraisal and adverse movements in the market or problems on site. The latter is probably obvious. The former refers to the vulnerability of developers to errors in their own assumptions or calculations. Scenarios are more realistic; they examine the effects of movements in the assumed values of pairs or groups of variables. Simulation, on the other hand, can be used in quite sophisticated decision-making techniques. We will examine each in turn and look at the way they can be used to make informed decisions.

SIMPLE SENSITIVITY ANALYSIS

Introduction

Simple sensitivity analysis is the bare minimum that should be done in an appraisal. Even so, it is very limited in its utility. Simple sensitivity analysis examines the effect of changing one variable at a time on the outcome of the appraisal, very much as was done in the example above.

Single variable analysis – fixed amounts

The standard way of carrying out sensitivity analysis is to use a set fixed amount, usually a percentage figure, and alter the figures for each selected variable by this fixed amount. Below, six key variables in our development have been selected and their values adjusted in the appraisal by plus or minus 10 per cent. The effect on the overall profit level is calculated for each individual variable, which is then returned to its original value.

Variable	Effect of changing variable on profit	
	+10%	−10%
Rental value	+62.4%	−62.4%
Investment yield	−59.0%	+72.2%
Interest rates	−6.0%	+6.0%
Construction cost	−25.9%	+25.9%
Letting period	−7.6%	+7.5%
Land value	−18.6%	+18.6%

This type of pattern of sensitivity is quite common. Usually, the factors that have the greatest impact on the profitability of a scheme are those concerned with its end value. Factors such as interest rates usually have very little effect, at least directly. Interest rate movements often indicate wider movements in the economy, which may have an impact on the key value variables.

A number of variations in approach exist in the use of simple sensitivity analysis. Sometimes monetary variations are used (for example, moving rents in £5/m^2 intervals) although it is hard to achieve consistency between variables when this is done. A common approach is to produce a table of sensitivity for each key variable, looking at the effect of 0, 2.5, 5, 7.5 and 10 per cent changes in the variables value on profitability or land value.

Use in appraisal and decision-making

Simple sensitivity has considerable value to the appraiser but has limited utility in terms of being realistic in the risk assessment for the development. Simple sensitivity enables the developer to identify the key variables in the development, i.e. those that have the greatest potential impact on end value. The developer can also quantify the degree of sensitivity to the variable, i.e. how little or much the variable needs to move in value before serious consequences arise. It is not, however, realistic. Variables such as rent very rarely move in isolation, they tend to move in complex ways with other variables. For example, if rents fall investors tend to become nervous about future rental growth prospects and tend to adjust their yield requirements upwards. This has a double effect on capital values (see the section on property valuation, page 183).

Single variable – profit extinguishments or break-even analysis

A valuable variation on the single point sensitivity analysis is to adjust the key variables values until they produce figures that extinguish the profit produced from a development. This is illustrated below:

Variable	Values required to reduce profitability to zero
Rental value	£197.37/m^2
Investment yield	8.27%
Interest rates	25.91%
Construction cost	£1,340/m^2
Letting period	31 months
Land value	£4,611,911

Use in appraisal and decision-making

Al though this does not appear unduly different from simple sensitivity analysis, it does provide the appraiser with more information about the nature of the scheme. The developer can identify exactly the point at which the scheme will fail to make a profit if there are movements in the key variable. For example, it can be seen that rents would have to fall by between 20 and 25 per cent to extinguish the profits of the scheme, *ceteris paribus*. In most market conditions such a drop seems unlikely but in extreme conditions this sort of movement can occur. The yield would only have to move from 7 per cent to around 8.25 per cent to see this occur. Developers can ask themselves whether this is feasible. This sort of analysis adds considerably to the knowledge about the scheme.

SCENARIOS

Introduction

Scenarios are a further step in sophistication in analysing the sensitivity of the scheme. They solve some of the problems that were identified earlier regarding the tendency of the individual variables to move together. They require the developer or appraiser to consider what might happen to the key variables in the scheme under differing economic conditions, for example higher or lower levels of economic growth than are currently being experienced.

Basic scenario analysis

This process is illustrated below. The expected values, those that form the appraiser's best judgement of how the scheme will be executed, form the base of the analysis. Two further scenarios have also been generated: one that assumes higher than average levels of growth (the optimistic forecast) and one that assumes a lower growth future (pessimistic). The appraiser has formed judgements as to what would happen to the values of the key variables under each of these conditions and the appraisal has been re-run to produce NPV and profit figures under each of these three possible views of the future.[14]

Scenario summary	Expected values	Optimistic	Pessimistic
Changing variables:			
Rental value (£/m^2)	£235.00	£250.00	£220.00
Car space annual rent	£2,500.00	£3,000.00	£2,000.00
Investment yield	7.00%	6.50%	7.75%
Incentive	−£940,000	−£600,000	−£1,300,000
Total development costs	−£9,712,189.85	−£9,200,000.00	−£10,500,000.00
Result variables:			
NPV (profit)	£2,047,933.87	£4,912,159.31	−£1,216,400.30
Profit on cost	19.861%	50.128%	−10.959%

Use in appraisal and decision-making

Scenarios are a valuable additional step in understanding the risk characteristics of the scheme. They are particularly useful in identifying more reliably the 'bottom line', 'worst case' scenario for the development than the simple approach. In this case, it is apparent that the scheme could make a considerable loss under the pessimistic scenario. The developers could use this information to make a judgement about whether this is a risk they are willing to take.

Scenarios of this form are still limited: they offer only three (in this case) discrete views of the future when we know that the future courses are much more diverse. They also say nothing about the probability of each of the scenarios occurring. Similarly, the scenarios are only as good as the underlying constructional assumptions made within them. Notwithstanding this, scenarios are a vital part of the appraisal process and should really be the minimum that an appraiser ought to use in their assessment of financial risk.

Probability-linked scenario analysis

Some of the problems that are identified above can be addressed by the ascribing of probabilities to the scenarios generated. This is illustrated below. This approach enables the calculation of expected net present value (ENPV), expected profit and expected IRR (not illustrated). This calculation of what are risk-weighted assessments of profit (or land price) can add valuable information to the developer's decision-making processes. It is not a perfect process, there are some serious questions as to the validity of the assessment of probabilities, but it is another valuable aid to decision-making.

Scenario summary	Expected values	Optimistic	Pessimistic
Changing variables:			
Rental value (£/m²)	£235.00	£250.00	£220.00
Car space annual rent	£2,500.00	£3,000.00	£2,000.00
Investment yield	7.00%	6.50%	7.75%
Incentive	−£940,000	−£600,000	−£1,300,000
Total development costs	−£9,712,189.85	−£9,200,000.00	−£10,500,000.00
Result variables:			
NPV (profit)	£2,047,933.87	£4,912,159.31	−£1,216,400.30
Profit on cost	19.861%	50.128%	−10.959%
Probability	50%	25%	25%
NPV (profit) × prob	**£1,023,996.94**	**£1,228,039.83**	**−£304,100.08**
Profit on cost × prob	**9.93%**	**12.53%**	**−2.74%**

Expected NPV £1,947,906.69
Expected IRR 19.72%

SIMULATION

Introduction

Although scenarios do represent an advance on the single point estimate, particularly for a DCF valuation, the scenario and probability approach is still fairly limited. Only three alternative views of the future are examined, each of which are discrete value assessments. Even taking the limited number of variables we chose, there is an almost infinite number of alternative combinations of values, each of which can produce a distinctly different NPV calculation. To carry out individual calculations for each of the possible alternatives, having decided on its probability of occurrence, is possible in theory but impractical.

TABLE 4.10 Possible alternative values for rental values and investment yield

Rental value (£)	Probability of occurrence (%)	Ascribed probability numbers
210	2	1–2
215	5	3–7
220	7	8–15
225	10	16–25
230	15	26–40
235	21	41–61
240	15	62–76
245	10	77–86
250	7	87–93
255	5	94–98
260	2	99–100

Terminal (sale) yield (%)	Probability of occurrence (%)	Ascribed probability numbers
5.75	1	1
6.00	4	2–5
6.25	7	6–12
6.50	10	13–22
6.75	15	23–37
7.00	21	38–58
7.25	15	59–73
7.50	10	74–83
7.75	7	84–90
8.00	5	91–95
8.25	2	96–97
8.50	1	98
8.75	1	99
9.00	1	100

There is an approach that does move a long way towards examining a larger sample of the possible outcomes. This is the Monte Carlo simulation. Simulation has been used since the 1960s to explore many areas of uncertainty. Until recently it has been a cumbersome method. It requires the range of probable values for a variable to be identified, for probability to be ascribed to each and then for random numbers to be generated in order to select the value to be used in the calculation. Taking our example as an illustration, the possible alternative values for rental values and investment yield, two of the key variables, are as shown in Table 4.10.

With our two variable models, two sets of random numbers between 1 and 100 would be generated, one for each distribution. For example, for a single 'run' these might be random numbers of 22 and 67. For rental growth this would equate to a rent of £225. For sale yield the appropriate figure would be 7.25 per cent. Combining these in the cash flow would produce an NPV of £1,063,885, a reduction in profitability of 48 per cent.

To produce the final answer this process would have to be repeated at least 100 times which would give an array of NPVs that could then be analysed. In particular, the mean figure is important as this would be the report value figure, but the distribution of the NPVs would give a valuable insight as to the certainty or reliability of the value figure.

The big problem with this approach (leaving to one side the problem of forecasting and probability assessment which will be addressed later) is clearly how time consuming it is. It is possible to construct Excel spreadsheets incorporating macro functions that will take some of the drudgery out of the task but this does require a relatively high level of spreadsheet knowledge and skill. Fortunately, there is software available as an add-in to spreadsheets like Excel at reasonable costs that allows simulations to be carried out relatively easily. One of the best examples is Pallisade Corporation's @Risk™ software. @Risk allows any input cell in a spreadsheet to be expressed as a probability distribution and will then use these to quickly recalculate the spreadsheet and analyse the results on any selected output cell. In this case we would clearly select the NPV calculation as the output cell.

An @Risk analysis was carried out on our example appraisal. The two variables were selected as probability distribution. Other variables were also set as being open to variation (construction cost, time, incentives, etc.). The software allows you to choose from a wide array of possible distributions. For this example a simple triangle distribution was chosen for each. For this distribution the minimum, maximum and most likely values are required, the software then calculating the probability distribution. The variable values chosen are illustrated below:

Name of variable	Minimum	Mean	Maximum
(Input) Building cost	£901.27	£950.00	£998.97
(Input) Rental value	£215.38	£233.33	£249.29
(Input) Investment yield/investment yield	6.52%	7.50%	8.96%
(Input) Rental incentive/rental incentive	6.21	14.00	23.66
(Input) Planning period	5.06	7.67	11.97
(Input) Construction/construction	10.06	12.33	14.95
(Input) Letting/letting	0.26	6.00	11.75

The simulation can then be run, selecting the NPV calculation cell as the @Risk output. In this case 1,000 iterations or individual calculations of NPV were carried out. On a modestly powerful PC this process takes 5–10 seconds. The software reports the mean NPV plus a wide range of other statistics including the standard deviation. In this case the mean profit predicted was £1,058,871 with one standard deviation of ±£812,019. The distribution of profits is represented in Figure 4.17 and the summary of the outcome given below. This level of analysis provides a powerful weapon for the appraiser in the assessment of the inherent risks in the project. We can only touch on the potential of these techniques in this medium.

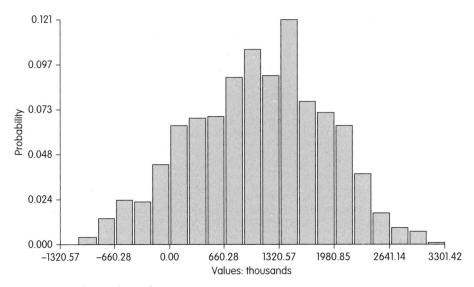

FIGURE 4.17 Distribution for profit

Name	Minimum	Mean	Maximum
Profit (Today)	−£1,097,949	£1,058,871	£3,301,421
Non-discounted profit on cost	−13.31%	12.82%	39.48%
Non-discounted profit on value	−13.41%	9.83%	26.97%
Profit on cost	−11.00%	10.60%	32.63%
Profit on value	−11.09%	8.13%	22.29%

Standard deviation £812,019

Use in appraisal and decision-making

This section is not intended to be a commercial for @Risk. There is no doubt, however, that this software greatly increases the ability of the appraiser to carry out very sophisticated tasks. What does the use of simulation add to our appraisal? First, we have explicitly addressed the uncertainty contained within the appraisal. Second, we have revealed more about the reliability of this appraisal based on our assessment of future uncertainty. This can be used as a benchmark to compare the reliability of the appraisal with other developments. For example, we can calculate the coefficient of variance of this project by dividing the standard deviation by the mean. This produces a figure of 130.4 per cent, illustrating a relatively high percentage of potential variance from the expected result. If most simulations were producing coefficients of variation below this level then the commissioner of this appraisal would be able to gauge that the development was subject to a relatively higher level of uncertainty. Analysing the overall results, however, shows that, given the distribution of variables chosen, only about 11 per cent of the 1,000 calculations of the profit produced a loss. This type of information would assist lenders on development, in particular, in arriving at more rational decisions.

There are, of course, drawbacks with this approach. Although this extension of the DCF technique counters some of the problems with the scenario approach – namely the problems of accurate forecasting – other problems are peculiar to risk-explicit approaches. The principal problem is the assessment of probabilities. There is insufficient reliable data available to assess the likelihood of certain factors occurring in the future. Past performance and relationships may, indeed, not be a good way of assessing what will happen in the future. In essence, although the knowledge and experience of the valuer is helpful in assessing what the near future is going to be like, no one has perfect foresight. The assessment of probabilities is likely to be subjective.

Despite these drawbacks, simulation is a very powerful and valuable technique. Just as DCF requires the appraiser to be explicit about what assumptions have been made concerning the future timing and extent of the key variables, so simulation requires the valuer to be explicit about the reliability of these forecasts. It is a logical extension of DCF that adds much to the single point estimate of NPV produced.

CONCLUSIONS TO THIS SECTION

It is essential that developers and appraisers should carry out some kind of sensitivity analysis on their financial appraisals. Development appraisals are inherently unstable and unreliable. A single point estimate of profit or land value may represent the appraiser's best guess as to how the development will proceed but it is likely that the outcome will differ from that projected because of the length of time involved in the development process and the degree of inherent sensitivity to key variables that the process possesses. The bare minimum that should be done is to carry out a simple sensitivity analysis. As noted, it is unlikely in reality that single variables change in isolation. It is therefore recommended that scenario building is undertaken for all development appraisals. Time invested in exploring the financial characteristics of the project can protect the developer from later losses.

Residential appraisal

Introduction

This section provides an illustration of a bid for residential land as it might be carried out in early 2007 by a small but sophisticated developer.

It is important to lay out the background to this scenario. One of the handicaps that previous books on the development process and development appraisal have had is that they have been overtaken by technological change and by changes in the way information has been collected and distributed. This is certainly true of the first edition of *Contemporary Property Development*. It was written with an acknowledgement to the internet age (with reference to marketing of property) but when it was written (late 2000 to the end of 2001) there was a very limited use of the web as a source of data for prospective developers. This is not true now. Although there is still the need to seek out experts in certain aspects of the market, the sheer quantity (and now also quality) of data available to the developer/appraiser/valuer through their PC is astonishing.

Similarly, with regard to the mechanics of carrying out the appraisal, most older books concentrated on the detail of calculation and the techniques that could be used to calculate the final figure. Up to the mid-1980s this was essential because the calculation had to be mainly done manually using valuation tables and utilising the traditional residual layout. The limitations imposed by the lack of calculation ability resulted in the rather odd creature that is the residual calculation; relatively easy to read and understand but inaccurate because of the short-cuts and simplifications that had to be incorporated within it.

With the development of spreadsheets and the proliferation of PCs it was at last possible for developers and appraisers to carry out much more accurate estimates of development site value and development profitability by the use of cash flows. There was still the need to know what formula to use where and to fully understand compounding and discounting in the construction of the cash flows and also how and why a cash flow would produce a different answer to the traditional residual approach.

Virtually every book that has been written in the past 40 years on this subject has covered both the traditional and cash flow models in their texts, with a heavy concentration on the mechanics of the calculation, including this one! There was an attempt, albeit perhaps a clumsy one, in the original edition of this text to try to spend more time talking about the factors that affected the input rather than the actual calculations themselves, but the underlying philosophy was continued. In the meantime, the real world, as it always has an annoying habit of doing, has moved on. From the very early days of widespread mass market desktop computers, proprietary development appraisal software was being developed to help the hard-pressed developer and appraiser. By the mid-1990s these were becoming very sophisticated and increasingly more widely used. At the time of writing the first edition, a review was made of the software available and it was only the pressures of meeting the publication date that prevented this information being used in some form in the book.

Today, the decision is even clearer. The majority of appraisals in the market are now done using some proprietary form of software. The reasons are obvious; the software produces more reliable answers, the modelling allowed is more sophisticated and the entire process can be carried out much more quickly. When we drive a car we do not need to be able to calculate the right proportion of air and petrol to put into each cylinder and the right moment to send power to the spark plug. We just know that somewhere this is being done; all we are really interested in is the output. Developers and appraisers no longer need to be experts in calculation. They need to know the effect of the assumptions they make and they need to know what the output of the software is telling them, but that is about all. We have moved out of an age where we needed to concentrate on the means of calculation to one where we can concentrate more on the input and the results.

This is the intention of this section, which illustrates how a contemporary appraisal is likely to be carried out using sources of information available to all via the internet and also using the products of the industry's leading software supplier, ARGUS Software (formerly Circle Software).[15] The software used is ARGUS Developer version 3.0, launched towards the end of 2006. This section illustrates how a developer collects information on the development opportunity to determine what they can bid for the site.

THE DEVELOPMENT OPPORTUNITY

The potential development site is located in the village of Culcheth, some 5 miles north of Warrington in Cheshire. The developer has identified a mature house in a poor state of repair with a large garden that is on the market. The site borders a site that has recently been developed and the developer understands that the house falls within an area identified by the local planning authority as one suitable for future development. This is confirmed by accessing the local planning authority's website where the Unitary Development Plan (UDP) is available (see Figure 4.18).

The developer knows that Culcheth has a buoyant residential property market and that property prices have risen markedly in recent years. It has a good location for

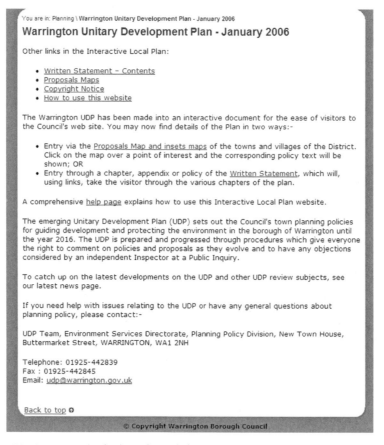

FIGURE 4.18 Warrington Borough Council UDP link. Source: Warrington Borough Council: www.warrington.gov.uk. Copyright, 2008 Warrington Borough Council. All rights reserved.

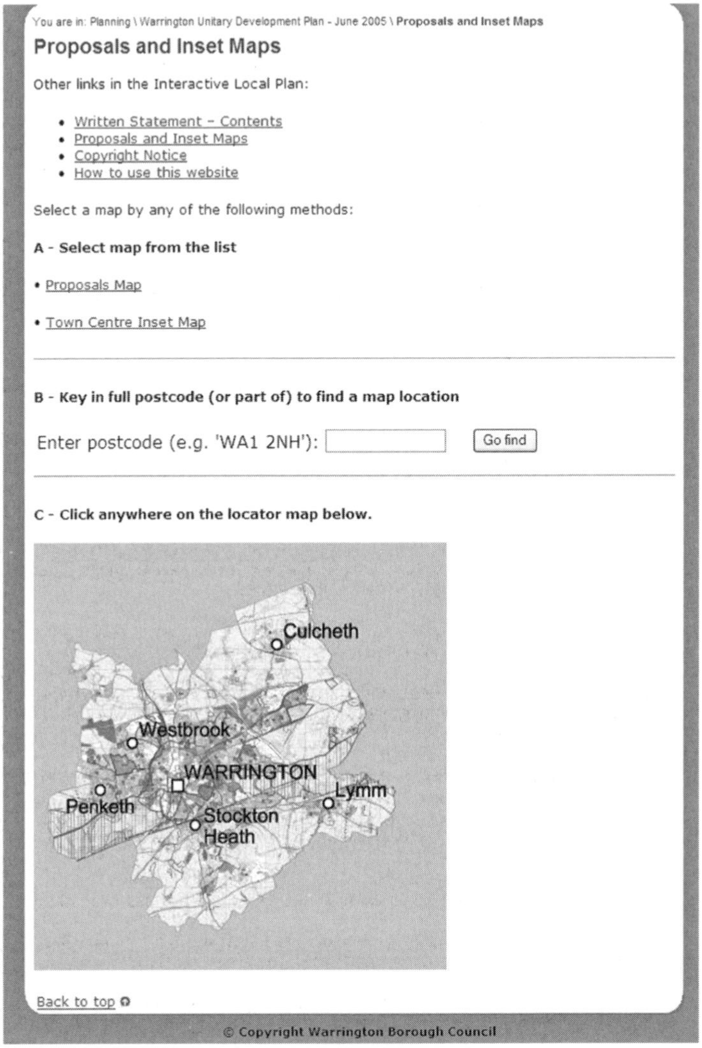

FIGURE 4.19 Map variant of the UDP . Source: Warrington Borough Council: www.warrington.gov.uk. Copyright, 2008 Warrington Borough Council. All rights reserved.

commuters, being 5 miles from Warrington and also within easy commuting distance of Manchester and Liverpool via the M62 and A580 East Lancashire road. It has three primary schools, a high school and a sixth form college. It has a strong commercial centre, including a new Sainsbury's supermarket, a Co-op, several restaurants and pubs. Further reference to the borough council's website, where the Unitary Development Plan is available, also shows that it is surrounded by green belt land, as well as giving important planning guidelines (Figures 4.19 and 4.20).

The plan version of the website allows the developer to focus down on the site and identify its planning status. Links within the plan allows the developer to call up information pertinent to the development of the site, including the development control strategy and any other relevant policies (Figure 4.20).

DCS1 DEVELOPMENT CONTROL STRATEGY

Development proposals should be designed to a high standard and should:

1. preserve the amenites of near neighbours;

2. preserve or enhance the character and appearance of the area;

3. conserve the natural, and the historic built environments;

4. make efficient use of land and other natural resources;

5. integrate efficiently with existing public utilities and the highway network;

6. avoid undue reliance on the private car;

7. where appropriate incorporate attractive landscaping and spaces;

8. aim to deter crime;

9. be accessible.

SOC1 SOCIAL PROGRESS

In making provision for development and in determining planning applications, the Council will aim to ensure that:

1. jobs, shops, services and community facilities are accessible to those without access to private motor transport;

2. the primary focus for essential services and amenities continues to be the town centre and other recognised centres well served by public transport;

3. new development does not increase the risk of crime or prejudice public health or safety;

4. the particular needs of children, women and the elderly are not overlooked;

5. the special needs of people with impaired mobility are catered for;

6. the provision of homes in the borough responds to identified local needs in terms of mix, quality, location and affordability;

7. provision is made for minority groups with identified needs that can be met within the land-use planning system.

< Prev Chapter | Next Chapter >

Back to top ◎

FIGURE 4.20 Planning policies and development strategies relevant to the site . Source: Warrington Borough Council: www.warrington.gov.uk. Copyright, 2008 Warrington Borough Council. All rights reserved.

Although this provides a lot of information, the developer would be wise to talk directly to a planning officer regarding the potential development of the site. There are a number of investigations that should be made prior to this discussion in order to make the discussions as focused as possible. As we have seen in the earlier sections, a key element in an appraisal is the determination of the type and quantity of property that can go on the site and what the market is for the type of properties

231

that can be built. This is not a simple task but is one that requires a host of enquiries to be made. In particular, an investigation of the site is a key element. The shape, size, topography and accessibility of the site will have a significant impact on what can be developed. The developer will therefore have visited the site prior to opening discussions with the planning authorities. Potential barriers to development should be considered, such as mature trees that might have tree preservation orders, a historic building that might be listed or the presence of some areas of special scientific interest or archaeology. In this case the site was flat with no obvious mature trees and with a fairly nondescript 1940s house on the site. The site has good access onto Hob Hey Lane, which is a good sized suburban road.

The micro location of the site was also investigated. The locality is dominated by large detached houses to the north of the site, while immediately to the south of the site is a new development of three-, four- and five-bedroom detached houses, three-storey town houses, flats and a terrace of four-bedroom houses developed over the previous twelve months. The development has been carried out by a major national firm of house builders and is of medium to high quality. The development still has an active website and on-site marketing presence.

It is clear that any development must be in keeping with the surrounding area and must also have a market. The neighbouring properties and the new development (and any others in the area) are pertinent in this. Other developments may have absorbed all the demand. The local development is relatively sizeable and consists of a range of properties, the last phase of the development consisting of four-bedroom terraced houses and terraced mews properties. All properties have sold well. Enquiries of the local estate agents revealed that there had been no other sizeable developments in the previous five years, the only other developments being small-scale infill schemes and a luxury farm conversion to the north of the village. There are some future potential sites for larger-scale housing development within the centre of the village, including one site that is currently in commercial use but could be developed for residential development under policy GRN4 (Policies for Inset Villages):

> The following development will be allowed within inset villages:
> 1. Housing development and redevelopment of an appropriate scale, character and design, provided the loss of a site previously providing employment is not detrimental to the rural economy or the development of sustainable communities;
> 2. Conversions of existing buildings to housing, provided their loss is not detrimental to the rural economy through the loss of viable premises for business or commerce;
> 3. New employment or mixed-use development of an appropriate scale and type;
> 4. Development providing local services and facilities of an appropriate scale and type.

Policy Derivation:
http://www.warrington.gov.uk/news/udp/interactive/interactive2/written/cpt7.asp#grn4

As yet, however, no applications have been made on the site, therefore there appears to be no danger of the market becoming over-supplied in the foreseeable future.

This was confirmed in discussion with the relevant planning officer at the council. They also confirmed that the site being considered by the developer was in the

TABLE 4.11 House prices achieved for Hob Hey Lane, May 2000 to Sept. 2006

Detached houses	Semi-detached houses
£525,000 (2006)	£268,000 (2006)
£400,000 (2004)	£120,000 (2002)
£212,000 (2002)	£131,000 (2001)
£218,000 (2000)	

Source: email4property.com

area identified for development and that the planning officers would accept the construction of up to six dwellings on the site, subject to them being in keeping with the properties in the surrounding area. The planning officer also indicated that they were keen to improve the positioning of the bus stop along the neighbouring Hob Hey Road and were seeking some land and a contribution from the developer to build a pull-in area for buses.

Talking to the estate agent who is selling the property, the developer was able to satisfy themselves that there was no legal barrier, such as a restrictive covenant on future development of the site, that the agent was aware of that would prevent future development of the site, although this would need to be checked with the solicitors prior to completing the acquisition. The agent also provided information regarding the current conditions in the market – the types of properties which were most sought after in particular areas.

This information was reinforced by examining property websites that provide free property information regarding house prices in the area. Sites such as www.email4property.com allow developers (and prospective purchasers and vendors of properties) to build up a full picture of transactions in the area over recent years. This is very useful in establishing a picture of the market and particularly in tracking down recent developments. Data was collected on sales in Hob Hey Lane itself (Table 4.11), and also on trends in the locality (Table 4.12).

TABLE 4.12 Comparative local house prices (top 10)

Street	Average price: £	Change from last average: %
Ivy Farm Gardens	835,000	–
Broseley Lane	670,000	–
Main Lane	475,000	–
Petersfield Gardens	445,000	+21
Holcroft Lane	425,000	−11
Twiss Green Lane	412,500	+54
Langden Close	400,000	+25
Hob Hey Lane	396,500	−1
Culcheth Hall Drive	379,375	+28
The Limes	372,500	+13

Source: email4property.com

THE APPRAISAL

This information in total quickly enabled the developer to determine what could be built on the site. The site was clearly suited to a small-scale residential development. The most efficient use of space on the site was a terrace of six modern three- and four-bedroom town houses with car parking at the rear. The current market analysis suggested that the houses would sell at about £320,000 each, with price inflation running at between 3 and 10 per cent p.a. The developer was therefore able to commence the appraisal using ARGUS Developer (Figure 4.21).

ARGUS Developer is a project-based system which enables the user to construct a development appraisal in a much simpler, quicker and usually more accurate way than constructing the appraisal manual. The user also requires less technical knowledge regarding calculation, although it is, of course, vital to have a thorough understanding of the impact of the assumptions that are made in the appraisal. Indeed, although relatively inexperienced users can successfully carry out an appraisal using ARGUS Developer, the software allows experienced developers and appraisers to model future schemes in a very sophisticated manner.

The running of the appraisal is very similar to that described in the earlier sections, except that many of the parts are automated to speed up the process of appraisal and incorporating templates that allow data collected to be slotted into the appraisal.

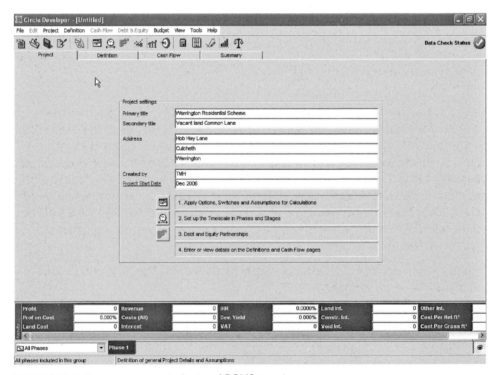

FIGURE 4.21 Setting up an appraisal using ARGUS Developer

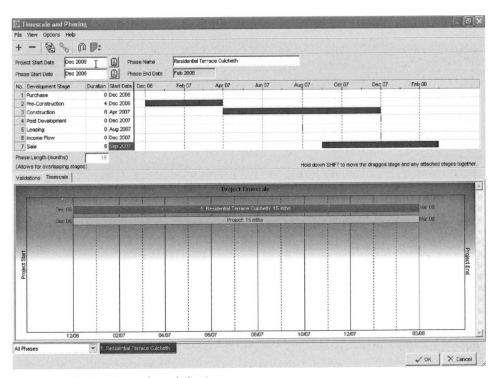

FIGURE 4.22 Setting timescale and phasing

The program works in a Windows environment with drop-down menus and icons and has four tabs, Project, Definition, Cash Flow and Summary, the former two being primarily entry tabs, the latter being primarily the results of the appraisal (although much fine tuning can be done in the cash flow).

In the project tab, as well as allowing the project to be referenced, the calculation assumptions and timescale are set up. Dealing with the timescale first, the developer expects that the project will be carried out in a single phase. Getting planning consent, designing the scheme and appointing a building contractor is expected to take four months, with the actual construction period being anticipated to take eight months. The developer expects sales to be brisk and anticipates the first sale being completed three months before the end of construction and then assumes that the sales will continue at the rate of one per month. This is entered into the table as shown in Figure 4.22.

Note that the assumption allowing sales to overlap earlier periods is very difficult to achieve in a conventional appraisal.

The next requirement is to set up some of the basic assumptions for the calculation. Many of these are standard and can remain unchanged for most developments but some need to be set up for each scheme. One that does need attention is the interest rate which calculates the cost of finance for the project (Figure 4.23). Multiple loan or interest sets can be set up, or else a single rate can apply throughout the

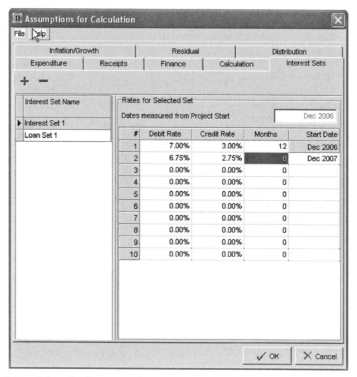

FIGURE 4.23 Setting interest rate assumptions

project. The developer here anticipates that interest rates will be at 7 per cent for the first year of the project then fall slightly for the rest of the project life and this is reflected in the calculation. Note that the credit rate is for any interest received on any project surpluses experienced.

In most cases the standard distribution assumptions can stay the same. This deals with key items such as the expenditure pattern during the construction period (which classically is an s-curve, Figure 4.24) and also the pattern of income (sales receipts and deposits, Figure 4.25). The standard assumption is a single period receipt but here it is expected that receipts will be spread over the sales period and received monthly. Similarly, the developer has assumed an even distribution of deposits spread over a length of time.

ARGUS Developer can calculate development profit or residualised land value (or a mixture in multi-phased schemes). In our case we are calculating the maximum bid that can be made for the site so the developer selects the Residualised land value option. This requires a target figure for profit to be stated, and here the developer has chosen a figure of 15 per cent.

Once the project has been set up then the bulk of the calculation and assumptions are entered via the definitions tab (see Figure 4.26). The top left-hand areas are where the main calculations of construction cost and scheme value are made, either using the Capitalised Rent (for commercial schemes) or Sales (for, as here, residential

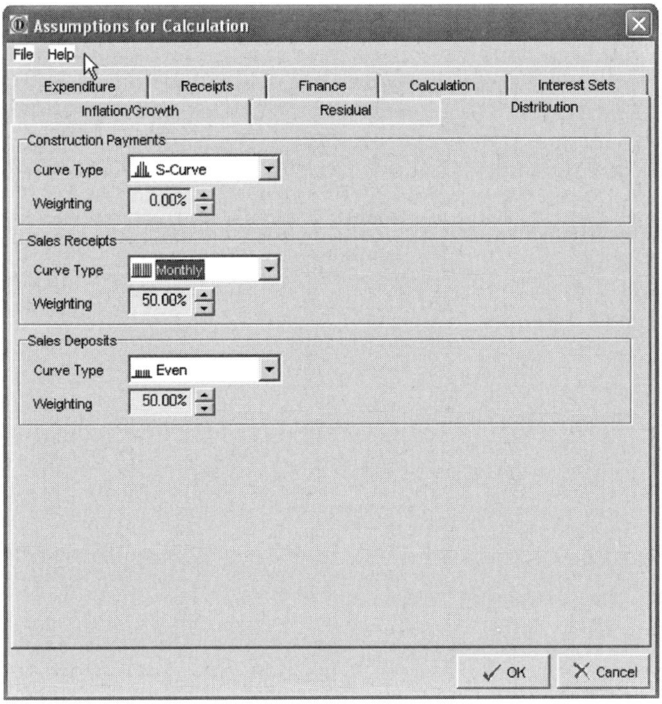

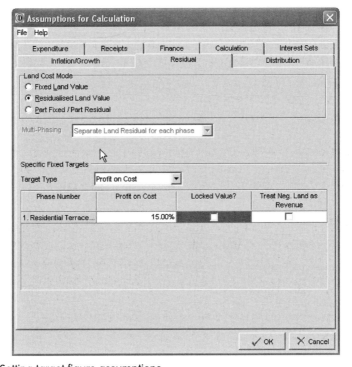

FIGURE 4.24 Setting expenditure pattern assumptions

FIGURE 4.25 Setting target figure assumptions

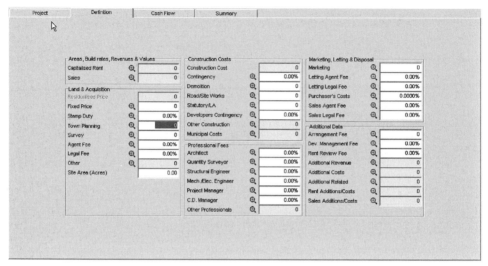

FIGURE 4.26 Definitions tab

property) areas. The magnifying glasses indicate that there are more detailed calculation areas underneath.

Opening up the Sales area (Figure 4.27) allows the assumptions over the number and areas of the houses to be entered as well as the assumed sale costs (£320,000 plus a

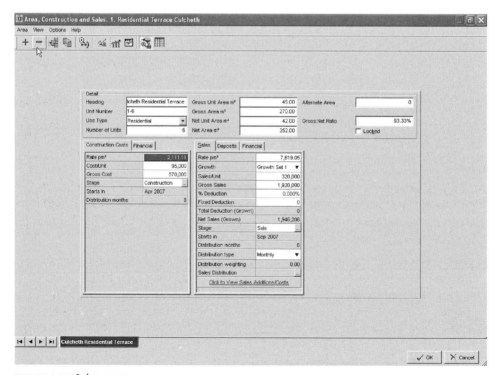

FIGURE 4.27 Sales area

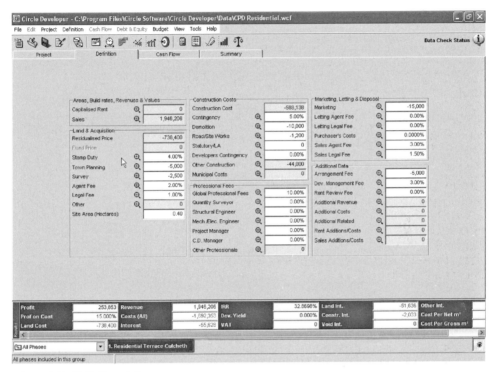

FIGURE 4.28 Definitions tab

small amount of growth in value) and building costs (assumed to be £95,000 per unit). There is also the option to fine tune the assumptions about the timing of expenditure and receipts at this stage (although this can also be done in the cash flow.

Returning to the definitions tab (Figure 4.28), the remainder of the key cost assumptions can be entered. These include the stamp duty and acquisition costs on the land and any planning or survey costs. Other costs accounted for include a 5 per cent contingency, a sum for the demolition and also a timed calculation for a section 106 agreement for the construction of the bus pull-in. A major cost is the professional fees and this has been done as a global 10 per cent of construction cost rather than making detailed assumptions about the individual professionals. A timed budget for marketing has also been decided and allowances made for fees on sale and a project manager. Once these have all been entered then the initial calculation is complete. This is shown in the summary in Table 4.13.

This summary is often sufficient for most developers' purposes. The appraisal shows a land value of £748,000 based on the assumptions made, which is the maximum bid that the developer can make. The developer has the ability to fine tune the assumptions in the cash flow, but as a quick baseline assessment of the viability of the scheme and whether the asking price of the land can be met and the profit targets still achieved. Perhaps more useful at this stage is a quick sensitivity analysis, which can be carried out to test the reliability of the land value assessment (Figure 4.29).

TABLE 4.13 Appraisal summary

Warrington Residential Scheme
Vacant land, Common Lane

Appraisal Summary for Part 1 Culcheth Residential Terrace

REVENUE

Sales valuation	m²	Rate m²	Gross sales	Adjustment
‡ Culcheth Residential Terrace	252.00	£7,619.05	1,920,000	26,206
Net realisation				**1,946,206**

Outlay

Acquisition costs

Residualised price (0.40 ha, £1,845,999.77 per ha)				738,400
Stamp duty		4.00%	29,536	
Agent fee		2.00%	14,768	
Legal fee		1.00%	7,384	
Town planning			5,000	
Survey			2,500	
				797,588

CONSTRUCTION COSTS

Construction	m²	Rate m²	Cost	
‡ Culcheth Residential Terrace	270.00	£2,111.11	588,138	**588,138**
Contingency		5.00%	29,407	
Demolition			10,000	
Road/site works			1,200	
				40,607

Section 106 costs

Section 106			44,000	
				44,000

PROFESSIONAL FEES

Global professional fees		10.00%	58,814	
				58,814

MARKETING AND LETTING

Marketing			15,000	
				15,000

DISPOSAL FEES

Sales agent fee		3.00%	58,386	
Sales legal fee		1.50%	29,193	
				87,579

Other cost

Arrangement fee			5,000	
				5,000

FINANCE

Timescale	Duration	Commences
Pre-construction	4	Dec. 2006
Construction	8	Apr. 2007
Sale	6	Sep. 2007
Total duration	15	

TABLE 4.13 Continued

Multiple finance rates used (see assumptions)		
Debit and credit rates varied throughout the cash flow		
Land	51,636	
Construction	2,033	
Other	1,958	
Total finance cost		55,628

TOTAL COSTS   **1,692,353**

PROFIT   **253,853**

Performance measures	15.00%
Profit on cost%	13.04%
Profit on GDV%	13.04%
Profit on NDV%	
IRR	32.87%
Profit erosion (finance rate 7.000%)	2 years 0 months

‡ Inflation/growth applied	**Ungrown**	**Growth**
Growth on sales		
Culcheth Residential Terrace growth set 1 at 3.00%	1,920,000	26,206
Inflation on Construction Costs	**Uninflated**	**Inflation**
Culcheth Residential Terrace inflation set 1 at 5.00%	570,000	18,138

Table of Residual Land Price and IRR %					
Constr. Rate → Sales Rate ↓	-4.000% £2,026.67 m²	-2.000% £2,068.89 m²	0.000% £2,111.11 m²	+2.000% £2,153.33 m²	+4.000% £2,195.56 m²
-4.000% £7,314.29 m²	£705,865 32.912%	£693,774 33.162%	£681,682 33.417%	£669,590 33.678%	£657,499 33.944%
-2.000% £7,466.67 m²	£734,224 32.651%	£722,132 32.891%	£710,041 33.135%	£697,950 33.384%	£685,858 33.639%
0.000% £7,619.05 m²	£762,583 32.405%	£750,491 32.635%	£738,400 32.870%	£726,309 33.109%	£714,217 33.353%
+2.000% £7,771.43 m²	£790,942 32.174%	£778,850 32.395%	£766,759 32.620%	£754,667 32.850%	£742,576 33.084%
+4.000% £7,923.81 m²	£819,300 31.955%	£807,209 32.188%	£795,118 32.385%	£783,026 32.608%	£770,935 32.831%

FIGURE 4.29 Sensitivity analysis

CONCLUSION TO RESIDENTIAL SECTION

This is a good illustration of how relatively simply and quickly a modern appraisal can be undertaken using the range of information available and using the power and ability of contemporary software. The developer needs to understand the nature of the calculation being undertaken but modern tools make the process both easier and more informative than was possible in earlier times.

Conclusions

Development appraisals are very important to the development process. They are not simply calculations, they represent an examination of the outcome of the bringing together of the development's components. This process is complex, the components can be fitted together in a number of ways and many assumptions have to be made. These assumptions that the developer/appraiser makes about an uncertain future must be soundly based; it is easy to be misled and over-optimistic, and the highly sensitive nature of the financial appraisal can lead people into disaster. All developers should spend time gaining a full understanding of both the process and mechanisms of the appraisal process and develop a feeling for what the outcome of the process actually means.

EXECUTING THE DEVELOPMENT
CHAPTER 5

Introduction

In many respects, to a developer the bulk of time and effort involved in carrying out a development is in the stage prior to the construction. The actual execution of the scheme is, however, the whole purpose of the development and should be treated with the requisite care. This chapter examines how development schemes are taken from existing only in the minds of their promoters to their physical completion.

General principles

A number of general guiding principles exist that developers should follow in executing a development. These are prepare, plan and plan and prepare again! It is vitally important for the success of the development that the groundwork is done before the scheme commences and that all the key components necessary to execute the development are in place at the time it commences. These include the following items.

(a) A development team must have been assembled possessing the appropriate skills and knowledge to complete the scheme.
(b) After this team has been identified, two important issues need to be resolved before the relationship can develop and the scheme proceed:
> the terms of engagement must be agreed between the team members and the developer. This document details the roles, responsibilities, duties and timescales required of the development team members. These documents are vitally important and each must be consistent with the others;
> professional indemnity (PI) insurances should be confirmed for each member of the professional team. PI insurance is an essential safety net for the developer to ensure that if a member of the development team fails to meet their professional requirements any cost consequences will be covered. Property development involves high stakes: an architect, for example, whose design was defective, could be faced with a multi-million pound damages bill. An individual or partnership will probably not have the resources to cover such a claim and it is essential therefore to have adequate insurance in place.
(c) The key goals, timescales and milestones must be established. Good planning is essential to ensure that the project is successfully completed on time and within budget, although the need for flexibility must be incorporated into the team's thinking in order to be able to accommodate unforeseen events.

(d) All the necessary components to complete the scheme need to be in place before the on-site work commences. In an ideal set of circumstances, to minimise the risk to the developer, the key elements should be in place before even the land is purchased. These include such items as:

> finance – it is impossible to proceed to the contract stage unless the finance is in place to pay for the construction work and the professional team. To do so would risk trading fraudulently;
> planning consents;
> proof of the resolution of any legal issues (ownerships, leases, rights of way, etc.);
> archaeological reports – as noted in the section on land acquisition, the UK has a long history of occupation. In many areas, even in so-called 'new towns' there may be an impact on archaeological remains. In historic towns it is almost inevitable that works in the ground or even alterations of existing older structures will have heritage consequences. The commissioning of reports from the local archaeological unit can clarify the situation;
> ground contamination investigations – similarly, it is wise, given the current attitude to contaminated sites, to commission a specialist report on potential contamination of the site;
> geo-technical investigations – a report on the geology and ground conditions on the site. As this has a major impact on the design this is a key report for most developments.

Other components that should be in place prior to commencement on site include:

> detail design of the building and all its components;
> detailed costings and projections;
> Building Regulations application – construction work in the UK requires several stages of approval from the authorities. This is in addition to planning consent. Local authorities are charged with the responsibility of ensuring that construction is carried out safely and that the buildings are structurally sound and meet health and safety requirements. This is in terms of both design and construction. The building control office of the local authority will therefore need to approve the plans of the scheme prior to commencement and will need to approve the construction of elements of the work as it progresses. They will also certify the final building;
> specifications and drawings;
> bills of quantity;
> cost plan;
> draft contract.

If these items are not in place then expensive delays or interruptions to the project may be experienced.

(e) An appropriate contractor should be selected who is able to successfully complete the work within the specified time period.
(f) The most appropriate procurement method should be chosen for the project.
(g) The most appropriate contract for the project should be selected.

Once these key components have been put in place then further material is required:

> Tender report – this is the report prepared by the cost consultant/quantity surveyor on the tenders received (depending on the contract procurement route chosen).
> Programme.
> Draft collateral warranties from main contractor, suppliers and subcontractors with design liability. (Collateral warranties are documents that enable subsequent users or owners of a building to be protected against latent defects in the design or construction of the building. Parties to a contract are protected; there is a duty of care from professionals that they will do their work properly for their client. No such duty is owed to third parties such as subsequent tenants or owners of the building. Collateral warranties give that contractural comfort, albeit of a generally weaker nature. Recently, an insurance route has been followed to cover this area – decennial insurance, so called because its cover runs for 10 years.)
> Insurances – all-risks cover for the works, endorsement of the existing building policy (if applicable), third party, loss of liquidated damages, terrorism cover, non-negligent damage and business interruption.

Some of the key items in connection with this will be covered in this chapter. The focus will be on items not specifically covered to date. The obvious starting point is the development team, given that many of the items listed above are heavily connected with the choice of the team.

The development team

The development team is made up of a group of professionals with very different backgrounds, attitudes and outlooks.

The development team can be broken down into five loose categories. These are management, design, economics, construction and others. We will examine each grouping in turn, focusing on identifying the key member of each group and outlining their main roles and responsibilities. We will try to identify the qualities that a developer should seek when appointing each member of the team. We will also attempt to define the working characteristics of each of the main members of the groups. This will inevitably involve a degree of stereotyping but the process is useful in general to appreciate some of the dynamics of working with such a diverse group of professionals. This diversity of backgrounds can potentially lead to conflict. Each constituent member may have a different role to play during the project. Sometimes there is a requirement to change personnel as these roles change. All of this can make building the team very difficult and, without careful management, can lead to conflict.

DEVELOPMENT MANAGEMENT

The diverse nature of the team and the complexity of most development projects mean that some kind of project manager is required.

In many traditional projects it was the architect who acted as project manager; increasingly this has changed. It is still quite common for the developer themselves to be the project manager. They are, after all, the entrepreneur and catalyst for the project and it is usually the developer who has the best of overall picture of how the project is to be completed and executed. This is acceptable and achievable only, however, in small projects and with smaller developers where considerable time can be devoted by the developer to oversee the project on a day-to-day basis. In other circumstances, where a number of schemes are involved or are being undertaken simultaneously or where the project is large and complex, then it is not feasible for the developer to be able to devote sufficient time to adequately supervise the project.

In these circumstances it is best to appoint a specialist project manager to be overall coordinator and planner. Project management is a discipline which has developed greatly over the past 10–20 years. It is used in many aspects of business as well as in the construction and the development field. Project managers are professionals in their own right and many universities have started to run postgraduate programmes in the discipline. In the UK, the Royal Institution of Chartered Surveyors (RICS) has set up a separate project management faculty from the year 2000.

The project manager fulfils the coordination and planning role that used to be undertaken by architects. Although there is an additional fee to be accounted for in the development budget, most large projects find it essential to employ a project manager.

DESIGN

A number of designers are involved in the development process. The key designers will be outlined below:

> architects
> space planners and interior designers
> landscape architects
> structural engineers
> services engineers
> mechanical and electrical engineers.

Architects

Key roles

Architects fulfil the key traditional design role in many projects. They are important in shaping the concept and idea of the client into the final scheme. They produce the drawings for pricing the scheme and for the construction of the building. The architect's traditional method of working is to take the concept as defined by the commissioning client from an overall outline as to how the building should look and how it should function, then to work towards that concept, creating more concrete designs as more information becomes available and as the client's ideas crystallise.

Another important role of the architect is to provide a record of what has actually been constructed, something that is essential for future management of the building and for carrying out future alterations.

A summary of the key roles of the architect in the development can be seen in the RIBA Outline Plan of Works, reproduced in Figure 5.1, which lays out the role of the architect at each stage of a scheme.

For different types of procurement the roles may differ. Figure 5.2 illustrates different sequences for completion of work stages for various procurement methods, but these are not representative of time. In arriving at an acceptable timescale, the choice of procurement method may be as important as other, more obvious, factors such as the amount of work to be done, the client's tendering requirements, risks associated with third party approvals or funding, etc.

Further key roles

> Project management (see above).
> Planning consultation and planning application – because of the interaction between the design, the project and the planning issues, it is common, especially in small projects, for the architect also to deal with the planning application. In a large project this role is more usually carried out by specialist planning consultants (see separate description, page 259).
> Issue of certificates of progress, practical completion and final completion – the architect has a very important role during the construction of the building in monitoring the progress of the building and the degree of conformity with the design, especially in traditional projects. In the majority of projects that are subject to monthly stage payments from the client to the contractor, it is the architect who certifies the amount of work that has been done and this is used by the quantity surveyor in pricing up the amount of work completed. Other important certificates issued by the architect include the certificates of practical and final completion. The certificate of practical completion is issued at the end of the main construction phase of the project. It certifies that the building contractor has completed the majority of building works and that, with the exception of minor 'snagging' items (relatively insignificant items that require to be completed or re-done), the works have been completed to the architect's satisfaction. The building then passes from the contractor to a client or developer. The building contractor has no further interest in the building with the exception of a relatively small sum (usually about 5%) of the contract money that is retained for a period that is agreed under the original contract. This money is only passed to the contractor when the architect issues a certificate of final completion. The issue of certificates therefore is a very important role that is fulfilled by architects under most development projects. That is particularly true of the certificate of practical completion that effectively marks the end of the construction phase of the project and the beginning of the occupation or investment phase.
> The architect sometimes acts as a planning supervisor under the CDM[1] regulations.

RIBA ✠ **Outline Plan of Work** 2007

The Outline Plan of Work organises the process of managing, and designing building projects and administering building contracts into a number of key Work Stages. The sequence or content of Work Stages may vary or they may overlap to suit the procurement method (see pages 2 and 3).

RIBA Work Stages			Description of key tasks	OGC Gateways
Preparation	A	**Appraisal**	Identification of client's needs and objectives, business case and possible constraints on development.	
			Preparation of feasibility studies and assessment of options to enable the client to decide whether to proceed.	**1** Business justification
	B	**Design Brief**	Development of initial statement of requirements into the Design Brief by or on behalf of the client confirming key requirements and constraints. Identification of procurement method, procedures, organisational structure and range of consultants and others to be engaged for the project.	
				2 Procurement strategy
Design	C	**Concept**	Implementation of Design Brief and preparation of additional data.	
			Preparation of Concept Design including outline proposals for structural and building services systems, outline specifications and preliminary cost plan.	
			Review of procurement route.	**3A** Design Brief and Concept Approval
	D	**Design Development**	Development of concept design to include structural and building services systems, updated outline specifications and cost plan.	
			Completion of Project Brief.	
			Application for detailed planning permission.	
	E	**Technical Design**	Preparation of technical design(s) and specifications, sufficient to co-ordinate components and elements of the project and *information for statutory standards and construction safety.*	**3B** Detailed Design Approval
Pre-Construction	F	**Production Information**	F1 Preparation of detailed information for construction.	
			Application for statutory approvals.	
			F2 *Preparation of further information for construction required under the building contract. Review of information provided by specialists.*	
	G	**Tender Documentation**	*Preparation and/or collation of tender documentation in sufficient detail to enable a tender or tenders to be obtained for the project.*	
	H	**Tender Action**	*Identification and evaluation of potential contractors and/or specialists for the project.*	
			Obtaining and appraising tenders; submission of recommendations to the client.	**3C** Investment decision
Construction	J	**Mobilisation**	Letting the building contract, appointing the contractor.	
			Issuing of information to the contractor.	
			Arranging site hand over to the contractor.	
	K	**Construction to Practical Completion**	Administration of the building contract to Practical Completion.	
			Provision to the contractor of further Information as and when reasonably required.	
			Review of information provided by contractors and specialists.	**4** Readiness for Service
Use	L	**Post Practical Completion**	L1 Administration of the building contract after Practical Completion and making final inspections.	
			L2 Assisting building user during initial occupation period.	
			L3 Review of project performance in use.	**5** Benefits evaluation

The activities in *italics* may be moved to suit project requirements, ie:
D   *Application for detailed planning approval;*
E   *Statutory standards and construction safety;*
F1   *Application for statutory approvals;* and
F2   *Further information for construction.*
G+H *Invitation and appraisal of tenders*

FIGURE 5.1 RIBA Outline Plan of Works

RIBA ✠ Outline Plan of Work 2007

Work Stage Sequences by Procurement Method

The diagrams illustrate different sequences for completion of work stages for various procurement methods, but are not representative of time. In arriving at an acceptable timescale the choice of procurement method may be as relevant as other more obvious factors such as the amount of work to be done, the client's tendering requirements, risks associated with third party approvals or funding etc.
✠ This symbol indicates that prior to commencement time should be allowed for appointing consultants.

Fully designed project single stage tender

Select advisors ✠ A B | Planning
Select / confirm consultants ✠ C D E F1 F2 L3
G H J K L1+2

Fully designed project with design by contractor or specialist

Select advisors ✠ A B | Planning
Select / confirm consultants ✠ C D E F1 F2 F2
Pre-contract design by Specialist G* H* F1 H2
Post-contract design by Contractor or Specialist F2 L3
Competitive single stage tender G H* J K L1+2
Two stage main contract tender G* H* F1 G H2

G* First stage documentation, H* First stage tender may include Contractor's Proposals, H2 Second stage tender

Design and build project single stage tender

Select advisors ✠ A B | Planning Design review
Select / confirm consultants ✠ C D L3
Employer's requirements G H J K L1+2
Contractor's proposals E F

Note: final design activity by Client may be at stage C, D, E or possibly F. These stages not repeated by contractor

Design and build project two stage tender (all design by contractor)

Appoint consultants ✠ A B Design review L3
Employer's requirements G H1 H2 J/K L1+2
Contractor's proposals C D/E F
Planning

Partnering contract

Output specification by client
Appoint consultants ✠ A B | Planning
Appoint partnering team H C D E F1 F2
Select specialists H E F1 F2 L3
Agree guaranteed maximum price G/H J/K L1+2

Design and construction sequences may be as shown for Management contract/ Construction management

FIGURE 5.2 RIBA Work Stage sequences by procurement method

RIBA ⚎ Outline Plan of Work 2007

Work Stage Sequences by Procurement Method

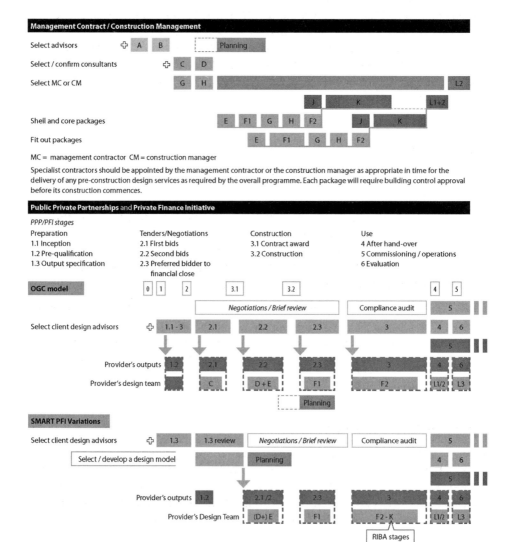

FIGURE 5.2 Continued

Key skills

The key skills to look for when selecting an architect really depend on the nature of the development project being considered.

Architects are trained to have artistic flair, a feel for space utilisation and the ability to translate and interpret ideas into reality. As with many professions, there are many different types of architect with different levels of skill and different strengths. Some architects are very good at aesthetics and design but less good at producing practical solutions to meet the needs of clients. If the project requires strong design and a striking appearance then it is essential to select an architect with flair and imagination. If, however, the project requires a practical solution within a tight budget then it is very important to appoint a pragmatic, experienced professional who is used to working within such constraints. To appoint a 'flair' architect in these circumstances is a recipe for disaster. Is well worth taking the time to talk over ideas with a range of architects and also to consult previous clients of these architects before an appointment is made, if no previous working relationship exists.

Characteristics

A number of potential problems exist in working with architects of which a developer should be aware. These are as follows:

1. buildability issues – it is not uncommon for architects to design buildings and details that cannot practically be constructed on site;
2. with architects, costs tend to be secondary to aesthetics;
3. similarly, commercial requirements and market requirements are secondary to design considerations in many architects' minds.

Members of the development team often find the architect the most difficult member to work with and to understand. This is largely the result of different backgrounds and different outlooks; it is the architect alone, of the whole development team, who has a background in humanities rather than construction, engineering or economics.

Space planners/interior designers

The design of the interior of buildings may be carried out by the main scheme architect. On larger schemes a specialist is sometimes employed. It is, however, rare for a developer to carry out a fit-out of a commercial building. This is normally left to the occupier. There will be occasions, however, when the developer is working to a brief produced by the client and will need to employ such skills.

Landscape architects

Landscape architects are a specialist branch of the architecture profession and, as the name implies, they deal with the external environment of the development. Where the development has fairly minimal external works, the planning and layout of the hard and soft landscaping can be carried out by the lead architect. However, with buildings such as office parks a much higher level of landscaping is required and a specialist landscape architect is essential.

251

Structural engineers

Key roles

The structural engineer, or civil engineer, has a key role in many commercial projects. They are specialists in the design of the structural elements of the building. Normally, the architect will design the general layout of the building, but then pass the responsibility for the structural elements to the structural engineer. The engineer will be responsible for the design, for example, of the structural frame of a building and also for calculating things such as floor loadings and the wind loadings of the structure. Architects have very limited knowledge and qualification in these areas. The second key role that structural engineers play in the development is in monitoring and checking progress on site. Engineers will make regular visits to the site to check calculations provided by the contractor and to inspect and approve the installation of the structural elements.

Key skills

A good structural engineer will need a sound level of experience in the type of development being undertaken. They will need to have an established track record in producing practical solutions to engineering problems.

Characteristics

Structural engineers are a vital part of the development team. Like other members of the team they have their own characteristics. Although education is changing, engineers have a background in calculation and mathematics with little emphasis on financial and management skills. Although some have financial awareness, many do not. A developer should be aware of this fact. The actions of civil engineers may be in conflict with the financial aims of the project. Another characteristic which can be applied to engineers is that they tend to be cautious and over-design some elements of their responsibility. This, too, can have financial implications.

Services engineers

Key roles

Services engineers design elements such as air conditioning, heating, lighting and other service elements. They work hand in hand with mechanical and electrical engineers who design lifts and air conditioning systems. The work of these engineers quite frequently overlaps.

Key skills and characteristics

Many of the key skills and characteristics of services and mechanical and electrical engineers are similar to those for civil and structural engineers. In particular, it is vitally important in complex buildings that these engineers have relevant practical experience of the type of project concerned.

ECONOMICS

There are a number of professionals who work in this area, most being related to the quantity surveying or construction economist professions. The two main types are quantity surveyors and value managers.

Quantity surveyors

Key roles

Quantity surveyors have for many years considered adopting the alternative title of 'construction economist'. This is because they feel this title more accurately reflects their function than 'quantity surveyor'.

The key roles of the quantity surveyor in the development team are:

> cost forecasting
> cost planning
> cost monitoring.

At the initial feasibility stage the quantity surveyor will produce the initial budget and cost forecast. At the outline design stage this forecast will be updated and more detail will be supplied by the client. At the detailed design stage the quantity surveyor will prepare a much more detailed cost forecast and estimate. This may include a month-by-month projection of future costs. This cost prediction is essential for the client to maintain an understanding of the current viability of the project and the effect of any design changes. This information is also vital in budgeting and in arranging finance.

In the conventional procurement route (see later section, page 261), one of the main tasks of the quantity surveyor is to prepare a bill of quantities. The bill of quantities is a detailed document where all the amounts and quantities of materials and construction elements of the proposed building are measured and described using standardised terms.

The bill of quantities has two main functions in the construction process:

> The bill of quantities acts as a tender document. The document is supplied to contractors along with the drawings and specification of the building. The contractors enter prices against the measured quantities. This enables a rapid estimate of the total lump sum cost to be arrived at.
> Once the building contract has been agreed and the work awarded to the successful contractor, the bill of quantities, priced up by the successful contractor, becomes the main method of development monitoring and payment for the contractor. Each month, or whatever the appropriate interval between payments happens to be, the amount of work done will be assessed against the bill of

quantities. A percentage estimate of the amount of work completed is then calculated. This allows the rapid calculation of stage payments. It also allows variations to be calculated relatively quickly using the rates supplied by the contractor in the document.

We will see when we look at alternative methods of procurement below, that the bill of quantities is only really applied in the traditional methods of procurement. When other methods are used by the developer, although the quantity surveyor is still a vital member of the development team, their role is somewhat different. They still have the same areas of responsibility as before but the method of working has to be adapted.

Further key roles

Other roles normally carried out by the quantity surveyor are detailed below.

> Tender scrutiny and checking – despite the presence of the bill of quantities, it is common for mistakes to be made by contractors when pricing work. One of the roles of the quantity surveyor is to audit contractors' bids and to identify errors. These are usually brought to the attention of the contractor who is given the opportunity either to stand by their original estimate, to alter it or to withdraw. Another role of the quantity surveyor is to assess the viability of the estimates submitted. Although it is normal to take the lowest estimate, it is sometimes obvious that contractors have mispriced work and that it cannot be done for the sum submitted. In these circumstances it may be best to take a more viable tender from an alternative contractor.
> Quantity surveyors are responsible, as we have already seen, for stage payments under the majority of building contracts. This normally requires the quantity surveyor to undertake monthly valuations of work completed on site. These valuations are supplied either to the architect or project manager or whoever is responsible for approving payments.
> Quantity surveyors are also responsible for the pricing of the variations. These are changes in design, quantity or timing of the construction work for which the main contractor will require additional payment.
> Quantity surveyors also have responsibility for agreeing the final account with the contractor.
> A further role is in dispute resolution.
> As well as the initial forecast and cost estimate, the quantity surveyor provides regular updates of the forecast and monitors the expenditure on a week-by-week basis. This is an essential tool of project management.
> In certain circumstances, the quantity surveyor can also act as the project manager.

Key skills

The characteristics of a good quantity surveyor are essentially related to thoroughness and diligence.

Characteristics

With quantity surveyors, cost dominates everything else. They will attempt to save money at every turn. This can conflict with the aims of the development as a whole. Another characteristic of quantity surveyors is the confrontational nature of much of their dealings with contractors. Contractors also employ their own in-house quantity surveyors, whose role it is to carry out the financial side of the contract process on behalf of the contractors. This includes agreeing monthly valuations with the developer's surveyor and also preparing and calculating claims for variations, which are subsequently negotiated with the developer's surveyor. All of these functions do tend to be confrontational and this can spill over into other working relationships.

Notwithstanding this, the quantity surveyor is an essential element of the development team. It is almost impossible to undertake development work and to manage a large project without their services.

Value managers

A further member of the team who deals with the economics of development is the value manager. These professionals had their origins in the USA. Value managers attempt to scrutinise a design before it goes to the tender stage in order to determine whether costs can be saved, i.e. whether the design is efficient or if some alternative, better solution can be found. Value management has been increasingly used in the UK to save costs in construction. It is, however, rare to make use of this in commercial investment developments.

CONSTRUCTION

Contractors

Contractors are often in an odd position in the development environment. To many outsiders, contractors are the physical embodiment of development; they are the 'developer'. It comes as something of a surprise to many to find that, in fact, the contractor is most frequently only a component of the development, the tip of the iceberg in a way, in that they represent only the visible 10 per cent of the whole effort. The contractor is a key part of the development process, which goes almost without saying. The development team needs the acquired skills, knowledge and experience of the contractor to complete the project successfully. In many ways, however, the status of the contractor is ambiguous.

In 'conventional' contractual arrangements (this term will be explained below) the contractor is almost a third party, an outsider, perhaps even considered to be the 'opposition' to the development team. This is because in traditional developments the contractor is not part of the design team but is the last element of the team, brought in later. If we repeat a diagram that we used in Chapter 1 (Figure 5.3), we will see that the contractor's position is quite separate from the rest of the team in the traditional arrangement. This is something that the construction and development

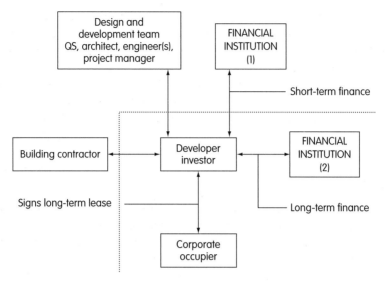

FIGURE 5.3 Speculative development: developer trader

team have long considered to have undesirable characteristics, not least of which is that this arrangement lends itself to conflict. It also means that contractors' inputs into the design process are limited; a good contractor can suggest alternative solutions to design or alternative methods of working. It is because of this that alternative methods of procurement have been developed that will be reviewed later in this section, which integrate the contractor into the development at an earlier stage. We will also explore why these alternatives have had a limited impact on many types of development.

Key roles

The key role of the contractor is, naturally, to complete the scheme as per their contract. They will need to employ the requisite skills, personnel and equipment to do so. How they do so is largely up to the contractor as long as they fulfil the terms of the contract. The client/developer has only limited powers to influence the way the contractor actually conducts the development.

Key skills

The developer should spend considerable time and effort reassuring themselves that the contractors they select to go on the tender list (assuming this is the approach adopted) have sufficient experience and sufficient resources to complete the scheme to the standard required and within the requisite time period. Not all contractors are the same, even at the larger end of the market. The large contractors have different strengths and it is worth reviewing the type of contracts they have recently undertaken to see where their experience really lies. Smaller contractors are far more variable in terms of their skills, experience and resources.

Taking the latter as a factor, many of the problems that exist at the domestic and smaller commercial-type end of the market in terms of delayed completion and intermittent progress is due to contractors taking on too much work and spreading themselves too thinly trying to keep everyone happy. Contractors do not like turning work down for fear of not being considered for future work. They therefore sometimes make irrational decisions about workloads. Although most building contracts contain provision for imposing penalties for late completions, these clauses are difficult to enforce, time consuming to pursue and usually give inadequate compensation for the true impact of late delivery on the developer. Late delivery may mean the loss of a tenant or a sale. It is best to do as much as possible to avoid these problems before the contract is placed.

Similar over-optimism also exists with regard to skills. The skill requirements for a contractor will vary from development to development. It is important for the developer to identify exactly what the critical skills are for the scheme and match these requirements against the list of potential tenderers. Other members of the development team, particularly the architect and quantity surveyors, are important in this process because they often have prior knowledge from previous schemes of contractors in the market-place. Even if no direct prior experience has been gained, the members of the development team are often able to use their contacts with professional colleagues in other organisations to obtain this information.

It is vitally important to most schemes that this investigation work is done. Selecting a contractor blindly without prior research is like playing Russian roulette. Usually one can get away with it but the consequences of making an incorrect selection can be severe. The building industry has a bad reputation, and with good reason. Choosing a big name contractor will usually give some guarantees. Below this, taking up references and doing plenty of research is absolutely essential.

Characteristics

Many of the points to beware of have been covered in the previous section. There are, however, other points to take into account when dealing with contractors.

Perhaps the most important is that many contractors acquire work with low or sometimes zero profit margins. The reason for this is simply to capture turnover in competition with other firms. Of course, they then need to find a profit margin. They do so in a number of ways.

Squeezing subcontractors' margins Subcontractors are contractors to contractors, employed by the main contractor to do elements of work. Many large contractors do not retain many staff directly but instead operate essentially as management shells employing personnel and equipment as required. Many tradesmen and labourers are 'labour only subcontractors'. Main contractors also employ smaller firms to carry out specific or specialist tasks. It is these bodies which tender for work from the main contractor and who then find their contract sums reduced by negotiation. These organisations have little power and are open to manipulation.

Failure to pay subcontractors on time   Related to the above, is a tendency for contractors to delay paying subcontractors even though the work has been done and the main contractor paid by the developer. This enables extra interest and credit to be obtained.

Although neither of the above practices is illegal or strictly the concern of the developer, these practices can cause bad working relations on site and also force subcontractors to take short cuts and reduce the quality of the finished product. A wise client would put pressure on the main contractor not to follow these practices.

Exploitation of variations and disputes   This is perhaps the most popular of the methods employed by contractors to maintain margins. Contractors also employ quantity surveyors whose main role is to negotiate interim and final payments for the contractors and also to negotiate variations. Variations, as we have seen, arise out of things such as design changes and changes in, for example, the order of work. Another common source of variation claims are errors in the contract documentation. These include items such as misdescription or mismeasurement of work or mistakes on drawings. Once the contract documentation is received, many contractors scour the material searching for errors. Some contractors are more litigious than others, this can be determined at the pre-tender selection enquiry stage.

OTHER MEMBERS OF THE DEVELOPMENT TEAM

Just because the members of the team fall into this category does not downgrade their importance. These parties have a significant impact on the design, cost and execution of the project if used correctly. A number of bodies fall into these categories but two of the key ones are property agents or consultants and planning consultants.

Property consultants

A number of different types of property consultants are used by developers. The roles of many will be considered later in the post-construction section, but the roles within the development process will be considered here.

The most common types of consultants used are listed below.

> *Residential agents* – used in marketing residential property but also in terms of input into the design process and make up of the development.
> *Residential land agents* – these consultants specialise in the identification and acquisition of land, with or without planning consent, for residential development. Specialist knowledge is required to successfully fulfil this role, particularly of the practicalities of development and the attitude of the planning authorities.
> *Valuation surveyor* – used during the process mainly to value the site for loan security purposes.
> *Development surveyors* – these are members of the surveying profession who specialise in development work. They are multi-skilled in terms of the tasks they can undertake, which range from valuation and appraisal work, to advice on

development form and design, marketing of the completed scheme and planning advice and applications.

> *Commercial agency surveyors* – these are probably the most important of the property consultants in commercial schemes. They have three main roles:
  - to secure an acceptable tenant for a scheme
  - to negotiate the heads of terms[2] with the occupiers, particularly the rental level and the outline lease terms (period (term) of the lease, rent review details, user clause, repairs and maintenance, etc.)
  - to advise the development team on current market requirements and trends at all stages of the development but particularly at the feasibility stage, final design, pre-tender stage and also during the course of the development.

  Getting these professionals involved at an early stage of a development will pay dividends, avoid costly design mistakes and negate the need for late changes in design. They form a key interface between the market and the production team.

> *Commercial investment agents* – these professionals are not usually the same as commercial letting agents. They have different roles and possess different skills. Commercial investment agents tend to be rather more technically adroit and numerate than letting agents as they have to deal with financial analysis and investment appraisal. Their two main roles are:
  - to advise the development team on the market requirements of investors
  - to secure the sale of the investment (as opposed to occupational) interest in the scheme (if, of course, the property is not to be retained by the developer or sold on to owner occupiers) at an acceptable rate and within an acceptable time period.

Characteristics

The main potential problem with property consultants is their tendency to be over-confident and over-optimistic about property markets and therefore the prospects for development. An important function of an agent is to 'talk up' markets to maintain confidence. This will enable turnover and activity in the market to be maintained. It can, however, be overdone, which can increase the tendency for property markets to crash by allowing unsustainable values and prices to be maintained for too long.

Planning consultants

Planning consultants play an increasingly important role in development. Planning consultants are the private sector side of the planning profession. Traditionally, planners were only employed by the public sector to fulfil the standard planning role of urban and economic development of an area. Over the past two decades in particular planners have crossed over to the developers' side to assist in the navigation of schemes through the planning process. Just as agents give invaluable early input about market requirements into the design process, so planning consultants perform a similar function in advising the planning authorities on what is and what is not acceptable.

PROJECT STAGES	A Appraisal	B Design Brief	C Concept	D Design Development	E Technical Design	F Production Information	G Tender Documentation	H Tender Action	J Mobilisation	K Construction to Practical Completion	L Post Practical Completion	Letting and/or sale
	PREPARATION		DESIGN			PRE-CONSTRUCTION			CONSTRUCTION		USE	LETTING
ARCHITECT'S ROLE	CLIENT BRIEFING PERIOD		SKETCH PLANNING PERIOD		WORKING PLAN PERIOD LEADING TO PREPARATION OF FINAL DESIGN				SITE OPERATIONS PERIOD			
	Outline sketches		Revisals	Scheme design plans	Detail design			Contract drawings issued	Monitor/late revisions/issue of details	Certificate of practical completion	'As built' drawings issued	Certification of final completion
QUANTITY SURVEYOR'S ROLE			COST PLANNING PERIOD						COST CONTROL PERIOD		COST RECONCILIATION PERIOD	FINAL ACCOUNT
	Initial cost limits set		Cost limits finalised		Cost checks	Outline cost plan finalised	Bills of quantity prepared		Cost monitoring and preparation of periodic valuations for stage payment of contactor		Preparation of final account	Release of retention
						Cost checks		Cost analysis				
AGENT/PROPERTY CONSULTANT'S ROLE	INITIAL APPRAISAL		FINAL APPRAISAL AND MARKET FOCUS						MARKETING			
	Briefing by client	Preliminary valuation advice	On-going valuation and marketing advice as the scheme develops					Final valuation and market advice before commitment to build made	On-going valuation and marketing advice as the scheme develops — Monitoring of market	Marketing and letting programme begins	Negotiations with occupiers and investors	Agreement of sale and/or leasing
		Market analysis		Monitoring of market								

FIGURE 5.4 Roles of the main project team members during a typical traditional property development project

The main roles of planning consultants are to:

> provide planning input to the design process;
> conduct schemes through the initial application process including leading negotiations and consultation with the local planning authorities;
> assist in the preparation of reports supporting planning applications; and
> prepare and argue the case for development during planning appeals.

There are now few large schemes where planning consultants are not involved. A trend is for local authorities and other public bodies to also employ planning consultants to counter the arguments of developers' consultants, particularly where a planning application is rejected and an appeal is made.

Other professionals employed by developers include environmental assessment consultants, archaeologists and market researchers.

INTEGRATION AND COORDINATION OF THE DEVELOPMENT TEAM IN THE DEVELOPMENT PROCESS

This is a difficult issue to summarise, but an indication of how some of the key members of the development team and the sequence of the development process fit together is given in Figure 5.4.

Methods of procurement

At some stage, a method of project selection must be decided on for procuring the building work, i.e. the process of physically realising the development. There are numerous ways of achieving this, the choice being dependent on a number of factors related to the objectives of the developer. The key factors include time, cost, quality, level of control and risk.

All of the methods of procurement have different characteristics related to these variables. Some are good for reducing cost; some allow the development to retain a high level of control, etc. Which one is chosen depends on the nature of the individual contract or development and sometimes even on the personal preferences of the developer involved. To give an example of this, many institutional investors prefer the conventional methods of procurement. The conventional methods of procurement see the separation of the design and construction elements of the project. In such cases, the contractor is placed outside the development team, as we have seen, leading to a more adversarial and confrontational relationship. Institutions need to have both certainty and control, something provided by the traditional methods, despite their other, acknowledged flaws. The conventional method also has the benefit of familiarity, therefore, despite the criticisms, it continues to be used.

The various methods of procurement can be summarised as follows:

> conventional methods
  - single-stage selective tendering
  - two-stage selective tendering

- negotiation
> integrated procurement systems
  - design and build
  - package deals
  - turnkey method
  - develop and construct
> management-orientated procurement systems
  - management contracting
  - construction management
  - design and manage.

CONVENTIONAL PROCUREMENT METHODS

The main feature of these methods, called conventional because these methods have a long history of use, is the separation of the design from the construction element. The design is largely completed by an architect, assisted by other specialist designers such as civil engineers and mechanical and electrical engineers, and prior to the on-site work commencing. The design work is usually completed prior to tendering. The contractor's main role is managing the project rather than assisting with the design, giving little scope for the designers and contractors to become involved in each other's activities.

The conventional method tends to be a sequential process involving four main stages of work:

1. preparation
2. design
3. preparation and obtaining of tenders
4. construction.

Preparation

This is where the inception of the project takes place. The client, in this case the developer, establishes his or her concept of the type of building that is required. With most developers this is market-led, but where there is an identified end user this process involves working directly with the intended occupier. This process will establish or at least outline their requirements. An architect and project manager are appointed to draft the outline of the building required to establish the feasibility of the scheme.

Design

The main outcome of this stage is the establishment of a design that meets the needs of the client. This must be done before obtaining tenders or commencing work on site. It is essential for the design to be completed before site work commences.

It is in this area where the traditional approach is most heavily criticised. There is a lack of consultation and involvement between the design team and the contractors. This is due to four factors:

1. The client usually chooses to retain control of design.
2. A list of tenders is not usually available until the design is completed.
3. The contractor's identity is not finalised at this stage. Different contractors being involved at this stage are likely to give different input which may confuse the design process.
4. By the time the on-site work has commenced it is really too late to alter the scheme design. Any input from the contractor changing the design will cause increases in cost and delays.

Preparation of tender documents and obtaining tenders

In conventional procurement this usually consists of the preparations of drawings, specifications and bills of quantities. Sometimes, for smaller projects, the bill of quantities is dispensed with and the tender documentation consists of drawings and specification only. This documentation needs to be accurate as tenders are prepared using these materials. Changes made later and mistakes corrected will be expensive.

Usually between four and six contractors are selected, contacted and invited to prepare a tender. These tenders usually consist of sealed bids prepared without collusion and submitted before a specified time.

Construction

This phase is the actual execution of the works. This is frequently carried out under a standard building contract, usually prepared by the Joint Contracts Tribunal (JCT) such as JCT 2005. These contracts include things such as time to complete, payment methods, standards required, relevant authorities during construction and also methods of dispute resolution. It should be noted that during the contract the site belongs to the contractor. The contractor is responsible for issues such as safety and therefore can exclude anyone from the site, including the client.

Characteristics and qualities of this method of procurement

Cost

When the design is fully developed and a bill of quantities prepared then the tendering costs are reduced for contractors. There is also a clear definition of the scope and character of the works. This greatly reduces uncertainty and gives a level playing field for true competition between contractors. In other methods, the contractor has to interpret far more, which gives rise to differences between tenders. On the downside, preparation costs for the client are higher and the design must be frozen earlier.

Time

There are two elements involved when considering the time characteristics of this method of procurement: the pre-contract and on-site works. There is no real difference between this method and others for the on-site work, although the methods and sequence of working may be more strictly defined than with other methods. The main difference is in the pre-contract preparation work, which makes this one of the slowest methods of procurement.

Quality and control

This method of procurement gives the highest degree of control over the finished product. It is for this reason that this method continues to be preferred by investment clients.

Advantages

1. This method is understood by most members of the team. It has the clear attraction of familiarity.
2. The main advantage has to be the ability of the client to control the output of the development process very closely.
3. The client can select the design team to suit the needs of the development.
4. The client can decide when to commit to the contract.

Disadvantages

1. The main disadvantage is speed. This is generally regarded as the slowest of the procurement methods.
2. It is not a good method for achieving cost savings.
3. It is difficult to deal with later design changes that may be required in the scheme.
4. The contractor is remote, and has very little opportunity to influence the project or to make an impact or have an input into the design or other aspects of the scheme until a very late stage.

Although heavily criticised, this method continues to be used. This is because many clients find that the advantages greatly outweigh the disadvantages. It is particularly true of investment clients, where control is far more important than, for example, cost saving. Many members of the construction team, particularly those concerned with cost, find this a difficult concept to understand. If, however, the relative impact of changing cost and changing values in an appraisal are investigated, in the great majority of cases it is the latter which has a much greater impact. For this reason, control of the output is the major requirement of procurement methods used for the construction of investment properties.

Variants

Two-stage selective tendering

As the name implies, two-stage selective tendering involves two distinct stages of the tender process. It is used in a number of circumstances. One example is where the design is not finalised. A second example is where the control of the finished product by the client is not as critical as in the above scenario. A final reason for use is where the building is complex and more input in terms of design and advice from the contractor is required.

In the first stage of the tender process, outline sketch drawings and bills of approximate quantities are sent out to between three and six contractors who are invited to submit tenders. The successful tenderer is notified of the client's intention to enter into a binding contract, subject to conditions. An acceptable final tender figure is agreed between the client and the potential contractor. The chosen contractor then agrees to cooperate with the design team. They give advice on issues such as buildability, materials, costs, programming and the detailed design.

This approach is worthwhile where the project is complex and where experience exists among contractors which will assist in the design and construction. The disadvantages of this approach are that the competitive element is lost after the first stage of the tender process.

Negotiated contracts

These proceed as per the conventional single-stage tender process, at least until after the outline design stage. At the detailed design stage a contractor is appointed. The appointment is based on the contractor's past expertise and past record of similar projects.

This type of contract is most effective in unusual, innovative or complex projects where the contractor's prior experience of similar situations allows their advice to be provided at the critical design stage. This helps in buildability issues, timing of work and programming as well as cost forecasting.

There are a number of ways of appointing the contractor including interviewing a range of suitable contractors and negotiation with a single contractor which is known to the team or the client.

This method of procurement saves time and reduces risk but can be more expensive as the competitive element is reduced.

Continuity contract

These types of contracts are used where a number of phases are involved. For example, a project with two similar phases may see the first phase contract awarded using a single-stage selective process, as per the traditional approach, then the second phase of the contract being negotiated. This usually involves modifying or updating the first set of priced tender documents.

This approach reduces the time required and the cost of preparing a second tender process. There are drawbacks with the approach, given that the competitive element is reduced. In addition, there is no guarantee that a contractor, having behaved well in the first contract, will do so in the second, particularly if there is no further phase of work to consider in the future. A contractor remaining in the second phase of the work might divert labour and machinery to other contracts. What might seem a sensible approach to the client may in fact go badly wrong.

Serial contracts

These are similar to the above but, in this case, there is a series of contracts, some consecutive and some occurring simultaneously. In these cases it is cheaper to work to a master bill of quantities. This document contains the rates for a series of activities across the various contracts.

Cost reimbursement contracts

There are a number of types of cost reimbursement contract.

One is the cost plus approach. Here, the contractor tenders for work at an agreed cost and rates supplied by the client's quantity surveyor. The contractor, as part of the tendering process, just adds a percentage for overheads and profit as required. The contract is awarded usually to the lowest percentage bid.

A second type of cost reimbursement contract is the target cost procurement method. Here, the contractor is given a target cost. Any savings actually achieved are shared as an additional profit between contractor and client. There are problems with this approach, the principal one being that, if the contract goes wrong and the target cost is exceeded, then the contractor may lose motivation to complete the project on time.

INTEGRATED PROCUREMENT SYSTEMS

Another name used for these approaches is integrated procurement systems. This is because the design and construction elements are the responsibility of a single organisation, usually a contractor. These methods have multiplied over the past 30–40 years. The impetus has come from two sources: first, contractors who feel that greater and earlier input into the design and development process will increase efficiency and reduce costs; and, second, the wish of some clients to reduce both costs and time. Although these methods give distinct advantages, the use of the conventional methods still continues, much to the chagrin and sometimes bewilderment of academics, Government and contractors.

The reasons for the continuing use of the conventional methods have been outlined above, namely the issues of controlling the project output and familiarity. Cost, as we have seen, is not the key element in many investment projects, **control** of the project is. In addition, fund managers (who make the key decisions on many development projects) are cautious, risk-averse people. Conventional contracts are a known entity with relatively low levels of risk to the client. Their argument is why, therefore, bother taking on more risk to save a relatively small amount of money?

To illustrate this point we will examine a typical industrial investment project:

Project values

End value	£3,000,000
Cost of land	£1,000,000
Cost of construction	£1,000,000
Professional fees	£250,000
Finance cost	£250,000
Profit	£500,000

Taking a non-conventional route may save 5 per cent of the construction costs. There may also, however, be the risk of losing 5 per cent of the value due not quite meeting the requirements of the market. As we have seen, these methods do not allow the client the same degree of control. If we examine the impact of this on the project viability we can see the type of risk that the client is running:

Project values

End value	£2,850,000
Cost of land	£1,000,000
Cost of construction	£950,000
Professional fees	£237,500
Finance cost	£250,000
Profit	£412,500

In this scenario, although the costs are reduced, profits have fallen because of the impact on the end value. Of course, this will not always occur, but why take the risk? Why should investors give up their control? Contractors are not in touch with the market and do not normally share in profits so why should they worry?

This factor does not rule out the use of these methods nor do these problems occur with every type of project; however, the developer should carefully consider the potential downside risk before adopting these methods of procurement.

We will consider four main types of integrated procurement systems:

1. design and build
2. package deals
3. turnkey method
4. develop and construct.

Design and build

This is one of the best known of the integrated procurement systems. In this approach the client develops a brief as to the type of building required. This brief needs to be clearly presented with regard to what is required and also sufficiently comprehensive for tender bids to be prepared on a competitive basis. The contractor bids a lump sum to cover the design and construction of the building based on information supplied. The bid is on a fixed price basis, i.e. it cannot change unless there is a substantial change in a requirement from the client. The process produces a simplified contract and functional relationship. The contractor who is successful commences the detailed design in consultation with the client.

Advantages

> A considerable amount of time can be saved as the contractor is also responsible for the design. This means that the contractor is not waiting for details and it is therefore possible to overlap elements of the design and construction due to the integration of the two processes.
> As long as the brief is comprehensive and accurate it is possible to achieve certainty in project costs for the developer.
> A closer working relationship is developed between the client and the contractor.

Disadvantages

> Perhaps the major disadvantage of this approach is that the client loses detailed control of the finished product.
> In this approach, no bill of quantities is produced. This makes the pricing of any variations on the contract very difficult.
> There have been questions about the quality of the finished product produced using this procurement method. The contractor is primarily concerned with cost reduction and maintaining or increasing the margin between actual costs and the agreed tender sum. This can impact on the building produced.

There are other points to be aware of when using this procurement method. An important factor to establish prior to the appointment of the contractor is whether the organisation has sufficient depth of design expertise to adequately complete the work. There are organisations which possess the requisite know-how and depth of experience of design and build, and indeed are design and build specialists. There are many other organisations who do not specialise in this field. Many contractors have gone down the design and build route to obtain work then buy in the design expertise by employing outside firms of architects. In this situation the advantages of design and construction integration that design and build can offer are largely lost. There is little real advantage over the traditional approaches, other than potential cost savings.

Package deals

Package deals are very similar to the above; however, a bespoke design is not produced. The contractor instead uses an 'off the shelf' solution, i.e. a design used elsewhere in another building. Using a ready-made design should be both cheaper and also a lower risk option in that any technical defects should have been eradicated in the previous attempts. The main downside of these approaches is that the product may not fully satisfy the client's needs.

Turnkey method

This is a more comprehensive approach to the production of a building. Effectively, it involves a full facilities management set-up of the building, including installation and commissioning of all operational equipment and sometimes goes as far as recruiting and training staff to run the facility. The PFI/PPP approaches are extensions of this. The approach allows a rapid use of the facility by the user. It is therefore particularly useful in complex buildings or facilities such as advanced manufacturing or medical facilities. It has not been widely used in mainstream investment type properties, usually because the end user has often not been identified prior to the development commencing and also due to a lack of demand by end users for these types of services.

Develop and construct

This is another variation on the same theme. In this case the client's consultants are provided with a brief from the concept drawings and an indicative site layout is produced. Contractors, as part of the tender process, develop the initial design, producing detailed drawings and specifications and submit this as part of their bid. The contractor then effectively becomes the developer, coordinating the scheme as a traditional developer would do, sometimes including arranging finance and employing other contractors.

MANAGEMENT-ORIENTATED PROCUREMENT SYSTEMS

This section deals with a group of procurement methods that sees the main contractor act more as a manager of the construction process than as a direct contractor.

Management contracting

This method has increased in popularity since the early 1970s. The main feature is that the management contractor does none of the construction work, instead operating as a coordinator and procurer of subcontractors. This service is provided on a fee basis as part of the developer's management team. The management contractor provides and maintains all necessary site equipment such as offices, storerooms, roads, etc., and is appointed either because of previous relationships with the client or because of bids on a competitive fee basis for the contract. The management contractor then takes all the steps necessary to complete the building to the client's specification and budget by employing a series of subcontractors to carry out the various sub-tasks of the building.

This approach offers a number of advantages:

> the contractor becomes part of the development team, adding valuable practical knowledge and input to the planning and design process;
> it is possible that time will be saved by overlapping elements of design and construction;
> it is a useful method when the details of the works are not finalised at the time of the initial tender;
> splitting up the works into component parts and subcontracting them out allows the early work to be completed without hold up, while the plans for the later stages are defined.

There are, however, disadvantages to the method:

> the final cost of the project is not known until the final contracts are placed;
> the method's flexibility invites variations in design to be made.

This can lead to problems with keeping costs under control and may lead to variation claims from individual subcontractors due to changes in the design in other parts of the works.

Construction management

Construction management is not, in fact, a procurement system. It refers to the service offered to the developer by a professional construction manager, who is often, but not always, working for a major contracting organisation. The service offered is very similar to the situation described in the management contracting section above.

Design and management

Design and management is a variation on the same theme. In this case, however, the construction manager or management contractor also procures the design of the building, either on an in-house basis or, more commonly, with the architect/designer as a further subcontractor.

With these last two methods, the main advantages are related to the closer integration of the construction process into the management of the development. Time should be saved with the input of the construction professionals, particularly with regard to the more rapid identification of practical problems and with the opportunity for design and construction to proceed in parallel. Again, there are problems with the number of subcontractors involved (instead of just one main contractor) and with the lack of certainty about the project cost until late on in the process.

CONCLUSIONS TO THE PROCUREMENT SECTION

As we have seen, a number of procurement methods are available to a developer. Each has its own strengths and weaknesses. The developer should aim to match their goals with the appropriate procurement strategy when selecting a method. For example, if speed and cost minimisation is the goal, then one of the integrated procurement systems should be followed. If certainty of output is required, then the choice should be one of the traditional methods. Certainly, the investment industry in the UK has tended to stay with the traditional methods, which seem to confirm that certainty and familiarity are more highly valued. There has been some movement towards more contemporary methods of procurement in the investment and speculative market, however. This tends to happen when the buildings produced across the market are similar and where profit margins are made thin by relatively low rents. This tends to be the situation with the decentralised office market and the industrial market. It seems that the preference for traditional methods in higher value situations such as city centres will be maintained.

Contracts and contracting

The final component in the execution of the project is the contract itself. This is a specialised area, one that the professional team, particularly the quantity surveyor, will advise the developer on. A brief summary of the main contract types will be included here.

It is worth reviewing the overall purpose of the contract as this often gets missed in the detail. The purpose of the building contract is simply to ensure that the employer obtains the building or structure that they desire at the cost predicted, and that the contractor is able to provide this and receive payment for this work, either as a final lump sum or, more frequently, in stages as the works proceed.

The contract should therefore be a clear and binding document that avoids any ambiguity. It should lay out the work to be done. It should define the information to be provided by each party. It should identify who is responsible for what activity. It should clearly define the moneys to be paid and the basis on which the money is to be released. It should lay down the procedures and processes to be followed should there be any dispute. All of this is a well worn path for many in the construction field. Essentially, it means that, although individual bespoke contracts for work can be drawn up by a developer, they would be very unwise to do so. It is far better to use standard forms of contract.

STANDARD FORMS OF BUILDING CONTRACTS

Most building contracts in the UK involve the Joint Contracts Tribunal (JCT). Using a standard contract form has to be the recommended path. It provides consistency for all parties and also provides a reliable framework for dispute resolution.

The JCT was established in 1931 and has produced standard forms of contracts, guidance notes and other standard documentation for use in the construction industry ever since. In 1998 the JCT became incorporated as a company limited by guarantee. The company is responsible for producing suites of contract documents and for operating the JCT Council.

From 2005 the JCT started to issue a revised series of contracts under the blanket title of JCT 2005. The JCT 2005 contracts available are:

> Standard Building Contract (SBC)
  - SBC/AQ Standard Building Contract With Approximate Quantities
  - SBC/Q Standard Building Contract With Quantities
  - SBC/XQ Standard Building Contract Without Quantities
> SBC Sub-Contracts
  - SBCSub/A Standard Building Sub-Contract Agreement
  - SBCSub/C Standard Building Sub-Contract Conditions
  - SBCSub/D/A Standard Building Sub-Contract with sub-contractor's design Agreement
  - SBCSub/D/C Standard Building Sub-Contract with sub-contractor's design Conditions
> Intermediate Building Contract (IC)
  - IC Intermediate Building Contract
  - ICD Intermediate Building Contract with contractor's design
> IC Sub-Contracts
  - ICSub/A Intermediate Sub-Contract Agreement
  - ICSub/C Intermediate Sub-Contract Conditions
  - ICSub/D/A Intermediate Sub-Contract with sub-contractor's design Agreement
  - ICSub/D/C Intermediate Sub-Contract with sub-contractor's design Conditions
  - ICSub/NAM Intermediate Named Sub-Contract Tender and Agreement
  - ICsub/NAM/C Intermediate Named Sub-Contract Conditions
  - ICSub/NAM/E Intermediate Named Sub-Contractor/Employer Agreement
> Minor Works Building Contract (MW)
  - MW Minor Works Building Contract
  - MWD Minor Works Building Contract with contractor's design
  - MWSub/D Minor Works Sub-Contract with sub-contractor's design
> Design and Build Contract (DB)
  - DB Design and Build Contract
> DB Sub-Contracts
  - DBSub/A Design and Build Sub-Contract Agreement
  - DBSub/C Design and Build Sub-Contract Conditions
> Major Project Construction Contract (MP)
  - MP Major Project Construction Contract
> MP Sub-Contracts
  - MPSub Major Project Sub-Contract
> JCT – Constructing Excellence Contract (CE)
  - CE JCT – Constructing Excellence Contract
  - CE/P JCT – Constructing Excellence Contract Project Team Agreement
> Construction Management (CM)
  - CM/A Construction Management Appointment

- — CM/TC Construction Management Trade Contract
- > Management Building Contract (MC)
  - — MC Management Building Contract
  - — MCWK/A Management Works Contract Agreement
  - — MCWK/C Management Works Contract Conditions
  - — CWK/E Management Works Contractor/Employer Agreement
- > Prime Cost Building Contract (PCC)
  - — PCC Prime Cost Building Contract
- > Measured Term Contract (MTC)
  - — MTC Measured Term Contract
  - — MTC/G Measured Term Contract Guide
- > Housing Grant Works Building Contract (HG)
- > Repair and Maintenance Contract (Commercial) (RM)

An excellent guide to selecting the appropriate contract is available from the JCT's website (www.jctltd.co.uk).[3]

Although there are important detailed changes in this new family of JCT contracts, the main changes made from previous JCT contracts (known as JCT 1998) are largely designed to make life easier on the reader:

- > The Conditions have been divided into Sections and the same section headings have been adopted across the entire JCT 2005 suite of contracts, making it easier to locate specific provisions when working on different contracts.
- > The Sections have been simplified and there are fewer of them. The effect of this has been to completely re-arrange the 1998 Conditions.
- > The majority of statutory and procedural material has been deleted because they were deemed unnecessary and their removal benefits the user by reducing the overall length of the contracts.

For more in-depth guidance on the main groups of the JCT 2005 contracts, it is worth referring the excellent series of contract guides written by Sarah Lupton and produced by RIBA Publishing (www.ribapublishing.com).

The JCT standard forms of contract are meant to be comprehensive but they can be amended by the parties. Amendments are common and are often successful but they are also often a source of litigation and should be avoided or, at least, very carefully considered.

Conclusions

The execution stage of the project represents the culmination of what is often a long, difficult process. It is a stage where the project vision becomes, literally, concrete. In order for the completed project to realise the developer's vision, this stage must be carefully planned. It is a stage that rewards attention to detail and careful preparation. If this is not done considerable delays can result, costs can mount and the end product may not be that required by either the developer or the market.

Of all the areas in this phase of the project, it is perhaps those concerned with the personnel elements that are the most critical. Time taken to assemble the right team, with the right knowledge and skills, will be well spent. The right team will greatly ease the burden on the developer and ensure that all the requisite pieces of the development jigsaw are put in place.

POST COMPLETION
CHAPTER 6

Introduction

What is a successful development? There are many definitions, but one overrides the rest. A successful development is one that does not lose money! Part of the process that results in a successful development is related to how the completed product of the development process is treated after completion. This chapter looks at this post-completion phase.

Activities involved in the post-completion phase

There are three main options at the end of the development process. These are:

1. to sell on the building to an owner occupier;
2. to lease the building to an occupier and sell the freehold investment interest on to a third party;
3. to lease the building to an occupier and retain the freehold as an investment.

A number of variations on these options exist but these are the fundamental choices. Each requires different activities to be carried out by the development team in the post-development phase.

a. Option (1) requires marketing and advertising to be carried out to find occupiers and/or purchasers for the completed scheme.
b. Option (2) requires:
   i.   the setting up of an acceptable investment vehicle that will be suitable for occupiers and acceptable to investors,
   ii. marketing and advertising to find occupiers, and
   iii. marketing and advertising to find investors willing to purchase.
c. Option (3) requires (i) and (ii), as above, and also requires the creation of an ongoing management system. This is necessary to service the property as an investment. This system will need to cover income collection, tenant monitoring, assessment of maintenance, etc. These are all factors necessary to maintain the value of the investment in the future.

These activities and processes are ones that should not be tacked on as an afterthought but must be integrated into the design and planning process.

Responsibilities for the main activities in the post-completion phase

The activities introduced above are largely typical functions of a good chartered surveying firm, although a separate marketing consultancy may need to be employed for specialist areas. Even where this is the case, it is best to coordinate this through a partnership with a commercial agent.

Is worthwhile acquiring a thorough understanding of the make-up of chartered surveying firms. Traditionally, firms involved in this area would be termed 'general practice' or GP firms. Strictly, today this type of surveyor does not exist as the professional body, the Royal Institution of Chartered Surveyors (RICS) has reorganised its divisions into several faculties. These are:

> Antiques and Fine Art
> Management Consultancy
> Building Surveying
> Minerals and Waste Management
> Commercial Property
> Planning and Development
> Construction
> Plant and Machinery
> Dispute Resolution
> Project Management
> Environment
> Residential Property
> Facilities Management
> Rural
> Geomatics
> Valuation.

It is likely that the majority of surveying people involved in the post-completion phase will be drawn mainly from the commercial property faculty, although surveyors from other disciplines will be used. It should also be noted that surveyors can and do have multiple membership of several faculties.

As we have seen in the development team construction, surveyors are an integral part of the team, which is important to involve at the design stage. The list of the functional specialisations of surveyors involved in the process is quite extensive:

> residential land agents
> residential sale agents
> residential letting agents
> commercial agents
  − retail[1]
  − office
  − industrial
> investment agents

TABLE 6.1 Fees involved in some of the key functions

Residential letting	Typically 10–15% of gross rental value
Commercial letting	Approximately 10% of annual rent (excluding advertisements, marketing fees and disbursements) although more complex structures can be used to incentivise an agent
Sale to owner occupier	Typically 1–2% of capital value (commercial)
Sale to owner occupier	Typically 1–5% of capital value (residential)
Sale to investors	Typically 1–2% of capital value
Management fee	Either a lump sum is agreed or a percentage of annual rent is taken
Rent reviews/lease renewals	A typical figure is 10% of the new rent or a percentage of the uplift or a fixed fee with overage over a certain figure or a fixed fee
Valuation	Varies from a lump sum to 0.25–0.75% of the capital value

> investment and portfolio managers
> management surveyors
> professional surveyors
>   – valuation
>   – rent reviews
>   – lease renewals.

Although general practice surveyors can technically carry out work in all these areas, usually specialisation occurs. If the development is complex and requires many different areas of work in the post-completion phase then it is worthwhile ensuring that the firm employed can service all of the areas required.

The level of fees charged by each function is rather complex. There is also no centrally agreed scale of fees, instead each rate is agreed by negotiation. Table 6.1 gives an idea of the level of fees involved in some of the key functions.

Each of the main functions needed in the post-completion phase will be examined in turn.

Sales and letting

This is one of the more important areas of commercial development. The timing and amounts of rent achieved can make a huge difference in the success or failure of the scheme. The agency selected should have the right blend of experience, specific to the type of development being undertaken.

In agency work, particularly commercial agency, staffing and personal issues are critical. Good agents are like gold dust. They are well-organised, well-motivated, with good contacts in both the offices of potential occupiers and also other firms who may act for potential occupiers. These contacts make life much easier than firms that are less experienced or less well-respected and who rely far more on 'cold calling'. In many aspects of the property world success is based on building up a network of contacts. Property is a 'people' profession, requiring a melding of technical skill and knowledge with a gregarious nature that stresses the importance of good oral and written communication. This is especially true of commercial agency work.

It is these agents who should have the greatest input into the design and planning of the project. This allows the application of information on current market requirements and future trends. They can also give advice on timing issues, e.g. at what time of year the developer should aim to finish the scheme in order to capture the greatest interest from potential occupiers.

Marketing

When to start the marketing phase, who to involve and what form the marketing of the property should take depends on the type and size of the project being undertaken.

RESIDENTIAL

With residential property the preference is to 'sell off the plan', particularly if the scheme is being undertaken by a well-known developer who produces a type of project end product with which the market is already familiar. An example of this would be a major house builder, or a leading player in the apartment market or a developer of retirement flats. This type of organisation is usually a national player with which many of the potential market members will be familiar.

Usually projects such as this start with an initial announcement being made; often this is when site works commence. This is not usually done earlier because of the risk of the image problems that might be created if the project was abandoned for some reason. This most frequently occurs due to market conditions changing; for example, if the economy went into a period of recession or if there was a marked rise in the cost of borrowing. It is only practical to stop a development before the building works commence. Normally only an extreme situation such as bankruptcy will stop a project when it is on site.

Once the on-site work has started then advertisements are placed in local newspapers. Quite frequently a marketing suite is placed on site.

COMMERCIAL

The decision on when to commence marketing in commercial property involves similar considerations.

In a poor market, or one that follows a downturn in the market, there is effectively no choice but to try to secure at least an agreement to lease (pre-letting) or an agreement to buy (pre-sale) prior perhaps even to the site purchase. As we have seen in the finance section (Chapter 3), the developer will not be able to obtain funding for a speculative scheme without these agreements being in place in weak markets or where financial bodies have suffered recent losses, such as may follow a market downturn.

In a rising, strong market the initial marketing may occur at the beginning of the project in order to attract expressions of interest, but most developers will wait until towards the end of the construction phase before the main marketing is undertaken. This is because the developer will wish to capture any rise in market values and will not want to enter into a premature agreement which may be at a lower rental level than could be achieved. The marketing expenditure made too early would be premature and may well be wasted.

FORMS OF MARKETING

There are several forms of marketing that can be used for the different types of development project. Examination of these methods is separated below into residential and commercial types of project.

Marketing residential developments

> The preparation of brochures giving a description of the project, a layout of the site, the types of houses and flats being built, the numbers of each type, a floor plan with outline specifications and a price schedule.
> Large feature hoardings with an artist's impression of the completed project on or near the site. Many developers have found this to be one of the more useful types of marketing that targets the core market for the project.
> Advertisements in local newspapers and magazines advertising the existence of a project, the type of building being produced (sizes, layout, quality) and also indicative prices.
> On-site marketing presence. This usually consists of either a temporary marketing suite or a completed suite within the development manned by a representative of the developer. This representative can introduce the scheme to prospective buyers, take details of these people's requirements and ensure that follow-up calls are made as the scheme approaches completion. This approach requires good promotional literature to be available for distribution to callers.
> Appointment of a local agent or agents who will promote the scheme through their offices.
> Web-based advertising – this has become more far more important over the past two to three years, given the number of people who initially search for new property using this medium. For larger schemes it is worth having a dedicated site, for smaller schemes advertising through some of the more general residential sales sites may suffice. Most schemes now have electronic versions of their marketing brochures either in HTML format or PDF files allowing on-screen browsing and self-printing if required.

Marketing commercial developments

The first step in commercial marketing is to appoint a suitable agent. This may be a single agent or it may be a joint agency, for example a local agent of a national agent.

There are a number of advantages in this. These agents will prepare the following marketing material:

> A brochure with an artist's impression, initially giving a brief specification.
> A one-page 'flier' for posting to other agents and potential occupiers or purchasers. This will give outline details of the development which will then hopefully translate into further interest on contact with the appointed agent.
> A hoarding will be erected, usually containing an artist's impression and an outline of the floor areas and specification of the building.
> A detailed technical specification should be drawn up for parties displaying serious interest. This can be a limited print run.
> Where the property is to be leased and to be sold on to investors it is useful to prepare an outline lease with outline 'heads of terms' indicated.
> As with residential development, web-based advertising has become increasingly important. Again, for larger schemes it is worth having a dedicated site, for smaller schemes advertising through some of the more general commercial sites may suffice. Many schemes have electronic versions of their brochures which can be viewed, downloaded or printed by prospective purchasers or tenants.
> For larger schemes, other advertising media may be considered. A number of schemes have had CD-ROMS prepared that allow the brochure material to be presented in a more interactive way. This may duplicate or substitute what is done in the web advertisement and may include, for example, animations or films of the scheme. 'Walk through' three-dimensional design material used by the designers on computer-aided design systems may be incorporated in this material.

The appointed agent will prepare mail-shot lists of parties to receive information. These will be potential occupiers or purchasers who are known to have a requirement, or other agents who are known to act for such parties. Agents will tend to prepare a telephone contact list to follow up these parties.

The agent may wish to place advertisements in the trade press. There are two main national property publications in the UK (*Estates Gazette* and *Property Week*, both published weekly) with a number of smaller, sometimes regional, publications. Both of the national publications also have websites offering the opportunity to advertise schemes. Advertisements for commercial schemes are not always required. Targeted marketing via mail-shot and telephone is usually far more effective, and, certainly for the very large schemes, press advertising is almost seen as an admission of failure. With smaller schemes that appeal to local markets this approach may, however, tease out occupiers from the local market who had not registered interest with agents and who may not have even considered moving prior to becoming aware of the scheme. In these cases, advertising in the local press and local trade magazines may prove useful. Very occasionally radio or even TV advertising may also be undertaken.

Later on in the development process of a speculative building the agent may promote the use of a launch party. This is usually done on completion of the scheme where part or all of the building remains vacant. The launch party should invite local businesses, potential occupiers and their agents. These events are popular with agents in particular and are useful in getting the development known in the market-place, but these events can be expensive.

It is worth defining the terms 'retained' and 'un-retained' agents at this point. Retained agents are those employed directly by the property developer or investment client. In this case they are retained to secure a successful letting of the scheme and will be paid a fee by the client when they do so. Occupiers searching for space can also retain agents to find space on their behalf. These agents are paid a fee by their own clients when they successfully fulfil their instructions but not by the developer.

There are also 'un-retained' or free agents who operate somewhere in the middle ground and who are not under instruction by any party. What these agents try to do is bring together two parties who are not aware of each other. They will try to introduce a building to a potential occupier and an occupier to a building. If the letting proceeds they will try to obtain a fee from one or the other of the parties. It is at times a precarious existence but one that many agents survive and thrive on and these agents do receive the protection of the law for the introductions they make, even if they do no more than get verbal confirmation over the telephone.

Whatever the type of property or the approach taken, time taken to establish a coherent marketing strategy with a good firm of agents early in the development scheme will pay dividends later on. Rapid leasing or sale of the scheme does more than anything to save money and maximise profitability.

Marketing for investment sales

It should be noted that preparing a development for sale as an investment is not usually carried out by the same team which deals with the leasing of the property, unless a smaller firm of agents is employed. This is not simply because firms aim to make multiple fees out of the same property instruction (although admittedly this is the effect) but simply that investment agents have different skills and have different contacts to those possessed by letting agents. How the marketing is approached depends on the nature of the scheme. An investment grade building will only appeal to a relatively narrow range of potential purchasers and therefore a relatively limited marketing programme can be instituted. This will effectively involve personal contact between the retained agent and investors and their agents. With smaller projects that may have wider appeal, a marketing programme similar to that outlined for commercial and residential letting above may be required.

Methods of actually achieving sales or lettings of properties will be discussed in the next section.

Disposing of development projects

Most developments will involve some kind of disposal process. Properties for sale to owner occupiers, whether they are residential or commercial, require the sale of the occupational freehold or long leasehold interests. Investment properties will involve at least the disposal of the occupational interest on a lease. If the investment is not retained the freehold reversionary interest will also require disposal. This next sub-section looks at the methods of disposal and gives a thumb-nail guide to the processes and procedures involved.

SALES OF FREEHOLD AND LONG LEASEHOLD INTERESTS

For the purposes of this section, sales of these two types of interest will be considered to be the same. As a brief explanation, fee simple absolute (feuhold in Scotland) or freehold interests are the highest bundle of rights that can be held in the UK below the Crown. Leaseholds (term of years absolute) are a lesser interest created out of freeholds where a consideration passes from the leaseholder to the freeholder (or higher landlord as tiers of leaseholds can be created) in return for a grant of lease giving the rights to occupy the property for a given term of years. Long leaseholds are those created for a period usually in excess of 99 years. Long leaseholds can be created for a number of reasons but the two commonest are:

1. development leases where the landowner wishes to retain overall control of the site, and
2. in properties that are in multiple occupation such as residential flats.

TABLE 6.2 The three main types of sale

Sale by private treaty	No fixed date of sale. The property is marketed as described in the text and the price is agreed by private negotiation	This is by far the dominant form of sale used in the UK
Sale by tender	The vendor asks for 'best bids' for a property by a given date. Usually these are submitted sealed and opened at a given time	Tenders are not frequently used for the sale of completed developments unless the property type concerned is rare in the area and substantial levels of interest are generated. Tenders are, however, widely used for selling development sites where developers are competing for the opportunity to develop
Sale by auction	The property is offered for sale on a specific day and time and will be sold at this time unless a previously set reserve has not been reached	Auctions have an odd position in the UK market. In other parts of the world auctions are a sensible and widely used method of selling. In the UK there is a cultural problem with auctions. Auctions are viewed as a last resort to sell 'problem' property such as repossessed homes, secondary investment properties and student houses. Despite this 'blight', auctions are widely used in the UK and good prices can be achieved. Several of the leading surveying practices run auctions in which some good quality property is sold

In the latter case, this approach is required due to the peculiarities of UK common law that does not allow the enforcement of positive covenants such as to repair or to provide support. The lease contract *is* enforceable; hence, at present all flats for owner occupation should be leasehold. The consideration, the rent, is usually nominal in the cases that we are considering here and the interest for sale is taken to be a virtual freehold.

There are a number of ways of achieving sales, although in the UK one dominates. The three main types are sale by private treaty, sale by tender and sale by auction, as summarised in Table 6.2.

With private treaty sales, and sometimes following the receipt of tender bids, the client's agent will normally negotiate the terms of the sale with the prospective purchaser, with the ultimate approval of the instructing client. These 'heads of terms' will then be passed to the parties' solicitors for agreement of the detailed contract of sale and the final conveyancing of title.

LETTINGS

Where the property is to be leased, the retained agent has a key role to play. The agent identifies prospective occupiers and deals with general enquiries arising from other sources. The agent will arrange viewings and will supply information to the potential lessees. Where the party is interested, the agent will lead the negotiations based on the parameters laid down by the client. If the negotiations proceed to a point where the party agrees to take space then the agent will agree 'heads of terms'. These will usually include:

> the initial rental level;
> the demise of the property (the definition of what is actually being let under the lease;
> the term of the lease (its length);
> key details such as the period and mode of the rent review clause, the alienation clause, repairs and maintenance responsibilities, etc.;
> any special features of the deal such as rent-free periods given at the start of the lease, or fitting out contributions paid for by the landlord, break clauses, etc.

Once agreed, these terms will be passed to the other parties' solicitors for the full preparation of the lease document. The basic lease documentation will be prepared by the developer's solicitor but its final form will be developed in an iterative process between the parties, the lease being passed between each side with alterations being made until agreement is reached as to the final form of the contract.

It should be noted that in multi-let properties that are to become investment properties, it is important to keep the lease terms as similar as possible across the building. Variations in lease terms, particular key clauses such as rental values, rent review clauses and terms and the repairing clause, will impact on the overall value of the investment, investors seeking a discount for the management problems created.

Essentially then, the actual changes that result from this iterative process must be limited.

The interaction between the letting and the subsequent management and investment performance of the property are closely interrelated. The properties' characteristics in these areas must be set up correctly from the beginning otherwise the problems will persist over most of the investment life of the building. These areas will be covered in a section below.

One of the other key roles that the agent needs to fulfil at this stage is related to this. The agent needs to carry out investigations into the quality of the potential occupiers. They will need to ensure that the tenant will:

1. be able to pay the rent both now and in the future, and
2. be a conscientious tenant who will obey the lease covenants and look after the building.

This is again where the agency, management and investment requirements overlap. Although the agent will want to let the property as quickly as possible to secure their fee, the investment and management departments will want the best possible quality of tenant to maintain the investment value. The value of a cash flow is not dependent on the quantum of money but also on the quality of that income flow, i.e. the quality of the party that is paying it. A local company with little track record in business may be able to pay the same rent as a large PLC corporation, but the cash flow from the latter will be worth more because it is more secure. A managing agent will not want a tenant to fall into arrears or fail to maintain a property or to use it in breach of the terms of the lease, as this will create additional management costs and problems, for example with neighbouring tenants. All of this means that good quality tenants (good covenants) are to be preferred even if they pay less rent.

The investigations that agents should undertake will depend on the identity of the proposed tenant. With larger PLCs little investigation should be required, although it is worthwhile to check whether the lease is with the parent company or a subsidiary, the former naturally being preferred. With smaller companies the agent should seek to obtain at least the past three years' trading accounts where possible. This should give information as to how solvent the companies are. Larger companies can be investigated using credit rating and company analysis agencies such as Dun and Bradstreet and Standard and Poors. References should be obtained from previous landlords where possible and the companies' accountants and bankers. Many of these references are often too general to have much utility. Decisions over tenants often become a matter of personal judgement. Where there is doubt it may be possible to obtain additional security using things such as performance bonds, simple deposits or personal guarantees from the directors of the companies signing the lease.

Successful management of investment properties

The following guidelines are aimed at developers who intend to retain their investment properties. They are equally valid, however, for situations where the property is to be disposed of. As we have seen from the preceding section there is a strong interrelationship between investment performance and the management structure.

There is insufficient space here to do more than give an outline of good management practice with regard to commercial and residential property. We will concentrate on the key factors that affect the performance of commercial investment property. It is these areas that the developer should concentrate on getting right at the commencement of the investment life of the project as it makes the transition from the development phase.

An important starting point in the proper management of investment property is to hire in good quality managing agents. These agents have experience and the systems in place to ensure the smooth operation of the property during its life.

When looking at how to manage a commercial property the following points should be considered:

> lease length
> covenant strength
> service charges
> repair and maintenance
> rent review clause
> user clause
> alienation clause
> alterations and improvements
> other clauses.

What we are essentially looking at is the structure of a commercial lease. It is the lease that is at the heart of good management practice with commercial property. It is the document that must be correctly constructed at the beginning in order to ensure smooth management in the future. It is very important to get advice from the management surveyor when these leases are being constructed.

FACTORS RELATED TO THE QUALITY OF INCOME FLOW

Cash flow from a property investment is the thing that gives it value. As we have already seen, this value is related to both the quantum of the cash flow and also its quality. Quantum issues are partly a question of management and, in the main, they are determined by market forces. Quality, however, is mainly determined by management decisions, although these, of course, are heavily influenced by market conditions. The two main areas that affect the quality of the cash flow are the lease length and the covenant strength of the tenant.

Lease length

Fundamentally, one of the key issues with regard to leases is their length. The lease length must both satisfy occupier requirements and also be long enough to suit investors. Commercial tenants want both flexibility and security. This is slightly contradictory: security comes from having a long lease. A long lease, however, is inflexible. An ideal situation for tenants is to have the ability to give up the lease with no penalty at their choice but also to have the option of continuing occupation if so required. Investors, on the other hand, value the certainty that comes from a long lease. The requirements of both sides of the letting equation have been in conflict for many years in the UK. The strengths of each party have varied according to market conditions; effectively, whether the market is considered to be a 'landlord' or a 'tenant' market. The former exists where there is strong competition for space and the latter when there is an oversupply in the market. The situation is made more complex by the intervention of the Government in the operation of the free market. There is a substantial amount of landlord and tenant legislation that exists and which investors and occupiers need to take into account. Some of this legislation affects this issue of security of tenure and flexibility in the actions of occupiers and landlords.

As noted, this is a complex area. Some of the issues require particular attention as we stand at the beginning of the 21st century in the UK:

1. Most business tenancies in England and Wales have an automatic right to renew their leases under Part II of the Landlord and Tenant Act 1954. The landlord has only limited grounds to oppose the grant of a new lease and therefore even a short lease taken out by a business tenant can be extended. In many respects this gives the best of all worlds to business tenants.
2. The market in the early 1990s in the UK was very weak. The UK saw a reduction in the length of leases from 25 years to 10–15 years at the prime end of the market. This is effectively the leases that would be granted on investment grade property. Even following the recovery in the market in the second half of the decade, the trend for shorter leases has been maintained.
3. Another feature of the market at this time was the fact that break clauses in commercial leases became far more frequently applied. These break clauses were invariably in the tenant's favour. This allowed far more tenants to terminate their leases early.
4. Changes in legislation in the 1990s in England and Wales further altered the balance in favour of the tenant. The Landlord and Tenant (Covenants) Act 1995 ended something called 'privity of contract' for leases granted after 1 January 1996. If the tenant wants to dispose of a lease they effectively have two choices. One is to sublet the property. This creates a lower level of interest below the tenant's lease. The other alternative is to assign the lease. This is effectively the sale of the lease with, in theory, the original tenant dropping out of picture with the obligations under the lease been taken on by the incoming purchaser of the lease. This was naturally the favoured option for tenants who no longer wished to have the liability of the premises. However, prior to the 1995 Act, although the original tenant was no longer in occupation nor paid the rent, and usually where the lease had actually been altered to note the change in occupier, the original tenant still had the residual responsibility for the premises. This was due to the original landlord and tenant alone having been party to the contract negotiations and agreement. As a result of this, the landlord could revert to the original tenant

if the assignee defaulted or breached a lease clause at some point in the future. In normal circumstances, therefore, it did not really matter if a PLC covenant assigned their lease to a much weaker tenant as the privity of contract acted as a virtual 'back stop' in the case of future default by the new tenant. This situation was felt to be onerous on tenants and much lobbying was done in the early 1990s which resulted in the legislative change.

All of the above factors have made it much more difficult for an investor to secure a good tenant on a long lease. The developer has to be much more conscious than in the past in the creation of the investment vehicle in order to ensure that its value is maintained. Some of steps that can be taken with regard to future security of income are listed below.

a. The inclusion of authorised guarantee agreements in the lease – these agreements arose out of the 1995 Covenants Act and are intended to mitigate the effect of the loss of primitive contract. They allow the landlord to require the initial tenant to offer limited guarantees as to the future payment of rent if they choose in the future to assign the lease to a third party.
b. A tighter alienation clause can be included in the lease requiring the landlord to give written approval of any assignee and granting landlord the right to reject the tenant on the grounds of quality. Prior to the 1995 Act, such clauses were illegal.
c. It is possible to jointly agree to operate the lease of the commercial property outside the terms of the 1954 Act, i.e. giving the tenant no security of tenure. This has to be done by joint application of the parties to the courts. This may seem perverse, in that it can swing the power of negotiation to the landlord if the tenant has no security at the end of the lease. However, the system has worked very successfully in Scotland where the 1954 Act provisions do not apply.

Quality of the tenant who signs the lease

As noted above, one of the main issues with regard to the management of an investment property is to ensure it that the highest quality tenant possible is signed up to the lease. This may even mean accepting a lower rent from a better quality tenant to ensure that the investment value of the property is maintained.

Where this is not possible there are mechanisms that can be put into place that can mitigate the effect of a weak tenant. Two ways of achieving this are outlined below:

1. By requiring the tenant to enter into a personal or third-party guarantee. This is particularly useful where the business signing up for lease is of dubious quality or where the business has not been in existence for many years. As there is a separate identity to a limited business and its directors, without a guarantee a default on business debt cannot be corrected if the business goes into liquidation or otherwise fails. Where a personal guarantee or a guarantee from a solvent third party exists, the property owner can at least cover some of the costs and recover some unpaid rent from this source.
2. A similar effect can be achieved by requiring the incoming tenant to take out a bond with a financial institution. The bond is effectively an insurance policy for

which the tenant pays a one-off or annual premium. The bond is made in favour of the landlord who can only access it if the tenant is in serious default.

COMMERCIAL LEASES: IMPORTANT CLAUSES

The following clauses in commercial leases should be very carefully considered in order to maintain the value of investment property.

Repair and maintenance clause

It is important to ensure that the buildings/premises are well maintained and are returned to the owner in an acceptable state. In most cases, investors in the UK seek to pass all of the costs of maintaining and repairing a building onto the tenant. In a single-let building this is done by way of the repairing clause; in multi-let building this is done using service charges (see below).

The majority of leases in the UK are what is termed 'full repairing and insuring' (FRI). This is a description of what has been outlined above, namely that the tenant is responsible for all outgoing costs including those of insuring the building. Most leases also require tenants to carry out periodic redecoration to maintain the image of the building. These maintenance clauses state the normal number of years to pass between redecorating internally and externally. The repairing clause normally defines the condition in which the building is to return to the owner at the end of the lease.

Again, it is good management practice not to be too strict or create too onerous repairing clauses. If the clause is too onerous it will make the premises difficult to let and reduce the value in the long term.

Service charges

Service charges are essential in multi-let buildings. A basic requirement of UK investors is that rents should be net rents, i.e. no deduction for repairing, maintaining, heating or lighting a building should be made from the rent. In a single-let building this is generally covered in the repairing clause which makes the tenant responsible for all repairs both inside and outside the building. In multi-let building, however, the work needs to be done by a central agency to ensure that it is carried out. The work must also be managed by the landlord's representative. To ensure that the rent received on the property is still a net rent, the costs of all of the work required to the building should be recovered from occupiers. This is done by way of a service charge. There should be no shortfall on the service charge otherwise the investment value of the building will be reduced.

There are various ways of calculating a service charge and constructing it for the actual recovery of work undertaken. This varies from an estimate of the annual or quarterly costs of maintaining the building with an up-front payment and mechanisms for additional recovery or repayment if required, to actual recovery of costs as the work proceeds. The service charge clause needs to be accurately constructed. It should also not be too onerous as this can reduce the attractiveness of the property in the market and impact on its investment value.

There are sometimes tendencies to make service charge provisions too clever. Some allow almost unlimited recovery of cost as the landlord sees fit, up to and including the complete rebuilding and redevelopment of the building. This can be especially true of residential buildings. As we have seen, multi-let residential buildings are leasehold. There must, however, an overriding freehold interest. The leaseholders normally only pay a nominal rent to the freeholder; it is the freeholder who is responsible for the maintenance of the building. The main source of trouble is connected with the quality of leases in residential property. They are often very loosely constructed compared with a commercial lease. They are therefore rather easily exploited by the unscrupulous. There are numerous examples of residential leaseholders finding themselves facing excessive bills under the service charge.

Rent review clause

The rent review clause is one of the critical areas of the lease, although its importance has waned as leases have become shorter.

The rent review clause is the mechanism that allows periodic reviews of the rent to take place. This is normally each year for residential property and also for poorer quality commercial property, every three years for secondary commercial property and normally every five years for top quality, prime property lets on longer leases (10–15 years).

There are various ways, in theory, of constructing a rent review clause. For example:

> an adjustment of the rent using an index (retail price index, building cost, etc.);
> fixed rate increases (e.g. 5 per cent p.a.);
> periodic comparison of the rent with the current market rental value of similar properties on the market at the time of the rent review.

Although all three are viable methods on paper, it is only the latter which is actually acceptable in UK practice. It is also, although deceptively simple, actually very difficult to successfully operate in practice. The reason why it is so difficult to achieve is that it requires a set of circumstances to be clearly defined so that each party knows exactly what is being valued.

Effectively, what the parties are asked to do in rent reviews is to assume that the premises are vacant and to let at the time the review occurs. What, then, would this property let for in the open market to an occupier acting with normal business motives in mind? This sounds straightforward, and indeed the original rent review clauses were very simple.

When things are considered more carefully, however, they become much more complex: what term of the new lease is to be considered? What state of repair is the demised property assumed to be in? Should incentives that are being given to tenants in the open market at the time of the review be taken into account in the calculation of the new rent? Should any improvements that have been undertaken by the tenant be included in the calculation of the new rent? These and a whole host of other questions have to be addressed in the clause. Modern rent review clauses attempt to cover all of these questions comprehensively. They lay down assumptions that the parties should make at the time of the review.

The rent review clause should be carefully considered as it is perhaps the single most important clause for investors.

Rent review clauses in the UK normally do not allow the rent to fall at review. Inaccurately, these clauses are referred to as being 'upward only' whereas in fact they are ratchet clauses whose normal wording is that the rent on review should be the higher of the current market rent or the existing rent passing on the property. Certain tenants and pressure groups have lobbied the Government to outlaw clauses such as these. The Government instigated a review of the workings of the property market that reported in 2005, which recommended that no changes be made in the workings of the market. As a result, these clauses are almost universal in the market-place and would only be at risk from future legislation or from changes in the landlord/tenant balance of power, as occurred in the early 1990s.

Although on the surface they do appear onerous, they are in fact only an issue where market rents have fallen severely and rapidly. In the UK, this situation has only occurred twice in the post-war period, and then only for fairly limited periods. They do, however, provide investors with considerable security and are highly valued by the investment community.

The detailed construction of the rent review clause should be left to the advice of a rent review surveyor and solicitor working in tandem. The review clause should have a timetable and also must have some mechanism for dispute resolution by a third party, either by resort to determination by independent expert or by arbitrator. The timetable should not be strictly construed otherwise the lease will be deemed to be onerous.

User clauses

The use of buildings or premises can be defined in two ways: fundamentally, by the land use planning system and also by the user clause that exists in the lease.

Why would a landlord wish to regulate the use of the building? The answer is to do with management. In a residential building the landlord would wish to ensure that no commercial use occurred that would interfere with other occupants in the building. In retail property, the mix between tenants is important in order to ensure that a wide range of shoppers will visit the shopping centre. With office property, landlords would not want an undesirable use to upset the other tenants. For example, an office building occupied by top quality leader or accounting firms, who rely on regular client contact, would not wish an office for the homeless to occupy the same building. Without any wish to be disrespectful to homeless people, this is an issue of image, and the image conflict is clear. The tenants in the building would not tolerate the situation and would almost certainly move out.

The user clause enables the building owner to maintain a balance between tenants. All user clauses, however, should not be 'closed', allowing no other use than the one defined. This also applies to all other clauses. Normally, clauses should be constructed to permit other uses to be considered on written application to the landlord. It should be written into the lease that the landlord's consent 'should not be unreasonably withheld'. These five magic words should be applied to many of the clauses in the lease as they allow the landlord to keep reasonable control but permit the tenant some leeway and flexibility.

Alienation clause

Alienation clauses deal with disposals. Normally, leases should allow the subletting of all or parts of the demised property but the assignment of the whole of the property only. All should require the landlord's consent but such consent should not be reasonably withheld, as per the above. As has been noted, the ending of privity of contract in England and Wales means that this clause requires greater scrutiny.

Alterations

Normally, leases should allow no structural alterations, e.g. work to internal partitioning, without additional permission from the landlord. All other alterations should require consent, particularly if they involve the alterations of pipework and wiring, the movement of fixtures and fittings or any work that involves any element of the structure of the building. The reason for this is to ensure the safety of other tenants, the structural integrity of the building and, indeed, the value of the building. While the landlord should retain an absolute right to prevent structural change to the building, any other work should require the landlord's consent, which is not to be unreasonably withheld.

Other lease clauses

Other clauses to include in the lease are such things as access rights, arbitration, issues to do with the landlord's interest disposal, and should also define the landlord's responsibilities. In general, commercial leases in particular are very thorough documents with a typical commercial lease being in excess of 100 pages long. However, landlords should resist the temptation to make leases too onerous as this tends to have a major impact on value.

Conclusions

There are some simple rules which affect the management of investment property:

> Good management and good investments go together.
> The value of investment is essentially determined by the quality of the income flow it produces. This is only partly determined by the quality of the building and its location. A very important element is the quality of the tenant and the terms

under which they occupy the premises, i.e. the lease. Each clause in the lease is important and the whole should be carefully scrutinised by both investors and occupiers.

> When the lease is signed it is too late to correct any mistakes, at least in all practical terms. Every effort should be made to get the lease structure correct even before the first draft is delivered to a prospective tenant's solicitor.

> Tenant selection and careful vetting of prospective tenants is essential to ensure that the building will be properly maintained and that the income flow will have as few interruptions as possible.

If these rules are followed then the management should be straightforward and the investment performance of the building should go smoothly.

Does everyone get this right? The answer may be found in the fact that considerable money can be made in the secondary property market by property companies who purchase older investments and 'work' them. 'Working' can mean refurbishment and remodelling but often means correcting errors in leases and problems in occupation, therefore adding back 'lost' value. Admittedly, part of this opportunity arises out of the passage of time and changing market practices but a proportion is due to the errors made when the building was first let.

The message is to be successful and get the investment vehicle right from the beginning!

RISK APPRAISAL AND RISK MITIGATION: A COMMON-SENSE APPROACH
CHAPTER 7

Introduction

Property development is a risky business. There are a number of ways that this can be observed. First, the returns from development are very high. There has to be a reason for this. People who are involved in property development are compensated for the high levels of risk that they run. You do not get something for nothing. The second evidence brought forward for the degree of risk involved in development can be found in the number of property developers who go out of business, often spectacularly.

A search through the recent past in the financial press will reveal a number of examples of companies who have failed. One example is the developer of Canary Wharf in London Docklands. The development company, Olympia and York, was one of the world's most successful property developers. They set up initially in Canada but undertook successful schemes all over the world, including most notably in New York. There were led by two of the most successful entrepreneurs, the Reichmann brothers. Both of the brothers, but particularly Paul Reichmann, were considered to be among the most astute, bold and indeed successful people in property. However, in early 1992 they became part of what was then the biggest private financial failure in world history. They were trapped by taking too much development risk, essentially, in the London Docklands project. There were not alone, with many developers going to the wall at this time. All essentially failed by taking on too much risk.[1]

The way fluctuations in the expected outcome of the development can impact on the profitability of the project can be illustrated in a simple example. Here, a simple commercial project is examined at the appraisal stage. The market and site have been analysed and Table 7.1 gives the values for the key variables that have been assessed.

When the figures of Table 7.1 are put into a simple residual calculation a healthy profit is predicted, as shown in Table 7.2. Given these figures, the project is given the go-ahead. The land is purchased and the planning stage of the scheme commences. Here is where the first minor problems occur. The planning negotiations take longer than expected. The developer is forced to make changes to the scheme that cause a small rise in construction costs. In the meantime, interest rates have moved up 2 per cent, a relatively small change but one that increases the costs of the scheme

TABLE 7.1 Speculative office project: key variables

Built area: m^2	1,000
Net area: m^2	800
Rental value: m^2	£250
Investment yield	7%
Interest rate	8%
Development costs (inc. all fees) per m^2	£900
Land cost	£1,000,000
Planning: months	6
Construction: months	12
Letting: months	3
Incentive: months	3

TABLE 7.2 Speculative office project: simple appraisal

Value on completion

	Rental value	£200,000
	Capitalised @ 7%	14.286
		£2,857,143
	Less costs @ 6%	−£161,725
		£2,695,418
Less costs		
Development costs	£900,000	
Interest charge (construction)	£36,000	
Land cost	£1,000,000	
Interest charge (land)	£122,369	
Void cost	£39,987	
Incentive	£50,000	
TOTAL COST	£2,148,356	£2,148,356
PROFIT		**£547,062**
Profit on cost		25.46%

a little more. When the scheme gets on site, unforeseen problems in the ground both delay construction and increase costs, again only slightly. By the time the scheme is completed the letting market has deteriorated slightly. Rents are some £20 per square metre less than expected. Lettings are taking longer to negotiate and tenants are wanting a little more as an incentive to sign leases. In the investment market, investors are now seeking 1 per cent more per annum as an initial return to compensate them for the lower rental growth they perceive will occur in the future.

The final, actually achieved, values for the key variables are given in Table 7.3.

This exemplifies, therefore, a fairly typical project that has not quite turned out as the developer expected but is not very far removed from the initial appraised figures. The consequences for the profitability of the project are, however, striking, as shown in Table 7.4.

TABLE 7.3 Speculative office project: actual values on completion

Built area: m^2	1,000
Net area: m^2	800
Rental value: m^2	£230
Investment yield	8.00%
Interest rate	10%
Development costs (inc. all fees) per m^2	£950
Land cost	£1,000,000
Planning: months	9
Construction: months	15
Letting: months	9
Incentive: months	6

TABLE 7.4 Calculation of actual return on project

Value on completion

	Rental value	£184,000
	Capitalised @ 8%	12.500
		£2,300,000
	Less costs @ 6%	−£130,189
		£2,169,811
Less costs		
Development costs	£950,000	
Interest charge (construction)	£60,099	
Land cost	£1,000,000	
Interest charge (land)	£210,000	
Void cost	£164,508	
Incentive	£92,000	
TOTAL COST	£2,476,608	£2,476,608
PROFIT		**−£306,796**
	Profit on cost	−12.39%

This is a graphic illustration of the degree of risk that developers run. For a small developer this loss of over £300,000 on the £2.476 million invested would probably mean financial disaster. Small changes are magnified. There also tend to be 'double hits' on the value of the completed schemes; if rents move down, so yield tends to move out, lowering the income multiplier applied. This is essentially what happened to many of the developers in the early 1990s, although what finally tends to drive developers out of business is their inability to service debt.

This example underlines the fact that, when doing any sort of development project, risk should always be taken into account. Risk should be considered at every turn. It should be avoided were possible. Where it is not possible to avoid it, it should be mitigated as far as is possible. It should only be accepted when no other course of action is open. You can never fully eliminate risk but you can be sensible with it. Risk should not be ignored or hidden from. This is the worst possible course of action. Risk should be identified, quantified and then either avoided, mitigated or accepted. This should be the standard process followed throughout the development.

Identifying risk

Risk can be dealt with in several clever ways. It is possible to break risk down into its component parts, as is done in the capital markets. This book will not take the high level theory approach, however, but will try to stay in the practical realm.

The concept of risk is not uniform. Some things have a high probability of occurrence but have a very low level of consequence. An example of this in development is a movement in interest rates. There is a reasonably high chance of interest rates moving during a project but the consequences are usually not serious unless the movement in rates is excessive. On the other hand, some things have a low risk of occurrence but when they happen the consequences are severe. For example, a military coup in the UK would have a huge impact on the investment market but the chance of this occurring is fairly minimal and can, to all intents and purposes, be ignored. One of the key skills in risk appraisal in property development is to identify those risks that are of major consequence and also have a significant likelihood of coming to pass. It is these factors that should be concentrated on.

The key goal of a development project for most developers is to minimise the risk of the development costing more than it is worth. Essentially, it is as simple as that.

What might cause this to occur? There are three main areas to consider:

1. delays in construction and in the overall development programme;
2. unforeseen costs;
3. a reduction in the value of the completed development as compared with the original appraisal.

It is these three areas, either singly or occurring in combination, where the greatest problems can occur. We will consider each of the three areas in turn.

DELAYS IN CONSTRUCTION AND DEVELOPMENT

Delays in the construction programme can create a number of problems: they tend to cause costs to increase; they add to the interest charges; they may also cause the developer to lose a tenant if the scheme is late and key dates are missed. Delays are to be avoided wherever possible. We will consider some of the most common reasons for delays in the construction and development programme below.

Problems in the ground

One of the most common reasons for delays in construction is problems in the ground. These include problems that arise from:

> poor ground-bearing capacity
> hard rock on site
> ground contamination
> archaeology.

The identification of all of these factors is down to thorough investigation beforehand. Money should be spent on proper, comprehensive surveys and testing of the site. This includes investigations and documentary evidence of the past users of the site, checking with the county archaeologist department and soil and geological surveys of the site. If possible a full site survey, both surface and subsurface should be undertaken. Basically, if any doubt exists about the site then investigations should be done wherever possible.

Quantification should be done at the appraisal stage. Any information that comes from the site survey should be incorporated into the design and fully costed. Those areas where there is uncertainty should see the variations in possible outcomes priced. The impact on the profitability of the scheme should be assessed using these different scenarios. The reader's attention is directed to Chapter 4 on appraisal where scenario analysis was examined. If the impact of the scenario is significant on the project outcome, the probability of the outcome occurring should be assessed.

Mitigation depends on the factors being considered. If the ground conditions are an unknown quantity it is important to have contingency plans, such as alternative designs for the execution of the project or key aspects of the project such as the foundations. With issues such as potential archaeology on site it is possible to programme in time for a 'rescue bid' period with the cooperation of the county archaeologist department. This body will then know the time period available for the excavation and also what funding is available.

Planning delays

Delays that arise from problems in planning are usually related to issues such as refusal of consent or the alteration of details of the design following the initial grant of planning permission.

To avoid the maximum impact on the programme, ideally it is best not to proceed with the scheme without detailed consent being in place. This is, of course, not always possible but certainly it is best to avoid major financial commitment if the planning situation is uncertain. A very important risk reduction technique is the basic consultation with the planning authorities. It is also advisable to enter into dialogue and discussion with any neighbours to the development. If possible, within the boundaries of commercial confidentiality, it is best to be as open as possible so that the application does not come as a surprise to the neighbouring occupants. This will reduce the risk of objections to the scheme being made at a late date. If planning issues are to be problematic, it is best to bring them out into the open as early as possible in order to avoid expensive disruption later in the programme. If it is perceived that planning may be a problem, then it is advisable to employ planning consultants as early as possible. This in itself is a good risk mitigation technique.

Problems with existing structures

The problems with existing structures can fall into two categories:

1. Problems with structures on site – these problems are related to the refurbishment, alterations or demolition of the structures that actually exist on site.
2. Problems with structures off site – these problems are related to the support of, damage to, the trading performance of, and rights such as rights of light, etc., enjoyed by neighbouring buildings.

Existing structures are extremely difficult to deal with. There are many unknowns in existing buildings, particularly with older ones. Refurbishment is particularly tricky, especially if major structural alterations are involved. The solution, although solution may be too strong a word, is to do as much prior investigation as possible, including partial dismantling of the building to reveal the internal structure.

Rights of third parties and the effects on neighbouring structures of the development should be very carefully investigated. A proper due diligence process should be undertaken for this area. This is due to the fact that the courts are very protective of third-party rights. Neighbours who have been affected by construction or are potentially going to be affected can take out injunctions to prevent the scheme proceeding until the issue has been resolved. This can be extremely expensive. With all of these issues the best mitigation is prior investigation.

Again, it is very important to test the impact of different scenarios on the appraisal where doubt exists. It is best to be realistic, rather than optimistic and find that the development is heavily exposed to risk. Risk is essentially uncertainty. Investigations should have the aim of reducing the uncertainty, of making known the unknown. It is only those items that cannot be fully investigated that should be appraised in this way. Appraisal and scenario analysis is no substitute for proper site investigation.

Failure of contractor/subcontractor

The failure of a contractor or a critical subcontractor can have dire consequences for the project. Problems that can occur include interruptions of work, additional costs incurred in finding a substitute contractor, failure to meet completion dates allowing tenants to walk away, among other things. One key problem is that it is very difficult to predict when such problems will occur and also what the delays and consequences may be. It is therefore almost impossible to quantify the impact of contractor failure.

The best mitigation and risk reduction technique to follow is, again, investigation. The list of potential contractors should be examined very carefully to check both the experience of the contractor and also their financial standing. Credit checks should be carried out to ensure that the contractor is paying bills within a reasonable time. If there is a doubt about the contractor but the client wishes to proceed with them then things such as performance bonds (an insurance taken out by the contractor and payable to the developer on the default of the contractor) can reduce the effect of failure.

Construction and buildability issues

This factor could fall into the cost element. It is mainly related to design issues, usually where the building is technically innovative or is designed to make a visual or aesthetic impact. All too often there is insufficient practical detail available to the contractor to actually build the building. This may seem unlikely to the outsider but it is not unusual for contractors, even with fairly modest buildings, to be waiting for details to be supplied from the design team when on site. Is also not uncommon for the contractor to resort to 'self design' elements of the building. This can lead to a delay in official working for the contractor for which the procurer will pay heavily.

The classic example of this is the Sydney Opera House. The original architect came up with the concept, reputedly by slicing up an orange and arranging the segments. However, this is just about all that he did. When construction commenced there was effectively no detail as to how all of the building should be built or what went inside. Not surprisingly, this project was extremely late and also well over budget. The project was a national scandal in Australia, perhaps similar to the Millennium Dome project in the UK. Fortunately, the building has enjoyed a happier life since it was completed.

How to mitigate or reduce the risk of this factor is difficult. The obvious answer is to keep the project simple and avoid unnecessary design problems. Where this is unavoidable, then it is the selection of the architect that is the critical factor. The past record of the architectural practice should be scrutinised, not only for architectural excellence in the field related to the project but also as to their record of practicality in construction. If the project is shown to be highly sensitive in the appraisal to changes in cost or in timing then the developer is running a very high level of risk if they choose to proceed with an innovative design. This is one of the reasons why the investment properties built in the UK tend to be bland and unadventurous. Investment clients tend not to want to make statements but instead prefer safe projects that make money.

Weather-related delays

Frustratingly, the business of the construction industry is largely carried out outside and is thus subject to the same difficulties that affect our sporting programmes. Cold, freezing weather can prevent concrete being poured; rain can prevent a whole host of activities.

Mitigation and risk reduction is again not easy. Careful consideration of the programme and timing of activities should be carried out where possible to reduce the risk of weather-sensitive construction being disrupted. If this is not possible then the design should be scrutinised in order to determine whether alternative solutions are possible which may avoid some of these problems.

Delays caused by poor project planning

This is more of an internal project problem but it can affect the overall timing of the project. While there is a certain degree of flexibility in some components of a building

299

as to when and in what order work is carried out, it is more common for tasks to be dependent on the prior completion of others. For example, a decorator needs the plastering completed, the plasterer needs all of the electrical and plumbing installation to be done, and both these trades need the internal walls and floors in place, etc. Failures and delays upstream in the project can have considerable knock-on effects.

Mitigation, like many of these factors, is down to good planning. In particular, a specialist project manager should be employed if the project has complex elements to interact and correctly sequence. One of the crucial functions of the project manager is to prepare a critical path analysis of the project. This process identifies the key tasks that need to be completed and also the logical sequence in which these tasks must occur. This will enable the project to proceed smoothly and without delays.

CHANGES IN COSTS OR UNFORESEEN EXPENDITURE

Many of the items mentioned above also lead to increases in the cost of the development. There are, however, specific factors that can occur during the development which will lead to increases in cost. These need to be identified separately and appropriate action taken.

There are two common causes of changes in cost. These are changes in the interest rate and changes in the actual cost of construction. Each of these will be considered in turn.

Interest rate movements

Interest rate movements are almost inevitable. It is extremely rare for interest rates to remain stable for more than a year. Interest rates are the primary tool of economic management used by contemporary governments.

In reality, interest rates themselves have very little effect on 'normal' development projects. This is despite a widespread belief that it is changes in interest rates and consequential rises in the cost of financing projects that are the prime causes of project failures. In fact, there is a relationship between interest rate movements and project failure, but it relates to the fact that interest rate movements are a symptom of wider problems in the economy. Rises in interest rates in recent years have been associated with financial constraints being imposed by the Government to control excessive demand and thus control inflation. There is a direct effect on the profitability of both projects and development companies generally, but perhaps the biggest effect comes from the consumers of the end product of the development process cutting back on demand. As we have seen from the appraisal section, development viability is most sensitive to changes in the value of the end product and a reduction in demand tends to have a consequent effect on prices. The effect is perhaps most direct and most marked on the residential market where consumers are directly influenced by the cost of borrowing on mortgages.

Although this section deals with factors that can lead to rises in construction costs, developers should also be concerned about proceeding with developments when interest rates are falling, even though this will, of course, lead to a reduction in construction costs generally. The cause of the concern lies in the reason for the cuts in interest rates. The reason for the reduction in rates is normally to stimulate demand in the economy. Small cuts in rates can be seen to be prudent economic management and fine tuning. Larger, more sustained cuts suggest an economy in decline with general reductions in levels of corporate and private spending and therefore a reduction in the demand for the products of development.

Rises in interest rates can be mitigated in a number of ways, many of which were reviewed in Chapter 3 on finance. These include fixed rate loans and hedging using financial instruments. These measures can deal with the symptoms of increasing costs but they can do little to mitigate the demand-side problems. This can be partly addressed in the letting and sale phase (see below) but, primarily, dealing with these factors is down to the developer making prudent decisions as to the timing and nature of the development produced, even down to making a decision on whether to proceed or not. Developers should keep up to date with trends in both the local, national and world economy and develop an understanding of how the economy works. An economically literate developer is likely to be more aware of potential risks and less likely to be drawn into the over-optimism that is the primary cause of failure within the sector.

Rise in construction cost

There are two slightly different circumstances to consider in this section:

1. when the final tender sums are in excess of the initial estimates; and
2. when the final contract sum is in excess of the initial estimate and/or the tender figure.

The first circumstance comes about when the project goes out to tender prior to the building contract being awarded. It can arise from a number of causes: the design of the building may not have been finalised at the feasibility stage; the quantity surveyor may have underestimated the practical problems of carrying out the project; and, finally, the market circumstances may be less competitive than expected. This occurs when there is a glut of construction work allowing contractors to pick and choose the developments for which they will tender competitively, putting in high prices for the remainder.

Mitigation or avoidance of this is difficult. Fully designing the project as early as possible is certainly a wise move, although taking one of the alternative procurement routes may be a possibility. This may also be the most appropriate route to encourage more competition for the contract. An alternative procurement route that offers a contractor the ability to make a better profit margin may, ironically, see the overall construction costs being reduced. The need to balance control with cost discussed in Chapter 5 should, however, always be paramount.

Regarding the second circumstance listed above, there are two major causes of fluctuation between tender prices and the final cost of construction. The first is due to the effect of unforeseen problems during the construction work. These may be caused by previously unknown problems in the ground (for example, contamination or unforeseen hard rock hindering excavation) or working with existing structures (conversion work is particularly prone to this). Largely, these risks can be mitigated by good site investigation, although the risks can never be completely eliminated. The second major clause of price changes is due to changes in design or client requirements between the tender process and final completion.

The public has become used to large, public contracts never seeming to come in on budget or on time. There is a myth that all construction is the same, that cost and time targets are rarely met. In fact, an examination of most investment development projects will show that there is rarely much difference between the initial cost estimates, the tender sums and the completed contract sum.

The reason for this is the way that the projects are organised and conducted. By their nature, public-type projects are subject to considerable consultation, discussion and thus design change throughout their lives. This is an undesirable state of affairs on a construction project, particularly where on-site work has commenced. Under the construction contract, the contractor is allowed to claim for disruption of work, additional head office and supervision time, abortive expenditures on material or plant order as well as higher rates for actually carrying out work that differs from the original contract documentation. This is how many contractors make an adequate profit margin on construction work. Contractors employ cost specialists to exploit these opportunities.

Although, again, an alternative procurement method other than the traditional approach could be considered (i.e. one that would allow a scheme to proceed prior to the final design being completed), often this is not appropriate. In most investment-type projects it is important to ensure that all of the design work has been completed prior to the tender process being initiated. The second factor to ensure that costs will not spiral out of control is strict control of the project during the construction phase. The temptation to change details of the project should be resisted unless the reasons for change are significant for the success of the project. These reasons may include changing the form or specification of the building to suit the requirements of a particular end user. All other changes after the tender documents have been finalised should be resisted.

REDUCTION IN VALUE OF COMPLETED DEVELOPMENT

The final factors that will be considered in this section are the most important. These are the factors related to the end value of the development. As we have seen, development appraisals are most sensitive to these factors and it is these factors that are biggest killers of development projects.

The main risk areas to the end value of a property development scheme are:

> due to adverse movement in the market – these include:
  − a fall in prices of properties for sale

- a reduction in rents achievable on properties to let
- an increase in the desired investment yield on investment properties for sale
> due to delays in letting
> changes in the quality of investment vehicle produced.

Adverse movement in market

Developers will always be vulnerable to adverse movements in the market. The timescale of the majority of development projects means that the market into which a property is introduced will almost certainly be different in some way from that envisaged at the time of the appraisal.

If the vulnerability must be expected then it is imperative for developers to fully explore the nature and extent of their exposure to adverse fluctuations. We have already seen how this is done – sensitivity analysis. It vitally important that developers do this at the appraisal stage, preferably using the most sophisticated technique that they can apply. The developer must understand how much they are at risk in order to take the basic decision as to whether to accept the risk and to proceed with the development.

There are things that can be done to mitigate the effect of adverse market movements during the course of developments. In good markets, most commercial developers will avoid making a decision about letting or selling the property until as late as possible for fear of reducing profits by accepting a price that might be exceeded later on. In poor markets the reverse is true: it will pay developers to try to achieve pre-lettings (lease agreements before the completion of the project) or pre-sales (sale of the long-term interest in the project prior to completion) to secure the income flow, the yield and the financial exit strategy from the project. When projects are commenced under poor market conditions many developers find that this is the only course of action that they can follow, as pre-lettings and pre-sales will need to be in place before finance can be secured. These actions greatly reduce the risk inherent in a development project.

Delays in letting

As we have seen from Chapter 4 on financial appraisal, in a speculative development it is the period from the end of the construction to the final letting where the finance charges on a conventionally funded development project increase at the greatest rate. Delays in letting a building can seriously jeopardise the success of a scheme.

One solution to this has already been discussed: attempting to agree pre-lets early in the scheme or before it has even begun removes this risk, albeit at the cost of agreeing the rent at potentially too low a level. The other main mitigation methods are really down to preparation and planning again. First, it is important to stress the significance of appointing a good letting agent at an early stage of the project. A good agent will target those occupiers who are genuinely in the market for space. They will also provide input into developing the marketing and advertising strategy that will see the property exposed to the right decision-makers at the right time as well as ensuring that the right product is produced at the right time.

Changes in the quality of the investment vehicle produced

This is not strictly a risk factor but is rather a step that a developer may consider as a reaction to a deterioration in the market. It is included, however, because it represents a type of risk that could be classified under the heading of 'temptation' and is thus one that a developer should try to identify and take steps to avoid. It concerns one of the most difficult areas for a developer facing a downturn in the market. It underlines the fact that, in commercial development at least, but increasingly in residential development, the developer is serving two markets: the occupation and the investment market.

The first impact of adverse movements in the economy on the property market is usually on the former. Developers frequently face a situation where good-quality tenants shelve plans for new space in the face of falling demand in their own market sectors. When this occurs developers may be tempted to secure a letting by compromising the assumptions originally envisaged. This may be by:

> accepting an offer from a lower quality tenant;
> agreeing to shorter lease lengths; and
> relaxing the terms of the lease away from those required by the mainstream investment market (i.e. away from an 'institutional' lease).

This is a dangerous step to take. All of these steps will have a major impact on the investment value. All of the above steps will result in a deterioration of the yield on an investment property. Our 'base' appraisal used throughout this book applied a yield of 7 per cent to the investment produced which assumed a letting to a good-quality tenant on an institutionally acceptable lease. This equated to an income multiplier of 14.286 times the annual income. Taking the three steps above, but keeping all else the same, might see the yield move out to 9–10 per cent because the security of the investment would be so eroded. This would equate to an income multiplier of 10–11.111, i.e. a reduction in value of around one-quarter. The changes may indeed make the investment unsaleable.

This, then, is a step that a developer should only take as a last resort when all other routes have been exhausted and when foreclosure is imminent. Alternative steps that may be considered are to offer more substantial rent-free periods or other incentives to take space.

Conclusions

This chapter of the book may have put prospective developers reading it off the idea of ever carrying out a development. It is often said that people who spend time considering all of the risks involved in a development would never do it. There is a grain of truth in this: it is easy to become obsessed with the downside risk of development. However, although this chapter has concentrated on downside risk because it is that which developers should be most concerned with, it should also be noted that property development is also subject to *upside* risk, i.e. that the factors we have considered here can move in favour of the developer, giving sometimes quite astronomic returns. Also, there is no excuse for a developer playing Russian roulette and ignoring risk. Risk is there; sensible decisions should be taken to deal with it. This means that it is important for developers to specifically address it.

Much of this chapter of the book keeps returning to the same thing: the need for diligence in the preparation and planning of the development project. In many ways a developer needs to be multifaceted in their personal qualities; they need the vision of an architect, the boldness of a gambler and the diligence of an accountant to succeed. It is perhaps the latter quality that should come to the fore as the scheme proceeds from idea to reality. This comment underlines the fact that there are no easy answers in development.

To misquote Einstein, success in development is down to the 90 per cent perspiration spent in getting all of the details of the scheme, including assembling the team, right at its commencement.

CASE STUDIES
CHAPTER 8

Case study 1: Macintosh Mill, Macintosh Village, Manchester, UK

Developer: Taylor Woodrow Capital Developments Ltd[1]

INTRODUCTION

This case study illustrates the depth of work required in the early stages of a development of a major city centre scheme. It illustrates the level of activity required to obtain the consents and establish the conditions required to bring a development to site.

PROJECT OUTLINE

The project is a mixed use development of Macintosh Mill and its associated buildings. The development was intended to provide 510 residential units in a mixture of new build and conversion of existing mill buildings. The new build sections included two 15-storey towers while three 19th century mills were to be refurbished and converted for residential use. Other parts of the complex were to be converted to offices while five three-storey live/work units were also to be built.

The formal description of the development included in the planning application was:

> Part demolition and redevelopment and part reconfiguration and refurbishment of Mackintosh Mill and redevelopment of land to the north of Macintosh Mill and East of Cambridge Street, for mixed use development, predominantly residential (510 units) – Use Class C3; offices and Live/Work units – Use Class B1; landscaping and environmental improvements; creation of public spaces; access works; highways works; and other related works.

The project had a number of problems to overcome prior to commencing construction works. Manchester was at the heart of the Industrial Revolution in the UK and retains many historic industrial buildings that are part of the country's historical heritage. The Macintosh Mill complex dated to the early part of the 19th century. The mill buildings were Grade II listed. The works involved substantial alterations to the buildings as well as demolition works. In addition, the financial viability of the scheme was dependent on the construction of the new build parts, particularly the towers. The imposition of these towers into the existing context of rather lower historical buildings was problematical. The site had also had over 160 years of virtually continuous industrial use, and therefore there was also the question of site contamination to resolve.

THE SITE

A location map and site plan are included in Figures 8.1 and 8.2. Essentially, the site consisted of the mill buildings and a cleared site on the opposite side of the street.

HISTORY OF THE SITE

The complex developed on the site commenced with the construction of a mill in 1825. The mill was to produce rubberised cotton by the Macintosh process. The site then had a long association with the production of 'Macintoshes' and was enlarged continuously into a complex of buildings. The original mill no. 1 was destroyed by bombing during the Second World War but many of the other older mill buildings dating from the 19th century survived on the site. These included:

Mill 2, built *ca.*1830
Mill 3, built 1850–55
Vulcan House, built *ca.*1849
Chimney, built *ca.*1851

The site was acquired by Dunlop in 1929 and was subsequently altered by additions, extensions and demolition. Dunlop initially produced solid tyres on the site. Later, much of the early plant and equipment were removed and a major part of the floor space was converted into administrative, testing and research facilities.

Although the buildings had some historic significance regarding their association with, initially, Macintosh production and later with the tyre industry, they were not in themselves highly significant buildings. They were relatively 'standard' mill or industrial buildings for their day. The mid-19th century buildings were constructed of double pile brick walls with timber floors. The spanning beams were supported on cast iron columns. The windows were timber casements with stone sills. The roofs were mainly pitched covered with Welsh slate, although some flat and bituminised roofs existed on site. The walls and structure were basically sound but were in poor condition in some places. The roof covering was generally in poor condition at the time of the site acquisition by the developers.

The site became redundant following the rationalisation of Dunlop's core business and thus became ripe for redevelopment.

THE SITE AND ITS RELATIONSHIP TO THE LOCALITY

The site is located in an area termed the 'Southern Gateway'. It is on the southern edge of the city centre, close to both the commercial areas and the university sector and forms part of the southern entry to the centre, hence the name. The main urban motorway, the Mancunian Way and the main railway line from the west pass close to the site. The University of Manchester and Manchester Metropolitan University are close to the site, with the University of Salford being only approximately one mile away.

The central urban area of Manchester has gone through a period of major change and development over the past 20 years. The surrounding area was one that showed the classic symptoms of inner urban decay until the formation of the Urban Development Corporation in the early 1980s and following the positive intervention of Manchester City Council to promote regeneration. This has led to a transformation in these areas of the city, characterised in particular by their repopulation. The surrounding suburbs have seen a huge increase in residential property with the resident population rising by literally many hundredfold over the period 1986–2001. Many redundant commercial and industrial buildings have been converted to residential use. This, in turn, has supported a vibrant entertainment and business sector expansion. Many of the occupants of these properties are young, affluent professionals, further boosting the trend to make the surrounding area economically viable.

The Southern Gateway area has not seen the intensity of development that some suburbs have. It has been identified by the city council as a priority area for regeneration. The city council developed a conceptual master plan for the area which had to be taken into account for development control purposes. The basic idea is to create an area characterised by relatively high-density residential schemes. Other, similar developments have taken place close by, including the development of the Student Village by the conversion of mill buildings. Other residential schemes completed within recent years include Chorlton New Mill and the Little Ireland scheme located very close to Macintosh Mill. The developer, Taylor Woodrow Capital Developments Ltd, also owns a number of other sites in the area and had other developments at various stages of completion underway at the time that Macintosh Mill was at the planning stage.

The area is not designated as a conservation area although individual buildings are listed.

THE PARTIES INVOLVED IN THE DEVELOPMENT

The following parties were involved in the development:

Landowner	Southside Regeneration Ltd
Developer	Taylor Woodrow Capital Developments Ltd
Local government	Manchester City Council
Development team	
Architect	Terry Farrell and Partners
Structural engineer	Waterman BBT
Environmental consultant	Waterman Environmental
Planning consultant	Drivers Jonas
Quantity surveyor	Rex Procter and Partners
Contractor	Taylor Woodrow Construction

DEVELOPMENT INCEPTION

The scheme essentially started with piecemeal assembly of the site by Westport Development. They acquired a number of sites in the area including cleared sites at Little Ireland and also Macintosh Mill, formerly the Dunlop works. Westport sought to bring a bigger player into the development to assist in the long-term programme. A scheme was drawn up for the smaller, less complex sites in the area and planning consent was gained for mainly new build development of these sites, while a partner was sought to assist with the more complex Macintosh Mill site.

Taylor Woodrow Capital Developments were soon identified as a potential partner. Taylor Woodrow had carried out a number of developments in London, including a number of residential developments as part of regeneration programmes. They were keen to expand into the regional markets and Manchester was particularly attractive as the city centre residential market was both well-established and buoyant.

Taylor Woodrow commissioned a master plan study of the area from Terry Farrell and Partners. The master plan covered a wider area than the site confines itself and was intended to identify the development capacity and potential of the area. Mackintosh Mill was identified as a key component of the development.

Ultimately, the developer's success in obtaining planning and listed building consent caused a rethink of the whole project. Taylor Woodrow took over the whole project and redesigned the layout of the scheme, including the new build section at Little Ireland, to maximise the scheme's appeal to both the planners and purchasers of the site.

SITE ACQUISITION AND INVESTIGATION

As noted, the site was already in the ownership of the original developer. Taylor Woodrow agreed to develop out the site on obtaining full planning consent.

A number of reports were prepared on aspects of the existing building and the site. They were mainly prepared by the engineers and environmental consultants, Waterman BBT and Waterman Environmental. These reports also formed part of the planning application. This was an important element of the due diligence process of acquiring the site, considering that the location had seen industrial processes carried out for around 160 years. Any contamination that presented a potential risk to health needed to be removed or remediated. This could affect both the programme and costs of the scheme and thus influence its viability. In addition, information was required as to the quality of the ground in order to assist the design and specification of elements such as the foundations.

The reports produced on these areas included:

> a structural report on the existing buildings;
> a site investigation and environmental assessment of Macintosh Mill;
> a site investigation and environmental assessment of the cleared part of the site (called Little Ireland Block C);
> a hazardous materials survey.

310

Structural survey of the existing buildings

As noted, the development works were partly new build and partly conversion of the existing mill structures. It was important to assess the state of the existing structures in order to gauge the degree of work required to be done to them.

The survey, carried out by Waterman BBT, structural engineers, found that the mill complex had exhibited heavy use over a period of many years. A number of defects were identified. Some of these were common to all buildings and included:

> spalling external brickwork
> eroded mortar joints
> vertical cracking of brickwork
> loose, missing brickwork
> bulging brickwork
> displaced coping stones
  degraded stone windowsills.

Some more serious individual defects were noted including fractured trusses and spalling, cracked concrete and exposed reinforcement in soffits in some buildings. In some buildings, notably the Solid Tyre Building, this was felt to be so extensive that repairs would not be economic.

All of the defects could be repaired but in many cases repair would be uneconomic based on the potential use of the buildings. The observations and information from the survey were incorporated into the schedule of works and design of the building.

Site investigation and environmental assessment of Macintosh Mill

The investigation was carried out by Waterman Environmental Ltd. This was done initially by a desk study that investigated the use history of the site. Subsequently, sampling and monitoring of the soil and groundwater was undertaken.

The principal areas of contamination found were:

> in areas of 'made ground', moderate contamination by metals and sulphates;
> under an area that was originally occupied by a gas holder (which overlapped with a neighbouring site) organic contamination (hydrocarbons) and inorganic contamination (metals, cyanide and sulphates) was found;
> hydrocarbon contamination was generally found to a depth of 4–9.8m within the eastern area of the site.

The contamination in the groundwater was found to be within EU limits by the time it drained into the River Medlock. No action was required. The contamination beneath the former gas holder was considered to be a greater risk and the contents of the soil required treating or their removal from the site. The majority of the site of the former gas holder was located off the boundaries of the site. It was therefore recommended that a cut-off wall be built between the two properties to protect the mill and its users from any residual contamination. The excavation of the basement car park would lead to the removal of other contaminated material from the site.

The high structural loadings that were envisaged for some elements of the new build of the site had implications for the design of the foundations. The site investigation reports suggested that piled foundations be used. Recommendations as to the grade of concrete to be used were included in the report, given the potential for chemical attack due to the condition of the ground and its contaminants.

Site investigation and environmental assessment of Little Ireland Block C

The findings for this site were similar to those of the main mill site. The investigations found evidence of contamination but, following remediation, the risk to the environment and end users would be negligible.

The site was greenfield until the 1820s. By 1829 the site had been developed and occupied by a large building. By 1948 the site was part of the Dunlop Rubber Works and remained as such until the 1990s. An underground naphtha tank and other underground storage tanks were either known or suspected to exist on the site. As per the main mill site, hydrocarbon contamination was found at a depth of 4–9.8m beneath the eastern part of the site. The recommended remediation was the removal and disposal of the underground storage tanks and the removal or treatment of soils and groundwater contaminated with hydrocarbons.

Hazardous materials survey

This survey was also carried out by Waterman Environmental Ltd. The survey assessed potential environmental and health risks at the site to be addressed by the site clearance/demolition contractors and site developers. The investigation comprised a site inspection, sampling, laboratory analysis and risk assessment associated with hazardous materials present within the existing buildings and structures on the site.

A number of hazards were identified, including lead in paint and elevated concentrations of metals, fractions of organic dust and some limited impregnation of concrete and wooden flooring surfaces.

Although the site was found to pose no more than a low risk to current site personnel it did present a risk to the health and safety of site operatives during the course of the development. Each of the hazards thus needed to be removed as part of planned remedial work and the site subject to revalidation prior to redevelopment.

SCHEME DESIGN

The scheme architect was Terry Farrell and Partners, the internationally renowned architecture practice. Farrells were responsible for the master planning of the scheme. The location map is shown in Figure 8.1 and the master plan in Figure 8.2.

The architects for the scheme worked to a number of overall design considerations. The new parts of the structures had to complement the existing, historical buildings

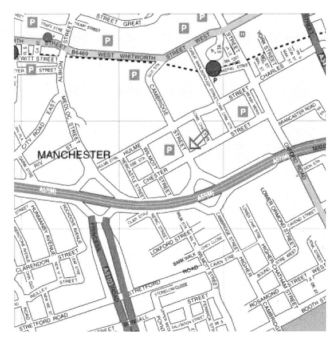

FIGURE 8.1 Location of Mackintosh Mill. Source: Taylor Woodrow Capital Developments

while providing an economic solution for the developers. In addition, the scheme as a whole had to fit within the context of the locality.

The Southern Gateway was perceived by the architects as connecting the city centre to three strands of new development on the south side of the city: along Chester Road, The Princes Parkway and the universities corridor. The Southern Gateway could also be viewed as an extension to the city centre. Cambridge Street itself was

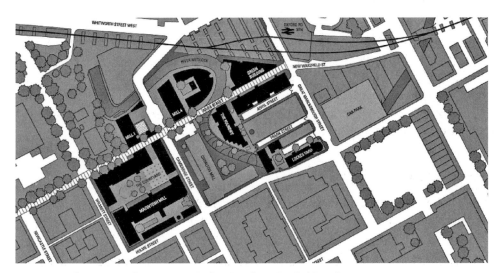

FIGURE 8.2 The master plan. Source: Taylor Woodrow Capital Developments

historically a gateway between the city centre and Hulme across the River Medway. It was separated from the city centre by the development of the railway, canal and urban motorways. The site is dominated by the railway viaduct in particular and the definition of a gateway has been lost. The architect thus proposed that twin towers be built, one on each side of Cambridge Street but set back and staggered to define a new urban square and re-establish the gateway feel, the towers forming a new urban marker for the city.

The new towers needed careful design to fit into the context of the site. The towers, or Campanali, were designed to be slender with recesses at the top and bottom to give a greater degree of elegance and remove the illusion of dominance created by a more imposing block. Tall buildings still retain the ability to better define the public domain. The podium height of the remaining new build was set by the height of the existing buildings. The towers were placed in gaps away from the main mill buildings, again to reduce the potential for dominance over the historic context.

In addition to these considerations, the design aimed to incorporate traffic calming measures into the Cambridge Street area to reduce the degree of speeding traffic. These included changes in material from the street to the 'square' area. The design also greatly improved pedestrian access to the river and the urban areas around the scheme.

Finally, Taylor Woodrow was keen to exploit the market for premium residential space in Manchester. They wanted to bring some principles used in their prestige London schemes to the Manchester market. These included both a high-quality specification and also rather larger floor areas than the market had generally seen to date. Rather than trying to maximise the number of apartments developed, there was concentration on producing a high-quality environment. This was additionally reflected in the provision within the design of a 'green' building on the island site opposite the mill that incorporated a wind-powered generator on the roof, natural ventilation and was to include a nursery and doctor's surgery as well as apartments. This, combined with small commercial premises to be included in the scheme, was intended to add to a village/community feel to the development.

This integrated approach certainly assisted in the planning consent process but also established the development in the market as something more distinct than just another residential scheme.

PLANNING APPLICATION AND PLANNING PROCESS

The planning application consisted of the statutory forms and the following supporting documentation:

> a plan showing the boundary of the application site;
> a set of drawings prepared by the architect illustrating the existing and proposed buildings;

> an environmental report that considered the impact of the proposals in relation to planning policy, townscape and cultural heritage, contamination, groundwater and water quality, air quality, noise and vibration, socio-economics, and the likely construction impacts and proposed mitigation;
> a transport statement dealing with the transport impact of the scheme;
> a statement on the proposals in relation to Planning Policy Guidance Note 15 (Planning and the Historical Environment);
> a condition survey of the mill buildings prepared in connection with the above;
> a landscape plan prepared by Edward Hutchinson, landscape architect;
> a landscape principles document;
> a note on the technical specification of the proposed electricity substation prepared by Arup Engineers;
> a structural report on the existing buildings;
> a site investigation and environmental assessment of the cleared part of the site (called Little Ireland Block C);
> a site investigation and environmental assessment of Macintosh Mill;
> a hazardous materials survey.

The planning application commanded a fee of £9,500.

Many of these items included in support of the planning application are statutory requirements of the planning process.

In addition, the developers were required to consult with a number of bodies, statutory, public and interest groups, as part of the planning consultation process. Some of this consultation was done directly by the developers, other issues were addressed by the planning officials of the city council as part of their decision-making process. The bodies consulted and their responses are listed in Table 8.1.

In addition to these specific consultations, the normal publicity requirements of the application process were followed. A notice bringing the public attention to the planning and listed building application was posted on the site and advertised in the local newspapers. Letters were sent to the neighbouring occupiers. Copies of these letters were included in the planning application. No representations were received.

A report was prepared by the head of planning of the city council for presentation to the council's planning committee. The report made recommendations based on the material presented by the applicants, the representations received by the consultation process and by the planning officers addressing the application against national planning guidelines. The recommendation from the head of planning was that the committee should be:

A. Minded to approve full planning application 062484 and listed building consent 062485 subject to the conditions laid out below;
B. Refer listed building consent application to the Secretary of State for the Environment for him to determine whether to call in the application for his determination;
C. Authorise the Head of Planning to determine the applications using the delegated powers should the Secretary of State not call in the applications for his determination.

TABLE 8.1 The bodies consulted and their responses

Body consulted	Comments
Director of Operational Services	No specific objections
Head of Engineering Services	No specific objections
Director of Housing	No specific objections
Environmental Health	No specific objections
Environment Agency	No specific objections
Coal Authority	No specific objections
Greater Manchester Passenger Transport Executive	No specific objections
English Heritage	Supported the principle of the development. No objection to the twin towers in principle but wanted to approve the material used, signage and the elevational details of the new build parts. The body had concerns about traffic flow and expressed a preference for Cambridge Street to be closed
Commission for Architecture and the Built Environment	No specific objections but would prefer the closure of Cambridge Street
Manchester Conservation Areas and Historic Building Panel	This body praised the quality of the information that was provided by the applicant. The applicant was clearly dealing sensitively with the site. They were concerned about the towers and debated the issue at length. They questioned the ability of the developers to deliver the new public space. They requested that a survey be done prior to development to record the industrial archaeology. They recommended that a condition be placed on the consent that no additions above the roofline of the listed buildings be allowed
Society for the Protection of Ancient Buildings	In general the society welcomed the conversion. They wanted more trees to be included in the landscaping and regarded the towers as too tall and too stark in contrast with the existing structures
Victorian Society	The society supported the principle of the proposal but objected to several elements. These included the West Tower and the Cambridge Street elevation

Source: Taylor Woodrow Capital Developments.

The referral of the listed building consent is normal procedure reflecting the fact that historical buildings in the built environment are part of the national heritage and not just a local concern. The majority of such referrals do not result in the call-in of the application.

Fifteen conditions were recommended to be applied to the main application. Similarly, 14 conditions were attached to the listed building consent. The principal conditions to the main application were as follows.

1. The development must be begun not later than the expiry of five years beginning with the date of permission.
2. The development should be carried out in accordance with the submitted drawings.
3. Details of the construction timetable relating to any phasing of the development should be submitted to and approved in writing by the local planning authority prior to the works under that phase being commenced.

5. The development shall not commence until detailed drawings of the external elevations … have been submitted to and approved in writing by the local planning authority.
6. Samples of the materials to be used in the external elevations … have been submitted to and approved by the local planning authority.
10. A scheme for acoustically insulating the proposed residential accommodation against noise … has been submitted to and approved in writing by the local planning authority.
14. The development … shall include a building lighting scheme and a scheme for the illumination of external areas during the period between dusk and dawn … have been submitted to and approved in writing by the local planning authority.
15. Before development commences full details concerning the layout and treatment of the Gateway Square across Cambridge Street shall be submitted to and approved in writing by the local planning authority. Details shall include how the continued use of Cambridge Street as a vehicle route shall be integrated into the physical layout and environmental treatment of this area.

The conditions recommended for the listed building consent were similar in character to those attached to the main application with regard to things such as time limits, construction plan and approval of drawings, etc. There were also requirements to provide statements and accurate drawings dealing with the proposed strip-out works for the internal features of the listed buildings and also works to provide fire protection, acoustic insulation and fume extraction in these structures. In addition, the city council required that schemes for the refurbishment and repair of the existing windows, brickwork cleaning, existing roofs and rooflights should be submitted to and approved in writing by the local planning authority. A full photographic and archaeological survey of the site and the buildings was also required.

The recommendations of the chief planning officer were approved and full planning consent and listed building consent (subject to the provisos made above) was granted at a meeting of the city council's planning committee in October 2001. This was much faster than was anticipated and the mill scheme was brought forward to development in the last months of 2001. The earlier sites with existing consent had already seen development start in the middle of 2001.

CONSTRUCTION PHASE

A modified design and build route was chosen, using the JCT 1998 contract with contractor's design. This was done for two main reasons. First, it enabled a rapid start on site with the contractors using the Terry Farrell design for the overall layout with the detail design provided by the contractor's design team as the work proceeded. The second reason for the adoption was that the sister company of Taylor Woodrow Capital Developments, Taylor Woodrow Construction, was selected as the contractor. The working relationship was thus different to the standard working relationship where the contractor is a separate company.

In common with many developers, the remaining members of the development team were selected from prior experience. With the exception of the main scheme architect, all of the team had worked on other projects with Taylor Woodrow.

POST-CONSTRUCTION PHASE

At the time of writing of the original version of this book (early 2002), the main scheme had been on site for around six months. The total development programme was of five years' duration, with the new build parts on the adjacent sites being built out first.

In early February 2002, a marketing suite was installed on the site. This was placed on part of the Mackintosh Mill site that was not due to be developed until later in the project. It was a two-storey structure furnished to a high standard, with models and plans of the scheme on one level and fitted out examples of the bathrooms and kitchens on a lower level. The marketing suite was open seven days a week from 11 a.m. to 6 p.m. Attractive brochures were available on each phase as they commenced. Prices in the early phases ranged from £87,000 for a ground floor one-bedroom flat to £189,500 for the larger upper storey two-bedroom apartments in the new build parts.

Around half of the apartments sold in the early stages of the project were bought as investments with the remainder going for owner occupation.

THE DEVELOPMENT IN 2007

The development has been released in phases over the course of its life. At the time of writing, the latest areas released included the converted Mackintosh Mill 2 and 3 where prices ranged from £135,000 for a studio up to £232,000 for a two-bedroom apartment (source: Bryant PLC), the new build Green Building (see below) where two-bedroom apartments were available at £400,000 to £450,000 and the nearby town houses. The brochure for the town houses (Figure 8.3, source: Knight Frank) illustrates how the area has become one of mixed commercial and residential use.

The Green Building at Macintosh Village designed by Terry Farrell is of particular interest for an urban development in that it is an ecological design and is one of the most environmentally advanced residential buildings in the country. A roof-mounted wind turbine generates electrical power for communal areas. Solar energy for hot water generation is harnessed using roof-mounted panels. The building is designed to achieve a 60 per cent reduction in CO_2 emissions compared to an average apartment building. Highly efficient communal gas boilers serve the underfloor heating system. Facilities throughout the building will separate waste to maximise recycling. There are expected to be considerable savings in water consumption – 40 per cent compared with the average home. Contained within a cylindrical drum, the central atrium allows plenty of natural light and ventilation into the apartments and a state of the art computerised system will optimise the control of active

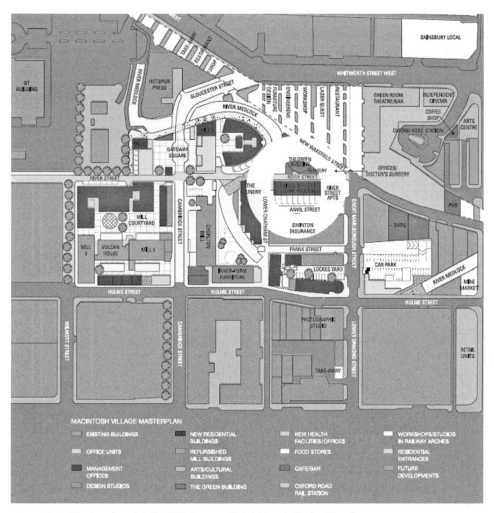

FIGURE 8.3 Master plan detail 2007. Source: Knight Frank/Taylor Woodrow

elements such as the atrium windows. Considering that the Green Building was in the original master plan of 2001, the developers proved themselves to be remarkably prescient as the building was launched into a market at a time when green issues and energy efficiency have risen to the fore (2007). It should be noted, however, that the Green Building is at the premium end of the market and that the remainder of the scheme is largely conventional.

CONCLUSIONS

The Macintosh Mill project was in its early stages at the time of writing the initial edition of the book and thus it was difficult to assess how successful it would be in commercial terms at that point. By 2007 the scheme has matured and has transformed the area and it appears to be a commercial success.

The main issues explored in examining the project are found in an appreciation of the amount of work that is required to get such a scheme to site. Obtaining planning and listed building consent while retaining commercial viability and meeting the timescale requirements needed the integration of a large team of diverse professionals. Each contributed to the work of the others and all had to work together to achieve the goal. This project is large, with likely end values in the £60–70 million range, but similar levels of coordination and effort can be found, and are required, in much smaller projects.

Case study 2: Investigating a residential development opportunity, Northern Quarter, Manchester, UK, late 2001 to early 2002

Prospective developer: Jon Berry, Berry Investments, Manchester

BACKGROUND

This case study examines how a smaller developer addresses a development opportunity.

Although the development examined here did not proceed, the study illustrates the steps that need to be followed to bring a development to reality.

The prospective developer, Jon Berry, had many years' experience running a family property business specialising in the acquisition, refurbishment and letting of residential buildings, predominantly for the student sector. For a number of years the developer had been looking at the prospects of moving into the development of houses or apartments for sale.

In many ways this represents a position in which many people with either professional or practical experience of the built environment or property industry find themselves – at the point of making the big step into the riskier world of development. This case study follows the steps taken in assessing the opportunity, the raising of the finance, the problems that arose during the feasibility study and the final decision that was made as to whether to proceed with the project or not.

PROJECT OUTLINE

The project concerned a residential development opportunity to convert the ground and upper floors of a former commercial building in the Northern Quarter, close to Manchester city centre, that was being marketed by a local agent. A separate sub-basement was given over to retail use and was held under a different lease, excluded from the interest in the property being offered.

The agents were offering a 99-year leasehold interest in the ground and upper floors of the property with a main street entrance. The owner had obtained planning consent for the conversion of the existing building to one- and two-bedroom apartments with the addition of two further new build floors to accommodate new build duplexes. This allowed for the construction of 14 apartments in total. The asking price for the leasehold interest was £500,000.

THE SITE AND ITS RELATIONSHIP TO THE LOCALITY

The existing building comprised the ground and three existing upper floors of a former commercial building in the Northern Quarter, an area in transition. Traditionally, the area was one of mixed commercial uses although it is now primarily associated with the textile and garment industry.

In recent years, a number of residential developments and conversions have taken place in the vicinity of the site, reflecting the move within Manchester as a whole towards 'City Living'. Manchester city centre has been transformed since the late 1980s with an enormous expansion in the number of residential schemes in many areas. The city became a fashionable place to live for young single professionals, young professional couples and older, wealthy business people wanting a second home closer to their place of work. The Northern Quarter had not, by 2002, been developed to the same degree as other areas but offered a number of development opportunities and generally lower prices than those around the universities and the 'Gay Village' area to the south of the city centre.

The site itself was located in the heart of the Northern Quarter. Some of the buildings in the vicinity had been converted to residential use for sale and/or letting while others remained in a variety of commercial uses, including many still being retained by the textile industry. The street where the building was located contained a mix of generally low-value secondary retail uses but with a number of vacant premises. The area is popular with many people, representing an affordable opportunity for city centre living. Apartments offered for sale in recent years tended to sell readily and good uplifts in prices had been achieved.

The building's structure was around 70 years old and was entirely conventional, consisting of load-bearing solid external walls, stone-faced on the ground floor and brick-faced above with timber floors, sash windows and a flat roof. The existing structure seemed to be in reasonable condition and was not listed nor was it in a conservation area.

The scheme as drawn, and for which planning consent was obtained, provided the accommodation listed in Table 8.2.

TABLE 8.2 Summary of accommodation

Apartment number	Floor	No. of bedrooms	Area (m^2)	Area (ft^2)
1	G	1	53	574
2	G	1	43	467
3	G	2	58	622
4	1	1	55	586
5	1	1	47	508
6	1	2	65	698
7	2	1	55	586
8	2	1	48	519
9	2	2	66	711
10	3	2	86	922
11	3	2	78	839
12	4 and 5	2	78	834
13	4 and 5	2	76	820
14	4 and 5	2	93	1,000

THE PARTIES INVOLVED IN THE DEVELOPMENT

Berry Investments was to be the sole developer of the scheme, subject to the provisions of the financing deal as described below.

DEVELOPMENT INCEPTION

The originator of the scheme was a local entrepreneur who ran a commercial property agency in the city. He acquired the property, employed an architect to design the scheme and then obtained planning consent. There was never any intention of the owners carrying through the development themselves; their interest was in the gain in site value that was achieved by obtaining planning consent, which would be realised by the re-selling of the site. As noted in the main text, this is common practice in the development sector.

APPRAISAL PROCESS

A number of steps were followed by Berry Investments to determine whether the scheme was viable and whether a purchase should go ahead. This involved consultation with a number of parties, principally involving seeking development advice from a firm of chartered surveyors, a cost consultant (via the agent), the planning department and financiers, and consultation with selling agents. The results of these consultations are outlined below.

CONSULTATION WITH SELLING AGENTS

A small developer working with a moderately sized development project has neither the time nor resources to carry out extensive market research. Establishing the nature and extent of the demand for the product is, however, one of the key parts of the development process both in assessing the overall viability and in determining the final design and specification of the scheme.

The best solution to this problem for a developer is to consult extensively with local agents – as did Berry Investments. This was done as part of the selection process for the agent who would handle the sale of the completed apartments at the end of the development. This process allows agents to reveal their knowledge about the local market and to explain how they would market the property, enabling the developer to get a range of views about the prospects for the scheme and the likely sale prices achievable on the apartments and duplexes.

The agents all commented on the increasing popularity of the Northern Quarter as galleries, bars and restaurants moved into the area, and its good location due to its proximity to the railway station and city centre. Advice was given on creating brochures and the fact that the apartments would appeal to the investment market with individuals seeking to 'buy to rent'. Most agents discussed strategies that would exploit this market, with a number highlighting their track record

TABLE 8.3 Agreed realistic selling prices

Apartment number	Floor	No. of bedrooms	Area (m²)	Area (ft²)	Price
1	G	1	53	574	£105,000
2	G	1	43	467	£90,000
3	G	2	58	622	£120,000
4	1	1	55	586	£105,000
5	1	1	47	508	£90,000
6	1	2	65	698	£125,000
7	2	1	55	586	£105,000
8	2	1	48	519	£95,000
9	2	2	66	711	£130,000
10	3	2	86	922	£175,000
11	3	2	78	839	£155,000
12	4 and 5	2	78	834	£160,000
13	4 and 5	2	76	820	£160,000
14	4 and 5	2	93	1,000	£185,000
		Totals	**901**	**9,686**	**£1,800,000**

and contacts in this area. Some recommended fitting out a show flat, although others considered this to be an unnecessary expense. All this advice was provided freely.

The selection of an agent was made by the developer and the prices given in Table 8.3 were agreed to be realistic selling prices, given the state of the market at the time that the development was being considered.

STRUCTURAL SURVEY OF THE EXISTING BUILDINGS

A structural survey would have formed part of the final site acquisition process and was budgeted for in the financial appraisal.

SITE INVESTIGATION, ENVIRONMENTAL ASSESSMENT AND HAZARDOUS MATERIALS SURVEY

These were not carried out. The building's structure was largely unchanged although a small passenger lift was to be incorporated in the scheme that did involve excavation. In addition, the existing fittings and fixtures were to be removed. Although both processes may have revealed deleterious material such as asbestos, this was not considered to be a major risk and, in any case, would have been picked up in the structural survey.

SCHEME DESIGN

The site sale included a set of plans commissioned by the vendor of the site that detailed the development scheme. It was these drawings that were used in the planning application and to which the full planning consent referred. The purchaser would receive the intellectual rights to the drawings and would be able to build out the scheme.

FINANCE

Berry Investments sought project finance to fund 100 per cent of the development costs. A number of banks were approached to secure funding but the best options seemed to lie with a smaller specialist lender which was more experienced in dealing with the risk involved in the scheme.

One specialist property fund was located which would provide 100 per cent development funding subject to the following criteria:

> X Limited normally chooses to invest in schemes that have sales revenue in excess of £1m ... for housing development, subject to the creation of a new company, usually a wholly owned subsidiary of the current operating company, which would act as the contractor for the development. X Limited would then enter into a joint venture agreement with this new company and, under this agreement, would arrange the finance necessary for the development.
>
> The following general criteria are usually required for an acceptable proposal:
>
> > The site is located where people choose to live.
> > The planned house types are consistent with the existing accommodation in the area.
> > The sale prices ... are reconcilable with those of existing surrounding properties.
> > The required rate of sale can be demonstrated to be achievable in current market conditions.
> > All permissions necessary to enable the foregoing assumptions to hold true are available.
> > The Joint Venture partner can demonstrate his financial standing, his ability to construct and manage the development and has a proven track record of successful projects.
> > The proposed development appraisal demonstrates an acceptable profit level.
>
> If these criteria are met, financing would be granted to the development company and would be secured by way of a first charge over the site to a joint stock bank, which would provide the primary loan. X Limited would be granted a second charge to cover the remaining top slice of finance, which would be provided from the company's own funds. A management charge would be made reflecting the interest rate applicable to the primary debt.
>
> Building costs and fees would be fixed and warranted by the contractor and would be paid by certified monthly valuation, by an independent surveyor. We would then share with you the risk of other time-related costs and selling prices.
>
> To enable us to evaluate your development proposal we would need to receive a viability appraisal from you. It should include a copy of any relevant planning permissions, a site layout, market research to establish and confirm sales income, a breakdown of building and development costs, your company profile, previous experience and track record and ... a detailed cash flow, tracking the development from start to finish, and including interest.

The guidelines, as laid down by the financier, have been extensively reproduced as they provide a very clear statement of what a developer must provide in order to gain finance. It can be seen that a blend of a viable project with a degree of prior experience is needed. It should be noted that, in this case, Berry Investments was judged to be an acceptable partner and, that in order to obtain 100 per cent finance (i.e. to cover all of the development costs), it was necessary to enter into a joint venture agreement, i.e. the requirement to give over the rights to 50 per cent of the profits (although these were to be shared on a vertical split, rather than giving the financier first call on the profits). Effectively, the financier is providing a viable level of security for a bank to advance funds for the scheme and, in return for a relatively small risk exposure, stands to gain a share of the profits.

PLANNING APPLICATION AND PLANNING CONSULTATION

As noted, full planning consent had been obtained by the current owner of the building. Planning permission was granted by Manchester City Council in October 2001.

The consent was subject to a number of conditions although most were standard (for example, the consent was limited to a five-year period following the date of the permission, and that the development should be carried out in accordance with the plans as submitted) but there were also requirements to agree to some of the details of the scheme on the execution of the project. These were seemingly minor issues such as the location of, and access to, bin stores and the provision of cycle stores on the premises.

In fact, consultation with the planning authorities showed that some significant changes were required to the layout of the ground floor that could have had an impact on both the marketability and the sale price of one of the apartments on this floor. There was also a small increase in construction costs. The negotiations with the planning department on this issue were protracted, being set back, in part, by the planning department's delay in retrieving documents on the scheme from archive storage. This information was received after the initial appraisal for the financiers had been completed. The figures included at the end of the case study are based on the original sale values and cost estimate – the loss of revenue allied to a rise in costs would have eroded the profit figure further from that given.

CONSTRUCTION ISSUES

The surveying firm providing development advice had the scheme costed for Berry Investments. This suggested a total build cost of around £900/m^2 to £950/m^2.

Berry Investments decided to follow a 'design and build' route for the project, should it choose to proceed. This provided a number of advantages, including certainty on cost and on speed of construction. It would also have greatly simplified the coordination of the project during its execution. There was also little need to keep strict control of the detailed output of the construction process. A shortlist of contractors was drawn up by Berry Investments' development consultants.

POST-CONSTRUCTION PHASE

A local firm of surveyors was to be appointed to advise on project management and construction costs. One of the agents who was consulted about the market potential of the project was to be appointed to conduct the marketing and sale of the completed apartments.

OUTCOME OF THE APPRAISAL PROCESS

Bringing together the various threads of the development project in the appraisal (the cash flow produced by Berry Investments is reproduced in Figure 8.4) caused the following conclusions to be reached:

> the development scheme in terms of the marketability of the product was viable;
> finance was available at an acceptable rate and on acceptable terms;
> Berry Investments was confident that it could successfully complete the scheme.

However:

> the purchase price for the land was too high at £500,000.

Allowing for all costs, an acceptable profit margin for residential schemes (around 15 per cent) was only approached when the land price was reduced to around £400,000. This gave the figures detailed in Table 8.4 and Figure 8.4.

Berry Investments attempted to secure the site at a lower price but the vendors were not willing to negotiate at this level. Berry Investments was unofficially advised that the vendors were expecting property prices to appreciate by 10 per cent over the next year, which would underpin the higher valuation.

Rather than buying the site at the full asking price and running the risk of house price inflation not being the amount expected, Berry Investments withdrew its interest from the property and the development did not proceed.

CONCLUSION

The study might perhaps have been more instructive if the scheme had proceeded in that it would have allowed an examination of how a small developer would have managed the execution of the scheme. It does, however, provide valuable insights in a number of areas.

It illustrates that a single individual can bring together all the components necessary to carry out a development, if they have the time, knowledge and expertise to do so. There is a considerable infrastructure of professional knowledge and sources of finance that can be tapped into and coordinated to complete a scheme. One of the main difficulties a new developer faces is in identifying these sources and establishing a working relationship with them. Berry Investments succeeded in this and the network of contacts built up was taken to the next development opportunity.

TABLE 8.4 Jon Berry Developments appraisal summary for Part 1

	m²	Rate m²	Gross sales	
REVENUE				
Sales valuation	**m²**	**Rate m²**	**Gross sales**	
Residential	901.00	£1,997.78	1,800,000	
NET REALISATION				1,800,000
OUTLAY				
ACQUISITION COSTS				
Fixed price			400,000	
Stamp duty		1.00%	4,000	
Agent fee		1.00%	4,000	
Legal fee		1.00%	4,000	
Town planning			3,000	
Survey			2,000	
				417,000
CONSTRUCTION COSTS				
Construction	**m²**	**Rate m²**	**Cost**	
Residential	901.00	£935.00	842,435	**842,435**
Contingency		5.00%	42,122	
				42,122
PROFESSIONAL FEES				
Fees		15.00%	126,365	
				126,365
MARKETING AND LETTING				
Marketing			5,000	
				5,000
DISPOSAL FEES				
Sales agent fee		2.00%	36,000	
Sales legal fee		1.00%	18,000	
				54,000
Additional costs				
FINANCE				
Multiple finance rates used				
Land			33,839	
Construction			30,636	
Total finance cost			64,475	
TOTAL COSTS				**1,551,397**
PROFIT				**248,603**
Performance measures				
Profit on cost%		16.02%		
Profit on GDV%		13.81%		
Profit on NDV%		13.81%		
IRR		30.21%		
Profit erosion (finance rate 7.000%)		2 years 2 months		

JON BERRY DEVELOPMENTS Row Heading	Category	Total	Jan 2002 0	Feb 2002 1	Mar 2002 2	Apr 2002 3	May 2002 4	Jun 2002 5	Jul 2002 6	Aug 2002 7	Sep 2002 8	Oct 2002 9	Nov 2002 10	Dec 2002 11	Jan 2003 12	Feb 2003 13	Mar 2003 14	Apr 2003 15
Revenue																		
Sale - residential	2	1,800,000	0	0	0	0	0	0	0	0	0	0	0	0	0	0	0	1,800,000
Disposal Costs																		
Sales Agent Fee	9	-36,000	0	0	0	0	0	0	0	0	0	0	0	0	0	0	0	-36,000
Sales Legal Fee	10	-18,000	0	0	0	0	0	0	0	0	0	0	0	0	0	0	0	-18,000
Acquisition Costs																		
Fixed Price	86	-400,000	-400,000	0	0	0	0	0	0	0	0	0	0	0	0	0	0	0
Stamp Duty	14	-4,000	-4,000	0	0	0	0	0	0	0	0	0	0	0	0	0	0	0
Agent Fee	16	-4,000	-4,000	0	0	0	0	0	0	0	0	0	0	0	0	0	0	0
Legal Fee	17	-4,000	-4,000	0	0	0	0	0	0	0	0	0	0	0	0	0	0	0
Town Planning	20	-3,000	-3,000	0	0	0	0	0	0	0	0	0	0	0	0	0	0	0
Survey	21	-2,000	-2,000	0	0	0	0	0	0	0	0	0	0	0	0	0	0	0
Construction Costs																		
Con - residential	24	-842,435	0	0	0	-18,213	-43,061	-63,290	-78,901	-89,894	-96,267	-98,022	-95,159	-87,677	-75,576	-58,857	-37,519	0
Contingency	25	-42,122	0	0	0	-911	-2,153	-3,165	-3,945	-4,495	-4,813	-4,901	-4,758	-4,384	-3,779	-2,943	-1,876	0
Professional Fees																		
Fees	32	-126,365	0	0	0	-2,732	-6,459	-9,494	-11,835	-13,484	-14,440	-14,703	-14,274	-13,152	-11,336	-8,829	-5,628	0
Marketing/Letting																		
Marketing	40	-5,000	0	0	0	0	0	0	0	0	0	0	0	0	0	0	0	-5,000
Net Period Total			-417,000	0	0	-21,856	-51,673	-75,949	-94,681	-107,873	-115,520	-117,626	-114,191	-105,213	-90,691	-70,629	-45,023	1,741,000
Total Interest (All Sets)		-64,475	0	-2,358	-2,371	-2,385	-2,522	-2,828	-3,273	-3,827	-4,459	-5,137	-5,831	-6,510	-7,142	-7,695	-8,138	0
Period total for IRR			-417,000	0	0	-21,855	-51,673	-75,948	-94,682	-107,872	-115,521	-117,627	-114,191	-105,212	-90,691	-70,628	-45,022	1,741,000
Period Total after Finance			-417,000	-2,358	-2,371	-24,241	-54,195	-78,777	-97,954	-111,700	-119,979	-122,263	-120,022	-111,723	-97,833	-78,324	-53,161	1,741,000
Cumulative Total		248,603	-417,000	-419,358	-421,729	-445,969	-500,163	-578,940	-676,895	-788,594	-908,574	-1,031,338	-1,151,360	-1,263,082	-1,360,915	-1,439,237	-1,492,397	248,603

FIGURE 8.4 Jon Berry Developments cash flow appraisal for Part 1

329

The study gives an insight into the requirements of financiers. Finance is the lifeblood of development and it is the one single component that can make or break a scheme. Finance was sourced in this case, although on terms that greatly reduced the overall return to the developer. It is also instructive to note that the financier required a detailed cash flow appraisal rather than the traditional residual with which most UK developers are perhaps more familiar.

Finally, the study illustrates the importance of researching the detail of a development project. Berry Investments had already found that the development was not really viable at the original asking price, based on its initial examination of the market using the scheme as drawn up. The minor alterations made by detailed application of the planning conditions showed that a considerable reduction in asking price was required. It was laudable that the prospective developer was not swayed into bidding closer to the asking price by being more optimistic about the rate of inflation in residential prices. Their sensitivity analysis had revealed that the project's profitability was extremely sensitive to this issue and they would be running a far greater risk if they proceeded at that price. Berry Investments decided to be patient and wait for a more viable, less risky alternative opportunity.

Case study 3: Industrial development, Wearside, UK, mid- to late 1990s

Developer: Edinburgh-based financial institution

BACKGROUND

This case study examines in outline the construction of an industrial scheme comprising eight units of differing sizes undertaken by an Edinburgh-based life assurance company. Some of the details of the scheme have been changed to respect the commercial confidentiality of the parties concerned.

The development was unusual in a number of respects. First, it is relatively uncommon for a financial institution to carry out direct development projects. In this case the property team of the organisation had built up many years of experience in direct development projects. It was also unusual in that the institution was developing investments to sell on rather than to retain and hold in an investment portfolio. The reason for this was tax driven. The site had enterprise zone status allowing the first owners of the buildings to claim capital allowances for their construction which could be offset against other tax liabilities.

Setting these distinct features to one side, however, the development does reflect a reasonable example of non-residential development of an investment grade property.

PROJECT OUTLINE

The project involved the development of 15,000m² of industrial B1, B2 and B8 buildings on a site of 35,000m² located on Wearside in the north-east of England. The six buildings making up the estate were to be let on full repairing and insuring (FRI) leases to manufacturing and warehouse companies and the freehold investment interests sold off to investors. The originally envisaged development period was 18 months, including letting voids.

THE SITE AND ITS RELATIONSHIP TO THE LOCALITY

The site was located close to the A19 trunk road and the A1231 about five miles from the centre of Sunderland. The site was thus close to the A1M motorway and the Nissan factory, a major employer in the Sunderland area. Mainline rail stations were to be found in Sunderland and Newcastle and airports at Teeside and Newcastle. The international freight port at Teeside is located approximately 30 miles to the north.

The Sunderland area was one that had been dominated by heavy industry, particularly ship building. These industries had been in decline for many years and most had closed by the time the development took place. New industries such as the Nissan factory had been established in the area but considerable development assistance was available and the Wearside/Sunderland area became one of the last Enterprise Zones to be dedicated in the UK. These zones encouraged occupiers and investors by providing tax breaks for new property construction and business establishment.

THE SITE PRIOR TO DEVELOPMENT

On first inspection, the site appeared to be a greenfield site prior to the development. In fact, it had been used for industrial processes for many years but had been cleared several years prior to the start of the development. The site was owned by Sunderland Borough Council, whose economic development department was promoting the area and trying to attract new investment into the region.

There were no existing structures on the site at the time it was brought to market.

DEVELOPMENT INCEPTION

The inception of the development arose from the investment requirements of the financial institution. Each year in January the institution held meetings among its investment staff to review the performance of its existing portfolio and to identify the sectors of the property market in which the portfolio was over- or underweight. This review meeting identified that the institution was underweight in industrial property. It was felt that this sector would perform well over the next few years and, in particular, that opportunities in the northern part of England offered the greatest possibilities of acquiring good-quality, high-yielding investments.

Over the next few months the property investment team examined a number of existing investment opportunities in the key areas identified. None were found to be satisfactory and a decision was taken to examine development opportunities that would allow the quality of the end product to be more strictly controlled.

During the course of the investigations the site at Sunderland was brought to the attention of the property team. The site had a number of advantages that were attractive to the institution. It was close to a major focus of other investment activity where mainly office buildings were being constructed. There was, however, a shortage of high-grade industrial and warehouse facilities in the area. Consultation with a local agent confirmed that there was considerable demand for higher grade properties from some of the newer industries in the area but that these were not being provided by the market. The downside to the site was that it had enterprise zone status. The institution had beneficial tax status as it was a pensions and savings product provider. Enterprise zone status suited higher rate taxpayers best.

The council was very keen to see a high-grade industrial development placed on the site and was willing to offer the site on very advantageous terms to the institution. The purchase price suggested was 5.5 per cent of the end value of the scheme, payable on sale of the investment. This offered the advantage to the developer of having very low initial costs and predictable cash flows. The initial feasibility study showed that the development returned an internal rate of return (IRR) in excess of 30 per cent and a return on cost of around 20 per cent.

Although it was an unusual step, the property team decided that there was an opportunity to act as if it were a developer trader, developing the scheme out with the intention of selling it on to investors with a different tax status to the institution. The institution could then gain benefit from the one-off developer's profit. The decision was ztaken to proceed and an agreement was signed with the city council. This agreement covered the purchase of the site and also covered the type of operator to which the properties were to be let. The council was keen to encourage employment in the area so the institution had to enter into a binding agreement only to lease to companies which met minimum levels of employment per square metre of let floor space.

THE DEVELOPMENT TEAM

The institution relied heavily on the local letting agent's advice regarding the form that the building should take. The agent was one that the institution had worked with before, having advised them on an acquisition made several years previously. The agent had considerable experience of the industrial market in the north-east region, having started his career with English Estates, a quango charged with the responsibility for the development of new industrial buildings in areas where the private sector market would not make provision. He had been working in the private sector for about ten years prior to the commencement of the development.

Later in the project it was decided to appoint a joint agent. This agent was one of the international central London property consultants. The reason for this appointment was that the likely buyers of the investment interests in the property would probably go through a London firm to obtain investment advice appertaining to tax shelters. The firm appointed specialised in tax shelters and had advised a number of other developers in this area over the previous few years.

The institution assembled a development team based mainly on prior working experience. The architects were one of the larger UK practices with whom the institution had worked on other projects in the south-east of England. The architects had a Newcastle office and a director of the practice from London worked with the local team on liaison with the institution in the early stages of the development of the design of the scheme in order to build a good working relationship. The relationship did develop very smoothly with a practical yet distinctive design.

The quantity surveyor was again derived from one of the UK's largest practices. Again, the institution had many years' experience of working with them on several projects throughout the UK. This practice also had a Newcastle office and, fortuitously, this was headed up by a surveyor with whom the institution had worked on a project in Birmingham. This person had impressed the institution with the accuracy of the cost forecasting and the way that he had managed an extremely difficult project.

The institution used its usual solicitors for the legal issues concerned with the development, such as conveyancing and the drawing up of leases, etc. This solicitors' practice was based in central London.

The engineers, both structural and services, were locally based. The institution had no prior experience of working with either. They were selected on the recommendation of the architect and quantity surveyor.

THE SCHEME DESIGN AND SPECIFICATION

The initial vision for the scheme was for relatively conventional steel portal frame industrial buildings with around 10 per cent of office space. This concept was later developed in discussions between the institution, the letting agent and the scheme's architect. It was decided that to achieve maximum market impact it was necessary to produce buildings that were of higher grade than was available elsewhere in the region. This development was to be the first private sector industrial scheme to be constructed by a financial institution in the region and it was felt that the higher quality buildings and image would attract tenants into the scheme more readily. This was backed up by informal market research carried out by the letting agent in meetings with occupiers in the region. These meetings also acted to bring the prospect of the development to the attention of people in the market, and were considered to be far more cost effective than advertising.

The final scheme design was for high-grade industrial buildings with brick cladding to two storey offices located at the corner of each building. Rather than produce terraces, the market research suggested that the larger occupiers preferred standalone buildings. The larger buildings were given distinctive 'towers' above their office areas to emphasise their individuality. Four larger standalone units where planned, with two further units subdivided to produce four smaller units.

A schedule of accommodation is given in Table 8.5.

The specification of the offices included:

> tinted double glazing
> prestige reception areas with feature staircases
> open-plan accommodation
> suspended ceilings with integral grid lighting
> quality carpeting
> gas central heating
> three-compartment perimeter trunking
> fully tiled male and female toilets.

The production/warehouse accommodation was finished to a shell specification allowing maximum flexibility of use. The features were:

TABLE 8.5 Schedule of accommodation

Unit	Area (m^2)
1	3,500
2	3,000
3	2,550
4	1,545
5	1,300
6	1,035
7	1,035
8	1,035
Total	**15,000**

334

> electrically operated high-lift loading doors
> good natural light provided by double skin translucent roof panels
> high specification insulated profile metal cladding
> separate production area toilets
> minimum internal clear height of 5.8m at eaves.

The yard areas were tarmacked. Landscaping and tree planting was provided at the site and unit boundaries and substantial areas of car parking were provided.

PLANNING AND PRE-CONSTRUCTION PHASE

Site assembly/acquisition

The land acquisition process took around 12 months from the commencement of negotiations. This was not due to any particular problem but rather because the institution wanted to ensure that the conditions for development were right. The local council was always keen for the development to proceed and recognised the institution as the preferred developer for the site. There were occasions when the council indicated that it was impatient with the lack of progress in proceeding with the scheme, but eventually the agreement to purchase was made.

The negotiation period enabled the detail of the scheme to be drawn up, a list of potential contractors to be compiled and site investigations to be made. The site survey revealed that the site had been used largely for open storage associated with railway use. No contamination was found, although an area of filled land associated with an old railway cutting was identified. This potential problem was incorporated into the works as described in the contract drawings and incorporated into the bill of quantities.

Planning/consents

The site had existing outline consent for the development of up to 15,000m² of B1, B2 or B8 buildings. Detailed consent was obtained prior to the signing of the agreement to purchase the land. The planning process was very straightforward with few objections from neighbouring occupiers and businesses. The enterprise zone status of the site in any case offered a simplified planning regime to applicants.

Finance

The scheme was financed using internal funds of the institution. Main board approval was gained to commit up to £8,000,000 of funds to the development. Later, additional funds were committed to the scheme. A notional opportunity cost of 9 per cent p.a. was applied to the finance.

Timescale

The timescale for the project is shown in Figure 8.5.

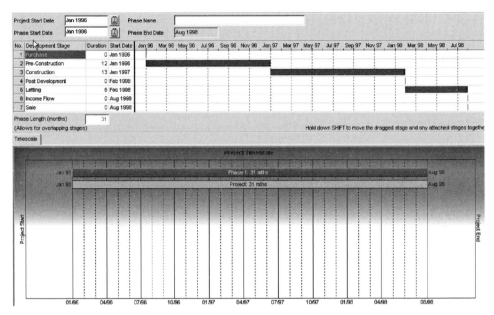

FIGURE 8.5 Wearside project timescale (screenshot from ARGUS Developer 3.01)

Appraisal

The final appraisal prior to the commencement of the scheme is outlined in Table 8.6. The appraisal was based on advice given by the letting agent, the investment agent and the quantity surveyor, who provided a detailed cost plan based on the design and specification provided by the architect and engineers. The letting agent advised that the scheme would attract rents of around £50/m² p.a. A six-month letting void was built into the appraisal. The yield on the scheme would be 7.75 per cent, reflecting the tax status of the scheme. The after-tax returns, after the capital allowances had been allowed for, were anticipated to be around 12.5 per cent for top-rate taxpayers. The cost of construction, including all external works, was anticipated to be £355/m². The result of the appraisal was considered to be acceptable and the scheme proceeded.

CONSTRUCTION PHASE

A conventional procurement route was chosen by the institution. This was due to the organisation's familiarity with the technique and the desire to maintain control of the finished product. The architect was responsible for the detailed plans, the engineers designed the structural frame and floors and the M&E consultant the services. A full set of construction drawings was prepared, as was a bill of quantities. These documents formed the basis of the tender documentation. The architect was to be the project leader of the development as the work continued and chaired the monthly site meetings. The institution also had representatives at these meetings.

A shortlist of six contractors was drawn up in consultation with the quantity surveyor and architect. All were national or international contractors with substantial experience of a range of commercial construction work. All indicated their willingness to

TABLE 8.6 Wearside industrial development appraisal

Condensed appraisal summary for Part 1

INCOME		
Annual rental income	750,000	
Net capital value		9,677,419
Less purchaser's costs		(290,323)
Net realisation		**9,387,097**
OUTLAY		
Acquisition		
Site purchase cost	532,258	
Site purchase fees	20,323	
Total purchase cost		552,581
Construction		
Construction costs	5,591,250	
Professional fees	367,958	
Total construction		5,959,208
Marketing and letting		
Marketing		25,000
Letting		112,500
Disposal		
Sales costs		187,742
Miscellaneous		
Rent-free costs	187,500	
		187,500
Finance		
Project length	32 months	
Debit rate 10.00%: credit rate 0.00% (nominal)		
Construction finance	291,038	
Void finance	317,212	
Total finance		608,250
Total expenditure		**7,632,780**
Profit		**1,754,317**
Performance measures		
Profit on cost%	22.98%	
Profit on GDV%	18.13%	
Profit on NDV%	18.69%	
Development yield% (on MRV)	9.83%	
Equivalent yield% (nominal)	7.75%	
Equivalent yield% (true)	8.14%	
Gross initial yield%	7.75%	
Net initial yield%	7.75%	
IRR	36.47%	
Rent cover	2 years 4 months	
Profit erosion (finance rate 10.000%)	2 years 1 month	

tender for the work. The tenders were all received on time and were all extremely competitive and close. The contract was awarded to the lowest tender received. The contract agreed used a standard JCT form of contract with quantities allowing for stage payment. A 12-month build period was agreed.

It should be noted that all of the design team and the contractor were required to enter into collateral warranties with the benefit lying with third parties, namely the future owners and occupiers of the building. This was important in order to pass comfort on design liability to these parties who were not party to the original contracts. These documents took time to agree, with the insurers of the consultants having a considerable input into the process.

On site, the programme of works generally proceeded well. The construction started in January and there were some weather-related delays in the early months. These concerned two main issues: January and February saw a number of days of extreme cold. On these days the temperature did not climb above zero and it was not possible to pour concrete during this time. Later there were problems with high levels of rainfall. As a result, the spend in the early months of the scheme was less than predicted. In the summer months the lost time on the programme was made up.

There were some problems with steel delivery for the portal frame and also some problems with the alignment of one set of frames in one of the larger buildings. This was not spotted by the consultant engineer until later in the programme when the sub-frames and cladding were installed. Although calculations provided by the steel subcontractor that were checked by the institution's engineer showed that there were no structural or safety issues with the misalignment, this issue did create problems at the end of the scheme.

By the time practical completion was approaching, all of the units had been sold to investors. The sale receipts were to be forwarded on practical completion. The prospective owner of the building raised objections to practical completion being granted because of the misalignment. Practical completion was delayed until satisfactory evidence was obtained to show that there were no significant structural issues to be resolved.

POST-CONSTRUCTION PHASE

The nature of the scheme led to a two-pronged approach to the marketing of the scheme. As capital allowances were only available on new buildings it was important that the building investment interest was sold first, so that the allowances could be claimed by those with the greatest beneficial motive. Letting the units meant that the capital allowances could only have been claimed by the tenants as first occupiers. This led to one case where a letting was lost because the unit that the tenant was interested in had not been sold.

Investment sale programme

In order to maximise the appeal of the scheme to tax shelter investors, certain components had to be put into place.

> As part of the sale agreements drawn up for the investors, the institution undertook to lease the properties to acceptable tenants. The institution provided a rental guarantee for the full outgoings on the property for a period of up to five

years after the sale of the investment interests. When an acceptable letting was in place, this rental guarantee would end.

> A draft lease was drawn up by the institution's solicitor. This document had to form part of the lease terms under which the properties were let. These leases were effectively of institutional grade, i.e. they were of long duration, on an FRI basis and contained 'upward only' rent reviews that occurred every five years. The sight of this documentation was intended to reassure the prospective investors of the quality of the income flow that was expected to be attracted to the scheme. It gave them an effective further guarantee that the institution would not lease the properties on weak occupational contracts to secure a quick letting and thus end the rental obligation of the institution early.

> Similarly, a specification defining an acceptable tenant was also drawn up and put into the sale documentation. Incoming tenants had to produce three years of trading accounts illustrating that they had been trading profitably, as well as providing trade and financial references. If this record was not available, the tenant was required to lodge a bond equivalent to six months' rent to be paid to the freeholder in case of default. This latter clause was very useful to the institution in the subsequent letting programme.

An investment brochure was prepared by the investment agent. The agents' clients were contacted and the scheme discussed.

The investment sale programme was extremely successful. All of the units had sale agreements in place prior to practical completion, which was much earlier than had originally been assumed to be the case in the cash flow. To a certain extent this complicated the practical completion process as many of the prospective owners sent representatives to the practical completion site meeting. These representatives were typically building surveyors there to represent their clients' interests.

Letting programme

The letting programme proceeded in parallel with the investment sale programme. An artist's impression was commissioned using the architect's elevation drawings. This was incorporated onto a large hoarding giving details of the development and the units available. This was visible from the main A19 road. The artist's impression was also included in the letting brochure for the development which provided details of the specification of the buildings and the lease details. Some 500 of these brochures were produced. In addition, a technical brochure was prepared with a limited production run of 50. A marketing consultancy was used in the preparation of the brochure. Advertising was taken in local trade publications and in the local papers. An initial marketing budget of £32,000 was set.

The target market comprised firms in the Washington, Sunderland and general Wearside area. Many such successful firms in the area were operating out of older industrial premises, often located on industrial estates built by the regional assistance agencies. While functionally acceptable, many of these premises presented a poor image for customers of the firms.

Wearside Industrial Development

Row Heading	Category	Total	Dec 1995 (0)	Jan/Mar 1996 (1)	Apr/Jun 1996 (4)	Jul/Sep 1996 (7)	Oct/Dec 1996 (10)	Jan/Mar 1997 (13)	Apr/Jun 1997 (16)	Jul/Sep 1997 (19)	Oct/Dec 1997 (22)	Jan/Mar 1998 (25)	Apr/Jun 1998 (28)	Jul/Sep 1998 (31)
Revenue														
MRV – unit 1	3	175,000	0	0	0	0	0	0	0	0	0	0	0	0
MRV – unit 2	3	150,000	0	0	0	0	0	0	0	0	0	0	0	0
MRV – unit3	3	127,500	0	0	0	0	0	0	0	0	0	0	0	0
MRV – unit 4	3	77,250	0	0	0	0	0	0	0	0	0	0	0	0
MRV – unit 5	3	65,000	0	0	0	0	0	0	0	0	0	0	0	0
MRV – unit6-8	3	155,250	0	0	0	0	0	0	0	0	0	0	0	0
RFree – unit 1	61	-43,750	0	0	0	0	0	0	0	0	0	0	0	-43,750
RFree – unit 2	61	-37,500	0	0	0	0	0	0	0	0	0	0	0	-37,500
RFree – unit3	61	-31,875	0	0	0	0	0	0	0	0	0	0	0	-31,875
RFree – unit 4	61	-19,313	0	0	0	0	0	0	0	0	0	0	0	-19,313
RFree – unit 5	61	-16,250	0	0	0	0	0	0	0	0	0	0	0	-16,250
RFree – unit6-8	61	-38,813	0	0	0	0	0	0	0	0	0	0	0	-38,813
Cap – unit 1	4	2,258,065	0	0	0	0	0	0	0	0	0	0	0	2,258,065
Cap – unit 2	4	1,935,484	0	0	0	0	0	0	0	0	0	0	0	1,935,484
Cap – unit3	4	1,645,161	0	0	0	0	0	0	0	0	0	0	0	1,645,161
Cap – unit4	4	996,774	0	0	0	0	0	0	0	0	0	0	0	996,774
Cap – unit 5	4	838,710	0	0	0	0	0	0	0	0	0	0	0	838,710
Cap – unit6-8	4	2,003,226	0	0	0	0	0	0	0	0	0	0	0	2,003,226
Disposal Costs														
Purchaser's Costs	8	-290,323	0	0	0	0	0	0	0	0	0	0	0	-290,323
Sales Agent Fee	9	-93,871	0	0	0	0	0	0	0	0	0	0	0	-93,871
Sales Legal Fee	10	-93,871	0	0	0	0	0	0	0	0	0	0	0	-93,871
Acquisition Costs														
Fixed Price	86	-532,258	0	0	0	0	0	0	0	0	0	0	0	-532,258
Stamp Duty	14	-5,323	0	0	0	0	0	0	0	0	0	0	0	-5,323
Town Planning	20	-10,000	0	-10,000	0	0	0	0	0	0	0	0	0	0
Survey	21	-5,000	0	-5,000	0	0	0	0	0	0	0	0	0	0
Construction Costs														
Con. – unit 1	24	-1,242,500	0	0	0	0	0	-159,885	-348,506	-392,467	-291,767	-49,875	0	0
Con. – unit 2	24	-1,065,000	0	0	0	0	0	-137,044	-298,719	-336,400	-250,086	-42,750	0	0
Con. – unit3	24	-905,250	0	0	0	0	0	-116,488	-253,912	-285,940	-212,573	-36,338	0	0
Con. – unit4	24	-548,475	0	0	0	0	0	-70,578	-153,841	-173,246	-128,794	-22,016	0	0
Con. – unit 5	24	-461,500	0	0	0	0	0	-59,386	-129,445	-145,773	-108,371	-18,525	0	0
Con. – unit6-8	24	-1,102,275	0	0	0	0	0	-141,941	-309,175	-348,174	-258,839	-44,246	0	0
Contingency	25	-266,250	0	0	0	0	0	-34,261	-74,680	-84,100	-62,522	-10,688	0	0
Professional Fees														
Architect	32	-213,000	0	0	0	0	0	-27,409	-59,744	-67,280	-50,017	-8,550	0	0
Quantity Surveyor	33	-79,875	0	0	0	0	0	-10,278	-22,404	-25,230	-18,756	-3,206	0	0
Structural Engineer	34	-39,938	0	0	0	0	0	-5,139	-11,202	-12,615	-9,378	-1,603	0	0
Mech./Elec. Engineer	35	-35,145	0	0	0	0	0	-4,522	-9,858	-11,101	-8,253	-1,411	0	0
Marketing/Letting														
Marketing	40	-25,000	0	0	0	0	0	0	0	0	0	0	0	-25,000
Letting Agent Fee	41	-75,000	0	0	0	0	0	0	0	0	0	0	0	-75,000
Letting Legal Fee	42	-37,500	0	0	0	0	0	0	0	0	0	0	0	-37,500
Net Period Total			0	-15,000	0	0	0	-766,831	-1,671,486	-1,882,326	-1,399,356	-239,208	0	8,336,773
Total Interest (All Sets)		-608,250	0	-250	-381	-391	-401	-4,483	-32,590	-78,233	-124,507	-153,393	-159,221	-54,400
Period total for IRR			0	-15,000	0	0	0	-766,832	-1,671,485	-1,882,326	-1,399,357	-239,208	0	8,336,774
Period Total after Finance			0	-15,250	-381	-391	-401	-771,314	-1,704,076	-1,960,559	-1,523,863	-392,601	-159,221	8,282,373
Cumulative Total		1,754,317	0	-15,250	-15,631	-16,022	-16,423	-787,738	-2,491,812	-4,452,372	-5,976,236	-6,368,836	-6,528,057	1,754,317

FIGURE 8.6 Appraisal cash flow

Wearside Industrial Development Row Heading	Category	Total	Dec 1995 (0)	Jan 1996 Mar 1996 (1)	Apr 1996 Jun 1996 (4)	Jul 1996 Sep 1996 (7)	Oct 1996 Dec 1996 (10)	Jan 1997 Mar 1997 (13)	Apr 1997 Jun 1997 (16)	Jul 1997 Sep 1997 (19)	Oct 1997 Dec 1997 (22)	Jan 1998 Mar 1998 (25)	Apr 1998 Jun 1998 (28)	Jul 1998 Sep 1998 (31)	Oct 1998 Dec 1998 (34)	Jan 1999 Mar 1999 (37)	Apr 1999 Jun 1999 (40)	Jul 1999 Sep 1999 (43)
Revenue																		
MRV - unit 1	3	175,000	0	0	0	0	0	0	0	0	0	0	0	0	0	0	0	0
MRV - unit 2	3	150,000	0	0	0	0	0	0	0	0	0	0	0	0	0	0	0	0
MRV - unit3	3	127,500	0	0	0	0	0	0	0	0	0	0	0	0	0	0	0	0
MRV - unit 4	3	77,250	0	0	0	0	0	0	0	0	0	0	0	0	0	0	0	0
MRV - unit 5	3	65,000	0	0	0	0	0	0	0	0	0	0	0	0	0	0	0	0
MRV - unit6-8	3	51,750	0	0	0	0	0	0	0	0	0	0	0	0	0	0	0	0
Cap - unit1	4	2,175,343	0	0	0	0	0	0	0	0	0	0	0	0	0	0	0	2,175,343
Cap - unit 2	4	1,864,580	0	0	0	0	0	0	0	0	0	0	0	0	0	0	0	1,864,580
Cap - unit3	4	1,584,893	0	0	0	0	0	0	0	0	0	0	0	0	0	0	0	1,584,893
Cap - unit 4	4	960,258	0	0	0	0	0	0	0	0	0	0	0	0	0	0	0	960,258
Cap - unit 5	4	807,984	0	0	0	0	0	0	0	0	0	0	0	0	0	0	0	807,984
Cap - unit6-8	4	643,280	0	0	0	0	0	0	0	0	0	0	0	0	0	0	0	643,280
Disposal Costs																		
Purchaser's Costs	8	-241,090	0	0	0	0	0	0	0	0	0	0	0	0	0	0	0	-241,090
Sales Agent Fee	9	-155,905	0	0	0	0	0	0	0	0	0	0	0	0	0	0	0	-155,905
Sales Legal Fee	10	-77,952	0	0	0	0	0	0	0	0	0	0	0	0	0	0	0	-77,952
Acquisition Costs																		
Fixed Price	86	-458,806	0	0	0	0	0	0	0	0	0	0	0	0	0	0	0	-458,806
Stamp Duty	14	-4,588	0	0	0	0	0	0	0	0	0	0	0	0	0	0	0	-4,588
Town Planning	20	-10,000	0	-10,000	0	0	0	0	0	0	0	0	0	0	0	0	0	0
Survey	21	-5,000	0	-5,000	0	0	0	0	0	0	0	0	0	0	0	0	0	0
Construction Costs																		
Con - unit 1	24	-1,242,500	0	0	0	0	0	-159,885	-348,506	-392,467	-291,767	-49,875	0	0	0	0	0	0
Con - unit 2	24	-1,065,000	0	0	0	0	0	-137,044	-298,719	-336,400	-250,086	-42,750	0	0	0	0	0	0
Con - unit3	24	-905,250	0	0	0	0	0	-116,488	-253,912	-285,940	-212,573	-36,338	0	0	0	0	0	0
Con - unit 4	24	-548,475	0	0	0	0	0	-70,578	-153,841	-173,246	-128,794	-22,016	0	0	0	0	0	0
Con - unit 5	24	-461,500	0	0	0	0	0	-59,386	-129,445	-145,773	-108,371	-18,525	0	0	0	0	0	0
Con - unit6-8	24	-367,425	0	0	0	0	0	-47,280	-103,058	-116,058	-86,280	-14,749	0	0	0	0	0	0
Professional Fees																		
Architect	32	-183,606	0	0	0	0	0	-23,626	-51,499	-57,995	-43,115	-7,370	0	0	0	0	0	0
Quantity Surveyor	33	-68,852	0	0	0	0	0	-8,860	-19,312	-21,748	-16,168	-2,764	0	0	0	0	0	0
Structural Engineer	34	-34,426	0	0	0	0	0	-4,430	-9,656	-10,874	-8,084	-1,382	0	0	0	0	0	0
Mech./Elec. Engineer	35	-30,295	0	0	0	0	0	-3,898	-8,497	-9,569	-7,114	-1,216	0	0	0	0	0	0
Marketing/Letting																		
Marketing	40	-25,000	0	0	0	0	0	0	0	0	0	0	0	0	0	0	0	-25,000
Letting Agent Fee	41	-64,650	0	0	0	0	0	0	0	0	0	0	0	0	0	0	0	-64,650
Letting Legal Fee	42	-32,325	0	0	0	0	0	0	0	0	0	0	0	0	0	0	0	-32,325
Net Period Total		-1,064,705	0	-15,000	-381	-391	-401	-631,475	-1,376,445	-1,550,070	-1,152,352	-196,985	0	0	0	0	0	6,976,022
Total Interest (All Sets)			0	-250	0	0	0	-3,764	-26,911	-64,500	-102,608	-126,397	-131,198	-134,478	-137,840	-141,286	-144,818	-49,480
Period total for IRR		-1,064,705	0	-15,000	-381	-391	-401	-631,475	-1,376,445	-1,550,070	-1,152,352	-196,985	0	0	0	0	0	6,976,022
Period Total after Finance		988,987	0	-15,250	-381	-391	-401	-635,239	-1,403,356	-1,614,570	-1,254,960	-323,382	-131,198	-134,478	-137,840	-141,286	-144,818	6,926,542
Cumulative Total		988,987	0	-15,250	-15,631	-16,022	-16,423	-651,663	-2,055,020	-3,669,592	-4,924,552	-5,247,933	-5,379,131	-5,513,610	-5,651,450	-5,792,736	-5,937,555	988,987

FIGURE 8.7 Actual cash flow

TABLE 8.7 Returns on the Wearside industrial development project

PROFIT	988,987
Performance measures	
Profit on cost%	14.53%
Profit on GDV%	12.31%
Profit on NDV%	12.69%
Development yield% (on MRV)	9.50%
Equivalent yield% (nominal)	7.75%
Equivalent yield% (true)	8.14%
Gross initial yield%	8.04%
Net initial yield%	8.04%
IRR	18.37%
Rent cover	1 year 6 months
Profit erosion	1 year 4 months

The letting programme went more slowly than was originally anticipated. By the time the development was underway there had been a downturn in the national and local economy. The terms of the investment sale restricted the room for negotiation with prospective tenants. The units did let, albeit more slowly than anticipated, and at the rental levels and on the lease terms that were anticipated. The quality of the tenants was, however, more mixed than anticipated, and the requirement for a rental bond was exercised on a number of units. The overall letting programme took six months longer than was anticipated, requiring the institution to face nearly a full year of paying the rent on the property to the investment owners. In addition, security was required for the site to prevent vandalism and break-ins. There was no liability for rates due to the enterprise zone status.

OUTCOME OF THE DEVELOPMENT

The earlier than anticipated sale of the scheme was more than offset by the increased letting programme. The appraisal and actual cash flows on the scheme are presented in Figures 8.6 and 8.7. The returns on the project are summarised in Table 8.7.

The early sale receipts had the effect of boosting the IRR figure. The extension to the letting programme did, however, have a considerable impact on the profitability of the development. The profit figures were reduced by the extension and by the institution's rental guarantee.

Conclusions

Although in some respects an unusual development, this outline case study does illustrate how a project goes from a concept to final execution. Some of the uncertainties of the process are illustrated, particularly with regard to the problems of predicting the letting up rates. Although enterprise zone tax shelters are largely a thing of the past, the study does illustrate generally how investment concerns can subordinate other issues in the development.

GLOSSARY

Bill of quantities

A detailed document produced by a quantity surveyor where all items in the construction are measured and quantified. This document is used by contractors to price the building works.

Break clauses

Special clauses in a lease which allow it to be terminated early instead of running its full course. These give the holder considerable flexibility in their occupation choices.

Caps

A vehicle used to limit the level of interest rates on a loan.

Certificate of final completion

A certificate issued by the architect that certifies that all the building works are completed to the architect's satisfaction.

Certificate of practical completion

A certificate issued by the architect that certifies that the building's construction is largely complete, except for very minor items that need correcting or completing. A sum of money is retained by the developer to cover these items, which will be released when the certificate of final completion is issued.

Collar

Similar to caps but cheaper as a lower limit is also agreed, below which the rate of interest cannot fall, which gives security to the lender.

Commercial paper

Short-term loans of less than three months' duration available in the money markets.

Competition survey

An analysis of the existing and potential competition to a property development scheme.

Debenture stock

Stock market issued debt.

Derivative-backed hedging

Using the futures and options markets to reduce the level of risk in interest rate movements.

Design and build	A method of procuring building works where the contractor is also responsible for the design of the scheme working to the client's brief.
Develop and construct	Similar to the above, except that the contractor fulfils a developer's function.
Discounted cash flow (DCF)	An important financial appraisal technique that requires a projection of future cash flows.
Equity returns	The return on an investor's own (as opposed to borrowed) funds used in a project.
Expected net present value (ENPV)	A probability weighted value of a cash flow.
Fee simple absolute interests	Another name for freehold interests, the highest level of land ownership able to be enjoyed by private individuals in England, Wales and Northern Ireland (in Scotland the equivalent is feuhold).
Fire sale	The rapid sale of assets, usually not at full market value, undertaken as a desperate measure to raise cash.
Forward fund	A way of securing cheaper funding for a development involving selling the scheme prior to construction to a financial institution which then provides the short-term project funding during the life of the development. On completion and letting of the scheme, the institution pays the balance owing to the developer and ownership is transferred.
Forward purchase and forward sale	Similar to the above, but the agreement is only to purchase the completed scheme at an agreed price and with an acceptable occupier and lease in place. The developer must secure their own project funding.
Full repairing and insuring (FRI)	A typical feature of UK leases that requires the occupier to carry out all maintenance and repairs, and to insure the building against loss.
General development order (GDO)	A planning instrument that allows certain activity, which would normally be deemed to be development, to take place without the requirement for making a planning application.

Gearing/leverage	The percentage of borrowed money to the developer's own money invested in a project.
General practice (GP) firms	A generic term used to describe UK commercial property consultants.
Highest and best use (HBU)	Refers to the highest value legal use for which a site may be reasonably used.
Interest-only mortgage	A property-backed loan where none of the principal sum is paid back until the end of the loan period, the borrower only paying interest on the loan.
Internal rate of return (IRR)	An important measure of investment return, representing the discount rate that produces a net present value of zero.
Investment yield	The return on an investment expressed as a percentage.
Joint venture	The practice of entering into a partnership with one or other development partners, such as a public sector body or bank, to carry out a development project.
Land value equation	Essentially, the residual value left after the cost of development is taken away from the end value of the scheme.
Limited liability partnerships (LLPs) and limited partnerships (LPs)	Two versions of special investment vehicles used to save tax on a development or investment project in the UK.
Limited recourse loans	A loan where the lender has limited ability to seek repayment from a parent company when a subsidiary defaults.
Loan stock	*See* Debenture stock.
Loan to value ratio (LTV)	The percentage of value or cost of a development scheme that forms the basis of how much a lender will advance to a developer. For example, if a scheme has an end value of £1 million and a bank has an LTV limit of 70 per cent, then the maximum that will be lent is £700,000. This ratio protects the banks' money from drops in value in the property market.

London interbank offered	The rate of interest that banks charge each other for loans between themselves. This forms an important benchmark for other, less secure lending.
Mezzanine finance	Debt financing of a project above the LTV limit, usually at a premium rate of interest.
Negative cash flows	Cash outflows, i.e. expenditure.
Net present value (NPV)	The sum of a future series of cash flows whose values have been discounted back to the present using the principles of the time.
Real estate investment trusts (REITs)	US tax-efficient property investment vehicle.
Rental incentive	A sum paid by a property owner to a tenant as an inducement to sign a lease.
Repayment/amortised mortgage	The traditional property-backed loan where the borrower pays off both interest and capital over a fixed time period.
Residual cash flow	A variation on the discounted cash flow approach.
Retail debt	Effectively, a corporate debt agreed for general business operations rather than project-specific debt.
Retention financing	Financing that allows a developer to retain, rather than have to sell, a development scheme.
Rolled-up interest	A debt where the interest is not paid each period but is instead added to the total amount owed which is then paid back as one lump sum.
Sale and leasebacks	Where a property owner receives capital by selling their property to an investor and immediately takes out an occupational lease on the property.
Special development orders (SDOs)	Special powers given to certain bodies to carry out development that would normally require consent without the requirement for making a planning application. Urban Development Corporations were given such powers.

Securitisation

Property investments divided up into shares like a company.

Senior debt

The main loan on a project, usually the debt that is not the mezzanine layer.

Sensitivity analysis

A test carried out by developers on appraisals of projects to see how sensitive the outcome of the calculation is to different values being experienced for the key components of the appraisal.

Spoiling bids

A bid for a site or component of a site put in by another developer who has no intention of bringing forward a development project on the site themselves. The bid either forces the hand of the developer who was working up a scheme on the site or else prevents the development completely.

Swaps

A form of derivative hedging for interest rates.

Taper relief

A tax allowance given on capital gains tax.

Texas agreement

A document drawn up for a partnership/joint venture that deals with what should happen if the partnership is terminated early.

Time value of money

Where there is a positive rate of interest, money received in the future has a lower value than the equivalent sum received today. For example, one would prefer to receive £5 today than £5 in one year's time, because the £5 today could be invested to accrue to a larger sum.

Turnkey method

A procurement system where the end user can move straight into the facility. All the design, financing, commissioning and construction of a building is carried out for the end user by a single provider.

Utilised securities market (USM)

A cheaper, less formal version of the main London stock market that allows smaller, less well-established companies to trade their shares and raise finance.

Value management

A division of the quantity surveying profession that analyses building design and procurement routes to ensure best value is delivered to the commissioner.

Void period

A period in which the developer assumes there will be no income received on a developed property. In practice, this is an allowance for risk and uncertainty in the development, the inclusion having the effect of reducing a potential bid price for land or scaling down profit expectations.

Year's purchase (YP) figure

A property term used to describe the number of times an annual income from a property is multiplied in order to determine its capital value.

NOTES

1 The background to property development in the UK

1 David Adams (1994), *Urban Planning and the Development Process*, London: UCL Press.
2 Note that under English land laws it is not possible to have freehold ownership of buildings in multiple occupation such as flats and apartments. All of them are technically leased to the occupier, and it is the leasehold interest which is purchased. These leases need to be long (99 years plus) to enable mortgages to be obtained on them as leases, unlike freeholds, are wasting assets, i.e. their value declines as the end of their term approaches. The need for leasehold tenure in these circumstances is due to the fact that positive covenants are not enforceable under English common law. A freeholder cannot be forced to repair their holdings; thus, in a multi-occupied building, neighbours could not rely on each other to ensure the building remained structurally sound or waterproof. Positive covenants to repair are, however, enforceable in leases, hence the need for this form of tenure.
3 'Commercial' is taken in this book to mean any type of property that is not residential, including shops, offices, industrial and leisure properties among others.
4 An innovative low-energy building that utilises natural ventilation rather than mechanical air conditioning.
5 1996 edition (annual publication).
6 The reason for this is the impact of use on the area. A2 and A3 are both seen to bring additional impacts: with the former the tendency towards bland, non-retail frontages, with the latter the additional litter and noise in unsocial hours. This requires local authorities to have additional powers to regulate these activities.
7 With income-producing properties, the value of the asset is usually found by multiplying the annual net income by an income multiplier based on the inverse of the investors' required initial return or yield. If investors seek a 7 per cent return this means that they should pay 1/7 per cent or 14.285 times the annual income when buying the property. As the investors' required return rises, so the multiple of annual income falls, so an 8 per cent required initial return equates to 1/8 per cent or 12.50 times annual income.

3 The finance and economics of development

1 Note that in Figure 3.6 building societies, which are a financial intermediary, have been excluded. This was to simplify the diagram but also reflects the fact that most of the larger building societies in the UK have in any case converted to banks under the powers given to them under the Building Societies Act 1986.

4 Financial appraisal of development projects

1 Periodically these requirements rise and fall depending on the state of the market. When the development market overheats then the profit margins that lenders will accept fall. At the time of writing (late 2006) many residential appraisals were being conducted at margins of 10 per cent or less.
2 The Government published revised guidance on the use of section 106 planning agreements during 2005. The new Circular 05/2005 – Planning Obligations (which applies to England only) replaced the previous Circular 1/97. It is, in the main, an attempt by the ODPM to clarify how section 106 agreements should be assessed for their acceptability in policy terms and to give further guidance on the process of securing obligations. This review followed the Barker Report (2004).
3 Note that ARGUS Developer V3.0 allows the user to define six elements within the development project. They still, however, fall into the three broad groupings described above. The addition of a Purchase, Post-Construction and Sale period allows more flexibility away from the norm to be included in the appraisal.
4 Spon, *Architects' and Builders' Price Book 2007*, 132nd edition, ISBN 9780415393782.

5 Laxtons, *Building Price Book: Major and Small Works 2007*, ISBN 9780750665612.
6 BCIS Wessex, *Comprehensive Building Price Book 2007*, BCIS Wessex, ISBN 1904829414.
7 The construction cost plus the professional fees, the demolition and the contingency.
8 Strictly, a void period only exists in a speculative building, i.e. one where there is no certain occupier known at the time of development inception. A void period may be included, however, as extra insurance when the building is being constructed for occupation under a lease where there is a tenant who has signed heads of terms but not a binding lease. A small void period may occur in other cases to allow for fitting out or legal delays, etc.
9 A 'fire sale' refers to rapid selling of assets to raise cash by organisations in financial difficulty. In these circumstances the organisation concerned tends to accept any bid for these assets even those that are at an amount well below the true market value.
10 Or at whatever point the actual land purchase occurs. It is not always at the beginning, in some cases the financial transaction may not occur until the very end of the development.
11 This is found by taking 1 + the interest rate (expressed as a decimal) raised to the power of 1/(number of interest periods in the year). In this case this is $1.10^{1/12}$ which gives a figure of 1.007974. Removing the 1 gives us 0.007974 or 0.7974 per cent. This represents the nominal monthly interest equating to a compound or APR figure of 10 per cent p.a. Most finance is on a compound interest basis, if simple interest is being applied (i.e. no interest on interest) then the 10 per cent can simply be divided by the number of cash flows in the year, e.g. 10%/12 which equals 0.8333 per cent per month.
12 See note 7 on the time value of money in Chapter 2 and earlier in this section.
13 Although in Japan in 2001 the central bank set interest rates at zero per cent, in order to boost consumer demand because of the serious deflationary environment and recession the country found itself in.
14 Note that scenario building is not confined to three alternatives, nor is it purely dependent on differing economic environments. It can be applied to a series of different views about the future.
15 ARGUS Software Ltd, 2/6 Granard Business Centre, Bunns Lane, Mill Hill, London NW7 2DQ, UK; e-mail information: infoEU@argussoftware.com

5 Executing the development

1 Construction (Design and Management) Regulations 1994, updated in 2007; a series of regulations designed to ensure site and construction safety.
2 'Heads of terms' refers to an outline agreement with the main parts of the contract agreed but requiring further negotiation as to the minor fine details.
3 Joint Contracts Tribunal (2007), *Deciding on the Appropriate JCT Contract,* Practice Note. London: Sweet & Maxwell Ltd.

6 Post completion

1 Larger firms will see separation of these functions. When specialisation is allowed by the size of the organisation, agents will concentrate on one or the other commercial sectors. The markets are so different that specialisations are required to work efficiently. In small firms agents will do work in all of these areas.

7 Risk appraisal and risk mitigation: a common-sense approach

1 It should be noted that Paul Reichmann has risen, phoenix-like, from the ashes of the Olympia and York fiasco having purchased Canary Wharf from the receivers. From being in serious difficulty the project has now gone from strength to strength and a substantial and very successful development programme has been undertaken. In many ways this underlines the fact that the concept of the project was correct and that the developers were simply overtaken by events.

8 Case studies

1 I would very much like to thank John Cooper and John Adams of Drivers Jonas, Manchester; John Letherland of Terry Farrell and Partners, Architects; and Mike Coulter of Taylor Woodrow for their generous assistance in obtaining the details of this project.

INDEX